American Psychopathological Association Series

THE VALIDITY OF PSYCHIATRIC DIAGNOSIS

American Psychopathological Association Series

Psychopathology and the Brain
Bernard J. Carroll and James E. Barrett, editors, 1990

The Validity of Psychiatric Diagnosis
Lee N. Robins and James E. Barrett, editors, 338 pp., 1989

Relatives at Risk for Mental Disorder
David L. Dunner, Elliot S. Gershon, and James E. Barrett, editors, 324 pp., 1988

Alcoholism: Origins and Outcome
Robert M. Rose and James E. Barrett, editors, 320 pp., 1987

Childhood Psychopathology and Development
Samuel B. Guze, Felton J. Earls, and James E. Barrett, editors, 320 pp. 1983

Treatment of Depression: Old Controversies and New Approaches
Paula J. Clayton and James E. Barrett, editors, 352 pp., 1983

Anxiety: New Research and Changing Concepts
Donald F. Klein and Judith G. Rabkin, editors, 440 pp., 1981

Psychopathology in the Aged
Jonathan O. Cole and James E. Barrett, editors, 332 pp., 1980

Stress and Mental Disorder
James E. Barrett, editor, 310 pp., 1979

Critical Issues in Psychiatric Diagnosis
Robert L. Spitzer and Donald F. Klein, editors, 355 pp., 1978

Psychopathology and Brain Dysfunction
Charles Shagass, Samuel Gershon, and Arnold F. Friedhoff, editors, 399 pp., 1977

Hormones, Behavior and Psychopathology
Edward J. Sachar, editor, 325 pp., 1976

American Psychopathological Association Series

The Validity of
Psychiatric Diagnosis

Editors

Lee N. Robins, Ph.D.
Washington University
School of Medicine
Department of Psychiatry
St. Louis, Missouri

James E. Barrett, M.D.
Dartmouth Medical School
Department of Community and
Family Medicine and Psychiatry
Hanover, New Hampshire

Raven Press ◆ New York

Raven Press, 1185 Avenue of the Americas, New York, New York 10036

© 1989 by Raven Press, Ltd. All rights reserved. This book is protected by copyright. No part of it may be reproduced, stored in a retrieval system, or transmitted, in any form or by any means, electronic, mechanical, photocopying, or recording, or otherwise, without the prior written permission of the publisher.

Made in the United States of America

Library of Congress Cataloging-In-Publication Data

The Validity of psychiatric diagnosis.

(American Psychopathological Association series)
Includes bibliographies and index.
1. Psychodiagnostics.   2. Mental illness—Diagnosis.
3. Mental illness—Classification.   4. Psychological
tests—Validity.   I. Robins, Lee N.   II. Barrett, James E. (James Elmer),
1934-   .   III. Series. [DNLM: 1. Mental Disorders—
diagnosis. WM 141 V172]
RC469.V34   1980   616.89′075   87-43322
ISBN 0-88167-499-0

The material contained in this volume was submitted as previously unpublished material, except in the instances in which credit has been given to the source from which some of the illustrative material was derived.

Great care has been taken to maintain the accuracy of the information contained in the volume. However, neither Raven Press nor the editors can be held responsible for errors or for any consequences arising from the use of the information contained herein.

Materials appearing in this book prepared by individuals as part of their official duties as U.S. Government employees are not covered by the above-mentioned copyright.

9 8 7 6 5 4 3 2 1

Preface

This volume, derived from the 1988 annual meeting of the American Psychopathological Association, is devoted to the problem of how to assess the validity of psychiatric diagnosis. This topic might have seemed utopian a generation ago when psychiatric diagnosis was believed by many to be so unreliable as to lack validity (since validity requires at least reasonable reliability). But even a generation ago a few hardy souls believed both that diagnostic reliability was achievable if criteria were clearly specified and that the validity of these diagnostic categories could be assessed. In 1970, Eli Robins and Samuel Guze proposed five indirect indicators for assessing the validity of psychiatric diagnosis. That paper has since become a classic and appears as the introduction to this volume.

Robins and Guze could envision assessing validity because they felt sure that the clearly defined diagnostic criteria which they used could be applied reliably. These criteria had not yet been published in 1970, but appeared two years later as the Feighner criteria. The Feighner criteria specified the symptoms that characterized a disorder, the number of symptoms that had to be present, and by what age and with what severity and frequency. These criteria became the foundation for a succession of diagnostic systems: the Research Diagnostic Criteria; the *Diagnostic and Statistical Manual, 3rd edition*, followed by the revision of that Manual—*DSMIIIR*; and some traces of these criteria probably will be found in the Mental Disorders section of *ICD-10* to be published in 1992.

It turned out that clearly defined diagnostic criteria alone were not enough to ensure diagnostic reliability across research groups that did not share common training. In addition, they had to be operationalized in standardized interview protocols and accompanying algorithms for combining interview responses. However, the clear diagnostic criteria were a necessary first step. Without an agreement on criteria, there could be no guides as to which symptoms should be explored by interview or how many positive responses should be required to make a diagnosis. In the last few years great strides have been made in constructing standardized diagnostic interviews that are based on the criteria that evolved from the Feighner criteria, largely solving the reliability issue. It is now time to ask whether these diagnoses that we can make reliably are worth making at all.

At one level, the answer has to be affirmative. Psychiatric diagnosis enables a wealth of facts regarding the patient's history and current state to be communicated in just a word or two. But we ask more of diagnosis than efficient communication. We want it to be valid, by which we mean that we want it to correspond to what exists in nature—to describe a "real" disorder. The difficulty is in determining whether or not that is the case. If we knew a specific etiology, a specific biological defect that caused susceptibility, or if there were observable adverse changes in physical structures or physiology on which we could rely, the problem would not be so difficult. But these are rarely available for psychiatric disorders. Indeed, one of the reasons we need valid classification is to enable us to select diagnostically homogeneous samples in whom to search for such correlates. The trick is to find indirect indicators that a diagnostic definition maps closely onto the "real" underlying disorder.

The current volume reviews applications of Robins and Guze's suggestions for five indirect indicators of validity. It asks to what extent those indicators have been tested and how the diagnoses tested measured up. It also reports on promising new indicators of validity that have been proposed in the interval. These reviews of efforts to assess validity have produced an additional dividend: suggestions for grouping some disorders into large categories that appear more coherent than those currently in use, and for splitting some current disorders that fail tests for homogeneity. Thus the volume spurs further methodological advances in detecting validity and suggests some improvements in current diagnostic categories. The final chapter asks what further studies of validity need be carried out to guide those charged with modifying the American psychiatric diagnostic system once again with the planned publication of *DSM-IV* in 1992. Such studies can assure that diagnoses in *DSM-IV* are as valid as our current knowledge allows. The resultant diagnostic categories would be an improved starting point for further efforts in the search for social and physiological correlates that may allow us to prevent or effectively treat psychiatric disorders.

Lee N. Robins
James E. Barrett

Contents

Conceptual Issues in Establishing Validity

1   Establishment of Diagnostic Validity in Psychiatric Illness: Its Application to Schizophrenia
    Eli Robins and Samuel B. Guze

9   Establishment of Diagnostic Validity in Psychiatric Illness: Robins and Guze's Method Revisited
    C. Robert Cloninger

19 Alternative Taxonomic Models of Psychiatric Classification
    Roger K. Blashfield

35 "The Problem of Validity in Field Studies of Psychological Disorders" Revisited
    Bruce P. Dohrenwend

Longitudinal Consistency

57 Stability and Change in Childhood-Onset Depressive Disorders: Longitudinal Course as a Diagnostic Validator
    Maria Kovacs and Constantine Gatsonis

77 Temporal Stability in the Major Mental Disorders
    Morton Beiser, William G. Iacono, and David Erickson

Descriptive Consistency

99 Internal Consistency of DSM-III Diagnoses
    Linda K. George, Dan G. Blazer, Max A. Woodbury, and Kenneth G. Manton

127 Quantitative and Qualitative Distinctions Between Psychiatric Disorders
    William M. Grove and Nancy C. Andreasen

Evidence From Family Studies

143 Psychiatric Diagnosis in the Age of Molecular Genetics
J. Gelernter and E. S. Gershon

163 Linkage Markers and Validation of Psychiatric Nosology: Toward an Etiologic Classification of Psychiatric Disorders
Richard D. Todd and Theodore Reich

Contributions From Laboratory Tests and Treatment Response

177 Laboratory Studies and Validity of Psychiatric Diagnosis: Has There Been Progress?
David J. Kupfer and Michael E. Thase

203 The Pharmacological Validation of Psychiatric Diagnosis
Donald F. Klein

217 Validating Affective Personality Types
Hagop S. Akiskal

229 Diagnostic Validity and Laboratory Studies: Rules of the Game
Bernard J. Carroll

New Directions

247 The Implications of Cross-National Research for Diagnostic Validity
John E. Helzer and Glorisa Canino

263 Diagnostic Grammar and Assessment: Translating Criteria into Questions
Lee N. Robins

279 Reliability Considerations in Planning Diagnostic Validity Studies
Joseph L. Fleiss and Patrick E. Shrout

293 Having a Dream: A Research Strategy for DSM-IV
Robert L. Spitzer and Janet B. W. Williams

305 Clinical Validity
R. E. Kendell

325 *Subject Index*

Contributors

Hagop S. Akiskal, M.D.
University of Tennessee
College of Medicine
42 North Dunlap Street
Memphis, Tennessee 38103

Nancy C. Andreasen, M.D., Ph.D.
University of Iowa
Department of Psychiatry
500 Newton Road
Iowa City, Iowa 52242

James E. Barrett, M.D.
Dartmouth Medical School
Department of Community and
Family Medicine and Psychiatry
Hanover, New Hampshire 03756

Roger Blashfield, Ph.D.
University of Florida
Department of Psychiatry
Gainesville, Florida 32610

Dan G. Blazer, M.D.
Duke University
Department of Psychiatry
Box 3003
Durham, North Carolina 27710

Morton Beiser, M.D.
University of British Columbia
Department of Psychiatry
2255 Westbrook Mall
Vancouver, British Columbia V6T 2A1
Canada

Bernard J. Carroll, M.D., Ph.D.
Duke University Medical Center
Department of Psychiatry
Durham, North Carolina 27710

Glorisa Canino, M.D.
University of Puerto Rico
Department of Psychiatry
Medical Sciences Campus
G.P.O. Box 5067
San Juan, Puerto Rico 00936

C. Robert Cloninger, M.D.
Washington University
School of Medicine
Department of Psychiatry
Jewish Hospital
216 South Kingshighway
St. Louis, Missouri 63110

Bruce P. Dohrenwend, Ph.D.
Columbia University
100 Haven Avenue
New York, New York 10032

David Erikson, M.D.
University of British Columbia
Division of Social Psychiatry
Vancouver, British Columbia V6T 2A1
Canada

Joseph L. Fleiss, Ph.D.
Columbia University
Division of Biostatistics
600 West 168th Street
New York, New York 10032

Constantine Gatsonis, Ph.D.
Carnegie Mellon University
Pittsburgh, Pennsylvania and
University of Massachusetts
Amherst, Massachusetts 01003

CONTRIBUTORS

J. Gelernter, M.D.
Yale University
School of Medicine
Department of Psychiatry
333 Cedar Street
New Haven, Connecticut 06511

Linda K. George, Ph.D.
Duke University
Department of Psychiatry
Box 3003
Durham, North Carolina 27710

Elliott S. Gershon, M.D.
National Institute of Mental Health
National Institute of Health
9000 Rockville Pike
Bethesda, Maryland 20892

William M. Grove, Ph.D.
University of Minnesota Medical School
Department of Psychiatry
Box 393, Mayo Memorial Building
Minneapolis, Minnesota 55455

Samuel B. Guze, M.D.
Washington University
School of Medicine
Department of Psychiatry
4940 Audubon Avenue
St. Louis, Missouri 63110

John E. Helzer, M.D.
Washington University
School of Medicine
Department of Psychiatry
4940 Audubon Avenue
St. Louis, Missouri 63110

William G. Iacono, Ph.D.
University of Minnesota
Department of Psychology
75 East River Road
Minneapolis, Minnesota 55455

Robert E. Kendell, M.D.
University of Edinburgh
Department of Psychiatry
Royal Edinburgh Hospital
Morningside Park
Edinburgh, EH10 5HF, Scotland

Donald F. Klein, M.D.
New York State Psychiatric Institute
722 West 168th Street
New York, New York 10032

Maria Kovacs, Ph.D.
University of Pittsburgh
Department of Psychiatry
3811 O'Hara Street
Pittsburgh, Pennsylvania 15213

David J. Kupfer, M.D.
University of Pittsburgh
Department of Psychiatry
3811 O'Hara Street
Pittsburgh, Pennsylvania 15213

Kenneth G. Manton, Ph.D.
Duke University
Department of Psychiatry
Box 3003
Durham, North Carolina 27710

Eli Robins, M.D.
Washington University
School of Medicine
Department of Psychiatry
4940 Audubon Avenue
St. Louis, Missouri 63110

Lee N. Robins, Ph.D.
Washington University
School of Medicine
Department of Psychiatry
4940 Audubon Avenue
St. Louis, Missouri 63110

Theodore Reich, M.D.
Washington University
School of Medicine
Department of Psychiatry
660 South Euclid
St. Louis, Missouri 63110

Patrick E. Shrout, Ph.D.
Columbia University
Division of Biostatistics
600 West 168th Street
New York, New York 10032

Robert L. Spitzer, M.D.
Columbia University
Department of Psychiatry
722 West 168th Street
New York, New York 10032

Michael E. Thase, M.D.
University of Pittsburgh
Department of Psychiatry
3811 O'Hara Street
Pittsburgh, Pennsylvania 15213

Richard D. Todd, M.D.
Washington University
School of Medicine
Department of Psychiatry
660 South Euclid
St. Louis, Missouri 63110

Janet B. W. Williams, D.S.W.
Columbia University
Department of Psychiatry
722 West 168th Street
New York, New York 10032

Max A. Woodbury, Ph.D., M.P.H.
Duke University
Department of Psychiatry
Box 3003
Durham, North Carolina 27710

Establishment of Diagnostic Validity in Psychiatric Illness: Its Application to Schizophrenia

Eli Robins and Samuel B. Guze

Department of Psychiatry, Washington University School of Medicine, St. Louis, Missouri 63110

A method for achieving diagnostic validity in psychiatric illness is described, consisting of five phases: clinical description, laboratory study, exclusion of other disorders, follow-up study, and family study. The method was applied in this paper to patients with the diagnosis of schizophrenia, and it was shown by follow-up and family studies that poor prognosis cases can be validly separated clinically from good prognosis cases. The authors conclude that good prognosis "schizophrenia" is not mild schizophrenia, but a different illness.

Since Bleuler (3), psychiatrists have recognized that the diagnosis of schizophrenia includes a number of different disorders. We are interested in distinguishing these various disorders as part of our long-standing concern with developing a valid classification for psychiatric illnesses (6,7,10,11). We believe that a valid classification is an essential step in science. In medicine, and hence in psychiatry, classification is diagnosis.

One of the reasons that diagnostic classification has fallen into disrepute among some psychiatrists is that diagnostic schemes have been largely based upon a priori principles rather than upon systematic studies. Such systematic studies are necessary, although they may be based upon different approaches. We have found that the approach described here facilitates the development of a valid classification in psychiatry. This paper illustrates its usefulness in schizophrenia.

THE FIVE PHASES

1. Clinical Description

In general, the first step is to describe the clinical picture of the disorder. This may be a single striking clinical feature or a combination of clinical features thought to be associated with one another. Race, sex, age at onset, precipitating factors, and other items may be used to define the clinical picture more precisely. The clinical picture thus does not include only symptoms.

2. Laboratory Studies

Included among laboratory studies are chemical, physiological, radiological, and anatomical (biopsy and autopsy) findings. Certain psychological tests, when shown to be reliable and reproducible, may also be considered laboratory studies in this context. Laboratory findings are generally more reliable, precise, and reproducible than are clinical descriptions. When consistent with a defined clinical picture they permit a more refined classification. Without such a defined clinical picture, their value may be considerably reduced. Unfortunately, consistent and reliable laboratory findings have not yet been demonstrated in the more common psychiatric disorders.

3. Delimitation from Other Disorders

Since similar clinical features and laboratory findings may be seen in patients suffering from different disorders (e.g., cough and blood in the sputum in lobar pneumonia, bronchiectasis, and bronchogenic carcinoma), it is necessary to specify exclusion criteria so that patients with other illnesses are not included in the group to be studied. These criteria should also permit exclusion of borderline cases and doubtful cases (an undiagnosed group) so that the index group may be as homogeneous as possible.

4. Follow-Up Study

The purpose of the follow-up study is to determine whether or not the original patients are suffering from some other defined disorder that could account for the original clinical picture. If they are suffering from another such illness, this finding suggests that the original patients did not comprise a homogeneous group and that it is necessary to modify the diagnostic criteria. In the absence of known etiology or pathogenesis, which is true of the more common psychiatric disorders, marked differences in outcome, such as between complete recovery and chronic illness, suggest that the group is not homogeneous. This latter point is not as compelling in suggesting diagnostic heterogeneity as is the finding of a change in diagnosis. The same illness may have a variable prognosis, but until we know more about the fundamental nature of the common psychiatric illnesses marked differences in outcome should be regarded as a challenge to the validity of the original diagnosis.

5. Family Study

Most psychiatric illnesses have been shown to run in families, whether the investigations were designed to study hereditary or environmental causes. Independent of the question of etiology, therefore, the finding of an increased prevalence of the same disorder among the close relatives of the original patients strongly indicates that one is dealing with a valid entity.

We hope it is apparent that these five phases interact with one another so that new findings in any one of the phases may lead to modifications in one or more of the other phases. The entire process is therefore one of continuing self-rectification and increasing refinement leading to more homogeneous diagnostic grouping. Such homogeneous diagnostic grouping provides the soundest base for studies of etiology, pathogenesis, and treatment. The roles of heredity, family interactions, intelligence, education, and sociological factors are most simply, directly, and reliably studied when the group studied is as homogeneous as possible.

We will demonstrate by examining certain studies that these principles concerning the validity of psychiatric diagnosis may be applied to schizophrenia. These studies show that it is possible to systematically divide cases of schizophrenia into a poor prognosis group and a good prognosis group. Further, these studies suggest that this differentiation is not simply a matter of severity of illness but that the two groups represent different illnesses.

NOMENCLATURE

Psychiatrists have recognized for many years that among patients given the diagnosis of schizophrenia there are two main groups—one with a poor prognosis and the other with a better prognosis. Different investigators have referred to these two groups by different diagnostic terms. The more common terms for poor prognosis cases are chronic schizophrenia, process schizophrenia, dementia praecox, and nuclear schizophrenia. For good prognosis cases, they are acute schizophrenia, reactive schizophrenia, schizo-affective psychosis, atypical psychosis, and schizophreniform psychosis.

DIAGNOSTIC VALIDATION BY FOLLOW-UP STUDIES

Table 1 summarizes those studies reported in English in which the authors attempted to define patients systematically into poor prognosis groups or good prognosis groups. These studies were prospective or retrospective. In the retrospective studies, the author, without knowledge of the outcome, made a prediction concerning prognosis based upon the original clinical manifestations in the clinical records. In the selection of patients for all of these studies, cases of organic brain syndrome (including delirium), mental deficiency, obsessional neurosis, and typical manic-depressive illness were excluded. It is worth noting that similar results

TABLE 1. Follow-up studies of patients given the diagnosis of schizophrenia

Authors	Country	Number of cases	Duration of follow-up (years)	Follow-up results (in percent)	
				Well	symptoms + incapacity
Cases predicted to have a poor outcome					
1. Clark and Mallett (4)	England	76	3	11	73
2. Eitinger and associates (5)	Norway	110	5-15	1	84
3. Stephens and Astrup (13)	U.S.A.	143	5-13	7	55
4. Astrup and associates (1)	Norway	435	6-22	15	68
5. Astrup and Noreik (2)	Norway	273	>5	6	66
6. Vaillant (14)	U.S.A.	35	2	14	—
7. Vaillant (15)	U.S.A.	48	8-15	13	74
		60	1-2	7	62
8. Johanson (8)	Sweden	100	10-18	<12	>88
9. Robins and Smith (12)	U.S.A.	35	6	9	91
Cases predicted to have a good outcome					
1. Eitinger and associates (5)	Norway	39	5-15	36	23
2. Stephens and Astrup (13)	U.S.A.	74	5-13	38	3
3. Astrup and associates (1)	Norway	398	6-22	—	26
4. Astrup and Noreik (2)	Norway	306	>5	—	17
5. Vaillant (14)	U.S.A.	30	2	83	—
6. Vaillant (15)	U.S.A.	24	8-15	83	17
		28	1-2	64	11

were obtained in different countries. This implies that the findings probably have universal application.

Patients with the diagnosis of schizophrenia who were predicted to have a poor outcome did so in from 55 to 91 percent of cases, whereas they were well at follow-up in from one to 15 percent of cases only (table 1). Clinical features of the cases in these studies associated with a poor prognosis are summarized in table 2.

Patients with the diagnosis of schizophrenia who were predicted to have a good

TABLE 2. Prognostic features in schizophrenia

Features associated with a poor prognosis	Features associated with a good prognosis
1. Insidious onset (more than six months of symptoms)	1. Prominent depressive symptoms
2. Hebephrenic clinical picture	2. Family history of affective disorders
3. "Massive" persecutory delusions	3. Absence of a family history of schizophrenia
4. Clear sensorium	4. Good premorbid adjustment
5. Schizoid personality	5. Confusion
6. Family history of schizophrenia	6. Acute onset (less than six months of symptoms)
7. Striking emotional blunting	7. Precipitating factors
	8. Concern with dying and guilt

outcome were found to have a poor prognosis in only three to 26 percent of cases, whereas they were well in 36 to 83 percent of cases (table 1). Clinical features associated with a good prognosis are summarized in table 2.

It is evident that in table 1, the figures do not add up to 100 percent except in three studies. This is because in the remaining studies, although the patients were not well, it was not possible to determine their incapacity. Therefore, we did not include them in the tables. It seems evident from the data in table 1 that, using the appropriate criteria, predicting a poor outcome is more likely to be correct than is predicting a good outcome.

The error in prediction for each group (poor outcome and good outcome) suggests two possibilities: either each group is not homogeneous, i.e., it includes patients with more than one illness, or each group represents a separate illness with a variable prognosis. The family studies described below permit, to a considerable extent, the resolution of these alternatives.

DIAGNOSTIC VALIDATION BY FAMILY STUDIES

There are many family studies of schizophrenia in the literature. We have limited ourselves for the present purpose to only two studies. We selected only studies in which the following three criteria were met: 1) There was a clinical differentiation made of poor prognosis from good prognosis index cases. 2) There was a follow-up of the index cases to establish the validity of the original differentiation. 3) There was a systematic study of schizophrenia and affective disorders among first-degree relatives. Since we believe that such family studies are very important in establishing diagnostic validity, we regret that there are so few to report.

The two pertinent studies are presented in table 3. The most striking finding in these studies is the great preponderance of affective disorders among the first-degree relatives of patients with a good prognosis. This indicates that many of the index cases with a good prognosis did not have schizophrenia but suffered from a different illness—an affective disorder. On the other hand, the finding of an in-

TABLE 3. Family studies of poor prognosis versus good prognosis cases

Author	Country	Number of cases	Percent of index cases with psychiatric illness in first-degree relatives	
			Schizophrenia	Affective disorder
Kant (9)	U.S.A.	50 good prognosis versus	8	38
		50 poor prognosis	32	6
Vaillant (14)	U.S.A.	30 good prognosis versus	20	50
		30 poor prognosis	23	7

creased prevalence of schizophrenia among the first-degree relatives of the good prognosis cases (eight percent in Kant's [9] series and 20 percent in Vaillant's [14] series) indicates that some of the good prognosis cases did, in fact, suffer from schizophrenia.

Another striking finding in these studies is the preponderance of schizophrenia among the first-degree relatives of patients with a poor prognosis (32 percent schizophrenia versus six percent affective disorder in Kant's [9] series, and 23 percent schizophrenia versus seven percent affective disorder in Vaillant's [14] series).

The only finding inconsistent with the two points just made is the similarity of the prevalence of schizophrenia among the relatives of good prognosis and poor prognosis index cases in Vaillant's (14) series. We have no explanation for this inconsistency. It suggests that Vaillant's (14) series of good prognosis cases included more patients with schizophrenia than did Kant's (9).

DISCUSSION

In this paper, we have reviewed selected studies written in English in which attempts were made to separate cases diagnosed as schizophrenia into two groups: one with a poor prognosis and the other with a good prognosis. These studies indicate that it is possible to achieve this separation with a high degree of success. The failure to achieve 100 percent success in predicting outcome and the overlap in the results of the family studies indicate that the criteria used for the separation need further refinement. The impressive results achieved, however, by using the method described in this paper for establishing diagnostic validity indicate that the method has great power.

The method shows its power not only by its ability to separate the two groups quite well but also by pointing up its failures, thus indicating where additional study is needed. This additional study may involve further refinement of clinical studies, of follow-up studies, or of family studies.

Even though at this time laboratory studies have not contributed reliably to the diagnosis of schizophrenia, without such reliable laboratory studies a completely satisfactory classification of schizophrenia may not be possible despite the refinements of clinical and family studies. Thus, as indicated earlier in the paper, a fully validated diagnostic classification will probably also require reliable laboratory studies. We hope we have demonstrated, however, that even in the absence of such laboratory studies, careful clinical, follow-up, and family studies have contributed importantly to our knowledge of schizophrenia. We believe that similar studies will accomplish as much in other psychiatric illnesses.

SUMMARY

A method for achieving a high degree of diagnostic validity for psychiatric illness was described. The method was applied to schizophrenia. It was shown that it is possible to separate poor prognosis from good prognosis cases of schizophrenia. Poor prognosis cases have a predominance of schizophrenia among their psychiatrically ill first-degree relatives. Good prognosis cases have a predominance of affective disorder among their psychiatrically ill first-degree relatives. Therefore, apparent "schizophrenia" with a good prognosis is not a mild form of schizophrenia, but is a different illness. Research in schizophrenia, whether genetic, psychodynamic, clinical, sociological, chemical, physiological, or therapeutic, must take this differentiation into account.

ACKNOWLEDGMENTS

This work was supported in part by Public Health Service Grants MH-13002 and MH-07081 from the National Institute of Mental Health.

REFERENCES

1. Astrup, C., Fossum, A., and Holmboe, R.: Prognosis in Functional Psychoses. Springfield, Ill.: Charles C Thomas, 1962.
2. Astrup, C., and Noreik, K.: Functional Psychoses: Diagnostic and Prognostic Models. Springfield, Ill.: Charles C Thomas, 1966.
3. Bleuler, E.: Dementia Praecox or the Group of Schizophrenias, trans. by J. Zinkin. New York: International Universities Press, 1950.
4. Clark, J. A., and Mallett, B. L.: A Follow-Up Study of Schizophrenia and Depression in Young Adults, Brit. J. Psychiat. 109: 491–499, 1963.
5. Eitinger, L., Laane, C. V., and Langfeldt, G.: The Prognostic Value of the Clinical Picture and the Therapeutic Value of Physical Treatment in Schizophrenia and the Schizophreniform States, Acta Psychiat. et Neurol. Scand. 33: 33–53, 1958.
6. Goodwin, D. W., Guze, S. B., and Robins, E.: Follow-up Studies in Obsessional Neurosis, Arch. Gen. Psychiat. 20: 182–187, 1969.
7 Guze, S. B.: The Diagnosis of Hysteria: What Are We Trying To Do? Amer. J. Psychiat. 124: 491–498, 1967.
8. Johanson, E.: A Study of Schizophrenia in the Male: A Psychiatric and Social Study Based on 138 Cases with Follow-Up, Acta Psychiat. et Neurol. Scand. 33: supp. 125, 1958.
9. Kant, O.: The Incidence of Psychoses and Other Mental Abnormalities in the Families of Recovered and Deteriorated Schizophrenic Patients, Psychiat. Quart. 16: 176–186, 1942.
10. Purtell, J., Robins, E., and Cohen, M.: Observations on Clinical Aspects of Hysteria: A Quantitative Study of 50 Hysteria Patients and 156 Control Subjects, J. A. M. A. 146: 902–909, 1951.
11. Robins, E.: "Antisocial and Dyssocial Personality Disorders," in Freedman. A. M., and Kaplan, H. I., eds.: Comprehensive Textbook of Psychiatry. Baltimore: Williams & Wilkins Co., 1967, pp. 951–958.
12. Robins, E., and Smith, K.: unpublished data.
13. Stephens, J. H., and Astrup, C.: Prognosis in "Process" and "Non-process" Schizophrenia, Amer. J. Psychiat. 119: 945–953, 1963.
14. Vaillant, G. E.: The Prediction of Recovery in Schizophrenia, J. Nerv. Ment. Dis. 135:534–543, 1962.
15. Vaillant, G. E.: Prospective Prediction of Schizophrenic Remission, Arch. Gen. Psychiat. 11: 509–518, 1964.

Establishment of Diagnostic Validity in Psychiatric Illness: Robins and Guze's Method Revisited

C. Robert Cloninger

Professor of Psychiatry and Genetics, Washington University School of Medicine, St. Louis, Missouri 63110

The work of Eli Robins and Samuel Guze on the validation of diagnostic criteria for psychiatric disorders stands as an important landmark in the history of psychiatry. Their classic 1970 paper, reprinted elsewhere in this volume, provided the first summary of their method and illustrated it by an analysis of the clinical features, prognosis, and family history of two distinct types of schizophrenic disorders (1). A general system of diagnostic classification of psychiatric disorders based on their method was published in 1972 (2), and became one of the most frequently cited articles in American psychiatry.

Robins and Guze's work contributed to a critical change in thinking about both the importance of psychiatric diagnosis and the value of explicit diagnostic criteria. By 1980 the American Psychiatric Association had adopted Robins and Guze's general approach to psychiatric diagnosis. In the third edition of the American Psychiatric Association's Diagnostic and Statistical Manual (DSM-III), disorders were classified according to explicit inclusion and exclusion criteria, yielding disorders that were either shown or presumed to be distinguished by other differences in course of illness, familial pattern, and predisposing factors (3). In accord with the 1970 proposal by Robins and Guze, the DSM-III was designed to be purely descriptive and atheoretical. This was a marked departure from earlier editions which had been guided by Freudian and Meyerian theories of psychopathology and based on general clinical descriptions without operational criteria. The extent of the change in diagnostic practice can be revealed by examining the conceptual roots of the method developed by Robins and Guze.

CONCEPTUAL ROOTS OF THE ROBINS-GUZE METHOD

Samuel Guze was trained first in internal medicine and later trained in psychiatry after studying psychosomatic medicine with the distinguished psychiatrist George Saslow.

Eli Robins was trained in psychiatry, neurology, and neurochemistry. During his clinical training, he worked closely with the neuropsychiatrist Mandel E. Cohen at Massachusetts General Hospital in Boston. Shortly before 1950, Cohen and his colleagues in Boston began a series of carefully controlled biomedical and descriptive studies of common psychiatric disorders, including anxiety neurosis (4), hysterical neurosis (5,6), and manic-depressive disorders (7). Cohen had studied the work of Emil Kraepelin (1856–1926) in a college course on abnormal psychology, and continued a Kraepelinian approach to psychiatric diagnosis despite training with Adolf Meyer at Johns Hopkins (C. R. Cloninger, personal communication, 1987). In his own work, Cohen emphasized the importance of detailed case description (8), follow-up studies (4), and family studies (8) of discretely defined groups of patients. He suggested that common neurotic and personality disorders were caused by heritable neurophysiological abnormalities, rather than reactions to life situations (8,9). This approach was strongly resisted by dynamically and socially oriented psychiatrists of the time, and Cohen and his colleagues published their work in general medical journals, not psychiatric journals.

Despite the general unpopularity of the biomedical approach to psychiatry in most of the United States, some psychiatrists found the work to be useful. One of these was George Saslow at Washington University in St. Louis. Saslow was active in the treatment of psychosomatic disorders, and began to use Robins and Cohen's diagnostic approach (5,6) in his work with hysteria (now known as somatization disorder). At this time, Samuel Guze, who was initially trained in internal medicine at Washington University, began work in psychosomatic medicine with Saslow. This eventually led Guze to specialize in psychiatry. In addition, Guze developed a close association with Eli Robins, who joined the psychiatry faculty at Washington University in 1951.

By 1970 Robins, Guze, and their colleagues had carried out sufficient empirical studies to demonstrate that about 80% of all psychiatric patients could be assigned to one of 15 specific diagnostic groups. These groups included neuroses (anxiety, phobic, obsessional, and hysterical), affective disorders (depressive, manic), schizophrenia, organic brain syndromes, substance abuse disorders (alcoholism, dependence on other drugs), sexual disorders (homosexuality, transexualism), eating disorders (anorexia, bulimia), and one personality disorder (antisocial personality). Each of these discrete diagnoses was differentiated by explicit criteria that had been validated by controlled descriptive, follow-up, and family studies (2). However, about 20% of psychiatric patients fit none of these 15 diagnoses, so that a residual class (called "undiagnosed" patients by Robins and Guze) was still required.

The descriptive biomedical approach of Robins and Guze to psychiatric disorders is actually an extension of the work of Thomas Sydenham (1624–1689), the English physician who is widely recognized as the founder of clinical medicine and epidemiology. Sydenham studied fevers by detailed longitudinal observations; as a result, he was the first to distinguish measles and scarlet fever. His method for studying the natural history of disorders became the standard basis for classifi-

TABLE 1. *Psychometric types of validity included in the five phases*

A. *Content validity*
   1. Clinical description
B. *Criterion-related validity*
   2. Laboratory study (concurrent validity)
   4. Follow-up study (predictive validity)
   5. Family study
C. *Construct validity*
   3. Delimitation from other disorders (discriminant validity)

cation in medicine in the absence of information about specific etiologic agents. Because psychiatry remains a clinical specialty in which specific etiologic agents are generally unknown, Sydenham's approach is especially useful in psychiatry. Kraepelin, Cohen, Robins, and Guze all share with Sydenham an emphasis on detailed observations of the clinical features and longitudinal course of medical disorders.

Kraepelin assumed that the disorders he distinguished, such as schizophrenia and manic-depressive disorder, were discrete entities like measles and scarlet fever. This theoretical assumption is not made by Robins and Guze, even though their goal has been to define mutually exclusive categories of illness to the extent that is justified by empirical results.

The five phases in the validation of psychiatric disorders proposed by Robins and Guze are (a) clinical description, (b) laboratory studies, (c) delimitation from other disorders, (d) follow-up study, and (e) family study (1,2). Table 1 relates these five phases to the concepts of content validity, criterion-related validity, and construct validity proposed by psychometricians (10). This table shows that the validation method of Robins and Guze is consistent with the basic studies that are advocated by both clinical epidemiologists and psychometricians.

IMPACT ON PSYCHIATRIC NOSOLOGY

The number of citations of the Robins and Guze (1) and Feighner et al. (2) articles are tabulated by year in Tables 2 and 3. The rate of citation in the research literature peaked during the period 1980–1984, coincident with the publication of DSM-III. Although the 1970 article setting forth the principles of validation and applying them to schizophrenia was the first to describe the method, the 1972 article, which summarizes the method and presents a general system of classification, has been cited more often (Table 4). The greater frequency of citation of the 1972 article is probably explained by its greater scope, which made it suitable for summarizing diagnostic criteria that were used widely in clinical research. No other journal article about diagnostic classification has enjoyed such frequent notice and application.

TABLE 2. *Annual citations of Robins and Guze, 1970*

Years	Number of citations[a]	Average citations/yr
70-74	26	5
75-79	49	10
80-84	59	12
85	11	11
86	9	9
Total	154	9

[a]Based on Science Citation Index.

TABLE 3. *Annual citations of Feighner, Robins, Guze et al., 1972*

Years	Number of citations[a]	Average citations/yr
70-74	97	32
75-79	785	157
80-84	1251	250
85	196	196
86	151	151
Total	2480	165

[a]Based on Science Citation Index.

TABLE 4. *Ratio of annual rates of citation Feighner et al./Robins and Guze*

Year	Ratio
70-74	6
75-79	16
80-84	21
85	18
86	17
Average	18

The method of Robins and Guze is likely to enjoy even broader application in the future because not only is the official American nomenclature now using explicit diagnostic criteria, but the international nomenclature (ICD-10) soon will also. However, these nomenclatures include disorders about which little or no validity data are yet available. These as yet unvalidated criteria should lead to collection of relevant data, provided the criteria are not changed too often and that alternative criteria do not proliferate.

CRITIQUE OF THE FIVE PHASE APPROACH

In this author's opinion, the great impact of the Robins and Guze method appears to be related to three important characteristics. First, because the method is strictly empirical and atheoretical, clinicians with different theoretical approaches have an objective basis for communication with one another. No assumptions are needed. In particular, no assumption about the discreteness of the categories of psychopathology described is needed for the method to be applicable as a research tool. However, the validation method proposed by Robins and Guze has usually been associated with a categorical system of classification, which does assume that psychopathology comprises discrete disorders. The method of five phases must be distinguished from the categorical classification system because the method can be applied to the validation of dimensional traits as well as discrete disorders. This distinction is critical because investigations guided by the five-phase approach may invalidate the assumption that psychopathology comprises independent, discrete disorders.

Second, the method has a strong appeal to both clinicians and researchers because it involves only clinical observations and, in some cases, laboratory tests. This is the standard Sydenhamian approach to clinical disorders which has proven useful over three centuries.

Third, this standard clinical approach includes aspects of content, construct, and criterion-related validity. This is the standard psychometric approach to clinical disorders which has proven useful in the behavioral sciences. Overall, the Robins and Guze method eschews unnecessary assumptions and satisfies both clinical and psychometric concerns.

What more could we want in a method for diagnostic validation? Four basic limitations of the approach are summarized in Table 5. First, alternative clinical criteria have proliferated because there is no absolute "gold" standard to which they can be compared. Since there are no single pathognomonic features for most specific psychiatric disorders, many different features must be combined to provide psychiatric criteria. Consequently, different clinicians working in different settings with different patients and interests develop overlapping, but nonidentical, criteria without the restraint of having to show that their criteria are better in any way than preexisting criteria. Although the alternative criteria may all be reliable, the use of different criteria impedes comparisons across studies.

TABLE 5. *Limitations of the five-phase approach*

1. Alternative clinical criteria have proliferated.
2. Substantial proportion of "atypical" or "undiagnosed" cases (20%) despite continued study.
3. Categorical system fully satisfactory only if disorders are truly discrete.
4. Hypothetico-deductive method of construct validation ignored (need to test pathophysiological or functional models).

Second, the proportion of psychiatric cases who are "undiagnosed," "atypical," or "residual" cases that do not meet any specific diagnostic criteria remains substantial (11). No additional disorders have been validated by the five-phase approach to reduce the proportion of "undiagnosed" cases since the system was first described in 1972. As a result, residual categories remain necessary as long as diagnosis must be based on clinical features and course. Of course, many unvalidated categories were added in DSM-III, but even that did not eliminate the need for residual categories (3).

Third, many individuals satisfy criteria for multiple disorders, rather than only one (12). This comorbidity means that it is often difficult to fit patients into mutually exclusive pigeonholes. A categorical system is fully satisfactory only if the disorders are truly discrete and mutually exclusive. Efforts to demonstrate the discreteness of different disorders have led to inconsistent results for both psychoses and milder anxiety and depressive disorders (13). This casts doubt on the Kraepelinian hypothesis that psychopathology comprises discrete entities. If that hypothesis is incorrect, a dimensional or profile approach provides a more exact description of an individual than does a single primary diagnosis. This calls into question the adequacy of categorical systems of classification, but not the validation method of Robins and Guze.

Fourth, by eschewing any explicit theoretical model, the five-phase approach does not provide any guidance for testing pathophysiological or functional models of the etiology and development of psychiatric disorders. The five-phase approach itself avoids theoretical assumptions and could be applied to dimensional traits as well as to categorical disorders. Therefore it does not guide us in deciding if overlapping pathophysiological processes underlie the risk for psychopathological disorders (14,15). Scientific progress requires a hypothetico-deductive approach that can be postponed, but not satisfied, by an atheoretical method. As a result the atheoretical method of Robins and Guze often needs to be supplemented by theoretical considerations that guide hypothesis formation. However, the atheoretical validation method is likely to outlive any particular theory.

Overall, the five-phase approach is a stepping stone to an etiological understanding of psychopathology. Robins and Guze emphasized the crucial nature of pathophysiological studies: "Even though at this time laboratory studies have not contributed reliably to the diagnosis of schizophrenia, without such reliable laboratory studies a completely satisfactory classification of schizophrenia may not be possible despite the refinements of clinical and family studies" (1, p. 987). The repeated failure of past efforts to identify laboratory tests that are both sensitive and specific for categorical disorders may be coming to an end as recent advances in clinical neuroscience and psychiatric genetics promise to make pathophysiological investigation fruitful.

Furthermore, Robins and Guze's method of validation transcends the categorical model of psychiatric illness with which it has usually been linked. In fact, the five-phase approach has revealed that there are systematic patterns of comorbidity that are predictable in terms of underlying dimensions of personality (14,15). An example of such comorbidity is the positive correlation of antisocial personality and somatization disorders in the same individual and in families; the probability of both disorders can be predicted by quantitative deviations on a dimension of personality that has been termed novelty seeking (14).

In summary, the five-phase approach of Robins and Guze can be expected to remain the mainstay of validation methods because it is strictly empirical and atheoretical. Their method defines a practical, clinically defined system of classification; it also provides a stepping stone to etiologically based classification.

ACKNOWLEDGMENT

This research was supported, in part, by Research Scientist Award MH-00048.

REFERENCES

1. Robins, E., Guze, S. B. (1970): Establishment of diagnostic validity in psychiatric illness: Its application to schizophrenia. *Amer. J. Psychiat.*, 126:983–987.
2. Feighner, J., Robins, E., Guze, S. B., Winokur, G., Woodruff, R. A., Jr., Munoz, R. (1972): Diagnostic criteria for use in psychiatric research. *Arch. Gen. Psychiatry*, 26:168–171.
3. American Psychiatric Association (1980): *Diagnostic and Statistical Manual*, 3rd edition. American Psychiatric Association, Washington, D.C.
4. Wheeler, E. O., White, P. D., Reed, E. W., and Cohen, M. E. (1950): Neurocirculatory asthenia (anxiety neurosis, effort syndrome, neuroasthenia). *J.A.M.A.*, 142:878–889.
5. Purtell, J. J., Robins, E., and Cohen, M. E. (1951): Observations on clinical aspects of hysteria. *J.A.M.A.*, 146:902–909.
6. Robins, E., Purtell, J. J., and Cohen, M. E. (1952): Hysteria in men. N.E. J. M., 246:677–685.
7. Cassidy, W. L., Flanagan, M. B., Spellman, M., Cohen, M. E. (1953): Clinical observations in manic depressive disease: A quantitative study of 100 manic depressive patients and 50 medically sick controls. J.A.M.A., 164:1535–1546.
8. Cohen, M. E., and White, P. D. (1950): Life situations, emotions, and neurocirculatory asthenia (anxiety neurosis, neurasthenia, effort syndrome). *Ass. Res. Nerv. Dis. Proc.*, 29:832–869.
9. Wheeler, E. O., White, P. D., Ried, E. W., and Cohen, M. E. (1948): Familial incidence of neurocirculatory asthenia (anxiety neurosis, effort syndrome). *J. Clin. Investigation*, 27:562–573.
10. Kerlinger, F. N. (1973): *Foundations of Behavioral Research*, 2nd edition. Holt, Rinehart and Winston, Inc., New York

11. Woodruff, R. A., Jr., Reich, T., Croughan, J. L. (1977): Strategies of patient management in the presence of diagnostic uncertainty. *Comprehensive Psychiatry*, 18:443–448.
12. Boyd, J., Burke, J. Gruenberg, E., Holzer, C., Rae, D., George, L., Karno, M., Stoltzman, R., McEvoy, L., and Nestadt, G. (1984): Exclusion criteria of DSM-III: A study of co-occurrences of hierarchy-free syndromes. *Arch. Gen. Psychiatry*, 41:983–989.
13. Kendell, R. E. (1982): The choice of diagnostic criteria for biological research. *Arch. Gen. Psychiatry*, 39:1334–1339.
14. Cloninger, C. R. (1986): A unified biosocial theory of personality and its role in the development of anxiety states. *Psychiatric Developments*, 3:167–226.
15. Cloninger, C. R. (1987): A systematic method for clinical description and classification of personality variants: A proposal. *Arch. Gen. Psychiatry*, 44:573–588.

DISCUSSION

Dr. Samuel Guze: I very much appreciate the chance to open the discussion. The question put to me by Bob Cloninger was, "If you were going to do it over again, how would you change the paper about the validation of psychiatric diagnosis?" Obviously there are many specific things that one could have wished we had done, including some of the points raised this morning. More broadly, however, we might have tried to imbed the emphasis on diagnosis within our theory of medicine. Blashfield's comments are well taken, because the medical model is itself a theory that has guided our work for the past 30 years.

As a theory, it has relatively few assumptions but many important implications. I think the continuing debate about the value of diagnosis in part reflects the fact that many colleagues are still uncomfortable with some of the implications of the medical model. Specifically, any hypothesis concerning etiology or pathogenesis must take into consideration variables involved in a diagnostic scheme and the assumption that there are many different disorders, with distinct etiologic and pathogenetic mechanisms.

I find myself somewhat disappointed that we continue to have substantial percentages of undiagnosed cases. But I would like to remind the audience that often in general medicine (I like to look to general medicine for experiences that might be helpful guides as to what to expect in psychiatry), even when a specific diagnosis depends on anatomical findings, further research more than occasionally reveals that the original diagnostic group was heterogeneous in etiology or pathogenesis.

In psychiatry, we are still struggling with signs and symptoms and mental status features; we have, as yet, no dependable laboratory tests. But even if we did have such tests, if the experience in general medicine is at all pertinent, we would probably learn that disorders defined by specific tests might very well still turn out to be heterogeneous.

It is very important not to lose sight of the basic justification of the process of diagnosis. Fundamentally it is to facilitate communication so that we can teach and compare, think and do research. As we learn more, our diagnostic schemes will change; in fact, if they remain static, it is a sign that we are not making progress. In the final analysis, a diagnostic scheme that is aesthetically satisfying would be wonderful, but that is not the primary goal. The primary goal is to facilitate communication, understanding, and treatment.

It is amazing and gratifying that in 20 years psychiatry has seen such a rebirth of interest in this field, something I did not think would happen so soon. Twenty years ago Eli Robins and I would not have predicted that in 1988 there would be an annual meeting of the APPA devoted to serious discussion and debate about psychiatric diagnosis.

Dr. Jan Loney: I think it would take a long time to try to assess the many positive effects of the St. Louis approach on the field in general. However, I did want to respond to Dr. Cloninger's list of its limitations, because I agree that there is a problem with the proliferation of diagnostic approaches. Compared to the development of a psychological test, for example, we are going about things somewhat backwards, in the sense that we are disseminating "official" criteria before their reliability and validity are assessed. I think that has caused some problems, because researchers then use a whole variety of alternative diagnostic approaches, and it is hard to pull together the resulting literature. If we adopted empirically validated interviews and procedures, it might reduce the confusion by discouraging some of these alternative systems and measures.

Dr. Cloninger: I agree.

Dr. Williams: On a slightly different topic, you both mentioned your disappointment with the fact that with the Feighner criteria you still have 20% undiagnosed cases. However, in the DSM-III field trials, (admittedly, a study not without its own problems), the rate of atypical diagnoses was only about 4%. Therefore, unless you think that all of the nonFeighner and nonRDC categories in DSM-III are invalid, I think you have to agree that we have made considerable headway since 1970.

Dr. Cloninger: When you say, "four percent" do you mean only 4% of cases received an atypical diagnosis and didn't receive a specific diagnosis?

Dr. Williams: No, I meant that only about 4% received an atypical diagnosis at all, regardless of whether or not they also received a more specific diagnosis.

Dr. Barrett: But those are in psychiatric clinic populations. You would expect that number to be quite a bit higher as you examine patients in the general medical sector or respondents in community studies.

Dr. Cloninger: And in family studies. I know in our studies we have still found 20% difficult to classify.

Dr. Guze: Or more.

Dr. Jean Endicott: This is the issue of "Let all flowers bloom," even if there are a few weeds. I feel that we are at a stage of development in which a lot is going on in diagnosis, in biological tests, in molecular genetics, and in the development of new treatments. Classification is an iterative process, and if someone comes up with a way of classifying patients that differentially predicts response to treatment, or differentially predicts familial aggregation, or predicts course of illness, then those sets of criteria should be made known to other investigators.

I think it also behooves investigators to use more than one classification system. If they are using something that is idiosyncratic or new, they should also use some of the standard categories. Usually one is collecting enough data that one can include RDC or DSM-III categories, in addition to the new ones, without that much excess work on the part of the clinicians. I am still at the stage of saying, "Let us keep developing new sets of criteria." I am a splitter instead of a lumper.

Dr. Spitzer: You listed family studies as an example of criterion validity. I have always thought of family studies as a wonderful example of construct validity because positive family findings do suggest a mechanism, and that is a theory having to do with etiology.

Dr. Cloninger: I agree with you. Family studies were originally proposed as a simple criterion for criterion validity, and it was only later that we began to appreciate that, in addition, they gave us a window on the important area of genetics and familial transmission.

Dr. Guze: Eli Robins and I have argued that the familiality of a disorder may not necessarily be evidence for any particular etiological mechanism. It suggests only that there is a common etiological nexus, whether environmental (including the social environment) or genetic or the interaction of the two. We proposed, therefore, that the familial aggregation of illness be an important diagnostic validator.

Dr. Joseph Schildkraut: A comment concerning the issue of undiagnosed cases. I don't think there is anything bad about undiagnosed cases in a diagnostic schema, depending upon what that schema was designed to do. Janet Williams indicated that in the field trials, DSM-III had only 4% atypical cases. DSM-III was designed to be a forced choice system, and consequently there should be fewer undiagnosed or atypical cases. This is a function of that diagnostic system and is not necessarily a function of the reality out there.

I also want to emphasize that in the validation of diagnostic categories we are dealing with an iterative process. Only by that means will we come to a clearer understanding of which diagnostic categories are "valid." To emphasize Sam Guze's point, I think that many of the cases that we now think of as clearly diagnosed, as clearly designated, may themselves be heterogeneous. They may be really unclassified, even though we think we are making a specific diagnosis.

Dr. Barrett: You are saying that even though the coverage is high for a diagnostic system such as DSM-III, it does not necessarily mean the diagnostic categories are "carving nature at the joints," to use that familiar phrase.

Dr. Donald Klein: With regard to communication, DSM-III is intended to aid clinical communication. It helps doctors understand what they are talking about, and it gives them some guidelines about how to treat the patient. It is not necessary that DSM-III categories be the best categories for family studies, because DSM-III is narrowly tied to the idea of impairment. To receive a DSM-III diagnosis there has to be some sort of impairment. Yet it is not clear that the unit of transmission necessarily includes impairment. For instance, in our studies about phobia, it is clear that irrational fears go in families more than irrational fears accompanied by avoidance. Somebody who simply has irrational fears, but who doesn't avoid anything, doesn't get a DSM-III diagnosis. In our consensus work, we have been rating separately symptom pattern and impairment to maintain that distinction. It is conceivable that many of the familial tendencies seen using DSM-III diagnoses actually relate to the impairment criterion rather than to the clinical syndrome.

I think it is very important that we not be locked into current diagnosis. Developing valid categories is an iterative procedure; everyone agrees to that. So, when we make diagnoses at our consensus conference, we end up saying that the patient fits the criteria. If the patient doesn't quite fit the criteria, but we really think they have it, then it's a "probable" case. If the patient doesn't fit the criteria at all, but we think they have it, then it's a "possible" case. We have not quite got to the point of a case that fits the criteria but we don't think they have it.

Dr. Cloninger: Those points are very well taken. Antisocial personality is one example where I think impairment relating to the unit of transmission is key. We have been able to identify continuously measurable personality dimensions which are predictive of antisocial personality traits and disorder. Whether or not a person meets the DSM-III criteria for antisocial personality disorder appears to depend on home environmental factors, whereas what is inherited seems to be these personality traits, with heritabilities of around 50%. What appears as a discrete disorder is really a combination of continuous personality dimensions and social impairment in the home.

Dr. Guze: One additional point. Studying the families of patients is a strategy for improving our diagnostic classification, but it can also identify certain nonimpaired individuals with specific traits who aggregate in the same families as impaired people. But we must check our findings by starting out with a selection of such nonimpaired people, to be sure that their families contain the expected frequency of impaired individuals. Once that has been confirmed, something very important has been learned.

The Validity of Psychiatric Diagnosis, edited by
Lee N. Robins and James E. Barrett.
Raven Press, Ltd., New York © 1989.

Alternative Taxonomic Models of Psychiatric Classification

Roger K. Blashfield

Department of Psychiatry, University of Florida, Gainesville, Florida 32610

Diagnostic validity refers to the extent to which diagnostic categories are related to the clinical reality of patients. A valid diagnosis helps in making treatment decisions, in knowing something about the etiology of the patient's disorder, and in predicting the course of the patient's problems.

In this paper, four alternative taxonomic models will be briefly presented. The four models are (a) biological classification, (b) folk taxonomies as examined by cultural anthropologists, (c) the prototype model as used by cognitive psychologists to study how children form classificatory concepts, and (d) the concepts of reliability and validity as presented in psychological testing. Associated with each model will be a brief comment on the meaning of validity within this model. Finally, the implications of these models for the validity of psychiatric diagnoses will be introduced.

BIOLOGICAL CLASSIFICATION

Within biology, the discussions of classification are much more elaborate than those occurring in psychiatric classification. Biologists, for instance, distinguish between the concepts of *classification, identification*, and *taxonomy* (1). Classification refers to the activity of forming groups (what the DSM-III Task Force did, for example); identification refers to the process of assigning individuals to groups (what is called *diagnosis* in psychiatry); and taxonomy refers to the theoretical study of classification systems.

To understand biological classification, an example is presented in Fig. 1. It is a partial representation of the classification of cats. The names in this figure are names of different categories: *Felidae* refers to the general cat family; *Felis catus* is the name for the category containing all domestic cats. There are three types of names in biological classification: (a) the names of individual organisms (such as Mehitabel, Mittens, Muffy, etc.); (b) the names of categories (in scientific biological classification, these names are all in Latin); and (c) the names of the ranks in the hierarchical organization of categories (for instance, "species" is the name of the lowest rank in Fig. 1).

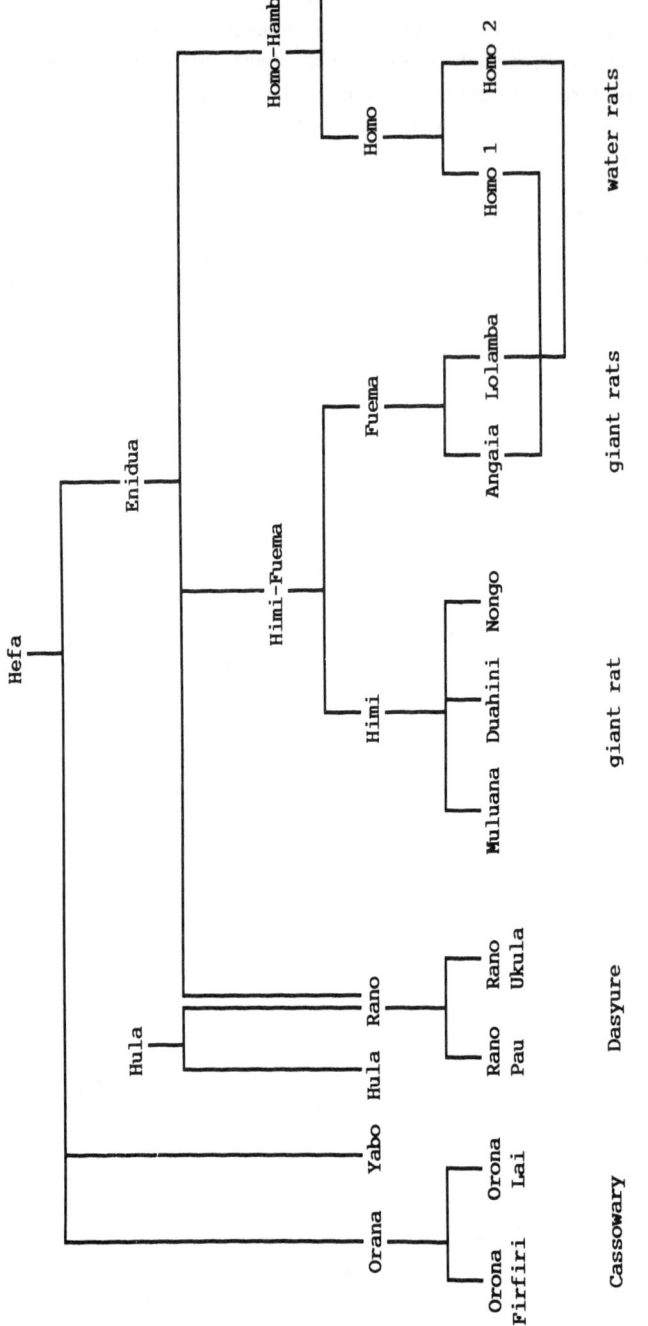

FIG. 2. A partial representation of the names of small mammals present in the New Guinea highlands.

pologists have described as the "unique beginner." This is the category at the highest level of the classification. Speakers in these non-Western cultures have a great deal of difficulty naming and defining the unique beginner. If asked for a name similar to our concept of "animal," for instance, a non-Western speaker is likely to generate a complex descriptive phrase (e.g., "rootless things with free spirits") that varies from speaker to speaker.

Berlin (4) suggests that the validity of categories in a folk classification can be studied using four approaches: taxonomic, linguistic, biological, and psychological. It is important to note that cultural anthropologists do not attempt to study the external validity of the concepts used by non-Western cultural groups (i.e., does a particular varietal concept of pig match something about the "reality" of pigs?). Instead, they study the classificatory concepts of speakers and the meaning of these concepts across different speakers of the same language.

PROTOTYPE MODEL

In 1980, Cantor, Smith, French, and Mezzich (5) proposed an alternative model for psychiatric classification. This model was called the *prototype model*. The best way to explain the prototype model is by example. Consider, for instance, that a mother is attempting to teach a child what a bird is. What the mother does not do is explain to the child that birds have feathers, they fly, they eat bugs, etc. Instead the mother is likely to point out the window at a robin and say, "Bird." Later the child may point at a cat and say, "Bird." The mother responds, "No, that is not a bird. That is a cat." Then she points at a sparrow and says, "Bird" to the child. After the child has learned to associate the word with different instances of the concept, the child is later able to abstract those features that separate instances of the concept from instances that do not fit the concept.

In effect, the prototype model proposes that classificatory concepts are not taught by teaching a list of defining features, but are taught through the presentation of exemplars of the concepts. (Explaining the prototype model by example in the preceding paragraph was intentional.) In more formal terms, logicians distinguish between *extensional* and *intensional* definitions of classificatory concepts (6). An extensional definition of a category is a definition in which all members of the category are listed. For instance, one could define the 1957 New York Yankees by naming all persons who played on that team. Generally, however, the standard view of classification is that extensional definitions are impractical. There are millions of birds in the world. To define this concept by attempting to list all members of this category would not be practical.

The other type of definition for a category is called an *intensional* definition. The standard or classic approach to defining classificatory concepts is to use intensional definitions in which the necessary and sufficient features for a concept are listed. Cantor et al. illustrate a classic intensional definition by describing how a square is defined. A square has four features: (1) four straight sides, (2) four angles, (3) all sides equal in length, and (4) all equal angles. All four features are necessary and are jointly sufficient for defining a square.

The prototype model suggests an alternative to the intensional definition approach favored by the classic model. Classificatory concepts can be defined through special extensional definitions by using exemplars. Crucial to the prototype model is understanding that not all instances of a concept are equally good exemplars of the concept. For instance, penguins and chickens are not good representatives of the bird concept in the way that robins and sparrows are. If one wishes to teach a child what a bird is, one does not point to a picture of penguin and say, "Bird."

Cantor et al. suggest that the representativeness of an instance of a concept is correlated with the number of features which the instance manifests. For instance, the features associated with the concept of bird are characteristics such as having feathers, flying, eating bugs, having wings, having a beak, being relatively small, etc. A sparrow is a good exemplar of a bird because it manifests all of these features. A penguin is not highly representative of the concept of bird because penguins do not fly, because they do not appear to have wings or feathers, and because they are moderately large animals.

The prototype model has attracted growing attention in the psychiatric literature. A series of papers have appeared in the journal literature of this decade discussing the prototype model and its relevance to psychiatric classification (7–12). An example of the use of the prototype model to study validity is presented later in this chapter.

PSYCHOLOGICAL TESTING

The fourth and final model relevant to psychiatric classification comes from the literature on psychological testing. The classic test theory approach to psychological testing is important because the concept of "validity" is most clearly enunciated.

In classic test theory, the fundamental assumption is that an observed score on a psychological test is a function of the true score and some error term. For example, the score of a child on an intelligence test is the sum of the child's true intelligence plus some amount of error.

The issue of error and its definition is quite important in classic test theory. The definition of error and how it is measured can have major effects on the explication of the particular theory of measurement.

Reliability is one of the major concepts in classic test theory. Using the algebra of classic test theory, reliability can be shown to have two important implications. The first is that reliability is equal to the ratio of the true score variance to the observed variance on a test. In other words, the reliability of a psychological test, when expressed as a correlation, is a measure of the degree to which the test is assessing the underlying concept associated with the test. If the reliability approaches 1.0, then the test is almost entirely measuring true score variance. If the reliability is closer to 0.0, then the obtained test scores are primarily a function of error variance.

The second theory is that reliability is related to an upper limit on the criterion validity of a test. More specifically, within classic test theory, the following equation can be proven: the criterion validity of a test, defined as the correlation of the test (x) with some criterion variable (y), must always be equal to or less than the square root of the reliability of the criterion or the reliability of the test, whichever is smaller.

There are three traditional ways of assessing reliability: parallel tests, test/retest method, and internal consistency. In the 1950s there was a standard intelligence test called the Wechsler-Bellevue scale. Two separate forms of the Wechsler-Bellevue existed. A way of assessing the reliability of this test would be to administer the two forms to the same individuals in order to see to what extent the scores of the individuals were the same. The problem with this approach to assessing reliability is that it is quite expensive because the test producers must create two forms of the same test.

The second way of assessing reliability is the test/retest method in which individuals are administered a test at time 1 and readministered the identical test at time 2. The extent to which the scores correlate across the two administrations is a measure of reliability. The pragmatic problem with this approach, however, is that subjects might remember their responses to questions from one administration to another.

The third way of assessing reliability is internal consistency. This can be measured by computing the average intercorrelation of the individual items on a test with the total score on the test. The higher the intercorrelations of the items, the greater the reliability. Basically this approach assumes that each item on a test is like a parallel test—in effect, each item represents an equally good measure of the concept being assessed.

The other major concept used in classic test theory is validity. Validity, according to the American Psychological Association's *Standards for Educational and Psychological Testing*, is defined as "the degree of evidence . . . which supports the inferences made from test scores" (p. 9).

Psychologists historically have discussed a wide range of types of validity: face validity, discriminative validity, convergent validity, predictive validity, concurrent validity, etc. However, there are three major ways of assessing validity that subsume all these other concepts: content, criterion, and construct.

Content validity refers to the extent to which the items on a test represent the domain of items that could be associated with a concept. For instance, suppose that you want to analyze the content validity of a self-report measure of depression. One way to accomplish this would be to interview a number of depressed patients and record their self-statements. "I feel bad most of the time." "Life is meaningless." "Things will never change." The extent to which the items on the self-report score represent the items appearing from the self-reports of depressed patients is the indicator of content validity.

Criterion validity is the most commonly used measure of validity. It is typically assessed by correlating a test score with a criterion measure. In intelligence testing, most of us would assume that if a child were highly intelligent then the child should do well in school and vice versa. Thus, the criterion validity of an IQ test can be assessed by correlating the test scores of children with their grades in school.

The third measure of validity is construct validity. Construct validity focuses on the extent to which a test measures a particular concept as that concept is explicated within a particular theory. For instance, suppose that the person creating a self-report measure of depression believes that depression is associated with a perceived loss. A way of assessing the construct validity of the depression scale would be to administer the scale to a group of people who are suffering the loss of a loved one and to compare those scores with a comparable sample of people who have not suffered a major loss.

Implications for Psychiatric Classification

Now that the four alternative models have been presented, the significance of these models for psychiatric classification will be presented. Five implications will be addressed: (1) in terms of its hierarchical structure, psychiatric classification is more similar to a folk classification than to scientific biological classification; (2) the claim that an unreliable system cannot be valid may not always be correct; (3) the dualism of reliability and validity, like most dualisms, becomes less clear when examined carefully; (4) the most fundamental type of validity for psychiatric classification may be content validity; and (5) the claim that psychiatric classification is atheoretical is absurd.

1. Psychiatric classification is more similar to folk classifications.

Figure 3 presents a partial representation of the classification of psychotic disorders in the DSM-III. Structurally, the hierarchical organization of mental disorders in the DSM-III and DSM-III-R is more similar to folk classifications than to scientific biological classification.

First, the DSM-III uses a hierarchical organization but the principles behind this hierarchical organization are not specified. Moreover, there are no "rank" concepts in psychiatric classification (i.e., there are no concepts formally analogous to concepts like "species," "genus," "order," etc.). Second, primary lexemes in psychiatric classification (e.g., "schizophrenia," "mania," "depression") are concepts that are first taught to new users of this classification (i.e., appear in all textbooks on psychopathology). Moreover, these concepts seem to be recognized cross-culturally. Third, the concept of the unique beginner (i.e., "mental disorder") is a very difficult concept, and the number of definitions of this concept are almost as variable as the number of users of the classification.

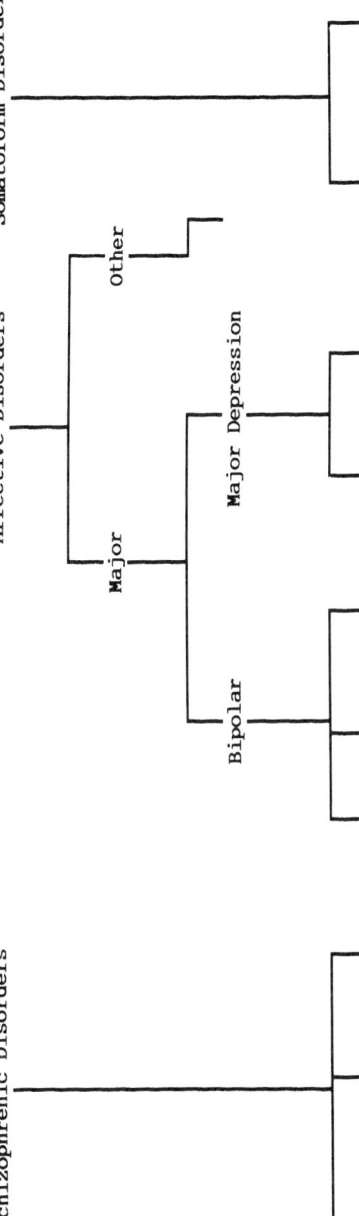

FIG. 3. A partial representation of the classification of psychotic disorders in the DSM-III.

2. *"There is no guarantee that a reliable system is valid, but assuredly an unreliable system must be invalid."*

In psychiatric classification, Spitzer and Fleiss (13) published an important review and analysis of the empirical studies of diagnostic reliability that had been performed during the 1950s and 1960s. They commented on the importance of assessing reliability by making the following, oft-quoted statement: "There is no guarantee that a reliable system is valid, but assuredly an unreliable system must be invalid."

In 1978, Carey and Gottesman (12) published an important but difficult to read article in the *Archives of General Psychiatry*. In their article, they presented an apparent counterexample to the claim by Spitzer and Fleiss (13). They presented a psychiatric diagnosis in which the reliability of the diagnosis had a kappa value of .08. This extremely low value would lead most of us to claim that this diagnosis was unreliable. However, they showed that the criterion validity of this diagnosis yielded a phi coefficient of .69. In other words, this diagnosis was unreliable, yet had moderately good validity.

How could this be? The apparent paradox, as Carey and Gottesman discuss and as Maxwell (14) also shows, has to do with the implicit assumptions about error that are made when using kappa as the statistical measure of reliability. Stated in overly simple terms, error as implicitly defined using kappa had a different meaning in this example than the implicit meaning of error used in the assessment of criterion validity.

3. Dualism of reliability and validity.

This leads to the next point: the problems associated with assuming the dualism of reliability and validity as if they are clearly separable concepts.

For instance, an area of growing research is the classification of the personality disorders. In the literature published in the 1980s, empirical studies appear in which the researchers administer structured interviews to a sample of patients with personality disorders and calculate the sensitivity and specificity of the individual diagnostic criteria of the personality disorders in terms of how well these criteria predict the diagnoses (8). These studies have been interpreted as studying the validity of the diagnostic criteria for the personality disorders.

Notice that this method of assessing validity is quite similar to the way in which the internal consistency method of assessing reliability is defined. Computing the specificity/sensitivity of diagnostic criteria, when the diagnosis is made by using the same criteria, is analogous to computing the average intercorrelation of the items on a test with the overall score on the same test.

To push this point further, in a recent study using structured interviews to assess the personality disorders, test/retest assessments of the reliability of these diagnoses were performed over a 4-month period (15). The resulting kappa values were low—most were about .4. This suggests that the reliability of the personality disorders is low. Or does it? From another perspective, these results might be seen as comments on the validity of the personality disorders. If the personality disorders refer to traits in people that are characteristic of long-term functioning, then would not marked fluctuations over time in the apparent diagnoses of these disorders be more of a comment on the validity of these diagnoses?

In modern views of test theory in psychology, the concepts of reliability versus validity are no longer seen as a clear and rigorous dichotomy. In fact, Cronbach, Rajaratnam, and Gleser (16) have proposed a generalizability theory that explicitly drops the dualism of reliability vs. validity. This approach to test theory suggests that in certain contexts, procedures often used to assess reliability can be better interpreted as indicating validity and vice versa.

4. Content validity as a fundamental type of validity for psychiatric classification.

Content validity is probably the most fundamental type of validity when applied to psychiatric classification. Content validity can be viewed as a method of assessing how well a psychiatric classification represents the consensus of mental health professionals. The governing principle behind the first two editions of the DSM classification was consensus. The DSM-I resulted from the dissatisfaction expressed by many psychiatrists during World War II with the plethora of competing classifications of psychopathology. During the war there were four major systems of classification in use within American psychiatry. The impetus for the DSM-I was to create a consensual system that all psychiatrists in the United States could use. The same principle was in effect in the creation of the DSM-II except that the context of consensus became international psychiatry.

How can the content validity of psychiatric classification be assessed? A group of us at the University of Florida are using the prototype model to study the classification of the personality disorders. In one of our studies, we created a scrambled list of all the DSM-III-R diagnostic criteria for the personality disorders and sent it to a random sample of psychiatrists and psychologists. The clinicians were asked to read each individual criterion, e.g., "Is uncomfortable in situations in which he or she is not the center of attention" (from Histrionic), and assign it to its parent diagnostic category. Using the data on the diagnoses which these clinicians associated with the different criteria, we were able to perform a multidimensional scaling analysis to visually represent the similarities among the criteria. The scaling solution is shown in Fig. 4.

In this figure, the antisocial criteria form one cluster on the top of the figure (denoted by capital "A"). At the middle right of the figure is a cluster of Borderline criteria. In the lower left is a cluster of Narcissistic criteria. And scattered over the bottom of the figure, with no clear clustering, are the Histrionic criteria. In fact, many of the Histrionic criteria, such as the one quoted above, are consistently seen by clinicians as better representatives of Narcissistic than of Histrionic. This suggests that Histrionic Personality Disorder, as defined in the DSM-III-R, lacks content validity.

5. Classification systems as atheoretical.

The authors of the DSM-III and DSM-III-R claim that their system is atheoretical. If psychiatric classification systems are to become scientifically useful, this

FIG. 4. A multidimensional scaling analysis visually representing the similarities among the criteria.

claim should be ignored. To understand why scientific theory and classification must be intertwined, consider criterion validity. There are two problems associated with criterion validity. First is the issue of assessing criteria. Criterion validity is not only limited by the reliability of the test but also by the reliability of the criterion. Unfortunately, experience in the area of psychological testing has often found that the psychometric properties of criteria are even worse than the psychometric properties of the psychological tests one is trying to validate. Certainly researchers should not assume that any particular criterion measures are perfectly reliable and valid.

The second problem concerns the choice of the criteria. Remember that validity was defined as "the degree of evidence which supports the inferences that are made from test scores." Crucial to assessing validity of a diagnosis is explicating what inferences might be made from this diagnosis. As soon as we begin to explicate the inferences, we are beginning to enunciate a theory—which brings up the issue of construct validity.

Modern psychometricians would generally agree that validating a psychological test cannot be viewed as an enterprise separate from exploring the validity of the psychological theory associated with the test. The attempts to create atheoretical tests have proven fruitless.

Moreover, all scientific classifications are intimately tied to theories within those sciences. What differentiates scientific biological classification from folk classification is that the organization of scientific biological classification is structured around a theory pertaining to the development of living organisms. Proposing a classification without a theoretical structure is rather like proposing a new language containing only nouns. Such a language would not contain sentences nor would there be any way of constructing sentences. To say that such a language is meaningless is probably too strong a claim, but the limitations of such a language would be severe. In short, if the validity of diagnostic concepts in the DSM-III classification are to be explored, scientists must begin to enunciate the theoretical suppositions that are implicit in this system of classification.

REFERENCES

1. Simpson, G. G. (1961): *Principles of Animal Taxonomy*. Columbia University Press, New York.
2. Sneath, P. H. A., and Sokal, R. P. (1973): *Numerical Taxonomy*. Freeman, San Francisco.
3. Dwyer, P. D. (1977): An analysis of Rofaifo mammal taxonomy. *American Ethnologist*, 4:425–445.
4. Berlin, B. (1977): Ethnobiological classification. In *Cognition and Categorization*, edited by E. Rosch and B. B. Lloyd. Wiley, New York.
5. Cantor, N., Smith, E. E., French, R., and Mezzich, J. (1980): Psychiatric diagnosis as prototype categorization. *Journal of Abnormal Psychology*, 89:181–193.
6. Buck, R. C. and Hull, D. L. (1966): The logical structure of the Linnean hierarchy. *Systematic Zoology*, 15:97–111.
7. Horowitz, L., Wright J., Lowenstein, E., and Parad, H. (1981): The prototype as a construct in abnormal psychology: 1. A method for deriving prototypes. *Journal of Abnormal Psychology*, 90:568–574.
8. Clarkin, J. F., Widiger, T. A., Frances, A., Hurst, S. W., and Gilmore, M. (1983): Prototypic typology and the borderline personality disorder. *Journal of Abnormal Psychology*, 92:263–275.
9. Livesley, W. J. (1985a): Classification of personality disorders: I. The choice of category concept. *Canadian Journal of Psychiatry*, 30:353–358.
   Livesley, W. J. (1985b): Classification of personality disorders: II. The problem of diagnostic criteria. *Canadian Journal of Psychiatry*, 30:359–362.
10. Livesley, W. J. (1985b): Classification of personality disorders: II. The problem of diagnostic criteria. *Canadian Journal of Psychiatry*, 30:359–362.
11. Blashfield, R. K., Sprock, J., Pinkston, K., and Hodgin, J. (1985): Exemplar prototypes of personality disorder diagnoses. *Comprehensive Psychiatry*, 26:11–21.
12. Carey, G., and Gottesman I. I. (1978): Reliability and validity in binary ratings. *Archives of General Psychiatry*, 35:1454–1459.
13. Spitzer, R. L., and Fleiss, J. L. (1974): A re-analysis of the reliability of psychiatric diagnosis. *British Journal of Psychiatry*, 125:341–347.
14. Maxwell, A. E. (1977): Coefficients of agreement between observer and their interpretation. *British Journal of Psychiatry*, 130:79–83.
15. van den Brink, W., Scoof, C., Hanhart, M., Rouwendael, J., and Koeter, M. (1986): Joint and test-retest reliability of DSM-III axis II disorders. Paper presented at American Psychiatric Association Meetings, 1986.
16. Cronbach, L. J., Rajaratnam, N., and Gleser, G. C. (1963): Theory of generalizability. *British Journal of Statistical Psychology*, 16:137–163.

DISCUSSION

Dr. Robert Spitzer: You mentioned that it is absurd to think that a classification can be atheoretical. Perhaps I am being a little defensive, but I have the feeling that you may be referring to the DSM-III-R concept, and, if that is the case. I think you are misrepresenting what we have claimed.

We have always used the phrase "generally atheoretical," to describe DSM-III and, more importantly, the atheoretical nature has to do only with *etiology*. We have never claimed that there are not a variety of theoretical constructs built into the way that the DSM-III and DSM-III-R classification is constructed. What we have argued, and I would like to hear a counterargument, is that, with the exception of organic etiology—which, of course, is built into the notion of organic mental disorders—and of three other disorders (adjustment disorder, post-traumatic disorder, and conversion disorder), there is no implicit theory regarding etiology for the other disorders. In fact, we think that is the reason people from a variety of etiological perspectives have been able to use the classification, such as people who have a social learning theory or a biological theory about the etiology of panic disorder. I don't think anyone has argued that there can be a classification system that is totally without theory, but we do argue that, with regard to etiology, it is possible.

Dr. Blashfield: I hope that I am not misrepresenting what you are saying. From my perspective, let me talk very briefly about biological classification. Biological classification was associated with a man named Linné who created descriptive systems, i.e., systems based on morphology. In terms of validity, biologists have become concerned with what is called a "natural" classification. A natural classification is a classification system in which the various concepts hold together across different lines of evidence: morphology, embryology, physiology, behavior, etc. The point at which biological classification became particularly important was when the hierarchical representation that Linné used was related to the theory of evolution. The result was that the concept of species became a concept whose meaning was crucial to the structure of biological classification. In psychiatric classification we can outline the system hierarchically so that it has a somewhat parallel structure. But what is analogous to the concept of species in psychiatric classification? Biologists have spent over a century arguing about the meaning of "species." Possibly the parallel concept in psychiatry classification is the concept of disease. Dr. Robert Kendell has written several important papers about the concept of disease as applied to psychopathology. Defining disease is not a trivial issue. Perhaps this issue does not have to be resolved in order to formulate a classification, but to ignore the issue will leave a psychiatric classification structurally incomplete.

Dr. Spitzer: Is it incorrect to state that the DSM-III and DSM-III-R classification is generally atheoretical with regard to etiology?

Dr. Blashfield: I would agree that it is. I would also claim that the Robins and Guze criteria represent levels of information associated with validating a classification. The Robins and Guze criteria are parallel to the levels of information (e.g., morphology, physiology) that biologists use when seeing if a system is a natural classification. Biologists hope that these different sources of information converge to support a common classification, much as we hope that family history data, clinical description, response to treatment, etc. dovetail to support a standard psychiatric classification. Ultimately though, we will want a classification to provide the structural basis of a theory of psychopathology or, at least, to form the concepts from which a comprehensive theory can evolve.

Dr. James Barrett: Conceptually how would you approach the issue of the criteria for the personality disorders, given some of the things that you have thought about and your work with these disorders?

Dr. Blashfield: The research that I have been doing with the prototype model tries to understand how clinicians think about the concept of the disorder. What I am explicitly trying to do is to learn how clinicians think about the personality disorders, and then extend the research to see how well clinicians' concepts match the real world of patients.

My own belief about the personality disorders is that the strongest evidence for the validity of these disorders would require longitudinal studies. If the personality disorders have meaning, it will be in terms of consistent patterns of interpersonal adaptation across time and across environmental circumstances. Longitudinal data are tremendously expensive data to gather. But in the area of the personality disorders I think that this type of data will have the most impact.

Dr. Barrett: That sounds like consistency over time. But the classification method that you presented—the use of cluster analytic techniques on cross-sectional data—would then be inappropriate for personality disorders.

Dr. Blashfield: What I am trying to do is take a look at how clinicians think about the concept underlying a particular disorder. It is clear from our work that clinicians have a fairly good core meaning for a concept like Antisocial Personality Disorder. They clearly have more problems with the way in which DSM-III or DSM-III-R define Dependent Personality Disorder. So, there are certain concepts in the DSM-III/DSM-III-R definitions which do not match the concepts which clinicians use.

Dr. Alexander Leighton: My comments have to do with your interesting parallel between diseases and species. These are of course different kinds of concepts, and so there are some problems about comparing them, an issue that has been hotly argued for about 200 years. As a matter of fact, I think the notion of disease syndrome came into medicine out of botany via Sydenham quite a bit before Linneaeus.

What is implicit and very worthwhile in your presentation is that these two concepts can be brought together if we move the level of abstraction to a higher level, namely the existence of patterns in nature—that there are regularly recurring patterns in nature that can be objectively determined. At this level, diseases on the one hand and species on the other do have in common the possibility of pattern classification. At this level some comparisons can be made. In natural history, pattern classification proved to be a procedure whereby processes were uncovered, such as organic evolution. With diseases, pattern classification can similarly offer help in approaching understanding of etiology. The thing we have to keep in mind is that classification is a tool, an aid in proceeding forward.

Dr. Blashfield: I would agree. I made two analogies in my talk. One was in terms of a psychiatric classification being like a psychological test, and the other was between the concepts of "species" and "disease." Arguing by analogy can always be dangerous, and I did not explore areas where the analogies may fail.

Dr. Robert Howell: A comment about your notion of classification theory. It seems to me that you are talking about a theory with models for each specific disorder rather than a theory that connects the disorders. There is no connecting link between schizophrenia and affective disorder, for example.

Dr. Blashfield: Those of us who are concerned with psychiatric classification have not spent much effort trying to understand the hierarchical nature of this system. All human beings seem to organize information in a hierarchical structure. But then what is the nature of the hierarchical relationships? In the area of psychopathology we have not devoted sufficient effort to defining node points in a psychiatric classification, nor how the node points relate to our theoretical perspectives about the nature of psychopathology.

Dr. Judith Rapoport: Your point about content validity seems particularly important with respect to the personality disorders. We are studying compulsive and obsessive-compulsive personality disorder in children and adolescents. In an epidemiologic survey of specific symptoms, we find that some of the items are checked significantly less by the patients diagnosed as obsessive compulsive disorder or compulsive personality than by the general population. For example, items that have to do with hoarding, money, and punctuality. A theoretical preconception by the clinicians making the diagnoses thus may have hampered research on the reliability and validity of these disorders. How does one solve this dilemma?

Dr. Blashfield: It is possible that what I am assessing in the prototype research are illusory correlations or stereotypes. One of the issues with stereotypes is that incorrect stereotypes are maintained, even in the face of contradictory evidence. You can provide people with evidence that their notion of the way in which things go together doesn't fit in the real world, and yet people will still insist that those things go together.

On the other hand, the literature in social psychology on stereotypes suggests that stereotypes almost always have something to do with the real world. Stereotypes don't appear out of nowhere. Stereotypes represent a kind of a low level theory about the objects being stereotyped. Part of the reason I am working with the prototype model in an area as fuzzy as the personality disorders is that this model hopefully will allow a better enunciation of the ways in which clinicians think things go together. The views of the clinicians may not match the ways in which things really do go together. But if we have enunciated what clinicians think, we can use bootstrapping techniques to gather evidence that will allow us as scientists to correct common clinical misconceptions.

The Validity of Psychiatric Diagnosis, edited by
Lee N. Robins and James E. Barrett.
Raven Press, Ltd., New York © 1989.

"The Problem of Validity in Field Studies of Psychological Disorders" Revisited

Bruce P. Dohrenwend

New York State Psychiatric Institute and Columbia University, New York, New York 10032

It is over 20 years since Barbara Dohrenwend and I published an article titled, "The Problem of Validity in Field Studies of Psychological Disorder" (1). We had occasion to update this review in 1974 (2), with other colleagues in 1980 (3), and in 1982 (4). In these publications, we were concerned with what we came to term the "first generation" of pre-World War II studies and the post-war "second generation" in which researchers attempted to investigate the true prevalence of psychiatric disorders in communities all over the world (4). For the most part, these studies focused on prevalence within periods of a few months to a year. There were too few longitudinal studies to permit an examination of investigations of true incidence as well.

Epidemiological research is dependent on the accuracy of diagnostic methods which in turn depend on the progress of laboratory and clinical research. Each of the first and second generation studies tended to pioneer its own unique methods and procedures for counting cases, with very little attention in any of them paid to problems of validity. This anarchy reflected the state of diagnostic affairs in the wider mental health community. However, a number of developments were under way that changed the situation dramatically.

By 1980, with the appearance of DSM-III and the changes in epidemiological research procedures coincident with it, it became meaningful to talk about the beginnings of a new, third generation of studies in psychiatric epidemiology. In this chapter, the first and second generation studies and the validity problems with their case identification and diagnosis procedures will be briefly described. Then, some of the newer developments in diagnostic instruments that either are or should be influencing third generation studies will be considered. Finally, some of the problems of validity in third generation studies completed so far and considerations for the future will be discussed.

FIRST GENERATION STUDIES

Sixteen studies, all of which took place between the turn of the century and World War II, comprise the first generation. Investigators in these studies tended to rely on key informants and agency records to supply the information that would enable them to identify cases. Such procedures tend to underestimate untreated cases of disorders that are characterized mainly by subjective distress that would more likely be revealed in direct interviews. Direct interviews were used in only six of these studies. But even in these six interview studies, where rates tended to be higher than in studies using key informants and agency records, the median for all types of disorders combined was only 3.6% as compared to a median of close to 20% in the second generation of studies conducted after World War II. The difference is a dramatic illustration of the effects of the tremendous expansion of psychiatric nomenclatures following World War II on rates of psychiatric disorders counted in community studies. The expansion itself reflected the experiences of the mental health professions with psychiatric screening for selective service and with subsequent psychiatric casualties in World War II (5). It marked the transition from the first to the second generation of epidemiological studies.

SECOND GENERATION STUDIES

Unlike the researchers in first generation studies, most of the investigators in the more than 60 second generation studies conducted between World War II and about 1980 relied on direct interviews with all subjects. Only rarely in these studies were the interviews supplemented systematically by data from key informants and official records, although such information is extremely useful for identifying or confirming some types of psychopathology such as substance abuse and antisocial behavior. Two different types of interview were used.

First, in most of the European and Asian research, a single psychiatrist or a small team headed by a psychiatrist personally interviewed community residents and recorded diagnostic judgments on the basis of these interviews. As a rule, the interview procedures were not made explicit in this type of approach.

In the second type of research, standard and explicit data-collection procedures were used. Although the interviews were sometimes done by psychiatrists and clinical psychologists and sometimes by lay interviewers, in all instances case identification depended on psychiatrists' evaluations of protocols compiled from the interview responses and, sometimes, from ancillary data from key informants, official records, and interviewers' observations. The Midtown study and the Stirling County study (6,7) pioneered this approach, and some others adopted their procedures (8,9,10). The resulting classifications were made not in terms of diagnostic types but rather in terms of ratings of "caseness" and "impairment."

Even more economical than having clinicians rate protocols constructed from data collected by lay interviewers is dispensing with clinical judgments altogether and using objectively scored measures of psychopathology. A number of investigators in this second generation of studies took this route. The objective measure used most often is a 22-item screening instrument developed by Langner in the Midtown study on a purely actuarial basis to provide an approximation of their

Mental Health Rating of psychiatric impairment (11). A similar, although less widely used, measure consisting of 20 Health Opinion Survey questions was constructed by the Stirling County study researchers (12). Both have as their core a portion of the items from the Psychosomatic Scale of the Neuropsychiatric Screening Adjunct, developed as an aid to Selective Service screening during World War II (13).

There exists by now a small family of these brief screening scales that appear highly similar in content and have been used in between a quarter and a third of the second generation of epidemiological studies to measure such things as "mental health," "mental illness," "psychiatric disorders," "emotional adjustment," "symptoms of stress," and "psychophysiological symptoms" (14, p. 257).

PROBLEM OF VALIDITY IN FIRST AND SECOND GENERATION STUDIES

There is little evidence for any of the usual types of validity in the first and second generation studies. Content validity was precluded because there was little consensus at any of the times these studies were done about the population of signs and symptoms to be sampled. Different nomenclatures were used by different investigators, and some investigators bypassed nomenclatures, substituting "caseness" (7) and "impairment" (6) ratings. Nor is the picture much better for criterion-oriented or construct validity. Except for studies using the brief screening scales for case identification, no attempts were made to test the ability of the diagnostic procedures to identify and classify known cases of important types or to test whether the main measures agreed with very different measures of the same types of disorders.

There has been much more methodological research on the brief screening scales used in these studies. They show good internal consistency (typically between .80 and .85) and tend to correlate with each other as highly as their reliabilities permit (15). They are all measures of much the same thing. However, it is not readily apparent from their content (symptoms of depressed mood, anxiety, and psychophysiological disturbance) what this is. They certainly do not, for example, contain symptoms of all varieties of "mental illness" or "psychiatric disorders"; nor are they limited to "psychophysiological symptoms"; nor do they exhaust the variety of stress reactions. Moreover, while whatever they measure frequently converges with diagnosable mental disorders, convergence occurs with at least equal frequency with the absence of such disorders (15). It is intriguing to inquire, therefore, into exactly what it is that they are measuring.

We have found that these brief screening scales have an extremely high correlation with measures of self-esteem, helplessness-hopelessness, dread, anxiety, sadness, and confused thinking (16), all of which are major facets of what Jerome Frank (17) has called "demoralization." In Frank's theoretical formulation as well as in relevant research that we have reviewed with regard to the screening scales

(18), this type of nonspecific psychological distress is likely to occur in response to a variety of predicaments: severe physical illnesses, especially those that are chronic; a buildup of recent stressful life events; attempts to cope with psychotic symptoms; and being from the lower social class. It is something like physical temperature in that you know something is wrong when it is elevated but not what is wrong until you learn more about the context. Although these measures of nonspecific distress that this author prefers to call "demoralization" are interesting in their own right, they are often very imperfectly related to diagnosable mental disorders.

BEGINNINGS OF A THIRD GENERATION

Epidemiological studies are expensive and time consuming. It is unlikely that there have been more than a dozen since around 1980. There is lack of unanimity about the diagnostic procedures to be used. However, the procedures have tended to be very different from those used in the first and second generation studies.

There have been a number of developments in psychiatry and related sciences here and abroad that have changed the context of these studies. Concern with systematizing and refining diagnostic systems is no longer concentrated abroad, but, spearheaded by the Washington University group (19,20), it has spread in the United States. Its embodiment is DSM-III. Semistructured diagnostic interview and rating examinations such as the Present State Examination (PSE) (21) and the Schedule for Affective Disorders and Schizophrenia (SADS) (22), developed for clinical research with patients, have been adapted for epidemiological research. Psychometric instruments such as the SCL-90 (23) and the GHQ (24), also developed for clinical research and research with general practice patients, have been used in epidemiological studies. In addition, there have been attempts to build instruments specifically for epidemiological studies. These include psychometric instruments such as the CES-D scale (25) and the set of screening scales from the Psychiatric Epidemiology Research Interview (PERI) (26). They include the most influential of all and the most directly related to the new DSM-III, the NIMH Diagnostic Interview Schedule or DIS (27), which is a fully structured diagnostic interview designed to be administered by lay interviewers.

THE PROBLEM OF VALIDITY IN
THE BEGINNINGS OF THE THIRD GENERATION

There has already been more research on the validity of third generation case identification procedures than on those used in the first and second generation. This is, however, an instance of a little being a lot by comparison. This chapter will examine the methodological research on semistructured clinical examinations, the more recently developed psychometric screening scales, and the DIS.

Semistructured Clinical Examination

In the semistructured clinical interview, main reliance is placed on the experience and skill of the clinician to reduce measurement error. A degree of structure is introduced to increase reliability. Wing, Cooper, and Sartorius (21) describe the interviewing and rating procedure for one of the most prominent of these semistructured instruments, the PSE, as follows:

> Each of the items or symptoms is defined in greater or lesser detail (in a glossary of definitions of symptoms). For most of the items or symptoms, a form of questioning is suggested, so that it would be possible to carry out the whole of the interview without deviating from the schedule at all. In practice, this would never happen since no two interviewees are alike and the examiner must be able to adapt his technique to the situation. The wording of each question depends on the answer to the previous one. . . .
> A symptom should not be rated as present simply because the patient says "yes." A further description should be asked for, in the patient's own words, and further specific questions asked as necessary. Following this process of cross examination . . . the examiner should make up his own mind as to how the symptom should be rated. Similarly, the fact that the patient says "no" to the standard question does not mean that the symptom should be rated as absent. All available cues, in behavior and case record, and from all parts of the interview, should be used to determine whether a particular line of examination should proceed further.

There has been very little investigation into the validity of semistructured clinical interviews in third generation epidemiological research. By and large, it is assumed they bring their credentials with them from their development with psychiatric patients and their use in clinical research, even when administered by predoctoral-level clinicians, as has been the case in some epidemiological studies (28,29). Such validity is by no means assured in field studies of psychiatric disorders in general populations where the conditions under which diagnoses are made are very different from those that obtain in research with patient samples, and where the boundaries between normal and abnormal are an underexplored frontier.

Much of what has been learned about the matter comes from two methodological studies. One is the author's previous research with a DSM-III era forerunner of SADS called the Psychiatric Status Schedule (PSS) developed by Spitzer et al. (30) and used by colleagues and the author in New York City (31). The second is a study by Wing and his colleagues (32) with a shortened version of the PSE scored on their "Index of Definition" to assess whether a respondent is a case in whom more detailed criteria of specific syndromes should be investigated. It is interesting to note that this type of case-noncase determination, used again by Brown and Harris (33), harks back to the Stirling County study "caseness" rating (7) and has much in common with the Midtown Study mental health rating of impairment as well (6).

The PSS was an attempt to standardize interviews of the kinds used for intake and diagnosis in clinical settings and was designed to provide DSM-II diagnoses of each subject through the application of a computer program called DIAGNO (34). The PSS consists of fixed questions, many of them open-ended, together with suggested probes. The actual responses to these questions and probes, however, are not recorded. Rather, they form the basis for judgments by the interviewer as to whether each of the several hundred carefully described symptoms is "true" or "false" of the subject. These clinical judgments then become the basic data resulting from the interview.

A number of years ago, we chose to investigate the PSS on grounds that it was likely to have much in common with the less explicit and less reproducible types of clinical interviews used by a number of first and second generation epidemiological investigators, especially those working in Europe and Asia rather than in North America (35,36,37). It is similar in type to the PSE and SADS, which we noted above have only recently been used with samples from the general population. Like these instruments it was developed on the assumption that its users had clinical experience and would undergo intensive training in making the clinical judgments required. Thus, the interviewer of choice with such instruments is an experienced psychiatrist, clinical psychologist, or psychiatric social worker. In our own research, the interviewers who used it were psychiatrists.

Fortunately, the items in the PSS, unlike the PSE and SADS, were not contingent on each other. It is thus possible to test their internal consistency reliabilities and make direct comparisons on this basis with measures from such self-report interviews as PERI. In our research, we were able to test a large number of PSS scales—those developed by its authors as well as our own a priori symptom groups—on a small sample from the general population as well as on a sample of psychiatric patients (31). The most striking finding was the contrast in internal consistency reliabilities of the scales for psychiatric patient and nonpatient samples. For example, we were able to replicate the findings of Spitzer and his colleagues (30) that a large number of PSS scales they developed showed good internal consistency reliability in psychiatric patients; we found, however, that most of the same PSS scales proved unreliable in the general population.

This lack of internal consistency reliability of the PSS scales in samples from the general population is accompanied by problems of validity. For example, we found that the computer program, DIAGNO, developed on the basis of research using the PSS with psychiatric patients, tended to grossly overdiagnose "schizophrenia" in the community sample that we studied; the errors were most likely to occur among respondents who were black or Puerto Rican (38). We found earlier that scores on the PSS can be misleading about rates of mental disorder in different social classes (39).

To illustrate, DIAGNO diagnosed 10 of the 133 community sample respondents as currently being schizophrenic. This rate of 7.5% is far higher than average prevalence rates of under 1% reported for a similar period of time in samples of adults from the general population. It is also considerably higher than rates of 4.5% diagnosed by the psychiatrists who interviewed the respondents and 3% by a psychiatrist who independently reviewed the transcripts of the interviews. Even the last rate of 3% seems high and may reflect the use of relatively broad pre-DSM-III definitions of schizophrenia. In any case, of the 10 DIAGNO schizophrenics, only three were also diagnosed as schizophrenic by psychiatrists who interviewed them, and only two of these three were diagnosed as schizophrenic by both the psychiatrists who interviewed them and a second psychiatrist who independently reviewed the transcripts of the tape recordings of the original interviews. Moreover, the psychiatrists who interviewed the community sample subjects diagnosed three respondents as schizophrenic who were not classified as schizophrenic by DIAGNO, and two of these were independently confirmed by the second psychiatrist who reviewed the transcripts. If we take as the most conservative identification of schizophrenia those instances where there was a consensus between the psychiatrist who interviewed the subject and the psychiatrist who reviewed the transcript, then DIAGNO converged with this clinical consensus in only two of its eight schizophrenic diagnoses.

It is believed that these problems of reliability and validity of the PSS for use in the general population are not specific to this instrument but extend to other instruments modeled on the clinical examination and developed primarily on the basis of research with psychiatric patients. One may consider in this regard some results reported by Wing and his colleagues (32). They come from a study in which the Present State Examination (PSE) was used by trained psychiatrists to investigate mental disorders among women sampled from the general population of a district in London. Like the PSS, the PSE data can also be reduced by a computer program, this one called "CATEGO" (21). The results of the PSE for each subject are summarized first in terms of an Index of Definition and, if the subject is above a cut-off on this index, into one or more psychiatric syndromes that correspond to diagnostic groupings of the mental disorders contained in the International Classification of Diseases (ICD-9). Of the 123 women in this sample, 22 were cases of "depressive disorders" on the basis of their identification above the threshold on the Index of Definition and their categorization as depressive disorders by CATEGO. However, when Wing and his colleagues (32) examined the PSE scores in terms of widely used criteria for depressive disorders developed by Feighner, Robins, Guze, Woodruff, Winokur, and Munoz (40) for this sample and for a sample of in-patients and out-patients, the results were as follows:

> One of the 22 "depressive disorders" in the general population series meets the standard, while two are probable. On the other hand, 16 of the 23 above threshold depressive disorders found in the in-patient series are definite and three are probable, while one patient with severe depressive retardation could not be rated on the subjective symptoms. Of the 14 above threshold depressive disorders in the outpatient series, seven are definite, five are probable, and two show only three of the Feighner (40) criteria (32, p. 213).

So far as the depressive disorders are concerned, the PSE and its Index of Definition and CATEGO system of case identification and classification are clearly not measuring the same thing in this general population sample as they are in samples of psychiatric patients.

Psychometric Screening Scales

It has been evident for some time that the unidimensional screening scales of nonspecific distress developed in the second generation of epidemiological studies are very imperfectly related to clinical psychiatric disorders. Results that Bruce Link and the author analyzed from three studies showed, for example, that at least half of those registering distress as severe as that of psychiatric outpatients did not have diagnosable disorders (15). Later studies with the more recently developed CES-D also show very imperfect correspondence between the scale cut-offs and diagnosable disorders (41,42,43). Thus, while these scales are brief, easily administered, and highly reliable in contrasting sex, class, and ethnic groups, they do not converge closely with diagnoses based on clinical interviews and ratings.

However, we have shown that it is possible to develop symptom scales that measure not only nonspecific psychological distress, but also a variety of other meaningful dimensions of psychopathology. These are the symptom scales in the PERI (16). We have also shown that subsets of seven or eight of these scales can discriminate cases from noncases with much higher sensitivity and specificity than a unidimensional scale of nonspecific distress (26). However, the scales are not very precise in screening individual cases of particular disorders (44). The best they can do so far as individual disorders are concerned is isolate subsamples with much higher rates than the general population sample as a whole. Thus, while very economical of time and money to administer (about 15 minutes for all the items in seven or eight scales by a lay interviewer or even in self-administered format if comprehension and motivation can be assumed) and very reliable in different gender, class, and ethnic groups, the symptom scales cannot provide precise rates of particular disorders in the general population.

The Diagnostic Interview Schedule (DIS)

The DIS was developed as "a response to the desire to have an instrument that will, as closely as possible, replicate a psychiatrist's diagnoses for situations when the use of psychiatrists is impractical or impossible" (45, p. 666). Large-scale epidemiological studies are assumed to be such situations by its developers. The DIS is not a psychometric measure, nor is it a clinical examination. It is a fully structured interview administered by lay interviewers and designed to provide current and lifetime diagnoses of many DSM-III disorders, with adaptations that make it relevant to other nomenclatures as well. Unlike the other instruments that have been used for individual investigations, the DIS has been used in the ECA collaborative program which, in terms of number of settings and cumulative sample sizes, is the largest undertaking at any time or place in psychiatric epidemiology to date (46). Moreover, its influence has spread. Now translated into many languages, it is undoubtedly the most widely used procedure for case identification and classification in psychiatric epidemiology in this country, and its use is spreading abroad.

More research has been done on the validity of the DIS than on the validity of the semistructured clinical interviews used in third generation studies. Conducted concurrently with or following the ECA studies, these methodological investigations have usually taken the form of diagnostic follow-up interviews. A number have focused on patient samples. However, the most important of them have been done with general population samples.

Some of these checks have involved closely spaced test-retest designs which varied the type of interview and/or the type of interviewer. For example, in a study reported by Helzer and his colleagues (45) of a subsample of ECA respondents in the St. Louis site, psychiatrists using the DIS and a DSM-III checklist were compared to lay interviewers using the DIS (45). This study contrasts with a study reported by Anthony and his colleagues in which the follow up of the lay interview DIS with a subsample of respondents in the Baltimore site was done by psychiatrists using a semistructured clinical interview and other information (47). Other studies have been one year or more follow-ups with lay administered DIS interviews that permit checks on the accuracy of diagnoses of past disorders, essential to the DIS goal of estimating lifetime as well as current prevalence (48,49).

The studies reported by Helzer and his colleagues (45) and by Anthony and his colleagues (47) are particularly instructive. In these studies, the subsamples of ECA respondents designated for follow-up after the initial DIS lay interviews were drawn to overrepresent cases. Although the subsample selection procedures were different, in each report the investigators present kappas for agreement (50) between the initial DIS and the follow-ups based, for most findings, on subsample data suitably weighted to represent the population sampled. For the Baltimore study reported by Anthony and his colleagues (47), only the kappas based on weighted data are provided. In the St. Louis study reported by Helzer and his colleagues (45), kappas for both weighted data and unweighted data are given for most of the results. The kappas for the unweighted data are usually somewhat higher due to the oversampling of cases and consequent higher rates of disorders.

In this discussion of the two studies, weighted results are referred to for the most part, using unweighted results only when weighted data are not provided, as is the case with some of the St. Louis findings. Given the differing designs of the follow-up subsamples in the two studies, the weighted results are more comparable. In addition, the weighted results are the only ones that can be generalized to the populations studied.

In the Helzer (45) study in St. Louis, the subsample of respondents with various types of DIS lifetime diagnoses (including no disorder) based on lay interviews in the St. Louis ECA site were reinterviewed within a few weeks to a few months after the initial interview. The second interview was done by psychiatrists using the DIS. However, after they made a DIS alone diagnosis, they also make a diagnosis based on a DSM-III checklist that could be based on additional questions and observations. The first finding to note is that the psychiatrists agreed quite well among themselves, with a kappa of .73 with unweighted data for all diagnoses combined versus none (kappas for weighted data were not provided for all versus none comparisons) and over .60 with weighted data for most individual diagnoses. For example, the kappa for major depression was .70 with weighted data. When the psychiatrists' DIS diagnoses were compared with the initial lay interviewers' diagnoses, agreement was considerably less although overall agreement for any lifetime diagnosis versus no disorder remained reasonably good, as indicated by a kappa of .63 with unweighted data. It decreased only slightly, to .59 with unweighted data, when the initial DIS diagnoses by lay interviewers were compared with the checklist diagnoses these psychiatrists were permitted to make following the psychiatrists' DIS interviews. The kappas for individual diagnoses based on unweighted data tend to be much lower and, with weighted data, satisfactory to good only for alcohol abuse, drug abuse and, possibly, antisocial personality. For major depression with weighted data, for example, they are only .33 when the DIS is compared with itself, and only .28 when the checklist diagnosis is substituted for the DIS diagnosis. Kappas for most of the remaining disorders are even lower.

In the study by Anthony and his colleagues (47), previous-month prevalence on DIS-DSM-III lay diagnoses were compared with previous-month prevalence diagnoses made on the basis of clinical examinations of a subsample of ECA cases from the Baltimore site. Two-thirds of the follow-up examinations took place within 3 weeks of the initial DIS interviews, 75% within 4 weeks, and 93% within 90 days. The results indicate that agreement is considerably worse than in the study by Helzer et al. (45). Here, for example, alcohol abuse again does relatively well, but the kappa is only .35 in this comparison based on weighted data.

Robins has pointed out (personal communication, May 31, 1988) that a positive diagnosis according to the clinical examination used in Baltimore requires meeting *full* criteria for a particular disorder in the last month; by contrast, the DIS definition of 1-month prevalence requires that the criteria have been met in one's lifetime and that there was at least *one* relevant symptom in the last month. These definitions are different, and it is hard to know how much they would overlap in practice if the same instrument were used to operationalize each definition. Moreover, no methodological study has yet been conducted with a semistructured research diagnostic interview designed for making DSM-III diagnoses—an interview such as the SCID which is only now being developed by Spitzer, Williams, Gibbon, and First (51). The PSE portion of the examination described by Anthony et al. (47) that was used to cross-check the DIS was designed for making diagnoses other than DSM-III, and had to be adapted for that purpose. It may have been too much to expect that DIS diagnoses would converge well with this particular clinical examination, especially with the added problems of differing approaches to defining 1-month prevalence and a time lag of 3 weeks to 3 months for the clinical follow-up after the initial interview.

By the same logic, however, it would have been very reasonable to expect the Helzer study to show strong convergence for *lifetime* diagnoses in retests done with the *DIS itself* which, although the type of interviewer is varied, is more a test of reliability than validity. If the goal of the DIS, as Robins and colleagues (27) have stated, is to "enable lay interviewers to obtain psychiatric diagnoses comparable to those a psychiatrist would obtain" (27, p. 386), then these results from the St. Louis and Baltimore ECA studies cannot be considered reassuring. Where the problem lies and what should be done about it are other matters, however.

It may appear that Robins is having second thoughts about the appropriateness of the goal itself as described above. She has argued in a remarkable paper that the tests so far conducted are flawed, and that we cannot assess the accuracy of the lay-administered DIS with a test-retest design using clinician examiners (52). She gives three reasons:

1. The research diagnosis by the clinician is not a gold standard.
2. There are problems of time-gap or order effects in the design.
3. Available statistical methods for testing accuracy are inadequate (the base-rate problem).

Note that a test using the more appropriate SCID would not solve any of these problems.

Robins argues further that we do not need all that much accuracy for two of the important purposes of epidemiological studies, estimating prevalence and investigating correlates of disorders in risk factor studies. She notes that analyses of the St. Louis data show that the discrepancies are most frequent for respondents whose DIS scores fall just short of meeting criteria or just barely meet the criteria —that is, are close to the cut point between the presence and absence of the disorder—and that these errors tend to be balanced among false positives and false negatives. She points out that unbiased estimates of rates require that there be equal numbers of false positive and false negative cases so that they cancel each other out. When rates are low, as with most disorders, and you have good specificity, a modest sensitivity can bring you nearer this goal than a very high sensitivity, as she illustrates.

However, there is no assurance that error with an instrument such as the DIS is itself randomly distributed among subgroups of the population defined by such factors as age, sex, and class. Perhaps most sobering in this regard is a comparison of initial DIS lifetime diagnoses made in four ECA sites with 1-year follow-up diagnoses made again by lay interviewers using the DIS. In analyzing these data, Anthony and Dryman (49) defined as a discrepancy a positive lifetime diagnosis for a particular disorder at Time 1 that disappeared altogether at Time 2. On the basis of this measure, 69% of baseline cases were discrepant (2456 out of 3572 cases). For example, 61% or 322 out of 529 respondents who had a lifetime DIS diagnosis of major depression at baseline did not have a lifetime diagnosis of major depression on the basis of the 1-year follow-up DIS.

Some of the marked discrepancies are due to the decreased reporting of positive diagnoses in general in the follow-up interview. This often occurs in repeated interviews over time with instruments of imperfect reliability and has been described as regression effects. The tendency appears to be particularly marked with the lay interview-administered DIS; it did not occur in the test-retest designs used in St. Louis and Baltimore, where some diagnoses were more frequent and some less frequent upon follow-up. More important with regard to the present issue, however, is the fact that the discrepancies are not randomly distributed according to age, gender, education, and ethnic status. As Robins (52) pointed out, if you are interested in studying risk factors for particular types of disorder, you need high sensitivity to assure an adequate sample of cases. There is, it seems, no way around the need for highly accurate measures that can do the job of unbiased measurement in the diverse social and cultural groups that make up our society. In the absence of biological tests and under the circumstances where interviews and observations of behavior remain the tools available to us, how do we obtain them?

MULTIMETHOD APPROACHES

There are two very different ways of handling measurement error in interview approaches. One involves psychometric theory and method to develop and evaluate strong threads of truth in scales composed of self-report items which, taken individually, are error prone. The second involves cross-examination by expert clinicians and application of their clinical judgment to rating signs and symptoms. Each of these procedures was used in rather primitive forms in some of the first and second generation studies.

As reported earlier, the two approaches have different strengths and weaknesses even in their more sophisticated forms. For example, an instrument like the Psychiatric Epidemiological Research Interview (PERI), which is in the psychometric tradition and was developed through research with samples from the general population, can yield scales with high internal consistency reliabilities in contrasting subgroups and cover a wide variety of dimensions of psychopathology; but PERI does not provide psychiatric diagnoses on an individual basis. By contrast, we have diagnostic interviews such as the PSS, SADS, and the PSE, which were developed with psychiatric patients and yield reliable diagnoses for such patients but are unlikely to provide reliable measures over the entire range of psychopathology dimensions in samples from the general population, and can yield misleading results in such samples (39,31,38). A possible reason is that the expertise of the clinician that helps reduce measurement error in instruments such as the PSS and PSE is more limited than has been recognized. It may not extend to the full range and variety of symptomatology that are found in groups from contrasting social and cultural background in the general population.

There are strategies, however, in which the strengths and weaknesses of the two approaches can be used symbiotically to complement and cross-check each other. For example, a self-report interview like the PERI, based on a psychometric approach to measuring dimensions of psychopathology, can be used to economically screen samples from the general population. Such screening can be designed to yield subsamples of individuals with various types of severe symptomatology. Individuals with high scores on the screening scale can then be followed up in a second stage of the research and interviewed by experienced clinicians with diagnostic instruments like the SADS or the PSE to provide rates for particular types of disorder. Results with the PERI from a study in Israel lend credence to the possibility that it could with no more than seven of the 25 symptom scales, with a total of only 73 items, perform the first-stage screening function (44). Such a two-stage procedure capitalizes on the ability of a psychometric instrument to provide reliable measurement over the full range of important dimensions of psychopathology and on the ability of a clinical examination to provide reliable diagnoses in groups where the types of symptomatology involved are not rare.

While the potential practical advantages of two-stage procedures such as this have long been evident (53), there have been only a handful of systematic attempts to use them for case identification and classification in psychiatric epidemiology. Duncan-Jones and Henderson (54) have speculated that use of two-stage procedures is so rare because of fear of loss of respondents between the first screening stage and the follow-up diagnostic interview. They found, however, that with careful planning, they were able to conduct interviews with 91% of the respondents designated for follow-up on the basis of initial screening. This author and colleagues are using this type of two-stage approach in an epidemiological study in Israel.

Choosing Israel as the setting for the epidemiological research was based mainly on two considerations. First, an open-class, highly stratified urban society that contained a set of advantaged and disadvantaged ethnic groups was needed to test theoretical issues having to do with class distributions of various types of disorder (55). Second, a place with a Population Register that would make it possible to draw samples of birth cohorts from such ethnic groups was necessary.

Within this setting, we have focused on a full probability sample of about 5,500 Jews born in Israel between 1949, just after it became a state, and 1958. The goal was to contrast Jews of European background with Jews of North African background, when both were born in Israel during the same period. Our aim has been to identify and define cases of schizophrenia, major depression, substance abuse, antisocial personality, and severe nonspecific psychological distress or "demoralization" (16). The first step was to draw a random sample of 19,000 Israel-born adults in the desired age range from the Population Register. Demographic prescreening of 98% of those 19,000 was completed to obtain information that would permit appropriate stratification into the approximately 5,500 member study sample on the basis of gender, educational level, and ethnic background. Once selected into the stratified sample, respondents were given screening scales from the Psychiatric Epidemiological Research Interview (PERI) (26,44). Developed in the U.S., these had been recalibrated in a previous pilot study in Israel (26). Excluding the respondents who died or who are abroad (who will be studied separately), we have so far obtained the relevant PERI screening data from 93.3% of our cohort sample, as Fig. 1 shows.

All of the screened positives (over 40% of the sample) and a subsample of about 15% of the negatives were given follow-up interviews by psychiatrists trained to administer a modification of the shorter version (SADS-L) of the Schedule for Affective Disorders and Schizophrenia (22) and to make diagnoses accord-

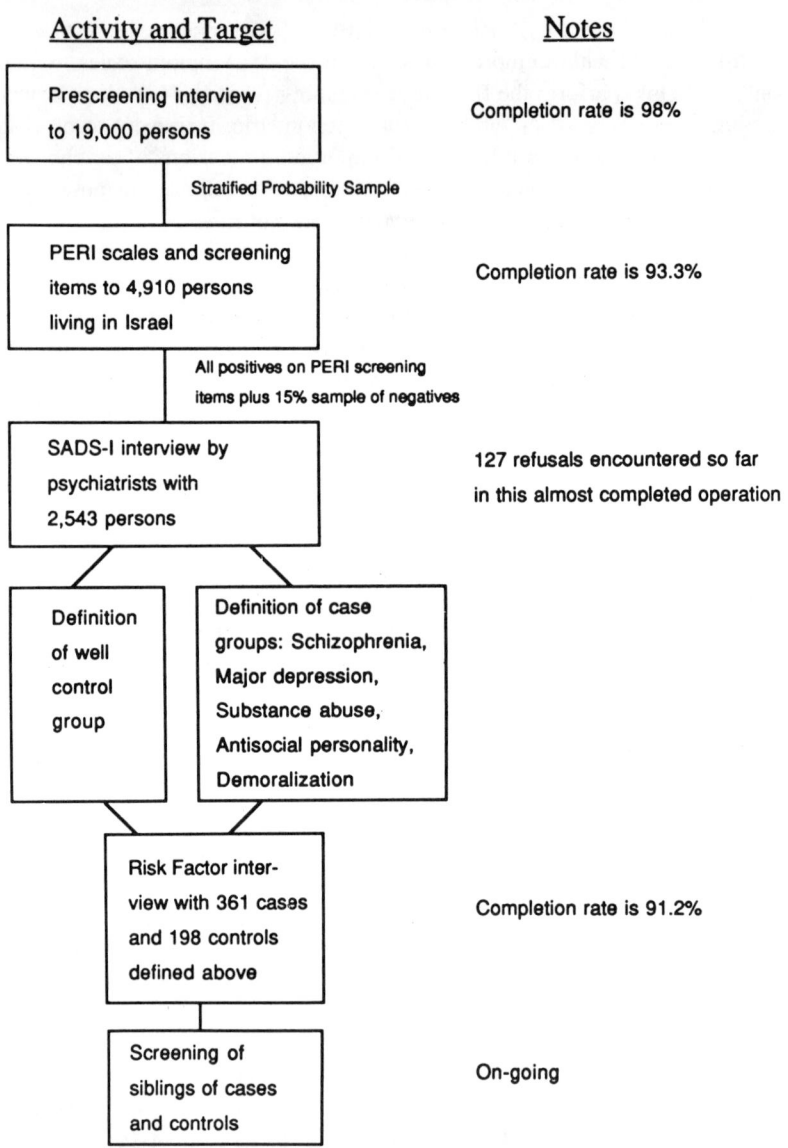

FIG. 1. Schematic chart of design and progress of epidemiological study in Israel.

ing to Research Diagnostic Criteria (RDC) (56). Since this instrument was modified to provide more introductory history and to permit the dating of onsets of episodes, we call it SADS-I (for Israel). The 40 or so psychiatrists involved in the research were intensively trained by Itzhak Levav, who was himself trained at the New York State Psychiatric Institute where SADS was developed. Their diagnostic interviews were tape recorded, permitting extensive quality and reliability checks. With 2,543 SADS-I's done and entered into our data files, we have so far encountered only 127 refusals. There are 62 that have been done but not entered into the file and 58 remain to be done. We expect to be able to report an excellent completion rate for this diagnostic follow-up.

From these diagnosed respondents, it has been possible to select a subsample of 361 persons for an intensive case/control study of risk factors for various types of disorder; most of the cases were chosen to have had a recent onset of the disorder. From those persons who were not screened as possible cases in the first stage, a stratified random subsample of about 300 has also been chosen for diagnostic follow-up. This follow-up of screened negatives serves two purposes: (a) it provides a check on the number of false negatives from the first-stage screening interview, and (b) it provides a sample of wells for use in the case/control study. As Fig. 1 shows, completion rates are excellent, and they will be even better before field work is over in this complex study.

The two-stage procedure that we are using in this research is, however, an economy. It would be best achieved following methodological research employing a multimethod strategy in which both types of interview were conducted with all subjects along, perhaps with a third method based on reports from family members or other key informants. In such a multimethod investigation, there would be two means of establishing validity.

One would be by testing the convergence of the three methods. This is illustrated in Fig. 2. The first method might consist of screening scales with the screened positives followed up at stage 2 by a clinical examination. When there is a divergence, categorization by a third method—perhaps informant reports—would be sought. The approach would be similar for screened negatives. "Truth" in Fig. 2 would be defined as a convergence across at least two out of three different methods of measuring the same thing—in the instance above, the diagnoses or other

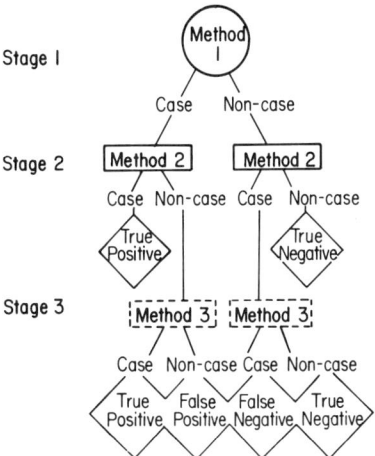

FIG. 2. Flow chart for a multistage-multimethod procedure for case identification and classification.
From Dohrenwend and Dohrenwend (4). With permission.

classifications dictated by the nomenclature or other theoretical constructs being used. Other things equal, the majority would rule.

However, other things are not likely to be equal in a situation where the different methods have different strengths and weaknesses. Thus a second procedure would be to establish not a gold standard of validity, but what has been called by Leckman, Sholomskas, Thompson, Belanger, and Weissman (57) a "best estimate" diagnosis in which the information from all three methods is assessed by two or more experts to arrive independently and then by consensus at a criterion diagnosis. It is something like the LEAD standard formulated by Spitzer (58) for testing SCID, and would be better with the longitudinal component Spitzer requires. The relative contributions of the separate methods to these best-estimate diagnoses can then be assessed for different diagnostic types and in different subgroups of the population as a basis for designing more economical two-stage procedures.

The validity achieved by such multimethod procedures would be relative to the validity of the particular diagnostic or classification system that dictates how the data on symptoms and signs are to be combined. Further tests of the validity of such systems are in order (19).

Other chapters in this volume discuss such tests. These tests can help those of us involved in epidemiological enterprises to use the more promising classification systems and even contribute to their selection. Whatever system is selected for a particular epidemiological study, however, epidemiologists will face the problem of how to validly classify people according to it. Perhaps someday there will be biological markers to provide gold standards. Meanwhile, some will be happy to settle for a combination of the democratic rule of the majority among methods and/or the authoritarian LEAD where a divergent minority method is too strong to be ignored.

ACKNOWLEDGMENTS

This work was supported by grants K05–MH14663 and MH30710 from the U.S. National Institute of Mental Health.

REFERENCES

1. Dohrenwend, B. P., and Dohrenwend, B. S. (1965): The problem of validity in field studies of psychological disorder. *J Abn Psychol*, 70:52–69.
2. Dohrenwend, B. P., and Dohrenwend, B. S. (1974): Social and cultural influences on psychopathology. *Ann Rev Psychol*, 25:417–452.
3. Dohrenwend, B. P., Dohrenwend, B. S., Schwartz Gould, M., Link, B., Neugebauer, R., Wunsch-Hitzig, R. (1980): *Mental illness in the United States: Epidemiologic Estimates*. Praeger, New York.
4. Dohrenwend, B. P., and Dohrenwend B. S. (1982): Perspectives on the past and future of psychiatric epidemiology. *Am J Pub Health*, 72:1271–1279.
5. Raines, G. N. (1952): Foreword. In: Committee on Nomenclature and Statistics of the American

Psychiatric Association. *Diagnostic and Statistical Manual; Mental Disorders.* American Psychiatric Association, Washington, D. C., pp. v–xi.
6. Srole, L., Langner, T. S., Michael, S. T., Opler, M. K., Rennie, T. A. C. (1962): *Mental Health in the metropolis.* McGraw-Hill, New York.
7. Leighton, D. C., Harding, J. S., Macklin, D. B., Macmillan, A. M., Leighton, A. H. (1963): *The Character of Danger.* Basic Books, New York.
8. Gillis, L. S., Lewis, J. B., Slabbert, M. (1965): *Psychiatric Disturbance and Alcoholism in the Coloured People of the Cape Peninsula.* University of Cape Town Department of Psychiatry, Cape Town.
9. Rin, H., Chu, H., Lin, T. (1966): Psychological reactions of a rural and suburban population in Taiwan. *Acta Psychiatr Scand,* 42:410–470.
10. Shore, J. H., Kinzie, J. D., Hampson, J. L., Pattison, E. M. (1973): Psychiatric Epidemiology of an Indian village. *Psychiatry,* 36:70–81.
11. Langner, T. S. (1962): A twenty-two item screening score of psychiatric symptoms indicating impairment. *J Health Human Behav,* 3:269–276.
12. Macmillan, A. M. (1957): The health opinion survey: Technique for estimating prevalence of psychoneurotic and related types of disorder in communities. *Psychol Rep,* 3:325–329.
13. Star, S. A. (1950): The screening of psychoneurotics in the army: Technical development of tests. In: *Measurement and Prediction,* Vol. 4, edited by Stouffer, S. A. et al. Princeton University Press, Princeton.
14. Seiler, L. H. (1973): The 22-item scale used in field studies of mental illness: A question of method, a question of substance, and a question of theory. *J Health Soc Behav,* 14:252–264.
15. Link, B., and Dohrenwend, B. P. (1980): Formulation of hypotheses about the true prevalence of demoralization in the United States. In:Dohrenwend B. P., et al., *Mental Illness in the United States: Epidemiological Estimates.* Praeger, New York. pp. 114–132.
16. Dohrenwend, B. P., Shrout, P. E., Egri, G., and Mendelsohn, F. S. (1980): Nonspecific psychological distress and other dimensions of psychopathology: Measures for use in the general population. *Arch Gen Psychiatry,* 37:1229–1236.
17. Frank, J. D. (1973): *Persuasion and Healing.* Johns Hopkins University Press, Baltimore, Maryland.
18. Dohrenwend, B. P., Oksenberg, L., Shrout, P. E., Dohrenwend, B. S., and Cook, D. (1979): What brief psychiatric screening scales measure. In: *Health survey research methods: third biennial research conference.* National Center for Health Services Research. DHHS pub. no. (PHS) 81–3268. U.S. Department of Health and Human Services, Washington, D. C.
19. Robins, E., and Guze, S. B. (1970): Establishment of diagnostic validity in psychiatric illness: Its application to schizophrenia. *Am J Psychiatry,* 126:983–987.
20. Woodruff, R. S., Goodwin, D. W., and Guze, S. B. (1974): *Psychiatric Diagnosis.* Oxford University Press, New York and London.
21. Wing, J. K., Cooper, J. E., and Sartorius N. (1974): *The Measurement and Classification of Psychiatric Symptoms.* Cambridge University Press, London.
22. Endicott, J., Spitzer, R. L. (1978): A diagnostic interview: The schedule for affective disorders and schizophrenia. *Arch Gen Psychiatry,* 35:837–844.
23. Derogatis, L. R. (1977): *SCL-90.R. Version Manual I. (revised)* Clinical Psychometrics Research Unit, Johns Hopkins University School of Medicine, Baltimore, Maryland.
24. Goldberg, D. P. (1972): *The Detection of Psychiatric Illness by Questionnaire.* Oxford University Press, London.
25. Radloff, L. S. (1977): The CES-D scale: A self-report depression scale for research in the general population. *Appl Psychol Meas,* 1:385–401.
26. Shrout, P. E., Dohrenwend, B. P., and Levav I. (1986): A discriminant rule for screening cases of diverse diagnostic types: Preliminary results. *J Consult Clin Psychol,* 54(3):314–319.
27. Robins, L. N., Helzer, J. E., Croughan, J., and Ratcliff, K. S. (1981): National Institute of Mental Health Diagnostic Interview Schedule: Its history, characteristics, and validity. *Arch Gen Psychiatry,* 38:381–389.
28. Weissman, M. M., and Myers, J. K. (1978): Affective disorders in a U.S. urban community: The use of research diagnostic criteria in an epidemiological survey. *Arch Gen Psychiatry,* 35:1304–1311.
29. Vernon, S. V., Roberts, R. E. (1982): Use of the SADS-RDC in a tri-ethnic community sample. *Arch Gen Psychiatry,* 39:47–52.

30. Spitzer, R. L., Endicott, J., Fleiss, J. L., and Cohen J. (1976): The psychiatric status schedule: A technique for evaluating psychopathology and impairment in role functioning. *Arch Gen Psychiatry*, 23:41–55.
31. Dohrenwend, B. P., Yager, T. J., Egri, G., and Mendelsohn, F. S. (1978): The psychiatric status schedule (PSS) as a measure of dimensions of psychopathology in the general population. *Arch Gen Psychiatry*, 35:731–739.
32. Wing, J. K., Mann, S. A., Leff, J. P., and Nixon, J. M. (1978): The concept of a "case" in psychiatric population surveys. *Psychol Med*, 8:203–217.
33. Brown, G. W., and Harris, T. (1978): *Social Origins of Depression*. Free Press, New York.
34. Spitzer, R. L., and Endicott, J. (1968): DIAGNO: A computer program for psychiatric diagnosis utilizing the differential diagnostic procedure. *Arch Gen Psychiatry*, 18:746–756.
35. Bash, K. W. (1967): Untersuchungen ueber die Epidemiologie neuropsychiatrischer Erkrankungen unter der Landbevoelkerung der Provinz Fars, Iran. *Aktuel Fragen Psychiatr Neurol*, 5:162–178.
36. Hagnell, O. (1966): *A Prospective Study of the Incidence of Mental Disorder*. Svenska Bokforlaget Norstedts-Bonniers, Stockholm.
37. Lin, T. (1953): A study of the incidence of mental disorder in Chinese and other cultures. *Psychiatry*, 16:313–336.
38. Dohrenwend, B. P., Yager, T. J., Egri, G. and Mendelsohn, F. S. (1980): Some problems of validity with the Psychiatric Status Schedule as an instrument for case identification and classification in the general population (letter to the editor). *Arch Gen Psychiatry*, 37:720–721.
39. Dohrenwend, B. P., Egri, G., Mendelsohn, F. S. (1971): Psychiatric disorder in general populations: a study of the problem of clinical judgment. *Am J Psychiatry*, 127:1304–1312
40. Feighner, J. P., Robins, E., Guze, S. B., Woodruff, R. A., Winokur, G., and Munoz, R. (1972): Diagnostic criteria for use in psychiatric research. *Arch Gen Psychiatry*, 26:57–63.
41. Breslau, N. (1985): Depressive symptoms, major depression and generalized anxiety: A comparison of self-reports on CES-D and results from diagnostic interviews. *Psychiatry Research*, 15:219–229.
42. Roberts, R. E., and Vernon, S. W. (1983): The center for epidemiological studies depression scale: Its use in a community sample. *Am J Psychiatry*, 140:41–46.
43. Myers, J. K., Weissman, M. M. (1980): Use of a self-report symptom scale to detect the depressive syndrome. *Am J Psychiatry*, 137:1081–1084.
44. Dohrenwend, B. P., Levav, I., and Shrout, P. E. (1986): Screening scales from the psychiatric epidemiology research interview (PERI). In: *Community Surveys of Psychiatric Disorders*, edited by M. M. Weissman, et al. Rutgers University Press, New Brunswick, New Jersey.
45. Helzer, J. E., Robins, L. N., McEvoy, L. T., Spitznagel, E. L., Stoltzman, R. K., Farmer, A., and Brockington, I. F. (1985): A comparison of clinical and diagnostic interview schedule diagnoses: Physician reexamination of lay-interviewed cases in the general population. *Arch Gen Psychiatry*, 42:657–666.
46. Regier, D. A., Myers, J. K., Kramer, M., Robins, L. N., Blazer, D. G., Hough, R. L., Eaton, W. W., and Locke, B. Z. (1984): The NIMH epidemiologic catchment area program. *Arch Gen Psychiatry*, 41:934–941.
47. Anthony, J. C., Folstein, M., Romanoski, A. J., Von Korff, M. R., Nestadt, G. R., Chahal, R., Merchant, A., Hendricks Brown, C., Shapiro, S., Kramer, M., and Gruenberg, E. (1985): Comparison of the lay diagnostic interview schedule and a standardized psychiatric diagnosis: Experience in Eastern Baltimore. *Arch Gen Psychiatry*, 42:667–675.
48. Pulver, A. E., and Carpenter, W. T. (1983): Lifetime psychotic symptoms assessed with the DIS. *Schizophrenia Bulletin*, 9(3):377–382.
49. Anthony, J. C., and Dryman, A. (1987): *Analysis of discrepancy in lifetime diagnosis of mental disorders: Results from the NIMH Epidemiologic Catchment Area Program*. Presented at the September 1987 meeting of the World Psychiatric Association; Section on Epidemiology and Community Psychiatry, Reykjavik, Iceland.
50. Cohen, J. (1960): A coefficient of agreement for nominal scales. *Educat Psychol Measurement*, 20:37–46.
51. Spitzer, R. L., Williams, J. B. W., Gibbon, M., and First, M. (1987): *Structured Clinical Interview for DSM-III-R (SCID)*. Biometrics Research Department, New York State Psychiatric Institute, New York.

52. Robins, L. N. (1985): Epidemiology: Reflections on testing the validity of psychiatric interviews. *Arch Gen Psychiatry*, 42:918–924.
53. Cooper, B., Morgan, H. G. (1973): *Epidemiological Psychiatry*. C. C. Thomas, Springfield, Illinois.
54. Duncan-Jones, P., and Henderson, S. (1978): The use of a two-phase design in a prevalence survey. *Soc Psychiatry*, 13:231–237.
55. Dohrenwend, B. P., and Dohrenwend, B. S. (1981): Socioenvironmental factors, stress, and psychopathology—Part I: Quasi-experimental evidence on the social causation-social selection issue posed by class differences. *Am J Comm Psychol*, 9:146–159.
56. Spitzer, R. L., Endicott, J., and Robins, E. Research diagnostic criteria: Rationale and reliability. *Arch Gen Psychiatry*, 35:773–782.
57. Leckman, J. F., Sholomskas, D., Thompson, D. W., Belanger, A., and Weissman, M. M. (1982): Best estimate of lifetime psychiatric diagnosis: A methodological study. *Arch Gen Psychiatry*, 39:879–883.
58. Spitzer, R. L. (1983): Psychiatric diagnosis: Are clinicians still necessary? *Compr Psychiatry*, 24:399–411.

DISCUSSION

Dr. James Barrett: As usual, Dr. Dohrenwend has given us some provocative issues to consider, and I would like to lead off with one. I agreed with your earlier comments, when you were discussing both the Index of Definition and the use of scales as case identifiers, that the literature is replete with studies which show that individual scales are not very effective identifiers of specific disorders, particularly when they are used in nonpatient populations. This is the issue I want to address, as in our work we have been involved with trying to use some of these measures in a general medical population. Our experience is that there are sizable numbers of individuals who appear to have a disorder, at least by the criteria that they have symptoms, distress, and some impairment, but they do not fit any of the official psychiatric diagnostic categories derived from the study of psychiatric patients. So, one rather critical issue, as you move from specialty sector patient categories into the general population, is: what is a disorder? One focus of the meeting is how are we going to decide what a valid disorder is? Would you address this question? Specifically, in your work, were there people who legitimately had disorders, but who were not able to be classified by the existing nosology which derives from the specialty sector of psychiatry?

Dr. Dohrenwend: The answer is very much yes. In our study in Israel, we have isolated persons who were high on our screening scale of nonspecific distress or demoralization but who did not meet RDC criteria for any of the types of disorder that RDC covers and thus were rated as having "no disorder" by the clinicians. These people did not even meet RDC criteria for what we consider demoralization equivalents, such as dysthymic disorder. Our distressed group I think is probably heterogeneous, and we are including them as a separate group in our case control study. We consider it extremely important to learn more about them. We don't know, for example, whether those who score high on our scale of nonspecific distress are on a continuum with clinical cases of depression or anxiety. We don't know if this kind of symptomatology, as may have been suggested by the Leightons a long time ago, is a risk factor for full-blown disorder. I think such groups of symptomatic general population respondents require much more investigation.

Dr. Bruce Pfohl: I would like to suggest that perhaps the problems of a clinical instrument's validity in the general population has little to do with the instrument per se but rather with the nature of diagnoses in the general population. It is easy to show that clinicians will have much better diagnostic agreement when dealing with severe cases than when dealing with milder cases of an illness. This holds for both medical and psychiatric diagnosis. The general population always has proportionally more mild and borderline cases of a disorder than are seen in clinical populations. Development of a better instrument is not going to solve this problem.

I suggest that all a multistage screening process may accomplish is to select cases that are sufficiently severe as to provide consistent pathologic responses to the screening questions over the various separate interviews. If this is true, you could make a three-stage screening process, such as the one you outlined, even simpler by giving the same instrument on 3 different days. The cases that met criteria for the disorder three times in a row would almost certainly be more likely to have "real depression" by other validating criteria than would cases that only met screening criteria one of the three times. My point is that the improved validity does not come from the choice of particular instruments at different stages of a screening process but rather comes from the multistage process itself, which increases validity by requiring that the patients meet the criteria three times in a row.

Dr. Dohrenwend: Let me say that I wouldn't advocate any procedure that ignored the threshold problem. The fact is that the discrepancies are concentrated around the cut points; these are cut point problems, and I would not allow the majority to rule in all cases. Where you have a unanimous majority of all methods, you don't have a problem of cut points. I don't think you need to adjudicate between three methods that agree; I agree that such unanimity would most likely occur for severe cases. Where the three methods do not agree, I think we must recognize that each method has strengths and weaknesses relative to the others. For example, informant reports certainly have clear advantages with regard to antisocial personality and certain acting-out disorders. Even if such reports were in the minority, I would not ignore them where such diagnoses might be at issue, or with regard to questions like accurate identification of cases in contrasting subcultural groups. Please don't forget that I said there were two criteria. One was a "majority rules" criterion and the other was a "best estimate" criterion. The best estimate assessment should be made with knowledge of the strengths and weaknesses of the different instruments.

Dr. Alan Frances: Two quick questions. When the results from clinical and nonclinical samples disagree, as they have, for example, in anxiety disorders and schizotypal personality, how would you balance or weigh the different results in establishing criteria for the official system of nomenclature? How much weight should one give to community sample results when they differ from results in clinical samples? A second related question is, if we want to talk about results applicable to "real" clinical practice, which would be more preferable: population survey results, or results generated from research patients in university settings? Do you think the populations in the real clinical world, the nonresearch clinical world, may be closer to the epidemiologic populations than the patient populations in the university research samples?

Dr. Dohrenwend: The only possibility of a representative sample is a general population sample. If there were a contradiction between the findings from a well investigated general population sample and a clinical sample, which is usually biased by selection factors related to who gets into treatment at any given time, I would go with the general population sample. Again, however, this decision assumes that our case identification procedures in the general population are adequate.

Dr. Frances: But are they, given the current state of case identification?

Dr. Dohrenwend: In the Israel study, I would go with the general population sample. Beyond that I am not willing to go.

Dr. Frances: And my second question; do you think that clinical samples in the community, those not obtained from university research settings, are closer to what you find in the epidemiological samples?

Dr. Dohrenwend: I think there would be some disorders where your general population sample isn't going to work. Schizophrenia would be an example. Even assuming good identification methods, your general population sample for such a rare disorder would have to be gigantic to obtain an adequate number of cases. The 20,000 member ECA sample isn't large enough, especially if you are interested in first episode cases or in repeat episode cases of recent onset. So the question is: how do you use what you can learn about who is treated from a general population sample to draw something approximating a representative patient sample from treatment settings? This information would preclude drawing cases from a university setting alone, since only a small minority of the cases of schizophrenia in a general population sample would be treated in such a setting. You would need to work in a place where there was prepaid, comprehensive coverage, such as the Scandinavian countries, England, or Israel.

Dr. Helzer: I would like to return to the difficulty of making diagnoses in the general population. The agreement between two lay interviewers, or between a lay interviewer and a clinician, in a clinical population is about comparable to what the agreement is in two independent examinations by clinicians. What we lack in the general population is a benchmark comparison of two independent examinations by clinicians to see how that would compare with the lay interviewer vs. clinician results. Concerning the problem of case thresholds, we have looked at the predictive validity of the lay diagnoses compared to clinician diagnoses by using the wave 1 follow-up data from the ECA. We find that when we look at outcome, the two sets of diagnoses predict about equally. This suggests that a lot of the diagnostic discrepancies between lay interviewers and clinician interviewers are probably those cases that are near the diagnostic threshold. For many of the kinds of things that we are interested in in epidemiology, that is not a serious issue.

Dr. Dohrenwend: I would agree with almost everything you said up to the last point. It is around the problem of threshold that epidemiology has a chance to make a unique contribution. Agreement is always going to be better at the extremes, but those at the extremes are a very selected sample of the population of people who may have the underlying problems that we are interested in.

Dr. Helzer: Of course, but to be able to identify the definite cases in the general population, and then look for risk factors and correlates of illness in those cases, may give us a lot of insight into the threshold issue.

Dr. Dohrenwend: If that is all you were doing, one would wonder why you wouldn't use patients as the "definite" cases?

Dr. Robert Hirschfeld: I want to emphasize the point made earlier, which was that the method of case identification to use depends on what you wish to measure. The discrepancy between cases identified by dimensional scales and cases identified by categorical or Stage 1 clinical interviews may have to do with the fact that they are measuring different things. I would like to point out that the SADS-L has been very effective in assessing over time specific categories of disorder, and so it is possible to do this in a community sample.

Stability and Change in Childhood-Onset Depressive Disorders: Longitudinal Course as a Diagnostic Validator

*Maria Kovacs,
**Constantine Gatsonis

*Department of Psychiatry, University of Pittsburgh School of Medicine, Western Psychiatric Institute and Clinic, Pittsburgh, Pennsylvania 15213; **Carnegie Mellon University, Pittsburgh, Pennsylvania 15213 and The University of Massachusetts, Amherst, Massachusetts 01003

INTRODUCTION

A major purpose of psychiatric diagnosis is to predict the outcome of the disorder, that is, to inform about prognosis (1, 2). In psychiatry, the concept of validity (which had been borrowed from psychometrics) can therefore be reformulated as the following questions: How well does a particular diagnosis attain its goals? (1) Does it predict outcome? We will address this aspect of validity by focusing on the longitudinal course of childhood-onset depressive disorders.

Because longitudinal course entails a temporal dimension, stability and change are two constructs of importance. On the one hand, there should be stability in the salient aspects or clinical features of the disorder, irrespective of the age of the patient, in order to ensure that the disorder is reliably identified. Stability can therefore be defined as within-episode or across-episode consistency in symptoms. Stability of a diagnosis can also be viewed as a predictable recurrence of the syndrome. The foregoing features then become part of the clinical course. And the characteristic disease course, as ascertained by follow-up, represents one phase in the validation of a psychiatric disorder (3–5).

On the other hand, change, as opposed to stability, is a concept which seems more suitable to children and adolescents. In the usual course of events, orderly progression on physical, psychologic, emotional, cognitive, and social parameters is the hallmark of the juvenile years. It has been proposed therefore that the salient aspects of psychiatric disorders should also vary as a function of normal developmental processes (6). Developmental-phase mediated features in the clinical picture ought to be evident for any young patient with the passage of time. If developmental stage affects symptoms, then groups of children with varying chronological ages should also differ symptomatically at any given point in time.

In the nosologic study of child psychiatric disorders, is it possible to reconcile the concepts of change and stability? This issue becomes particularly important if it can be demonstrated that developmental phases affect the course of psychiatric disturbance in the preadult years. A related question is whether longitudinal follow-up can provide prognostic and validational data about juvenile disorders, in the manner in which these approaches have been found fruitful with adults.

Because the characteristics of the depressive disorders among adult patients have been extensively explored, the extant information can serve as a backdrop in the interpretation of data from depressed juveniles. For example, it is well known that depressive disorders among adults are phasic. They are associated with high rates of recovery both with and without formal treatment, although some episodes may be protracted. However, there is also a high risk of subsequent relapse, as well as a risk of chronicity (7–15). Whether or not the features of depressive disorders in children and adolescents are comparable to the presentation of these disorders in the later years is therefore a practical nosologic issue.

Because we have been conducting a longitudinal prospective follow-up study of school-aged children with depressive disorders, we are in the position to explore several of the above noted issues. Specifically, we will address two areas of interest: (a) we will examine the symptom pictures of depressed youths as a function of chronological age in order to assess possible age-related changes, and (b) we will investigate whether the clinical course of these disorders is sufficiently stable to provide prognostic information.

With regard to the question of the possible effects of age on symptoms, it is worth noting that the symptomatic manifestations of depression in childhood are a controversial area in child psychiatry. For many years, it was believed that depressive disorders among juveniles were difficult to diagnose because of the absence of a stable and clear pattern of symptoms and signs. It was posited that due to developmental influences, the depressions presented in atypical and variable ways in the preadult years, were often being "masked" or concealed by acting-out behaviors (for reviews, see 16–18). Thus, for example, younger depressed children were expected "to act bad rather than sad" and were also presumed less likely than adolescents or adults to show the classic symptoms of depression (19, 20).

Notwithstanding putative age-dependent changes in symptom presentation, a psychiatric diagnosis must have prognostic implications. Otherwise its validity is questionable. A diagnosis, for instance, should convey information about the likelihood of recovery and the chances of recurrence, as well as the odds of new psychiatric illness developing. Such information is both clinically very important and nosologically pertinent. Variable or discordant outcomes among a group of patients with a given diagnosis have been interpreted as one indication that the original patient group was heterogenous (3). However, such outcomes have also been viewed as the natural consequence of a given disorder (2). In either case, outcomes that are logically consistent with the original diagnosis support its predictive validity.

We have already reported initial findings on the likelihood of recovery associated with the various types of depressions in part of our juvenile cohort (21). For the current presentation, we will briefly summarize the findings on recovery as reconfirmed by analyses on a larger portion of our sample. Then, as one approach to the study of predictive validity, we will report on the time-dependent risk of four different outcomes for each of the depressions we have studied: (a) a new episode of major depression or (b) a first episode of bipolar disorder, both of which would be entirely consistent with an initial diagnosis of depression, (c) secondary anxiety disorder or (d) conduct disorder, which have been reported to be the most common comorbid conditions in young depressed patients (17, 18, 22).

The validational schema of Robins et al. (3–5) gave the impetus for our present investigation and therefore we will place our findings in the context of that schema. We will also relate the nosologic issues raised by our work to the prototypical nature of the current psychiatric classificatory system.

METHODS

We briefly review salient methodological aspects of this study. Extensive descriptions of patient recruitment, instrumentation, and diagnostic procedures have already been provided elsewhere (21, 23, 24).

The subjects in this study were recruited through outpatient child-psychiatry and pediatric clinics. Our research staff evaluated all eligible cases and established their suitability for the study, which included being 8–13 years old at entry with no evidence of systemic medical illness or mental retardation. Children who met diagnostic criteria, according to the Diagnostic and Statistical Manual of the American Psychiatric Association, Third Edition (DSM-III) (25), for some type of depression constituted the *depressed* probands (total $N = 142$). A consecutive series of age-matched clinic referrals who failed to meet criteria for any type of depressive disorder constituted the psychopathologic controls ($N = 49$). In the first year of study participation, children were evaluated up to four times; in every subsequent year, up to two evaluations were done per subject per year.

Using a semistructured, symptom-oriented psychiatric interview, the Interview Schedule for Children (ISC), as well as pertinent diagnostic addenda (see 21, 23, 24), the probands were repeatedly assessed over the course of the study. At each evaluation, the parent was first interviewed about the child; then, the same clinician interviewed the child about himself or herself. The final symptom ratings at each assessment were therefore based on data from both informants. The data were routinely reviewed in clinical case conferences and the diagnoses were assigned by consensus. Examples of our diagnostic decision making in the case of multiple, contemporaneous disorders have been provided (21). Likewise, operational rules have been specified for dating onsets and offsets of disorders and for defining recovery (21, 23, 24).

Subjects and Follow-Up Interval

In this chapter, we report data only on the first 104 cases in the depressed sample. At study entry, average age was 11 years (range: 8–13 years) and the sex ratio was perfectly even. Whites made up 58% of the sample, and there was a slight overrepresentation of lower socioeconomic classes (as calculated by Hollingshead's index).

At initial case classification, 46 cases had major depressive disorder (MDD); 23 had dysthymic disorder (DD); 16 cases had both, a phenomenon which has been called double depression (MDD/DD); and 19 had adjustment disorder with depressed mood (ADDM). A high rate of comorbidity characterized the entire sample. Altogether 77% had one or more concurrent psychiatric disorders during their index depressions, with anxiety disorders being the most frequent comorbid condition (43%). Only 17% had comorbid conduct disorders (26).

The earliest of the cases entered the study in the spring of 1978. The data points used in the present analysis included all face-to-face interviews from study entry up to January 8, 1987.

Diagnostic Verification

In the study of the predictive validity of a diagnosis, the original diagnostic classification should be as accurate as possible, Several strategies in our protocol served to facilitate reliable and accurate diagnosis. First, the use of a semistructured interview and trained professional clinicians served to reduce information variance. Second, the use of the DSM-III helped to decrease criterion variance.

Furthermore, after a case was classified at study entry, we allowed a 6-month period of diagnostic verification. The purpose of this was to enable the gathering of further data, as needed, to verify that the patient *did* meet criteria *initially* for a targeted depressive disorder. For example, a parent may not have had sufficient information about impaired concentration in the child, which could however be verified from school report cards or teachers' notes. Or, at study intake, the parent who brought the child to the assessment may not have had sufficient contact with the child to report on all the areas of functioning, but an interview with the other parent would satisfactorily settle certain issues. Altogether 11 cases who passed our Phase II recruitment prescreen (23) eventually were found not to meet any criteria for depression and were deleted.

Finally, it has been our policy not to include a subject's data in publications until he or she has been in the study for a minimum of 2 years. This additional period provides time for the proper classification of outcomes.

Statistical Analyses

Fisher's exact test was used to compare the proportions of younger and older depressed children who manifested a certain symptom. The Bonferroni inequality (27) was used to account for the effects of multiple comparisons across symptoms. We report the odds-ratios for the symptoms on which there appeared to be age-related differences.

Rates of recovery from the depressive disorders, which we briefly review, and the time-dependent risk for the various psychiatric outcomes since the onset of the index episode of depression were estimated using the Kaplan-Meier estimator (28). This approach accounts for the fact that subjects were observed over time intervals of differing lengths, and that some dropped out of the study prior to the occurrence of interest while some others did not reach the outcome of interest by the end of the observation period.

RESULTS
Change in Symptoms of Depression as a Function of Age

To estimate the extent to which symptom patterns may vary as a function of age, we compared the incidence of selected symptoms for 50 youngsters, whose ages ranged from 8 to 16 years at the time of the symptom ratings. These cases were selected because they had a full-blown major depressive disorder (MDD) at the time of evaluation. The actual symptom ratings, as recorded on the ISC interviews, were made on 0-to-8 point or 0-to-3 point scales.

For these comparisons, the symptom ratings were collapsed into two categories: present (that is, a clinically significant rating) or not present. The children were divided into two age groups: 11 years or younger (N=31) and 12 years or older (N=19). Only five of these 50 children were above 14 years old at the time of the evaluation in question. The age cut-off point of 11 years was selected on two grounds: (a) it provided comparable sample sizes, and (b) it represented a conventionally accepted point for distinguishing between children and adolescents. (Note that we did consider one alternative cut-off point at the age of 10, but found the same results.) The list of selected symptoms and the odds-ratios for those symptoms with age-related differences are shown in Table 1.

It can be readily seen in Table 1 that the incidence of most of the classic symptoms of depression was not different in the two age groups. The only symptom with a drastically different age-related incidence was hypersomnia. Although the overall rate was low, older children were more than seven times as likely to experience hypersomnia as the younger ones (Fisher's exact p-value = .003 is significant even after accounting for multiple comparisons). There were indications that younger children were more likely to have reduced sleep, somatic complaints, and separation anxiety than the older ones, but these results were not statistically significant. Our findings that the clinical picture of MDD does not change substan-

TABLE 1. *Depressive and related symptoms among two age groups of young patients with MDD (N = 50)[a,b]*

Symptoms	Odds ratio (Older/younger cases)	Fisher's p-value
Depressed mood	.37	
Feels unloved	.78	
Anger	.61	
Temper tantrums	1.58	
Irritability	.53	
Guilt	.91	
Self-deprecation	1.03	
Pessimism/hopelessness	1.28	
Anhedonia	.90	
Social withdrawal	1.24	
Impaired concentration	.79	
Suicidal ideation	1.13	
Wants to die	.68	
Reduced sleep	.35	.07
Increased sleep	7.50	.003
Reduced appetite	.43	
Increased appetite	.78	
Fatigue	.70	
Somatic complaints	.31	.06
General anxiety	.76	
Separation anxiety	.38	.11
Disobedience	3.01	.06
Physical fighting	.91	
Truancy	(2 Older Ss)	.13
Drug Abuse	(4 Older Ss)	.02

[a] Aged 11 years or younger ($N=31$) vs. 12 years or older ($N=19$).
[b] Symptom ratings dichotomized as clinically significant or not.

tially with age are in general agreement with the conclusions by Ryan et al. (29) based on the analysis of their data on 6- to 18-year-old patients.

The Predictive Validities of the Diagnoses of Depression

Two aspects of a psychiatric disorder are of particular clinical importance, namely, the associated prognosis for recovery and the risk for recurrent or new episodes of psychiatric illness. We have already documented aspects of the prognosis for the diagnoses of depression in childhood (21) and, therefore, will only update these data briefly.

Recovery from the Index Depressions

The analysis of the data on the first 104 cases in the sample reconfirmed our previous report. That is, each of the diagnoses of depression which we studied in juveniles was found to be associated with a high rate of recovery. The estimated cumulative probability of recovery from the index episode of major depressive disorder (MDD) was .97 by 41 months since MDD-onset, with a median time to recovery of 9.54 months (S.E. = 0.71 months; $N = 62$).

Although the rate of recovery from the index dysthymic disorder (DD) was almost as high, the resolution time for dysthymia was considerably longer. For the 39 children with DD, the estimated probability of recovery was .93 at 81 months since dysthymia onset (median time to recovery = 45 months; S.E. = 4.8 months). This was partly confounded by the fact that the DSM-III requires a 1-year duration of symptoms for the diagnosis of DD, during which recovery is not possible, by definition.

The diagnosis of adjustment disorder with depressed mood (ADDM) also has high information value as far as recovery is concerned. Using data on the 19 cases with this diagnosis, we found an estimated cumulative probability of remission of .95 at 17 months from onset of ADDM (median time to recovery = 6.2 months, S.E. = 1.2 months).

In summary then, the follow-up information on the course of MDD, DD, and ADDM in school-aged children and adolescents suggests that each of these diagnoses has high predictive value, as far as recovery from the episode is concerned. In fact, the three diagnoses cannot be distinguished from one another in regard to the probability of eventual remission; only on the temporal dimension can they be differentiated. That is, compared to DD, episodes of both MDD and ADDM resolve in relatively short periods.

New Episodes of Psychiatric Illness Developing

In order to investigate the validity of the diagnoses of depression based on predicting new episodes of psychiatric illness, we selected four possible outcomes and estimated the time-dependent risk for the occurrence of each. The outcomes were: (a) a new episode of major depression, (b) a first episode of bipolar disorder, (c) secondary anxiety disorder, and (d) secondary conduct disorder.

The risk curves were constructed by reversing the Kaplan-Meier estimates of *not* developing the particular outcome. The analyses were carried out separately for cases with index MDD, DD, or ADDM. The outcomes were not mutually exclusive because a patient could have developed either none or up to all four outcomes. And, because for each index depression data from the *same cases* were used to calculate the risk estimates, we did not attempt formal within-group comparisons of the risk-curves.

Figure 1 shows the time-dependent risk estimates of the four outcomes among subjects with an index diagnosis of major depression. On the X-axis, time is depicted since the onset of the index MDD. Note that the risk of a *subsequent* episode of major depression in this group far surpasses the risk of the other outcomes, and reaches the cumulative probability of .72 at 68 months.

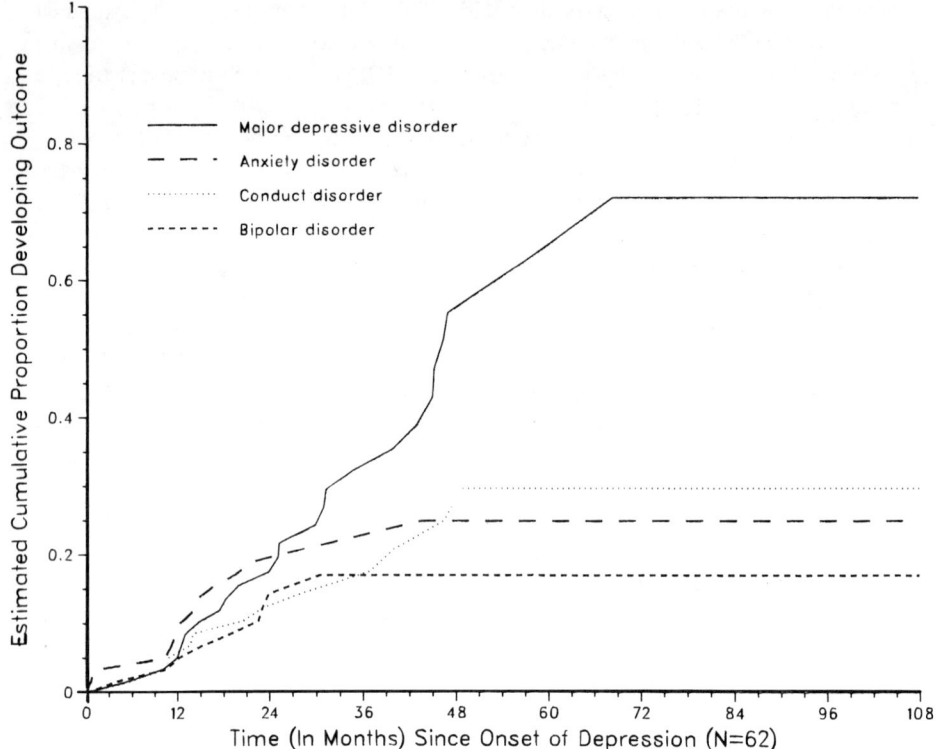

FIG. 1. Time-dependent risk of four different disorders developing among children with the index diagnosis of major depressive disorder.

It is notable that the risk estimate for a *new* episode of major depression among index MDD cases is high, although the risk-period for it is briefer than for the other outcomes. That is, the risk of a secondary anxiety disorder developing starts shortly after the onset of the index depression (by definition). On the other hand, before the child could have a *second depression,* he or she would have had to recover from the index episode, and then remain free of depressive symptoms for at least 2 months, the latter of which is part of our definition of recovery (21). Only *then* could the child develop a new episode.

As can be also seen in Fig. 1, the risk of bipolar disorder is .17 at 30 months. In view of the general rarity of bipolar illness and its even lower prevalence in children and adolescents, this outcome is unexpectedly high. Note that in classifying bipolar outcome, both "Bipolar I" and "Bipolar II" were included. Finally, the risks of a first episode of secondary conduct disorder or secondary anxiety disorder developing are virtually indistinguishable among these children with MDD.

In Fig. 2, the graphs depict the time-dependent risk of major depression, bipolar disorder, secondary anxiety disorder, and secondary conduct disorder develop-

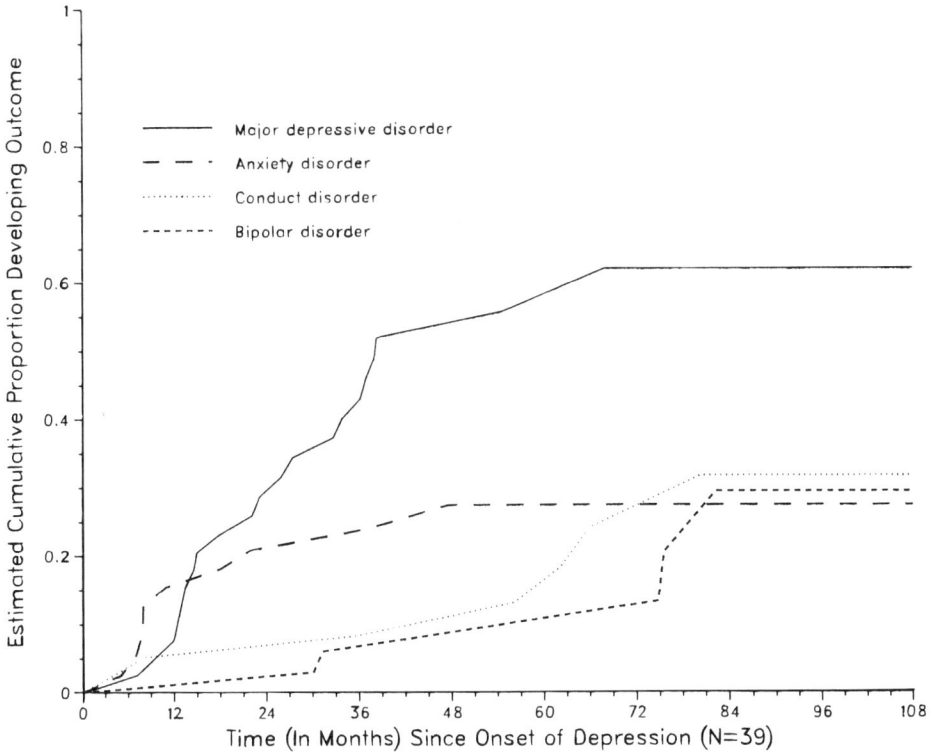

FIG. 2. Time-dependent risk of four different disorders developing among children with the index diagnosis of dysthymic disorder.

ing among the 39 children with index DD. Once again, the risk of an episode of major depression (with a cumulative probability of .62 at 68 months) among these children with dysthymia far exceeds the risks of the other outcomes. The risk of bipolar outcome is again higher than expected. About one-third of these DD cases run the risk of anxiety disorders or conduct disorders developing secondary to their dysthymia.

Very few children with index ADDM developed any of the outcomes of interest, and for that reason, no risk curves are presented for that group of cases. Instead, in Table 2 we present a brief numeric summary of the results for the three types of index depressions. The finding that readily emerges is that adjustment disorder with depressed mood is clearly different from the other depressions in terms of its predictive validity. That is, the diagnosis of ADDM in this cohort is associated with a very low risk for subsequent psychiatric illness of the types that we examined.

We did not attempt formal comparisons of the risk estimates *across* the different types of index depressions, in part because of the small size of the ADDM

TABLE 2. *Estimated probabilities of developing various psychiatric outcomes by maximum follow-up time since onset of index depressive disorder (Kaplan-Meier Estimates)*[a,b]

Outcome	Index depressive disorder		
	MDD (N = 62)	DD (N = 39)	ADDM (N = 19)
Major depressive disorder	.72	.62	.09 (1)
Bipolar disorder	.17	.29	.00
Conduct disorder	.30	.32	.11 (2)
Anxiety disorder	.25	.27	.06 (1)

[a]Parenthetic entries are frequencies.
[b]Duration of maximum follow-up time for index MDD = 104 months; for DD = 128 months; and for ADDM = 104 months.

group ($N = 19$). Additionally, there were overlapping cases because the 16 cases with "double depression" were represented both in the MDD and the DD analyses. We did, however, compute separate estimates of the four outcomes for the "pure MDD" cases, the results of which were not substantially different from the findings already presented. On visual examination, the estimates for the three types of index depressions do suggest that MDD and DD are indistinguishable in terms of their predictive validities, whereas both disorders are clearly different from ADDM.

DISCUSSION

The overall goal of the present volume is to review the progress that has been made in validating psychiatric diagnoses. A specific aim has been to examine the current status of the validational schema that had been outlined in the 1970s by Drs. Robins, Guze, and their associates (often called the "St. Louis criteria," "St. Louis approach," or the "Washington University approach"). Within that schema, a prominent role was accorded to longitudinal course as observed through prospective follow-up interviews (3–5).

The clinical course of a disorder, as it waxes and wanes with an eventually characteristic outcome, was apparently recognized by the French psychiatrist A. L. J. Bayle as an important classificatory principle as far back as the 1820s (30). By the late 1890s, the evolution and final state of a psychiatric illness became the backbone of Kraepelin's nosology (31). With the resurgence of interest in classification around the 1960s, Zubin (1) in the United States and Kendell (2) in the United Kingdom were influential in emphasizing the importance of prognosis in psychiatric diagnosis. Finally, by the 1970s the St. Louis group accorded long-term clinical course a prominent position in their empirically based proposal to establish the validity of psychiatric diagnoses. Thereby, the prognostic aspects of diagnoses took on nosologic significance in addition to their clinical importance.

The St. Louis approach has been extensively applied in adult psychiatry and has left a mark on recent refinements of psychiatric nosology. However, neither this approach nor its phenomenologic stance toward classification had a marked impact on clinical child psychiatry. Therefore, it has given us particular pleasure to be able to report that the "St. Louis approach" to validation is as potent when applied to children as it has been in the study of psychiatric disorders among adults.

Stability Versus Change in Childhood

The prognostic value of the diagnosis of depressive disorder in childhood cannot be discussed without addressing the issue of symptom stability. This is particularly important because for many years it was widely believed that depression in the preadult years expressed itself in various ways and lacked a stable and recognizable symptom configuration (16–18, 32).

The belief that psychopathologic experiences in childhood would be unstable and short-lived probably reflected the need to account for several issues, including the fact that there is discontinuity between juveniles and adults on multiple dimensions. Additionally, the process of change which characterizes development during the preadult years was thought to preclude stable and prolonged forms of mental disturbance.

Clinicians and researchers who studied depression in childhood were particularly emphatic that the expression of this disorder is subject to developmental factors (19, 20). It was noted, for instance, that younger children were more likely to act out (externalize) their distress by displays of anger and tantrums, whereas older ones would presumably run away rather than complain of sadness. Suicidal ideas and attempts were held to represent impulsivity, rather than hopelessness and the wish to die.

If such developmental stage-dependent symptom constellations were to be empirically verified, psychiatric diagnostic criteria would have to make accommodations for different age groups. It is notable, therefore, that contrary to views which were common in the past, the age-related variability in the clinical picture of major depression among school-aged and adolescent patients does not seem to be substantial. This conclusion, based on the findings we presented here, is also supported by previous analyses of related data along developmental lines (33) and by the work of others (29, 32, 34).

That is not to say that there are no age-related variations in symptom patterns at all. For example, in addition to us, Ryan, Puig-Antich, and their associates (29) also found in their sample of 187 depressed children and adolescents (aged 6–18 years) that hypersomnia was more frequent among the older children as compared to the younger ones. The fact that Ryan et al. (29) reported more age-related features than we found probably reflects methodological and statistical differences. Nonetheless, the trend toward more anxiety (also reported by Ryan et al. [29]) and associated complaints among the younger depressed children is interesting. This observation complements another finding in this cohort that contemporaneous anxiety and depressive disorders were associated with earlier onset of the depression (24). Developmental factors therefore probably play a role in symptom patterns and can be used to explain such differences across age-groups.

Psychiatric Diagnosis as a Prototypical Class

From the point of view of nosology, the findings concerning symptom stability and age-related changes lead to two important conclusions. First, stability in the *overall syndrome* of major depressive disorder seems to outweigh changes in its presentation. This stability, particularly in regard to the classic symptoms of depression (e.g., sadness, anhedonia, and neurovegetative disturbances), in fact facilitates reliable identification of the disorder. Second, the variations that have been documented are entirely consistent with the prototypical diagnostic schema that characterizes the RDC (35), DSM-III (25), and DSM-III-R (36). From a nosologic viewpoint, it therefore appears to be of marginal relevance whether or not the variability in the syndrome or in its associated features is due to developmental or other (nontreatment) factors.

What are the characteristics of a prototypical descriptively oriented classification such as the one currently used in psychiatry? A prototypical schema involves classes or categories that are *not* defined by a combination of singularly necessary and jointly sufficient features (37). Instead, a "prototype" taxon or diagnostic category is described by features which *correlate* with category membership (38, 39). The DSM-III diagnosis of major depressive disorder, for example, requires *any combination* of four or more (out of eight) clinical features (that is, symptoms or signs) together with one necessary (but not sufficient) symptom of dysphoric mood, resulting in many possible clinical variants. Moreover, in a prototypical classification system, "imperfect nesting" of features or classes may occur and some members of a class will be closer to the prototype than others (38).

The implications of a prototypical schema become clearer by comparing it with biologic taxonomy (40, 41). Currently, a living organism is classified into seven major categories that form an ordered and hierarchical set. The highest category (Kingdom) is the most inclusive and abstract, with subsequent categories being progressively more specific (that is: Kingdom-Phylum-Class-Order-Family-Genus-Species). Each category consists of biologic classes or taxa, the members of which are organisms.

The schema is characterized by a hierarchical, vertical organization which is *inclusive* (i.e., the Class "Mammalia" includes the genus *Homo).* There is also perfect nesting of features (i.e., the Genus *Homo* has all the features of bipedal, primate mammals, as specified by the Family of Hominidae). Moreover, a taxon is defined in terms of necessary and sufficient features which are possessed by all its members, which thereby characterize the class (taxon) and differentiate it from every other taxon in the same category. This results in taxonomically equivalent (horizontal) but *mutually exclusive classes*. Thus, at a species level, one cannot be both a *Homo sapiens* and a *Canis lupus* (wolf); or in the category of "Kingdom," one cannot be in both the class of animals and the class of plants.

In contrast, the structure of psychiatric or medical nosology is not hierarchical and vertically inclusive. Although certain psychiatric diagnoses override others, the rules refer to the *process* of diagnosis, rather than to class inclusiveness. For example, even if a patient is reacting to a stressor, if the syndrome meets criteria for a "specific" Axis I condition (e.g., a depressive disorder), that specific diagnosis is given. The presumably subordinate class of adjustment disorders is *not* automatically included in the class of affective disorders.

The major psychiatric diagnostic categories ("affective disorders," "anxiety disorders") are at present rarely mutually exclusive. For example, a patient may receive a diagnosis of both an anxiety disorder and an affective disorder at the same time. The classes within a diagnostic category are not mutually exclusive either, and therefore multiple diagnoses can be assigned from the same category (for example: simple phobia and overanxious disorder). Because diagnostic groups are described by correlational rather than by singularly necessary and jointly sufficient features (symptoms), psychiatric classes or subclasses do not show perfect nesting of features: for example, subclasses of schizophrenia do not all manifest the same central symptoms of "thinking disorder." And, there can be borderline diagnostic cases because the correlational approach permits overlap in the disorders' phenomenological attributes.

The final difference between psychiatric and biologic taxonomy concerns the *entity being categorized,* which is a given organism in biologic taxonomy. In medical and psychiatric classification, however, there has been a debate as to the nature of a disease or disorder (for overviews see 42–44) and whether the disease or the patient is classified. Although some philosophers and social scientists noted that in psychiatric nosology it is a *patient* who is classified (1, 45), the DSM-III is explicit that the members of diagnostic classes are *disorders* rather than patients (see p. 6). One consequence of this is to make possible multiple diagnoses for any one patient.

The major aspects of a prototypic diagnostic schema such as the DSM-III therefore include variability in the characteristic features (symptoms) of a disorder, multiple contemporaneous disorders, and possible atypical cases. Keeping these features in mind makes it easier to discuss our findings in regard to the prognostic value of the diagnoses of depression in childhood.

The Prognoses for the Depressive Disorders in Childhood

How does information on follow-up course help to answer the nosologic question of whether a particular diagnosis exemplifies a given diagnostic category? According to Robins and Guze (3), the purpose of follow-up is "to determine whether or not the original patients are suffering from some other defined disorder that could account for the original clinical picture." They briefly noted two findings that would argue against diagnostic homogeneity. There could be marked differences in outcome within a given group of patients "such as between complete recovery and chronic illness," and there could also be a "finding of a change in diagnosis." They felt that the latter outcome is the more compelling in suggesting diagnostic heterogeneity of the original group.

In our work, the general premise has been that prognosis, or clinical course, is a salient correlate of a psychiatric disorder. Therefore, to delineate the relationship of various diagnostic entities to each other, specific aspects of prognosis have to be examined; we focused on two of them, namely, recovery from the index episode of a disorder, and new psychiatric illness developing. Given the prototypical nature of DSM-III diagnostic classes, we did expect variability in outcomes.

Our data on the recovery of juvenile patients from the index episode of depression suggest a number of conclusions. First, the results parallel findings on adults, which show a good likelihood of recovery from major depression (8–11). Second, as a group, the children with the various depressions are clearly different from youngsters with conditions such as attention deficit disorder or conduct disorder, who show prolonged chronicity and poor prognosis (e.g., 46, 47). Moreover, because each of the three diagnoses of depression is associated with a very high likelihood of recovery, this aspect of prognosis does not distinguish them from one another. But, they can be differentiated on the temporal dimension because dysthymic disorder takes longer to remit than the other depressions.

In order to assess the subsequent predictive value of the diagnoses of depression, we selected four outcomes. On the assumption that depression is episodic in nature, we examined the risk of a new episode of major depression. We also examined the risk of bipolar illness developing because this outcome would be conceptually and clinically consistent with the diagnostic category of major affective disorder (although probably a rare event). Because all the children in this sample of 104 were initially unipolar, the latter outcome means a change in "polarity" during study observation. We chose to estimate the risk of secondary anxiety disorder partly in light of the literature in support of its frequent association with depression (22). Finally, we examined the risk of secondary conduct disorder because of the earlier child psychiatry literature which related it to depression. Other outcomes, such as the schizophrenias, which are generally rare, did not occur in our cohort.

With respect to a new episode of major depression developing, the findings suggest that, just as among adults (9, 10, 12, 48), the depressions in childhood are recurrent. The predictive validities of MDD and DD are similar in that regard, because they are associated with comparable risks of subsequent MDD. The finding that a new episode of depression was far more likely than several other outcomes also suggests considerable homogeneity in the original diagnostic groups.

Insofar as the onset of bipolar illness is concerned, MDD and DD once again represent diagnoses in the same general category, as compared to adjustment disorder with depressed mood. It is notable that the rate of bipolarity we found exceeds the rate of "switching polarity" that has been reported among depressed adults. For instance, in a recent 7-year follow-up of 50 previously hospitalized depressed adults, only 8% were found to have developed bipolar illness (15). However, among adolescents who have been hospitalized with major depression, the 3 to 4 year follow-up by Strober et al. (49) reported a 20% rate of bipolarity. These findings suggest that early-onset depressive disorder is a high-risk factor for bipolar illness.

The finding that secondary anxiety disorder and secondary conduct disorder were estimated to develop in about one-third of the cases with MDD or DD may simply represent the prototypical nature of the initial diagnostic classes. And these data also support previous reports that the depressions in childhood rarely present in "pure" forms but are often associated with multiple psychiatric problems. More importantly, the relative risks for these outcomes both across and within the index depressions once again support the similarity of DD and MDD as classes in the domain of affective disorders.

In conclusion, the data on the clinical course of children with MDD, DD, and ADDM suggest that major depression and dysthymia, as defined by the DSM-III, are diagnostic classes that have predictive validity and that MDD and DD probably belong in the same general domain. However, notwithstanding their similarities, MDD and DD should be treated as separate conditions because the temporal aspects of their recovery are different. And although close to two-thirds of children who have a dysthymic disorder appear to be at risk for developing major depression, only about one-third of the children with the diagnosis of major depression have a concurrent dysthymia (21, 23). Therefore, once other aspects of diagnostic validity are examined, including family history, childhood-onset DD and MDD could prove to be separate but overlapping disorders. Although diagnostic overlap may be an unavoidable correlate of the current prototypical nosologic system, further refinements in the definitions of these disorders might produce mutually exclusive categories, which would be the most desirable.

ACKNOWLEDGMENTS

This research was supported by grants MH-33990 and MH-15758 from the National Institute of Mental Health, Health and Human Services Administration; partial support has also been provided by a grant from the W. T. Grant Foundation.

A previous version of this chapter was delivered at the 78th Annual Meeting of the American Psychopathological Association, New York, New York, March 3–5, 1988.

REFERENCES

1. Zubin, J. (1967): Classification of the behavior disorders. *Annual Review of Psychology*, 18: 373–406.

2. Kendell, R. E. (1975): *The Role of Diagnosis in Psychiatry.* Blackwell, Oxford.
3. Robins, E., and Guze, S. B. (1970): Establishment of diagnostic validity in psychiatric illness: Its application to schizophrenia. *Am J Psychiatry,* 126:983–987.
4. Feighner, J. P., Robins, E., Guze, S. B., Woodruff, R. A., Winokur, G., and Munoz, R. (1972): Diagnostic criteria for use in psychiatric research. *Arch Gen Psychiatry,* 26:57–63.
5. Guze, S. B. (1978): Validating criteria for psychiatric diagnosis: The Washington University approach. In: *Psychiatric Diagnosis: Explorations of Biological Predictors,* edited by H. S. Akiskal and W. L. Webb, pp. 49–59. Spectrum, New York.
6. Rutter, M. (1986): The developmental psychopathology of depression: Issues and perspectives. In: *Depression in Young People: Developmental and Clinical Perspectives,* edited by M. Rutter, C. E. Izard, and P. B. Read, pp. 3–32. Guilford, New York.
7. Barrett, J. E. (1984): Naturalistic change after 2 years in neurotic depressive disorders (RDC categories). *Comprehensive Psychiatry,* 25:404–418.
8. Faravelli, C., and Poli, E. (1982): Stability of the diagnosis of primary affective disorder: A four-year follow-up study. *J Affective Disorders,* 4:35–39.
9. Faravelli, C., Ambonetti, A., Pallanti, S., and Pazzagli, A. (1986): Depressive relapses and incomplete recovery from index episode. *Am J Psychiatry,* 143:888–891.
10. Gonzales, L. R., Lewinsohn, P. M., and Clarke, G. N. (1985): Longitudinal follow-up of unipolar depressives: An investigation of predictors of relapse. *J Consulting Clinical Psychology,* 53:461–469.
11. Keller, M. B., Shapiro, R. W., Lavori, P. W., and Wolfe, N. (1982): Recovery in major depressive disorder: Analysis with the life table and regression models. *Arch Gen Psychiatry,* 39:905–910.
12. Keller, M. B., Shapiro, R. W., Lavori, P. W., and Wolfe, N. (1982): Relapse in major depressive disorder: Analysis with the life table. *Arch Gen Psychiatry,* 39:911–915.
13. Keller, M. B., Lavori, P. W., Endicott, J., Coryell, W., and Klerman, G. L. (1983): "Double depression": Two-year follow-up. *Am J Psychiatry* 140:689–694.
14. Keller, M. B., Lavori, P. W., Rice, J., Coryell, W., and Hirschfeld R. M. A. (1986): The persistent risk of chronicity in recurrent episodes of nonbipolar major depressive disorder: A prospective follow-up. *Am J Psychiatry,* 143:24–28.
15. Bronisch, T., Wittchen, H. U., Krieg, C., Rupp, H. U., and von Zerssen, D. (1985): Depressive neurosis: A long-term prospective and retrospective follow-up study of former inpatients. *Acta Psychiatr Scand,* 71:237–248.
16. Kovacs, M., and Beck, A. T. (1977): An empirical-clinical approach toward a definition of childhood depression. In: *Depression in childhood: Diagnosis, treatment, and conceptual models,* edited by J. G. Schulterbrandt and A. Raskin. Raven Press, New York.
17. Kashani, J. H., Husain, A., Khekim, W. O., Hodges, K. K., Cytryn, L., and McKnew, D. H. (1981): Current perspectives on childhood depression: An overview. *Am J Psychiatry,* 138:143–153.
18. Puig-Antich, J. (1980): Affective disorders in childhood: A review and perspective. *Psychiatric Clinics of North America,* 3:403–424.
19. Glaser, K. (1968): Masked depression in children and adolescents. *Am J Psychotherapy,* 1:565–574.
20. Toolan, J. M., (1962): Depression in children and adolescents. *Am J Orthopsychiatry,* 32:404–415.
21. Kovacs, M., Feinberg, T. L., Crouse-Novak, M. A., Paulauskas, S. L., and Finkelstein, R. (1984): Depressive disorders in childhood: I. A longitudinal prospective study of characteristics and recovery. *Arch Gen Psychiatry,* 41:229–237.
22. Maser, J. D., and Cloninger C. R., eds. *Comorbidity in anxiety and mood disorders.* American Psychiatric Press, Washington, D.C. (in press).
23. Kovacs, M., Feinberg, T.L., Crouse-Novak, M. A., Paulauskas, S. L., Pollock, M., and Finkelstein, R. (1984): Depressive disorders in childhood: II. A longitudinal study of the risk for a subsequent major depression. *Arch Gen Psychiatry,* 41:643–649.
24. Kovacs, M., Gatsonis, C., Paulauskas, S. L., and Richards, C. (1988): Depressive disorders in childhood IV. A longitudinal study of comorbidity with and risk for anxiety disorders. (*Submitted for publication.*)
25. American Psychiatric Association. (1980): *Diagnostic and Statistical Manual of Mental Disorders,* 3rd ed. The American Psychiatric Association, Washington, D.C.

26. Kovacs, M., Paulauskas, S. L., Gatsonis, C., and Richards, C. (1988): Depressive disorders in childhood: III. A longitudinal study of comorbidity with and risk for conduct disorders. *J Affective Disorders*, 15:205–217.
27. Snedecor, G. W., and Cochran, W. G. (1980): *Statistical Methods*, 7th edition. Iowa State University Press, Ames, Iowa.
28. Kalbfleisch, J. D., Prentice, R. L. (1980): *The Statistical Analyses of Failure Time Data*. John Wiley, New York.
29. Ryan, N. D., Puig-Antich, J., Ambrosini, P., et al. (1987): The clinical picture of major depression in children and adolescents. *Arch Gen Psychiatry*, 44:854–861.
30. Pichot, P. J. (1984): The French approach to psychiatric classification. *Brit J Psychiatry*, 144: 113–118.
31. Kraepelin, E. (1968): *Lectures on Clinical Psychiatry*. Hafner, New York.
32. Strober, M. (1985): Depressive illness in adolescence. *Psychiatric Annals*, 15:375–378.
33. Kovacs, M., and Paulauskas, S. L. (1984): Developmental stage and the expression of depressive disorders in children: An empirical analysis. In: *Childhood Depression: New Directions for Child Development*, no. 26, edited by D. Cicchetti and K. Schneider-Rosen. Jossey-Bass, San Francisco.
34. Mitchell, J., McCauley, E., Burke, P., and Moss, S. J. (1988): Phenomenology of depression in children and adolescents. *J Am Academy Child and Adolescent Psychiatry*, 27:12–20.
35. Spitzer, R. L., Endicott, J., and Robins, E. (1978): Research diagnostic criteria: Rationale and reliability. *Arch Gen Psychiatry*, 35:773–782.
36. American Psychiatric Association. (1987): *Diagnostic and statistical manual of mental disorders*, 3rd edition, revised. The American Psychiatric Association, Washington, D.C.
37. Rosch, E. (1978): Principles of categorization. In: *Cognition and Categorization*, edited by E. Rosch and B. B. Lloyd, pp. 27–48. Lawrence Erlbaum, New Jersey.
38. Cantor, N., and Genero, N. (1986): Psychiatric diagnosis and natural categorization: A close analogy. In: *Contemporary Directions in Psychopathology: Toward the DSM-IV* edited by T. Millon and G. L. Klerman, pp. 233–256. Guilford, New York.
39. Cantor, N., Smith, E. E., deSales French, R., and Mezzich, J. (1980): Psychiatric diagnosis as prototype categorization. *Journal of Abnormal Psychology*, 89:181–193.
40. Ruse, M. (1973): *The Philosophy of Biology*. Hutchinson University Library, London.
41. Sokal, R., and Sneath, P. (1963): *Principles of Numerical Taxonomy*. W. H. Freeman, San Francisco.
42. Kendell, R. E. (1975): The concept of disease and its implications for psychiatry. *Brit J Psychiatry*, 127:305–315.
43. Kräupl Taylor, F. (1980): The concepts of disease. *Psychological Medicine*, 10:419–424.
44. Engelhardt, H. T. (1974): Explanatory models in medicine: Facts, theories, and values. *Texas Rep Biol Med*, 32:225–239.
45. Hempel, C. G. (1961): Introduction to problems of taxonomy. In: *Field studies in the mental disorders*, edited by J. Zubin, pp. 3–26. Grune & Stratton, New York.
46. Gittleman, R., Mannuzza, S., Shenker, R., and Bonagura, N. (1985): Hyperactive boys almost grown up. *Arch Gen Psychiatry*, 42:937–947.
47. Quay, H. D. (1986): Conduct disorders. In: *Psychopathological disorders of childhood*, edited by H. C. Quay and J. S. Werry, pp. 35–72. Wiley, New York.
48. Zis, A. P., and Goodwin, F. K. (1979): Major affective disorder as a recurrent illness: A critical review. *Arch Gen Psychiatry*, 36:835–839.
49. Strober, M., and Carlson, G. (1982): Bipolar illness in adolescents with major depression: Clinical, genetic, and psychopharmacologic predictors in a three- to four-year prospective follow-up investigation. *Arch Gen Psychiatry*, 39:549–555.

DISCUSSION

Dr. James Halikas: What about eating disorders developing in this population? And what was the average number of diagnoses any one child accumulated?

Dr. Maria Kovacs: For eating disorders, there were about two cases among these children. The average number of diagnoses per child is about three. The highest number of diagnoses is seven.

Dr. Halikas: How would you compare this accumulation of diagnoses to what you would find starting with conduct disorder youngsters; what diagnoses do they develop, and how many?

Dr. Kovacs: Among our pathological controls we do have children with conduct disorders. We do not have affective disorders developing in them. What we basically have is a kind of bifurcated outcome, where some of them miraculously recover at age 18, when they realize that they are going to be put into jail, and the rest of them turn into adult antisocial personalities. What we do have in the conduct disorder children is substance abuse and mood lability, but none have turned into affective disorder, at least not yet.

Dr. Halikas: Do you see substance abuse in these youngsters?

Dr. Kovacs: Yes, when they became adolescents. But conduct disorder was one of the most frequent comorbid diagnoses in this cohort. Sixteen percent of these children had a diagnosis of conduct disorder at the time of study entry. It was not that unusual.

Dr. Altshuler: Did any of these kids stay well? I mean were there any in whom there was not a recurrence, and if so, from which categories and what were the percentages?

Dr. Kovacs: The children who tended to have the worst course were the children with bipolar illness. They were really very different from what you see in adults; they very rarely recovered.

Dr. Altshuler: Of your index cases with major depression as their initial diagnosis, about 69% had a recurrence. Did the other 31% not have a recurrence, or did they have a recurrence but with a diagnosis other than major depression?

Dr. Kovacs: Very few had no disorder. The interesting thing about the affective disorders in childhood is that the course of these children is much, much worse than adults. Even when they are asymptomatic and have recovered from an episode, they remain socially impaired. They don't do well in school. The next interesting question is what happens to them when they become adults. They don't seem to become schizophrenic.

Dr. Klein: I wasn't sure about your definition of bipolarity. Some people use that for both bipolar I and bipolar II. Did you, and did any of these kids require hospitalization or lithium treatment?

Dr. Kovacs: We used the term to include both bipolar I and bipolar II; because so little is known about these illnesses in childhood, we wanted to include both. About 80% of these children eventually do get hospitalized. Because we had trouble convincing people that these children had bipolar illness, we had children who were without any kind of treatment for about 5 or 6 years. By the time they become adolescents they usually do get treated, but in adolescence their bipolar illness is very, very difficult to treat. Typically they are treated with a combination of lithium and Tegretol. If you are very lucky they respond, but eventually almost all of them get hospitalized.

Dr. Pfohl: I was interested in your comments about adjustment disorder and wanted to be clear on your approach to the diagnosis. If you follow DSM-III strictly, the diagnosis excludes any cases that meet full criteria for major depression even if a clear psychosocial stressor is present. Did you follow that rule in your diagnosis?

Dr. Kovacs: Yes we did. The amount of life stress among these children was horrendous, but we followed DSM-III criteria. Irrespective of a stressor, if they met full criteria for an episode, we called them major depression.

Dr. Pfohl: So you found that the cases with major depression almost always had life stressors too?

Dr. Kovacs: Yes.

Dr. Barney Carroll: My question is also about the adjustment disorder category. Could you clarify for us how they were entered into the study? I thought I heard you say that they were not enrolled until they had been observed for several weeks after first contact.

Dr. Kovacs: All of these children were entered at the same time. Our procedure was as follows. We recruited children from our clinic and we screened all of them, looking for those who had several depressive symptoms. We then made systematic diagnoses, evaluating them at least three times over the first 6 months of study. The purpose of this diagnostic verification phase was to be certain that a child met criteria for major depression, dysthymia, or adjustment disorder. We had about 14 cases that we misdiagnosed, and we eventually dropped them from the study because we couldn't put them into any one of those categories. They were almost all anxiety disorders.

Dr. Carroll: Had you made a forced choice diagnosis of adjustment disorder versus major depression at first contact, would the composition of your groups have differed? This is an important differential diagnosis for people entering treatment.

Dr. Kovacs: In roughly 65% of the cases we could make a diagnostic decision at the time of the first assessment. In the other cases we could not, either because the mother was depressed, or she was vague and couldn't give adequate information, or the child was very uncooperative and wouldn't talk. This is a particular problem with diagnosing children. Our verification procedure was to use multiple sources of information to be sure that the study diagnosis was as accurate as we could make it.

The Validity of Psychiatric Diagnosis, edited by
Lee N. Robins and James E. Barrett.
Raven Press, Ltd., New York © 1989.

Temporal Stability in the Major Mental Disorders

*Morton Beiser,
**William G. Iacono and
*David Erickson

*Division of Social and Cultural Psychiatry, University of British Columbia, Vancouver, British Columbia V6T 2A1; and
**Psychology Department, University of Minnesota, Minneapolis, Minnesota 55455

Temporal stability is sometimes invoked as a criterion for assessing the validity of psychiatric diagnosis. In this context the question usually asked is: "How likely is it that a patient, having received a particular diagnosis at one point in time, will be categorized in the same way on another occasion?" The assumption underlying this question is that the more stable the diagnosis, the more likely it is to be reflecting a basic psychopathological or pathophysiological process, which will be found in all individuals categorized in the same way. Hence, the more stable the diagnosis, the more valid it is.

The present inquiry addresses three overlapping issues: (1) How stable are psychotic diagnoses? (2) How can stability be used, along with other criteria, to examine validity? (3) Is the diagnostic system which produces the most stable diagnosis the best system?

PREVIOUS RESEARCH IN DIAGNOSTIC STABILITY

While previous studies of psychotic disorders conducted over periods ranging from 2 to more than 30 years have produced impressive estimates of stability, conceptual and methodological questions limit the interpretability of many of the findings. Several investigations have focused upon the stability of diagnoses assigned to individuals who experienced repeated admissions to treatment facilities (Cooper, 1967; Kendell, 1974). Estimates of stability which derive from such studies are compromised by lack of standardization in data and by inconsistent application of diagnostic criteria. Cooper (1967), for example, discerned that hospital charts frequently lacked information to justify assigned diagnoses; his study demonstrated that a change in doctors accounted for more instability in diagnosis than changes in the patient's condition. Several assessments of diagnostic stability have utilized research-quality interviews at baseline and follow-up or a combination of clinical data and follow-up interviews (Helzer, Brockington, and Kendell, 1981; Cloninger, Martin, Guze, and Clayton, 1986; Kendler, Gruenberg, Tsuang, 1985; Perley and Guze, 1962; Tsuang, Woolson, Winokur, and Crowe, 1981; Winokur, 1974, 1985; Sheldrick, Jablensky, Sartorius, and Shepherd, 1977). Despite this methodologic advance, difficulties remain. Most studies include chronic as well as first episode cases of disorder. Since chronicity reduces variance in course and outcome, it is likely that chronic cases will exhibit more stable diagnoses than cases experiencing a disorder for the first time. Data deriving from chronic populations may overestimate diagnostic stability (McGlashan, 1984).

In many studies of stability, diagnostic assessments are made at only two points in time, with a long interval between baseline and follow-up. If a patient is assigned the same diagnosis on two occasions, it is difficult to know whether to interpret this to mean he or she has suffered from the same disorder for the entire period under study, or whether there have been periods of remission and relapse, during the most recent of which the original illness was re-experienced. Some investigators have bypassed this question by assigning a "best" diagnosis at the end of the study period, then comparing this final diagnosis with the one obtained at baseline (Tsuang et al., 1981). This procedure compounds the difficulty, since cases who never recover, those who remit and then become ill again, and those who have only one illness episode may all be included under one class of apparently stable diagnosis. In addition, it may be important to analyze changes in diagnosis, or progressions from diagnosis to no diagnosis and back again and the clinical factors relating to such patterns. For these purposes, several rating points, each one characterized by the diagnostic label relevant at that point in time, are desirable.

METHODS

For the current investigation of diagnostic stability, persons experiencing a first episode of functional psychosis were interviewed and assessed using standardized techniques during their initial illness as well as 9 and 18 months later.

This report is part of a study of biological and psychosocial factors implicated in the course of first-episode schizophrenia and first-episode affective psychosis. The sampling frame for the University of British Columbia Markers and Predictors of Schizophrenia (M.A.P.) study consists of all persons between the ages of 15 and 54 living in Greater Vancouver who experienced a first episode of nonorganic psychosis from February 1982 through September 1984. To minimize selection bias, we extended recruitment beyond the mental health care system to encompass the community-wide "administrative incidence" strategy proposed by the WHO (Sartorius et al., 1986). Our referral network consisted of psychiatric hospitals, psychiatric services of general hospitals, psychiatrists in private practice, university and college counseling centers, employment and immigration counseling agencies, and a one in six probability sample of physicians in general practice. To avoid missing potential cases, we supplied referral sources with very broad inclusion criteria. Agencies and practitioners were asked to refer anyone experiencing hallucinations or delusions, displaying grossly disorganized behavior, showing marked thought and speech disorder, or having two or more of the following: marked loss of drive, social withdrawal, severe excitement, overwhelming anxiety or fear, or gross self-neglect. Other criteria included the requirement that this be the first episode of a disorder, i.e., that subjects had never been previously treated with neuroleptic or antidepressant drugs; that they were not suffering from organic cerebral illness, chemical dependence, severe mental retardation, or a chronic physical condition; that they were between the ages of 15 and 54; and that they had lived in the Vancouver metropolitan area at least 6 months. Project research staff contacted each of the referral sources at regular intervals to receive updates on potential recruits for the study.

During the intake period, February 1982 through September 1984, we admitted 175 qualifying subjects.

After a potential recruit signed a consent to participate, one of the project clinicians, either a psychiatrist or clinical psychologist with a PhD, conducted an interview utilizing the Present State Examination (PSE), 9th edition (Wing, Cooper, and Sartorius, 1974). Trained Masters level research assistants then interviewed the subjects who were found to be appropriate for the study with a variety of instruments including a sociodemographic history, the SCL-90-R (Derogatis, 1977), Bradburn's Affect Balance Scale (Bradburn, 1965; Bradburn and Caplovitz, 1969), and Henderson's interview schedule to assess social interaction (Henderson et al., 1978, 1981). We derived two scales from the Henderson instrument: the extent of involvement prior to the illness episode (1) with family, and (2) with friends and acquaintances. The research assistants also obtained ancillary information from the hospital charts. Each study subject was asked to recruit at least one significant other, preferably a first degree relative, for the study. We also recruited a sample matched for age and sex who had never experienced a psychiatric disorder and who had no family history of illness. We gathered this sample from employment centers, family practices in middle-class and lower-class neighborhoods, and community centers.

Following the gathering of all intake data from psychotic subjects, treatment agencies, and significant others, the project staff, including at least one psychiatrist and one clinical psychologist, met to assign DSM-III (American Psychiatric Association, 1980), RDC (Spitzer, Endicott, and Robins, 1977, 1978), ICD-9 (WHO, 1978), and Feighner (1972) diagnoses. Our method resembles a "best estimate" diagnosis (Leckman et al., 1982) in that we assumed that the "best" diagnosis was the one made on the basis of the most complete information. In addition, we addressed the problem of reliability. While the explicit criteria of the DSM-III, RDC, and Feighner systems facilitate reliability, this is compromised by human failure to consistently follow diagnostic rules. We addressed the problem by creating a checklist describing each criterion required for any possible diagnosis in each of the four diagnostic systems. Using the checklist, the diagnostic team followed each of the algorithms in each system to determine which diagnosis applied to a particular case. Since ICD-9 diagnostic criteria are more abstract than those in the other systems, we developed a checklist of operational definitions for each ICD-9 symptom by using words and phrases that occur in the ICD-9 descriptions. The resulting checklist ensured that project diagnosticians covered all relevant inclusion criteria for ICD-9 diagnoses.

We utilized consensus diagnoses because other investigators have recommended that with large and complex data sets, consensus diagnoses are more reliable than single-rated assessments (Helzer, Brockington, and Kendell, 1981; Carey and Gottesman, 1978). We also developed a negative symptom scale consisting of blunted affect, poverty of speech, and lack of volition, ratings for which were derived from the first PSE and other data.

Nine months after intake, each subject was re-assessed with the SCL-90-R, the Affect Balance Scale, a series of questions covering illnesses subsequent to the initial episode, work history, and social relations during the interval. The research assistants, who had been trained in the use of the NIMH Diagnostic Interview Schedule (DIS)—a structured, lay-administered interview which yields DSM-III diagnoses (Robins et al., 1981)—administered the portions of this instrument which address severe psychiatric disorders. Limitations in our resources made it impossible to have psychiatrists re-interview the subjects with the PSE at 9 months. However, 18 months after intake we re-interviewed each subject with the PSE. We also re-administered the SCL-90-R and Affect Balance Scale and re-interviewed the study subjects' significant others for ancillary information. We also searched treatment files of each of the general hospitals with psychiatric services in the Greater Vancouver Area, the Provincial Mental Hospital, and the Community Mental Health Care System in order to document any illness episodes as well as treatment interventions. Table 1 summarizes the measures gathered at intake, 9, and 18 months reported in this study.

Longitudinal studies inevitably suffer from subject attrition. At 9 months, we located and interviewed 120 of our original 175 subjects, and at 18 months, 129. During the 18-month follow-up four of the subjects died. Since death is an analyzable outcome, our true attrition was 42 subjects or 24%. Compared to the drop-outs, those retained were slightly younger and came from families of slightly higher socio-economic status. However, there were no differences between the two groups in the distribution of DSM-III intake diagnosis.

Project staff, with at least two clinicians present, utilized all data to rate each subject's overall functioning on the Global Assessment Scale (GAS) (Endicott et al., 1976), as well as our own measure of occupational functioning at 9 and 18 months and to assign consensus diagnoses at these points.

In order to address the constraints on stability imposed by the diagnostic system employed, we compared the DSM-III, RDC, Feighner, and ICD-9 systems. RDC and Feighner "definite" and "probable" categories were combined and counted as cases of the diagnoses in question.

TABLE 1. M.A.P. study design

Time 1 (Intake)	Time 2 (9 Months)	Time 3 (18 Months)
1. Present state examination (PSE): S	1. Diagnostic interview schedule (DIS): S	1. PSE: S
2. Background information: S and S.O.	2. Illnesses, work, social history: S	2. Illnesses, work, social history: S and S.O.
3. SCL-90-R: S	3. Affect balance: S	3. SCL-90-R: S
4. Affect balance scale: S		4. Affect balance: S
5. Social interaction interview: S		5. Illness and treatment history: S, S.O., and treatment institutions

S = Subject
S.O. = Significant Other

In addition to tracing diagnoses over time, we were interested in studying possible correlates of stability, such as mode of onset and short-term outcome.

The clinical literature has placed a great deal of emphasis upon age of onset as a predictor of illness course and stability of diagnosis. In spite of the acknowledged importance of this factor in arriving at a diagnosis, most studies equate date of onset with the date of first contact for treatment. Since seeking treatment is often delayed because of psychosocial factors which have little to do with the disease itself. This is unsatisfactory. We developed our own method based on a content analysis of case summaries, from which we derived a checklist of behaviors signaling illness onset. Clinicians reviewed subject files to establish the date at which any item on the checklist of signs of illness first appeared. This was then taken as the date of illness onset. We followed the same procedure to derive a checklist of florid psychotic symptoms and to date their onset. The method yields highly acceptable measures of inter-rater reliability (Beiser, Erickson, and Husted, unpublished).

There are many scales for rating outcome. We felt, however, that the assumption underlying most scales—that adjustment can be placed on a continuum from "good" to "bad"—violates clinical reality, which is much more complex. Our measure of outcome, based on a cluster analysis (Ward, 1963) of the GAS, SCL-90, and Positive Affect Scales as well as ratings of occupational adjustment, consists of a four category typology. These categories, described in Table 2, are an attempt to harness nomothetic precision to the multifaceted richness of clinical description (Beiser, Iacono, and MacEwan, unpublished).

The first category is Superior Adjustment, in which symptoms are mild, feelings of well-being are high, and functioning is good. Subjects who at 18 months after an episode of illness fall into this category are performing as well as the normal comparison group. The Incapacitated group, who fall at the other end of the spectrum, suffer a large burden of symptoms, have little sense of well-being,

TABLE 2. *Cluster characteristics: 18-month outcome*

Cluster groups	n*	GAS** mean	(sd)	Occupational functioning† mean	(sd)	SCL-90‡ (Global symptoms) mean	(sd)	Positive Affect§ mean	(sd)
I. *Psychotic subjects*									
1. Superior adjustment	28	81.9	(4.7)	75.7	(10.8)	44.3	(9.3)	34.8	(2.9)
2. Working wounded	26	60.4	(12.9)	69.0	(14.5)	54.7	(11.4)	26.1	(6.5)
3. Walking wounded	33	53.7	(12.2)	26.5	(16.6)	51.0	(9.1)	30.3	(5.5)
4. Incapacitated	41	29.9	(9.3)	16.9	(16.0)	64.3	(13.4)	25.9	(5.8)
II. *Normals*	84	not rated		69.7	(18.1)	49.6	(10.4)	33.6	(4.4)

*d.f., differ slightly due to missing data
**F = 148.7; d.f. 3,124; p < .001
 Superior > Working Wounded > Walking Wounded > Incapacitated
†F = 112.8; d.f. 4,207; p < .001
 Superior = Working Wounded = Normals > Walking Wounded > Incapacitated
‡F = 16.4; d.f. 4,199; p < .001
 Superior = Normals < Working Wounded = Walking Wounded < Incapacitated
§F = 24.9; d.f. 4,196; p < .001
 Superior = Normals > Walking Wounded > Working Wounded = Incapacitated

are usually unable to work (or at best, work sporadically), and have poor social relationships. Two intermediate groups are of special interest. The Walking Wounded, although not quite so symptomatic as the Incapacitated, are functioning at a similar occupationally impoverished level. The Working Wounded, despite being troubled by a heavy burden of symptoms, are occupationally and socially at a level equal to that of subjects in the Superior adjustment category.

Table 3 summarizes the measures used for this report.

RESULTS

Sample Characteristics

The sample is young—three-quarters of them are under 30—mostly single, and predominantly lower social class. Males make up 68% of the total.

As Table 4 illustrates, ICD-9 has the broadest definition of schizophrenia: it generated more than twice as many schizophrenic diagnoses as DSM-III and almost three times as many as the Feighner system. DSM-III, on the other hand, provides the broadest concept of mania (bipolar disorder) and major depression, with the Feighner system again being the most conservative. A large number of cases are labelled unspecified psychosis according to Feighner criteria; this is because Feighner criteria used to make diagnoses of schizophrenic and affective psychosis are narrow and restrictive. Using this very conservative system, many psychotic subjects cannot be assigned a diagnosis.

TABLE 3. *M.A.P. study measures*

Time 1 (Intake)	Time 2 (9 Months)	Time 3 (18 Months)
1. Diagnoses: DSM-III, RDC, ICD-9, Feighner	1. Diagnoses	1. Diagnoses
2. Negative symptom scale		2. Outcome Categories
3. Involvement with family and with friends		
4. Interval between illness onset and emergence of florid psychotic symptoms		

TABLE 4. *Number of psychotic patients by diagnostic category for each diagnostic system (total n = 175)*

Diagnosis	ICD-9[a]	RDC	DSM-III	Feighner
Schizophrenia	114	64	54	41
Schizophreniform	—	—	31	—
Schizoaffective	—	54	6	—
Mania	28	25	37	16
Depression	23	20	35	21
Other (or unspecified)[b]	10	12	12	97

Note: Dashed lines indicate that the diagnostic category does not exist for the indicated diagnostic system.
[a]Manic depressive psychosis was broken into subtypes depending on whether the subject's first episode was manic or depressed.
[b]Mainly paranoid or paranoia.

How Stable Are Psychotic Diagnoses?

There are apparent differences in diagnostic stability among the three systems. Figure 1 analyzes, at 9 and 18 months, the diagnostic breakdown among those originally diagnosed schizophrenic according to the four different systems.

By 9 months, as many as one-third of the RDC and about 40% of the ICD-9 schizophrenics available for follow-up had recovered to the point where they no longer warranted a diagnosis. This was true for fewer than 20% of DSM-III diagnosed schizophrenics. About 5% of the RDC schizophrenics were reclassified "Other" by 9 months, and 5% of ICD-9 schizophrenics had an affective disorder. Twenty-three percent of Feighner-diagnosed schizophrenics had recovered at this point, and 37% were rediagnosed "Other."

Recoveries tended to be short-lived. At 18 months, 40% of the RDC schizo-

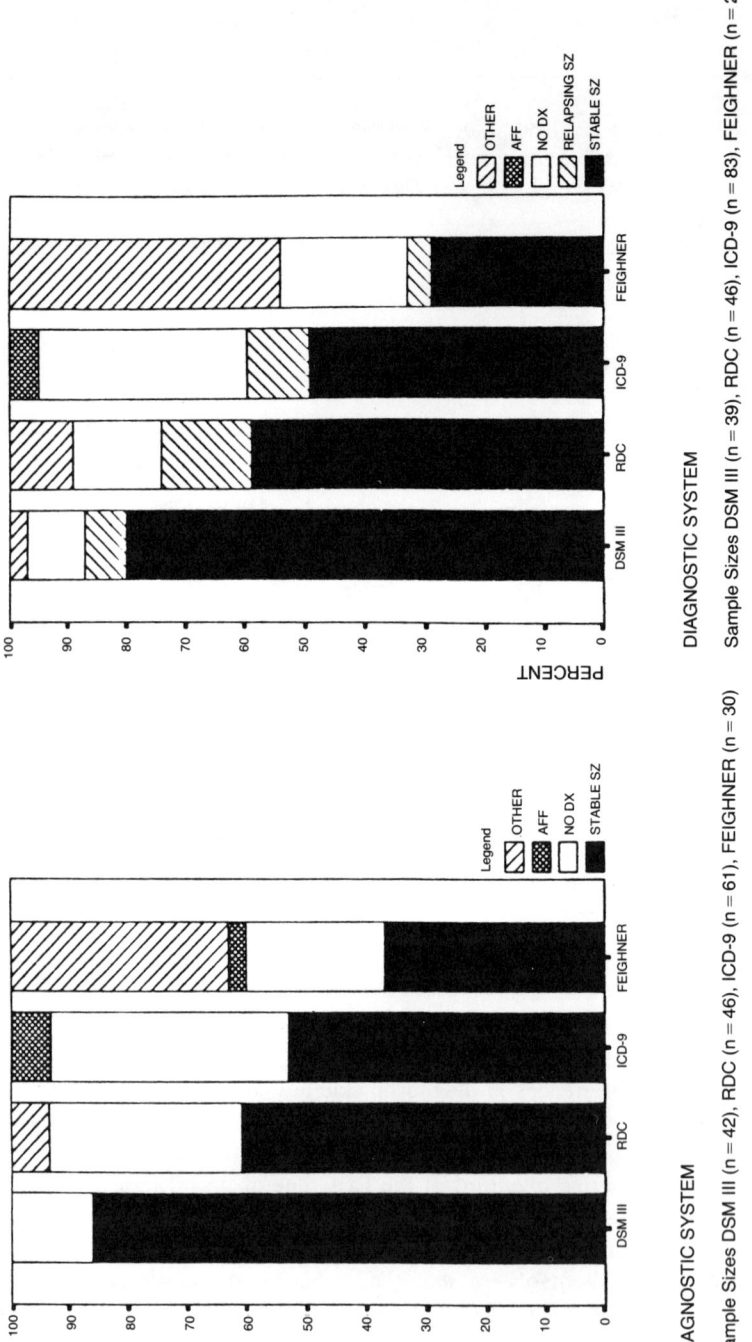

FIG. 1. Schizophrenia: Diagnostic stability.

phrenics who had recovered at 9 months were ill once again—most with a diagnosis of schizophrenia—a pattern which pertained to 25% of the ICD-9 schizophrenics, 5% of the DSM-III, and 4% of the Feighner cases. One RDC schizophrenic developed an affective disorder at 18 months and several others at this point exhibited symptoms more characteristic of psychoses other than schizophrenia.

We have classified people with an initial diagnosis of schizophrenia, at least one period with no diagnosis, plus one additional episode of schizophrenia as "Relapsing Schizophrenics," as contrasted with those with a consistent diagnosis, the "Stable Schizophrenics." Most people diagnosed schizophrenic under DSM-III criteria were stable schizophrenics, retaining this diagnosis throughout the 18 months of our study, whereas RDC and ICD-9 diagnosed schizophrenics split into relapsed and stable subgroups. Very few subjects initially diagnosed schizophrenic under the DSM-III, RDC, or ICD-9 changed diagnosis at the first or second follow-up.

Feighner diagnoses of schizophrenia proved less stable. Compared to the three other systems, only a small number of subjects were diagnosed as schizophrenic under the Feighner system at intake to the study. At follow-up, a large proportion of these Feighner-diagnosed schizophrenics were reclassified as having another or "undiagnosed" psychosis.

Comparison of Fig. 1 with Figs. 2 and 3 demonstrates that regardless of the diagnostic system employed, there are fewer recoveries from schizophrenia than from affective psychoses.

Figure 2 compares 9- and 18-month outcome among DSM-III, RDC, and Feighner-diagnosed depressives. A higher proportion of RDC and Feighner depressives display recovery than do those in the DSM-III category. There is relatively little shift into other diagnostic categories except in the DSM-III, where about 20% of people diagnosed as DSM-III Major Depressive Disorder at intake were, by the study's conclusion, reclassified as Bipolar Disorder.

The Feighner diagnosis of mania is the least stable of the four categories compared in Fig. 3. A relatively high proportion of Feighner-diagnosed cases of mania shift in and out of this category and "Other" during the follow-up period.

Stability as a Criterion for Validity

We turn to a consideration of stability as a criterion for validity by examining two diagnostic categories: RDC schizoaffective disorder and DSM-III schizophreniform disorder.

1. Schizoaffective Disorder

DSM-III focuses on separating affective from schizophrenic psychosis, a process which has always been difficult, especially when an affective syndrome appears concurrently with mood incongruent psychotic features. The other diagnostic systems handle this problem by assigning such patients to special classes: schizophrenia-schizoaffective subtype (ICD-9), schizoaffective disorder (RDC),

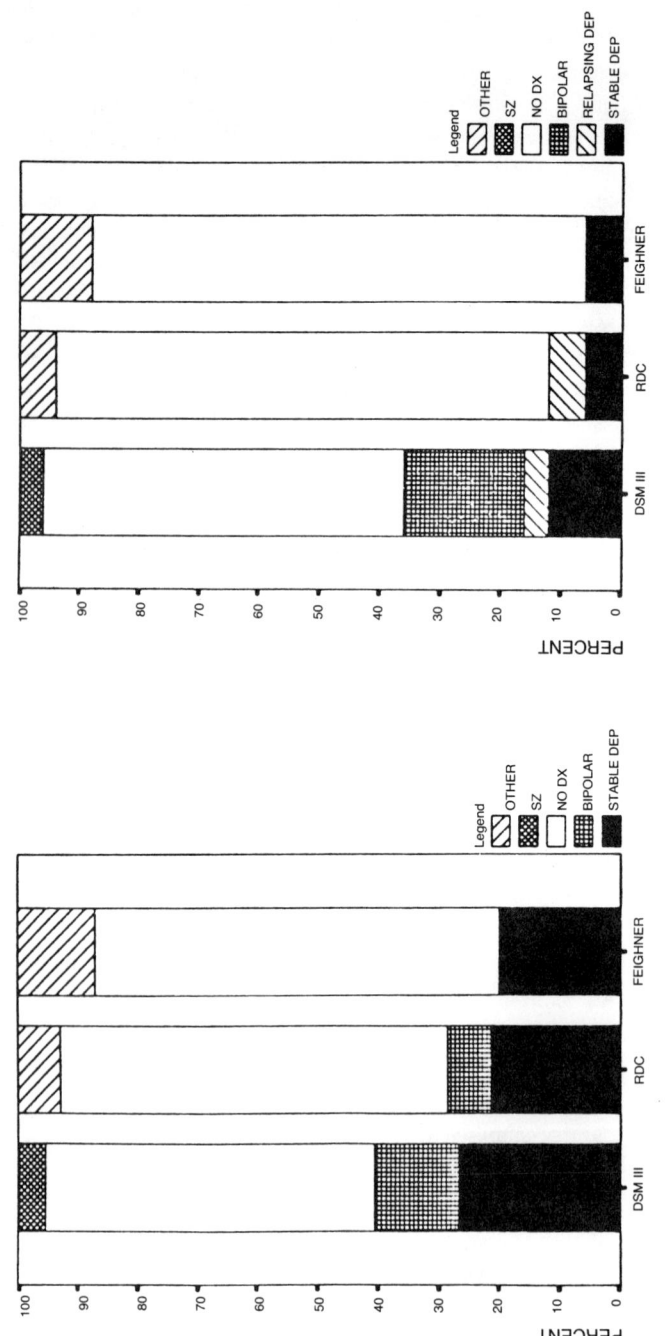

FIG. 2. Depression: Diagnostic stability.

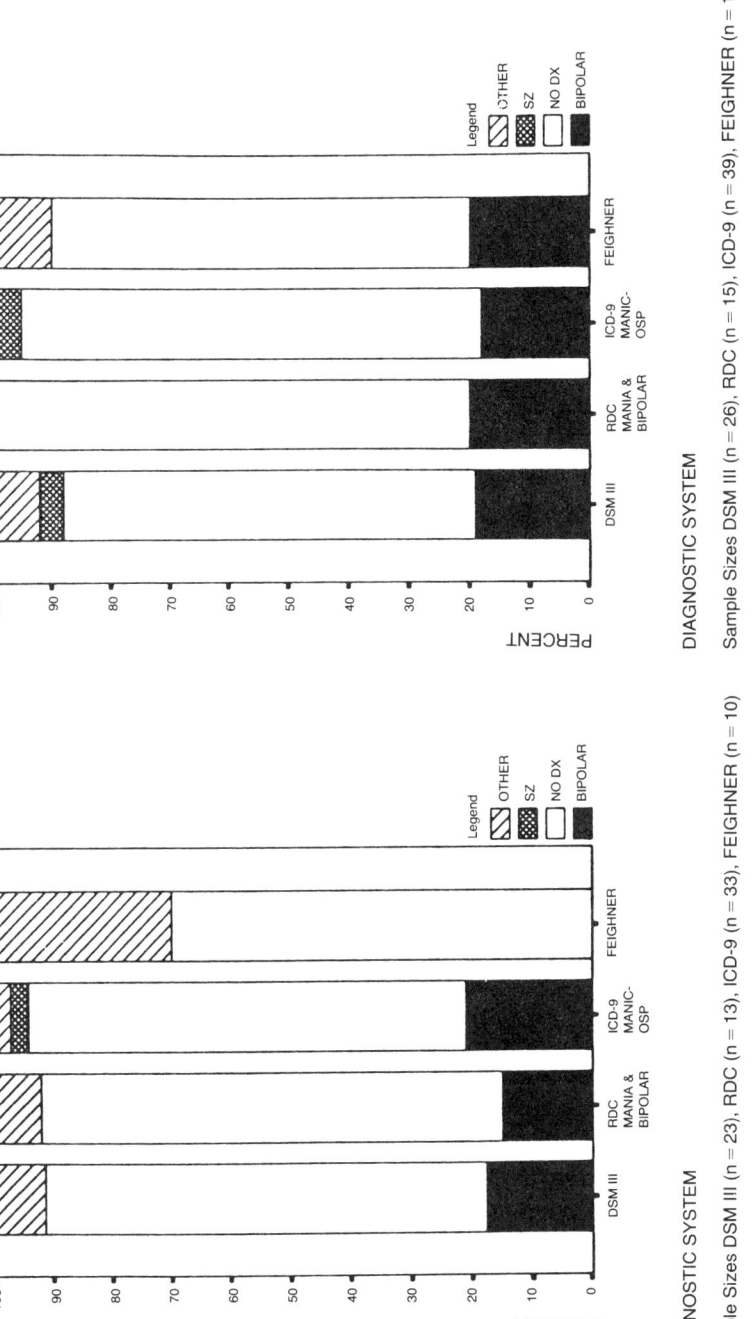

FIG. 3. Bipolar disorder, mania, manic-depressive psychosis.

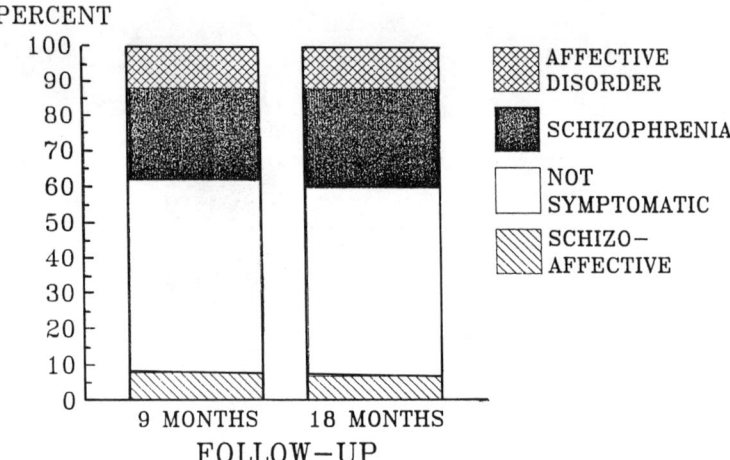

FIG. 4. RDC schizoaffective diagnostic stability.

and undiagnosed psychosis (Feighner). Although DSM-III also includes a schizoaffective diagnosis, it is a residual category with no defining criteria. In the case of first-episode patients, DSM-III deals with the dilemma of assigning someone to an affective or schizophrenic category primarily by determining when the affective syndrome appeared relative to the psychotic symptoms. The diagnosis of schizophrenia takes precedence if the psychotic symptoms came first; affective disorder is diagnosed if psychotic symptoms appear after the mood disturbance. The reasonableness of this approach is supported by the observation in our study that very few patients originally diagnosed with one of these disorders switched to the other at 9 or 18 months.

Figure 4 displays the diagnostic constancy for RDC schizoaffective disorder. Substantial fractions of subjects receiving this initial diagnosis are reclassified schizophrenic or affective over time. A subject initially diagnosed schizoaffective was less likely to stay in this category than to be reclassified as schizophrenic or as affective psychosis.

2. Schizophreniform Disorder

Schizophreniform disorder is an inherently unstable diagnosis since, by definition, one can only know in retrospect if the diagnosis was correctly assigned in the first place. The decision rests upon whether the short-lived schizophrenic symptoms which resulted in the diagnosis resolve in fewer than 6 months. This is ironic since rather than having the course of disorder postdict diagnosis, prognosis should be inherent in diagnosis. In other words, having established that psychopathology fits best within a particular diagnostic category, the clinician should then be able to forecast the probable course of illness. In an attempt to overcome this

TABLE 5. *Stability of schizophreniform, 18-month diagnosis*

1. "True" (stable) schizophreniform	7
2. Schizophreniform → schizophrenia	18
3. Schizophreniform → other	6
Total	31

conceptual difficulty, the DSM-III-R manual suggests that several factors thought to be associated with good prognosis be added when a diagnosis of schizophreniform disorder is made. These include a duration of less than 4 weeks between the onset of illness and the emergence of florid psychotic symptoms, evidence of good premorbid adjustment, absence of blunted affect, and evidence of confusion at the height of the psychotic episode.

The stability of this diagnostic category is addressed in Table 5.

Our series contained 31 cases who qualified for a schizophreniform diagnosis. As expected, the initial diagnosis was very unstable; over time, 18 of the 31 cases were reclassified as schizophrenia, 7 exhibited quick symptom remission and therefore retained the schizophreniform diagnosis, and 6 were reclassified as affective or other psychotic disorders. In this case, the stability criterion identified "true" cases of schizophreniform disorder, differentiating them from cases of schizophrenia who happened to be seen early in the course of their illness. The categories of true schizophreniform, unstable schizophreniform (cases who changed from schizophreniform to schizophrenia), and stable schizophrenics were, at admission to our study, remarkably similar in psychopathology and in sociodemographic characteristics. The only difference among the groups was that, as might be expected, at intake the stable schizophrenics had been ill a much longer period of time. [The mean ($\pm$s.d.) for the stable schizophrenic group was 68.1 ($\pm$52.3) weeks, 11.9 ($\pm$5.9) weeks for the unstable schizophreniforms, and 6.8 ($\pm$5.2) for the stable, i.e., true schizophreniforms. (F=14.8, d.f. 2, 55, p< .001)].

At 18 months, the unstable schizophreniforms were indistinguishable from the stable schizophrenics whereas outcome among the true schizophreniforms was markedly different. As Table 6 illustrates, all the true schizophreniforms fell into the superior or working wounded categories at 18 months, whereas those reclassi-

TABLE 6. *Outcome categories*

	Superior	Working wounded	Walking wounded	Incapacitated
True schizophreniform	4	3	—	—
Schizophreniform → SZ	—	1	7	10
Stable SZ	—	1	23	30

Chi square = 26.0, d.f. 6, p < .001

TABLE 7. *Prognostic indicators: true schizophreniform and schizophrenic groups*

Item	True schizfm	Merged schizophrenics (stable schiz and unstable schizfm)	Chi Square Tolerance	Probability
Axis V ratings (of "good" or higher)	86%	20%	10.6	<.001
Blunted affect	Yes = 28%	Yes = 63%	2.9	.10
Poor rapport	Yes = 14%	Yes = 57%	2.7	.10
Interval between first signs of illness and florid psychosis ≤ 4 weeks	Yes = 43%	Yes = 28%	.15	n.s.

fied schizophrenic and the stable schizophrenics became the incapacitated and the walking wounded.

Because the unstable schizophreniform group resembled the stable schizophrenics so closely, we considered them to be cases of true schizophrenia who happened to be caught early in the course of their first illness. For subsequent analyses, we merged them with the cases initially diagnosed as schizophrenia.

Table 7 examines differences between the true schizophreniforms and the merged schizophrenic group on three of the variables which, in addition to the presence of "schizophrenic" symptoms for less than 6 months, make up the DSM-III-R criteria for the schizophreniform diagnosis, i.e., premorbid functioning, blunted affect, and mode of onset. We also considered clinicians' ratings of rapport during the initial interview. Premorbid functioning is assessed by Axis V ratings. Poor rapport and blunted affect are items appearing in the PSE.

Premorbid functioning predicted group membership: almost all the true schizophreniforms scored good or better on Axis V at intake, whereas this was true for only 20% of the schizophrenia group. More than twice the number of schizophrenics compared with schizophreniforms displayed blunted affect while the difference in poor rapport was fourfold. The large differences in blunted affect and poor rapport do not reach conventionally accepted levels of statistical significance, probably because small sample sizes limit statistical power. The 4-week duration criterion does not differentiate the groups.

How Do the Diagnostic Systems Compare with Each Other?

Although there are overlaps among the DSM-III, RDC, and ICD-9 diagnostic categories, the areas of divergence are important.

During our longitudinal investigation, persons diagnosed as schizophrenic by RDC and ICD-9 split into two categories—a stable group which overlaps with the DSM-III-defined subjects, and a relapsing group, for which DSM-III has no counterpart. (Since only one Feighner-diagnosed schizophrenic displayed a relapsing course during our follow-up, the Feighner categories are not considered in this section.) While relapsing schizophrenics had the same sociodemographic characteristics and displayed psychopathology at intake which was equal to the stable group, there were marked differences in the 18-month outcome. While most of the RDC relapsing schizophrenics were categorized in either the superior or working wounded groups at 18 months, this was true for only a small percentage of the stable groups (relapsing group, good outcome = 58%; stable group = 22%; Chi square = 9.7, d.f.3, $p<.05$). This difference was even more striking for the ICD-9 groups, where four times more of the relapsing group than the stable group ended up being classified as either superior or working wounded (relapsing group, good outcome = 61%; Stable group = 15%; Chi square = 24.3, d.f.3, $p<.001$).

Even though at intake to the study the psychopathology of the two groups was the same, relapsing schizophrenics differed from stable schizophrenics along several important dimensions. Judged by Axis V ratings, the relapsing group had achieved a higher level of premorbid occupational functioning. Differences between relapsing and stable schizophrenics were significant and substantial for both RDC and ICD-9 defined cases. [For RDC: Mean ($\pm$s.d.) Axis V ratings, relapsing category = 4.2($\pm$1.1), stable category = 3.2($\pm$1.2); t = 2.7, d.f.43, $p<.01$; for ICD-9: relapsing category = 4.6($\pm$1.1), stable category = 3.5($\pm$1.2), d.f.78, $p<.001$.]

Comparisons of the relapsing and stable schizophrenics' quantity and type of social involvement also revealed illuminating differences. On average, schizophrenics were involved with between three and four family members at the time they entered our study: there were no differences between relapsing and stable groups in family involvement. However, the RDC relapsing group counted almost twice as many friends among their close and intimate relationships as the stable: [means for relapsing = 6.3($\pm$4.1); stable = 3.3($\pm$2.1)]. This difference is highly significant (t = 3.2, d.f. 43, $p<.005$). Results are highly similar in the ICD-9 category: [relapsing group friends and acquaintance = 5.2 ($\pm$4.3), stable = 2.3 ($\pm$2.0); t = 3.2, d.f. 78, $p<.005$].

Finally, the ICD-9 relapsing group had lower negative symptom scores than the stable [relapsing mean ($\pm$s.d.) = 2.6($\pm$2.2), Stable = 1.8($\pm$1.7); t = -1.7, d.f. 78, $p<.05$].

These data are summarized in Table 8.

DISCUSSION OF DATA

The data suggest a number of conclusions. First, as others have demonstrated, no matter whether one uses DSM-III, RDC, or ICD-9, schizophrenia and affective disorder display impressive stability over time (Winokur, 1974; Tsuang et al., 1981; Cooper, 1967; Munk-Jorgensen, 1985; Coryell and Zimmerman, 1987;

TABLE 8. *Stable and relapsing schizophrenia (RDC and ICD-9)*

	Stable	Relapsing
A. Outcome typology Categories	Mostly incapacitated and walking wounded	Mostly superior and working wounded
B. Intake variables		
1. Axis V	Low	High
2. Family involvement	3-4 persons	3-4 persons
3. Friends and acquaintances	Few	Many
4. Negative symptoms	Many	Few

McGlashan 1984). Our data demonstrate that this impressive stability applies to first onset, as well as more chronic cases. Feighner criteria, on the other hand, produce overly narrow as well as unstable diagnostic categories, particularly for schizophrenia and mania.

Secondly, stability is a useful tool for identifying diagnostic groupings and, in combination with other criteria, in establishing their validity. In our series, a small group of persons with a diagnosis of schizophreniform disorder recovered and did not develop another disorder. These "true" schizophreniforms demonstrated better premorbid adjustment, and less affective flattening, than others who were later rediagnosed, supporting the DSM-III-R introduction of these criteria as part of the schizophreniform construct. Although poor rapport is not one of the DSM-III-R criteria, it has appeared in many clinical conceptions of schizophrenia. For example, Kraepelin (1919, p. 259) spoke of the schizophrenics' "inaccessibility towards the reassuring statements of the physician" and Bleuler (1950, p. 299) noted the "absence of ability for discussion." Finally, among the criteria for schizophrennia, the DSM-II (APA, 1968, p. 33) included "constricted and inappropriate emotional responsiveness and loss of empathy with others." This web of meaningful relationships helps establish the construct validity of one of the more controversial DSM-III and DSM-III-R diagnoses. Although illness onset among the schizophreniforms was less insidious than among schizophrenics, applying a criterion of 4 weeks, as suggested in DSM-III-R, did not successfully separate the groups. A much larger series than ours will be required to effectively address the questions of which cut-point in duration will best serve to identify schizophreniform cases. In the meantime, the explicit incorporation of lack of affective flattening, good rapport, and evidence of good premorbid adjustment as criteria for the diagnosis of schizophreniform disorder should result in a more stable diagnosis.

Longer follow-up will be necessary in order to determine if the diagnosis of schizophreniform disorder will remain stable over a long time, if some or all of these people will suffer future episodes of schizophrenia, or if, as Fogelson (1982) has suggested, they will go on to manifest an affective disorder.

About one in five of the cases originally diagnosed under Major Depression in DSM-III went on to be reclassified as a case of Bipolar Disorder. Tsuang et al. (1981), in their 30-year follow-up of persons originally hospitalized for psychosis, report that 11% to 17% originally classified as depressed had to be reclassified as bipolar. This convergence of findings suggests an interesting question. Is it possible to find criteria which will identify those persons with a bipolar disorder who initially present with depression rather than mania? Since a diagnosis of bipolar disorder carries with it treatment and prognostic implications different from those which obtain for depressive disorder, investigations of this question appear warranted.

On the whole, psychotic diagnoses are stable categories. The overlap between diagnostic systems was less in this series than in some reports. This is probably due to our use of a first-episode cohort. Overlap is greatest in patients with chronic disorders (Endicott et al., 1982; McGlashan, 1984).

Given the narrowness of its definition, the stability of DSM-III schizophrenia is particularly noteworthy. As Kendler (1985) has noted, broadly defined diagnostic categories tend to be the most stable because even if some symptoms change over time, there is a good chance that others will remain sufficiently constant to satisfy the inclusion criteria for the initial diagnosis. The temporal stability of DSM-III schizophrenia diagnoses suggest that the defining criteria identify a particularly homogeneous category. Data on the course of illness support the impression of diagnostic homogeneity. Only one of the DSM-III schizophrenics followed over 18 months had, by the end of the study, recovered sufficiently that he no longer qualified for a diagnosis. Even this "recovered" case, however, made a marginal adjustment: one of the "working wounded," he was productively employed but with little sense of joy and at an apparent cost of considerable suffering.

By contrast, the even more narrowly defined Feighner schizophrenics display an unstable course over time. While Feighner-defined mania proves no more stable than the same system's diagnosis of schizophrenia, the DSM-III bipolar category is at least as stable as that found in RDC or ICD-9. In fact, both major depression and bipolar disorder in DSM-III appear to be impressively homogeneous and stable categories. In this respect, DSM-III has an edge over the RDC because its diagnoses of schizophrenia, major depression, and bipolar disorder are more stable and it does not include schizoaffective disorder, a diagnosis in RDC that proved disappointing when judged by the criterion of diagnostic stability.

If DSM-III diagnoses are, on the whole, more stable than Feighner, RDC, and ICD-9 (see also Helzer and Brockington, 1981), is DSM-III the best system? Possibly not. For example, despite its stability and demonstrable homogeneity, DSM-III schizophrenia may be an overly restrictive diagnosis, one which identifies only a subcategory of schizophrenia—those illnesses with a uniformly poor prognosis. It seems to be characteristic of restrictive diagnoses that cases with the worst prognosis will be included, and those with more variable outcomes excluded (Munk-Jorgensen, 1985).

While there is a good match between the stable schizophrenic groups in RDC,

ICD-9, and DSM-III, the RDC and ICD-9 systems identify a category of relapsing schizophrenia which has no counterpart in DSM-III, but which others besides ourselves suggest is a useful construct (WHO, 1973; 1979). Relapsing schizophrenia includes persons diagnosed schizophreniform under DSM-III, but is not limited to them. While there are no symptom differences between relapsing and stable schizophrenics, the former show evidence of much better premorbid work history. Differences in the amount of involvement with friends, but not with family, are striking and intriguing. Perhaps schizophrenics with relatively good prognosis differ from those with a poorer course in possessing more social skills or being better able to emancipate themselves from their family of origin.

Although it may seem paradoxical, relapsing schizophrenia is as stable a category as stable schizophrenia. Recurring illnesses in physical medicine, such as regional and rheumatoid arthritis, are analogies. People with these illnesses do not necessarily stay sick all the time. Instead, it is the pattern of recurrence, and the basic similarity of the symptom picture from episode to episode which defines stability.

The fact that stability is used as a criterion for validity reveals an implicit assumption about most, if not all, psychiatric illnesses. The assumption is that they are, or at least act like, chronic illnesses. This is why we expect them to endure for a long time in their original form. If, on the other hand, a patient with a psychiatric disorder recovers and then falls ill again, it should be with the same illness.

There is a third form of stability which the data in this study cannot address. It is possible to think of a diagnosis as remaining stable even if the symptoms of the original disorder bear little relationship to forms of illness which occur later. Syphilis is an example from physical medicine. In the course of this disorder, the original illness with its chancre and enlarged lymph nodes quickly passes, to be replaced by a second stage of rashes, to be replaced by a final stage with cardiovascular involvement, neurological deficit, dementia, and madness. Despite the changing clinical picture, the diagnosis is stable because clinicians can trace the pathophysiological process which unites the apparently dissimilar states.

Research into the evolution of various forms of psychiatric disorder demonstrates several interesting and convergent trends. For example, between 25% to 50% of cases of paranoia and 20% to 30% of cases of affective disorder evolve over time into schizophrenia. The reverse is rarely true. Within the category of schizophrenia itself, research suggests that some cases show a tendency to change from schizophrenia episodes dominated by positive symptoms into later forms where, at least in some cases, negative symptoms become the most prominent (Lindenmayer et al., 1986; Pogue-Geile and Harrow, 1985; Kolakowska et al. 1985).

Most studies support the approach of dividing schizophrenia into two subgroups, one with permanent, or at least long-lasting symptoms, another characterized by recovery and recurrence (Marengo and Harrow, 1987; Harrow et al., 1978; Westermeyer and Harrow, 1984; Kolakowska et al., 1985; Neuchterlein and

Dawson, 1984; Wynne et al. 1978). The possibility that these subgroups may overlap to some extent with the occurrence of negative syndromes, a trend suggested in our data, lends added weight to their importance (see Kay et al., 1986; Lindenmayer et al., 1986; Pogue-Geile and Harrow, 1985).

Even in this young population experiencing a first episode of schizophrenia, DSM-III seems to identify only one subgroup, the one with the worst course. If investigators exclude cases of schizophrenia with a good prognosis, it becomes impossible to examine the potentially important finding that premorbid characteristics and the presence of negative symptoms may help differentiate the subgroups and perhaps help explain how schizophrenic vulnerability evolves into different phenotypic expressions of illness.

Diagnostic stability is not the ultimate criterion for validity. However, in combination with other considerations, such as course of illness, family studies, and investigation of associated clinical features, it becomes a powerful clinical and investigative tool.

REFERENCES

American Psychiatric Association. (1980): *Diagnostic and statistical manual of mental disorders*, 3rd edition. American Psychiatric Association, Washington, D.C.
American Psychiatric Association. (1968): *Diagnostic and statistical manual II*. American Psychiatric Association, Washington, D.C.
Barrett, J. (1986): Case identification for category validation: The challenge of disorder-specific assessment. *Comprehensive Psychiatry*, 27(2):81–100.
Beiser, M., Erickson, D., and Husted, J. Dating the onset of schizophrenic illness (*submitted for publication*).
Beiser, M., Fleming, J. A. E., Iacono, W. G., and Lin, T. Y. (1988): Refining the diagnosis of schizophreniform disorder. *Am J Psychiatry*, 145(6):695–700.
Beiser, M., Iacono, W. G., and MacEwan, W. Descriptors and predictors of the eighteen-month course of first-episode schizophrenia (*submitted for publication*).
Bleuler, E. (1950): *Dementia praecox or the group of schizophrenias*, translated by J. Zinker. International Universities Press, New York.
Bradburn, N. M., and Caplovitz, D. (1969): *Reports on happiness*. Aldine, Chicago.
Bradburn, N. M. (1965): *The structure of psychological well-being*. Aldine, Chicago.
Carey, G. and Gottesman, I. I. (1978): Reliability and validity in binary ratings: Areas of common misunderstanding in diagnoses and symptom ratings. *Arch Gen Psychiatry*, 35:1454–1459.
Cloninger, C. R., Martin, R. L., Guze, S. B., and Clayton, P. J. (1986): A prospective follow-up and family study of somatization in men and women. *Am J Psychiatry*, 143(7):873–878.
Cooper, J. E. (1967): Diagnostic change in a longitudinal study of psychiatric patients. *Brit J Psychiatry*, 113:129–142.
Coryell, W. and Zimmerman, M. (1987): Progress in the classification of functional psychoses. *Am J Psych*, 144(11):1471–1474.
Derogatis, L. R. (1977): *SCL-90: Administration, scoring and procedures. manual I*. Clinical Psychiatric Research, Baltimore.
Endicott, J., Nee, J., Fleiss, J., Cohen, J., et al. (1982): Diagnostic criteria for schizophrenia: Reliabilities and agreement between systems. *Arch Gen Psychiatry*, 39:884–889.
Endicott, J., Spitzer, R. L., Fleiss, J. L., et al. (1976): The Global Assessment Scale: A procedure for measuring overall severity of psychiatric disturbance. *Arch Gen Psychiatry*, 33:766–771.
Feighner, J. P., Robins, E., Guze, S. B., Woodruff, R. A., et al. (1972): Diagnostic criteria for use in psychiatric research. *Arch Gen Psychiatry*, 26:57–63.
Fogelson, D. L., Cohen, B. M., and Pope, H. G., Jr. (1982): A study of DSM-III schizophreniform disorder. *Am J Psychiatry*, 139:1281–1285.

Harrow, M., Grinker, R. R., Sr., Silverstein, M. L., and Holzman, P. (1978): Is modern-day schizophrenia outcome still negative? *Am J Psychiatry*, 135:1156–1162.
Helzer, J. E., Brockington, I. F., and Kendall, R. E. (1981): Predictive validity of DSM-III and Feighner definitions of schizophrenia. *Arch Gen Psychiatry*, 38:791–797.
Henderson, S., Byrne, D. G. and Duncan-Jones, P. (1981): *Neurosis and the social environment*. Academic Press, Toronto.
Hendersen, S., Duncan-Jones, P., McAuley, H., and Ritchie, K. (1978): The patient's primary group. *Brit J Psychiatry*, 132:74–86.
Kay, S. R., Opler, L. A., and Fiszbein, A. (1986): Significance of positive and negative syndromes in chronic schizophrenia. *Brit J Psychiatry*, 149:439–448.
Kendell, R. E. (1974): The stability of psychiatric diagnosis. *Brit J Psychiatry*, 124:352–356.
Kendler, K. S., Gruenberg, A. M., and Tsuang, M. T. (1985): Subtype stability in schizophrenia. *Am J Psychiatry*, 142(7):827–832.
Kolakowska, T., Williams, A. O., Ardern, M. Reveley, M. A. et al. (1985): Schizophrenia with good and poor outcome I: Early clinical features, response to neuroleptics and signs of organic dysfunction. *Brit J Psychiatry*, 146: 229–246.
Kraepelin, E. (1919): *Dementia praecox and paraphrenia*, translated by M. Barday, from the 8th German Edition of the *Textbook of Psychiatry*, E. S. Livingston Ltd., Edinburgh.
Leckman, J. F., Sholomskas, D., Thompson, W. D., Belanger, A., et al. (1982): Best estimates of lifetime psychiatric diagnosis: A methodologic study. *Arch Gen Psych*, 39:879–883.
Lindenmayer, J. P., Kay, S. R., and Friedman, C. (1986): Negative and positive schizophrenic syndromes after the acute phase: A prospective follow-up. *Compr Psychiat*, 27(4):274–286.
Marengo, J. T., and Harrow, M. (1987): Schizophrenic thought disorder at follow-up. *Arch Gen Psychiatry*, 44:651–659.
Mazure, C., and Gershon, E. S. (1979): Blindness and reliability in lifetime psychiatric diagnosis. *Arch Gen Psychiatry*, 36:521–525.
McGlashan, T. H. (1984): Testing four diagnostic systems for schizophrenia. *Arch Gen Psychiatry*, 41:141–144.
Munk-Jorgensen, P. (1985): The schizophrenia diagnosis in Denmark. *Acta Psychiatr Scand*, 72:266–273.
Neuchterlein, K. H., and Dawson, M.E. (1984): A heuristic vulnerability/stress model of schizophrenic episodes. *Schizophrenia Bull*, 10:300–312.
Perley, M. J., and Guze, S. B. (1962): Hysteria—The stability and usefulness of clinical criteria. A quantitative study based on a follow-up period of six to eight years in 39 patients. *The New England Journal of Medicine*, 266(9):421–426.
Pogue-Geile, M. F., and Harrow, M. (1985): Negative symptoms in schizophrenia: Their longitudinal course and prognostic importance. *Schizophrenia Bull*, 11:427–439.
Robins, L. N., Helzer, J. E., Croughen, J., and Ratcliff, K. S. (1981): National Institute of Mental Health diagnostic interview schedule: Its history, characteristics and validity. *Arch Gen Psychiatry*, 38:381–389.
Sartorius, N., Jablensky, A., Kortin, A., Ernberg, G., et al. (1986): Early manifestations and first-contact incidence of schizophrenia in different cultures. *Psychol Med*, 16:909–928.
Sheldrick, C., Jablensky, A., Sartorius, N., and Shepherd, M. (1977): Schizophrenia succeeded by affective illness: Catamnestic study and statistical enquiry. *Psychological Medicine*, 7:619–624.
Siris, S. G., Rifkin, A., Reardon, G. T., Seshagiri, R., et al. (1986): Stability of the postpsychotic depression syndrome. *J Clin Psychiatry*, 47(2):86–88.
Spitzer, R. L., Endicott, J., and Robins, E. (1985): Research diagnostic criteria: Rationale and Reliability. *Arch Gen Psychiatry*. 35:773–782.
Spitzer, R. L., Endicott, J., and Robins, E. (1977): *Research diagnostic criteria*, 3rd edition. New York State Psychiatric Institute, New York.
Stromgren, E. (1987): Changes in the incidence of schizophrenia? *Brit J Psychiatry*, 150:1–7.
Tsuang, M. T., Woolson, R. F., Winokur, G., and Crowe, R. R. (1981): Stability of psychiatric diagnosis. *Arch Gen Psychiatry*, 38:535–539.
Turner, R. J. (1972): The epidemiological study of schizophrenia: A current appraisal. *Journal of Health & Social Behavior*, 13:360–369.
Ward, J. H. (1963): Hierarchical grouping to optimize an objective function. *J Amer Statistical Association*, 58:236–244.
Westermeyer, J. F., and Harrow, M. (1984): Prognosis and outcome using broad (DSM-II) and narrow (DSM-III) concepts of schizophrenia. *Schizophrenia Bull*, 10:624–637.

Wing, J. K., Cooper, J. E., and Sartorius, N. (1974): *The measurement and classification of psychiatric symptoms.* Cambridge University Press, New York.
Winokur, G. (1974): Diagnostic stability over time in schizophrenia, mania and depression. *New England Journal of Medicine*, 290(18):1027.
Winokur, G., Scharfetter, C., and Angst, J. (1985): Stability of psychotic symptomatology (delusions, hallucinations), affective syndromes, and schizophrenic symptoms (thought disorder, incongruent affect) over episodes in remitting psychoses. *Euro Arch Psychiatr Neurol Sci*, 234:303–307.
World Health Organization. (1973): *Report of the international pilot study of schizophrenia.* World Health Organization, Geneva.
World Health Organization. (1978): *Mental disorders: Glossary and guide to their classification in accordance with the ninth revision of the international classification of diseases.* World Health Organization, Geneva.
World Health Organization. (1979): *Schizophrenia: An international follow-up study.* John Wiley & Sons, New York.
Wynne, L. C., Cromwell, R. L., and Mathysse, S. (eds.) (1978): *The nature of schizophrenia: New approaches to research and treatment.* John Wiley & Sons, New York.

DISCUSSION

Dr. Zubin: When we talk about construct validity, what we really mean is the following: first, developing a scientific model for the disorder from which we then get certain hypotheses, and then searching for evidence for the hypothesis beyond the overt psychopathology. For example, a construct validity for a genetic hypothesis would consist of demonstrations that identical twins are more concordant for a disorder than nonidentical twins. Consistency of diagnosis over time is really a form of reliability. I don't see why you use it as an example of construct validity.

Dr. Beiser: I agree up to a point. I think that the application of a criterion like stability helps to create meaningful categories of illness. In that way, I think stability is a commentary on the validity of the original conceptualization.

For example, schizophreniform disorder is a construct—a short-lived psychosis with features resembling schizophrenia but which runs a different course. Finding that the stability of symptoms is different in the schizophreniform group from that in the schizophrenics is one aspect of construct validation. The demonstration that symptoms are relatively stable in schizophrenia, but evanescent in schizophreniform psychosis, is more than reliability. Since these features are part of the constructs themselves, they support their validity. The demonstration that features besides symptom stability also distinguish schizophreniform disorder from schizophrenia—factors such as differences in work performance, in rapport with the examiner, and in the distribution of affective flattening—is another exercise in construct validation. This step enables us to say that the category, schizophreniform disorder, is a useful psychopathological construct. The web of relationships accumulating around that construct is evidence of its usefulness.

Dr. Guze: A question to Drs. Beiser and Kovacs: did your research designs provide for a study of psychopathology in families?

Dr. Beiser: We have preliminary data on families in our data which lead us to feel that it is important to do a study of family patterns. It certainly is something we would like to do.

Dr. Kovacs: We have just completed a family study of these probands, but I don't yet have the results. There is one problem in doing family studies with these psychiatrically referred children, and that is less than one-third of them live with both biological parents. It is almost impossible to get hold of the fathers, and in many cases the mother doesn't know anything about the father. It is sad because information on the paternal line would enable us to have a much better understanding of the genetics of these kinds of disorders.

Dr. Guze: Dr. Kovacs, I am surprised at the unusually high rate of bipolarity in the children in your study. In our psychiatry clinic, where we have followed many patients with a variety of affective disorders, we have not found so high a percentage except in a very small subgroup. Have you any explanation for this unusually high rate of bipolarity?

Dr. Kovacs: There was a paper published by Mark Strober a few years ago on the rate of bipolarity among adolescents hospitalized with a depression. He also found a rate of 20%.

Dr. Guze: He found this in hospitalized patients, but your patients were not hospitalized.

Dr. Kovacs: They were not, but they were also much younger than his. I don't know exactly what these data mean, but my guess is that childhood onset depressive disorders are very severe. There were very few families that were not affected with something, and I suspect that we could be identifying a subtype of early onset affective illness which has a far worse outcome than we usually see in adults.

Ms. Lish: Dr. Kovacs, did the lack of differential outcome between dysthymia and major depressive disorder lead you to question the validity of that diagnostic distinction in children?

Dr. Kovacs: We thought a lot about the meaning of that finding. The problem is that about two-thirds of the children with dysthymia develop a major depression, but less than one-third of the children with major depression have an underlying dysthymia. So there are two overlapping groups, and at the present time, I don't know what the relationship is between the two of them, and so I prefer to keep both of the categories.

Dr. Beiser: Another comment on stability of diagnosis, after thinking about Dr. Zubin's comment about construct validity. Bob Hirschfeld pointed out that there is instability of diagnosis in field surveys. Certainly that is true for depression. In community surveys, a great many people who report depression at one time don't report lifetime depression when they are resurveyed. One recommendation is to take consistency of reporting as an indication that the psychopathology is more "real." My reading of the literature on this topic is that the major determinant of whether somebody who reported depression at Time 1 will report lifetime depression at Time 2 is whether or not they happen to be depressed at Time 2. If that is the case, then one is saying that the more chronic a condition, the more "real" it is. I am not sure that one should or can say that. After all, why should a depression which only happens once be somehow less "real" than a depression that continues? The short-lived and apparently easily forgotten depressions are likely different from more chronic conditions, but I am not sure that they are less "real." Likewise, a depression which recurs, but only after long intervals so that there is a diminished chance of being identified as depressed in repeated waves of a field survey, is not less real. It is a different kind of illness, perhaps, and that is where construct validation may come in. One may want to look at separate subgroups of depressive disorders, for example, to see whether these form distinct entities. I am proposing that one consider stability as a criterion for validity, but not to take it too seriously.

The Validity of Psychiatric Diagnosis, edited by
Lee N. Robins and James E. Barrett.
Raven Press, Ltd., New York © 1989.

Internal Consistency of DSM-III Diagnoses

*Linda K. George, *Dan G. Blazer,
**Max A. Woodbury, and †Kenneth G. Manton

*Department of Psychiatry, Duke University Medical Center, Durham, NC 27710; **Center for the Study of Aging and Human Development, Duke University Medical Center, Durham, NC 27710; and †Center for Demographic Studies, Duke University, Durham, NC 27706*

In 1970, Robins and Guze (1) proposed a five-stage procedure for establishing diagnostic validity for psychiatric disorders. Two of those stages were clinical description and delimitation from other disorders. Internal consistency analysis is relevant to both of these phases of validity assessment. It is relevant to clinical description because internal consistency analysis concerns the degree to which symptoms cluster to form empirically, theoretically, and clinically meaningful syndromes. It is relevant to delimitation or discrimination because internal consistency analysis can be used to document the boundaries (or lack of them) between symptom syndromes and to disaggregate clusters of symptoms into increasingly specific and homogeneous subsets.

This chapter addresses the internal consistency of DSM-III diagnoses and is organized in four sections. The first section briefly reviews the logic and general principles of internal consistency analysis. Extant evidence about the internal consistency of DSM-III diagnoses is reviewed in the second section. The third section describes a new procedure for internal consistency analysis: grade of membership analysis. This procedure is especially promising because it simultaneously examines the natural clustering of symptoms into syndromes and the distribution of individuals across syndromes. Our final comments attempt to place DSM-III and internal consistency analysis into broader perspective.

INTERNAL CONSISTENCY ANALYSIS: BASIC PRINCIPLES

As used in the clinical and social sciences, the term internal consistency has its roots in the psychometric literature. Internal consistency analysis is best known as a method by which the reliability of multi-item scales can be assessed (2,3). In that framework, internal consistency refers to the degree of intercorrelation among a set of indicators intended to measure the same phenomenon. The higher the correlations, the more internally consistent the set of indicators. The logic of using internal consistency as a measure of reliability or of psychometric adequacy more generally merits brief examination.

Internal consistency analysis can be used only when a phenomenon is measured on the basis of multiple indicators. The logic of internal consistency analysis rests on the assumed importance of *sampling content* and *homogeneity*. Most phenomena that scientists want to measure can be described in terms of multiple indicators. Indeed, many if not most constructs of scientific concern are sufficiently complex that multiple indicators are not only possible, but necessary for adequate measurement. To the extent that phenomena can or must be measured using multiple indicators, the total universe of relevant indicators must be representatively sampled. Note that not every relevant indicator must be included in the measurement tool; rather, the total universe of indicators must be representatively sampled (2,4).

There is a "flip-side" to the issue of representative sampling of indicators. The measuring tool should not include indicators that are not definitionally relevant to the phenomenon of interest (2,4). At an obvious level, a measuring tool should not include items that are not characteristic of the phenomenon to be measured. A more subtle issue, however, is the need to restrict the universe of indicators to those that are *definitionally relevant* to the phenomenon of interest. That is, the universe of indicators should include only those required to define the construct of interest; indicators of associated, but different phenomena should not be included in the measuring tool. The distinction between definitional and associated indicators is based on theory and substantive knowledge of the phenomenon of interest.

Internal consistency analysis cannot tell us whether the universe of indicators that are definitionally relevant to a particular phenomenon have been representatively sampled. Nor can internal consistency analysis tell us whether an investigator has included indicators of associated phenomena in a measuring tool or has appropriately restricted the instrument to definitionally relevant indicators. If an internal consistency analysis suggests that one or more indicators behave poorly, we cannot know with certainty whether those items are not definitionally relevant to the phenomenon of interest or whether they were poorly measured. Internal consistency analysis can, however, tell us if the relationships among indicators are sufficiently strong to suggest that they are tapping the same underlying phenomenon (2,4). Moreover, indicators can be systematically added to and removed from the analyses to examine the ways that inclusion and exclusion of particular indicators affect internal consistency.

As these comments imply, an internally consistent measurement tool is relatively homogeneous (2,4). One of the issues that investigators must confront is the degree of homogeneity desirable for their research purposes. It is often possible to disaggregate pools of items that exhibit adequate internal consistency into increasingly smaller and more specific dimensions. For example, the CES-D, a 20-item scale designed to measure current levels of depression, has been demonstrated to exhibit adequate internal consistency (i.e., alpha$>$.70) (5). Additional analyses, however, suggest that the scale can be further disaggregated into three or four more specific dimensions—and that each of those dimensions is somewhat more internally consistent than the total scale score (6,7). Depending on the research purpose, some investigators may wish to use total CES-D scores and others may find it advantageous to use one of the more specific dimensions in the scale. Moreover, it is also possible to have excessive internal consistency. If indicators are extremely highly correlated (e.g., $r \geq .90$), they may be redundant rather than representing different parameters of the same underlying phenomenon. Redundancy may be of minimal conceptual consequence, but it is statistically troublesome because it introduces multicollinearity into statistical models. Thus, investigators typically desire results that suggest excellent internal consistency but that also minimize redundancy.

As noted previously, the psychometric literature traditionally has treated internal consistency as one form of reliability assessment, with reliability referring to the degree to which measurement is free from random error. An internally consistent measure may be assumed to be relatively free from error because random error would lower the correlations observed among indicators (2,3). The traditional psychometric literature also draws a rigid line between reliability and validity. According to this perspective, a reliable measure is free from random error, but it may be totally invalid (2). In essence, reliable measures permit investigators to conclude that they are measuring "something" in a relatively error-free manner, but offer no evidence that the "something" is what they intended to measure.

More recently, however, psychometricians are increasingly viewing reliability and validity in a less rigid way. A number of psychometricians now view reliability and validity as ultimately inseparable because, by definition, a measure that is strongly affected by random error cannot be valid. Precisely because it is based on issues of sampling content, homogeneity, and the dimensional structure of sets of indicators, internal consistency analysis is relevant to validity assessment and hypothesis testing, as well as to estimating reliability (4,8).

It is perhaps worth inserting a caveat at this point. Though the logic of internal consistency analysis is important for multiple purposes, we are not claiming that it is the only important approach in social and clinical research. Indeed, internal consistency analysis, by itself, is rarely sufficient for addressing any research question. But it is a useful tool in many research studies—and its importance is broader than its traditional image as a form of reliability assessment.

A variety of statistical techniques, ranging from the simple to the complex, are used to estimate internal consistency. Indeed, most investigators who apply the logic of internal consistency analysis do not describe their efforts in those terms. It is perhaps worth noting briefly the major statistical techniques used for this purpose. Detailed descriptions of these techniques are beyond the scope of this chapter. For the reader's convenience, however, key references to each technique are provided.

Coefficient alpha is perhaps the statistical estimator most closely linked to internal consistency analysis (3). This coefficient is used to estimate the reliability of multi-item scales and is based on the average correlation among items and the number of items in the scale. A variety of techniques subsumed by the generic term item analysis (e.g., item-to-total correlations, item discriminability) also are an integral part of internal consistency analysis (2). Factor analysis is the technique most commonly used to examine the dimensional structure of a set of indicators (8). There are numerous types of factor analysis. One factor generating this heterogeneity is the variety of assumptions investigators may make about scale items and the restrictions that they can impose on the factor models. Another component of this variation concerns the purpose of the factor analysis. Differences in purpose have led to a common distinction between exploratory factor analysis (generally used for data reduction purposes and reliability assessment) (9) and confirmatory factor analysis (used in a hypothesis-testing mode) (10). Multidimensional scaling techniques are similar to factor analysis in that they are used primarily to identify the dimensional structures underlying a set of relationships. Unlike traditional factor analysis, however, multidimensional scaling is not constrained by assumptions of linearity (11). Latent trait models are designed specifically to relate a set of indicators to an underlying (or latent) construct that cannot be directly observed or measured and are, thus, a form of internal consistency analysis (12). Finally, cluster analysis is sometimes used to identify the structure of a set of indicators (13). In some ways, cluster analysis is similar to factor analysis. As noted below, however, cluster analysis is generally used to classify people whereas factor analysis is used to categorize indicators of the phenomenon of interest.

Internal consistency analysis has been frequently used in psychiatric research, though it usually is not described that way by those who employ it. Review of the literature suggests that most of the psychiatric research based on internal consistency analysis is described in terms of validity assessment, the identification of diagnostic subtypes, symptom profiles, and phenomenology. Regardless of the labels used, the logic in these studies is similar: a set of indicators proposed to measure one or more diagnostic constructs is examined in terms of dimensionality, distinctiveness, and/or homogeneity.

As used in psychiatric research, two issues with regard to internal consistency are the basis of continuing debate. These debates so thoroughly pervade the literature on the internal consistency of psychiatric diagnoses that they merit brief discussion.

One debate concerns the appropriateness of categorical versus continuous measures of psychiatric disorders. Some investigators argue strongly for a categorical or typological approach. In a recent paper on the history and operationalization of psychiatric syndromes, for example, Weber and Scharfetter (14) argue that:

> Factor analysis is used to construct syndromes and . . . these syndromes then possess the continuous quality of scales. . . . We do not regard this model as appropriate for the identification of syndromes, because a syndrome is typically non-continuous. If the subject is affected by the underlying illness . . . the symptoms are to appear; if he is not so affected, the symptoms should not be apparent. If we introduced the idea of continuity in the context of psychiatric syndromes, we would have to give them names like "schizophrenicity" or "manicity" in order to clarify their scale property. In our opinion, however, the medical syndromes as conceptualized by medicine itself generally do not share that quality. (p. 320)

Other investigators are not only comfortable with the notion of psychiatric disorders as continuous in nature, but suggest that any workable diagnostic system must come to terms with the fact that psychiatric disorders cannot be classified into discrete and mutually exclusive categories. In a recent study of DSM-III personality disorders, for example, Livesley (15) stated: "Personality categories are like fuzzy sets with indistinct boundaries; category membership is not an all-or-none occurrence but a matter of degree. . . . Patients also differ in how typical they are of a given diagnostic grouping, an observation reflected in such commonplace statements as 'a classical histrionic personality' or 'a typical borderline personality.'" (p. 728)

This is not a forum in which the merits and liabilities of categorical versus continuous nosological systems can be explored. It is important to note, however, that this distinction has implications for internal consistency analysis. Proponents of categorical diagnostic systems place greater restrictions on internal consistency findings than do advocates of continuous measures. For the latter, internal consistency is achieved so long as a pool of indicators is highly intercorrelated and empirically distinct from indicators intended to measure other diagnostic entities. Proponents of categorical diagnostic systems, however, require evidence that their diagnostic categories also are discrete and mutually exclusive.

A second, though often less explicit, debate concerns the distinction between categorizing signs and symptoms into diagnostic categories and classifying individuals into diagnostic groups. Some studies focus on the relationships among signs and symptoms of psychiatric disorder. In such studies, the goal of the investigator is to categorize symptoms into internally consistent groups that correspond to clinical syndromes. Other studies focus on individuals, with the goal of classifying them according to membership versus nonmembership in diagnostic categories.

This distinction also has important implications for conducting internal consistency analyses. Different techniques are needed to categorize symptoms than to classify individuals. Moreover, results based on one form of analysis will not necessarily correspond to those based on the other form of analysis. This point is clearly demonstrated by Good and associates in a recent study of the structure of depressive symptoms in the elderly (16). In that study, psychiatric symptoms were elicited using the Hamilton Depression Rating Scale and the Mental Test Score. Factor analysis was used to identify the structural dimensions underlying the items in those two measures. Four clinically relevant and statistically reliable factors were identified: depressive symptoms, anxiety symptoms, symptoms of cognitive impairment, and psychosomatic symptoms. Cluster analysis was used to categorize respondents on the basis of the symptoms in the two scales. Four clusters were identified: normals (i.e., relatively asymptomatic individuals), persons reporting anxiety symptoms, those reporting symptoms of both anxiety and cognitive impairment, and persons reporting symptoms from all four factors. As these results illustrate, respondents' symptom profiles often do not match the diagnostic categories generated by internal consistency analysis of symptom data.

Though the issues of categorical versus continuous measures of psychiatric disorder and of categorizing symptoms versus classifying persons have been described separately, there is a clear link between them. As the quote of Weber and Scharfetter illustrates, many proponents of categorical diagnostic systems want not only diagnostic categories to be discrete and mutually exclusive, they also want psychiatric patients to closely match those diagnostic categories. Advocates of continuous measures, however, are content to acknowledge "fuzziness" with regard to both the nature of diagnostic categories and the degree to which patients' symptoms are characteristic of those categories. This point was nicely illustrated by the Livesley quotation—Livesley's comments are directed as much to the ways that patients present symptoms of personality disorders as to the definitions of those disorders. Thus, both of these debates concern fuzziness versus discreteness and both can be explored in the context of internal consistency analysis.

INTERNAL CONSISTENCY OF DSM-III DIAGNOSES

The logic of DSM-III is described in ways that interface well with the basic principles of internal consistency analysis. Four points of convergence are found in the introduction of DSM-III. First, definitions of DSM-III mental disorders "consist of descriptions of the clinical features of the disorders" and the clinical features "are described at the lowest order of inference needed to describe the characteristic features of the disorder." (17, p. 7). Thus, DSM-III disorders are defined by multiple indicators, generally of a highly specific nature, suggesting that sampling content and homogeneity are relevant to the measurement of DSM-III diagnoses.

Second, a clear distinction is made between essential features of the DSM-III disorders and both associated and predisposing factors. Essential features are definitionally related to DSM-III disorders and are the signs and symptoms that should be included in estimates of the internal consistency of DSM-III diagnoses. Associated features are "often, but not invariably, present" (17, p. 31); predisposing factors are "characteristics of an individual that can be identified before the development of the disorder and that place him or her at higher risk for developing the disorder." (17, p. 31). Thus, DSM-III provides guidelines concerning those signs and symptoms that are definitionally relevant and those that are clinically relevant yet distinct from the definitions of DSM-III mental disorders.

Third, the issue of differing levels of homogeneity is addressed in DSM-III. One example of this is the grouping of specific mental disorders into diagnostic classes (e.g., affective disorders, anxiety disorders). Another example is the subdivision of some specific disorders into subtypes (e.g., major depression with and without melancholia). This hierarchical approach to diagnostic specificity (which is distinct from the exclusions hierarchy) suggests that internal consistency can be evaluated at multiple levels and investigators should not be surprised that disorders can be described at varying levels of abstraction.

Finally, the developers of DSM-III explicitly support the notion of "fuzziness" with regard to both the definition of mental disorders and the classification of patients presenting with psychiatric symptomatology. With regard to the definition of mental disorders, the developers note that, "In DSM-III there is no assumption that each mental disorder is a discrete entity with sharp boundaries (discontinuity) between it and other mental disorders, as well as between it and No Mental Disorder." (17, p. 6) Strong comments also are offered with regard to the classification of individuals: "A common misconception is that a classification of mental disorders classifies individuals, when actually what are being classified are disorders that individuals have. . . . Another misconception is that all individuals described as having the same mental disorder are alike in all important ways." (17, p. 6) These statements about discreteness versus fuzziness have important implications for internal consistency analyses, suggesting (a) that specific symptoms may be definitionally relevant to multiple disorders, (b) that the boundaries between diagnoses will be indistinct, (c) that diagnoses may be correlated, (d) that individuals vary in the degree to which they exhibit the defining characteristics of mental disorders, and (e) hence, that the presentation of mental disorders is ultimately continuous rather than discrete.

Evidence now is beginning to cumulate concerning the internal consistency of DSM-III diagnoses. In the following paragraphs, the major conclusions of that research base will be summarized. Three qualifications should be noted from the outset, however. First, though the literature review generating these conclusions was extensive, it is likely that some relevant research was overlooked. Second, this review was largely, but not exclusively, restricted to studies based on psychiatric disorders as defined by DSM-III criteria. In particular, because of its similarity to DSM-III, some studies based on RDC diagnoses also are reviewed. Finally, as noted previously, many investigators who apply the logic of internal consistency analysis do not describe their efforts in those terms. Thus, the studies included in this review reflect our definition of what constitutes evidence of internal consistency and our judgments may or may not be congruent with the orientations of the authors of those studies.

Depressive Disorders

Not surprisingly, given recent emphasis on affective disorders in general and depressive disorders in particular, there is considerable evidence concerning the internal consistency of DSM-III depressive disorders. In the most comprehensive study of this kind, Fabrega et al. (18) examined the internal consistency of five DSM-III depressive diagnoses. Analysis of these symptoms generated two factors. The first factor included the symptoms of adjustment disorder with depressed mood, dysthymia, and atypical depression. Symptoms of bipolar disorder and unipolar depression loaded on the second factor. The authors concluded that the two factors primarily reflect differences in severity and that the DSM-III diagnostic categories are generally supported although the boundaries among some disorders are relatively indistinct.

Several investigators examined the internal consistency of the distinction between melancholic and nonmelancholic major depression, as defined in DSM-III. Zimmerman et al. (19) report that internal consistency analysis of depressive symptoms does not support the assumption that melancholic depression is qualitatively different from nonmelancholic depression. Rather, their data suggest that patients rated as having melancholic depression exhibit more severe depression than those diagnosed as nonmelancholic. Young et al. (20) also examined the melancholic-nonmelancholic distinction (as well as the RDC definition of endogenous depression), using latent trait analysis. Their results also failed to support either distinction, though the latent trait analysis revealed two factors of depressive symptoms: anhedonic and vegetative symptoms. In a study of somewhat narrower scope, Davidson and Turnbull (21) report that vegetative symptoms do not distinguish between melancholic and nonmelancholic depression. Along these same lines, Clark et al. (22) used latent trait analysis to examine the structure of depressive symptoms among patients with alcohol abuse or dependence. They report that anhedonic symptoms are the primary indicators of depression in this patient group and that vegetative symptoms are of little use in identifying depression. Overall, then, internal consistency analysis does not support the melancholic subtype of DSM-III. The distinction between anhedonic and vegetative symptoms appears empirically meaningful, however, with the former comprising the core features of depressive disorders.

Using similar logic, Breslau and Meltzer (23) examined the reliability of the DSM-III subtype of depression with psychotic features. Their data failed to support the distinctiveness of this subtype though the distinction between bipolar and unipolar disorder was supported.

The distinction between depression and anxiety is a long-standing debate in the psychiatric literature. In factor analyses of depressive and anxiety symptoms, both Kendler et al. (24) and Good et al. report that separate factors emerge for the two syndromes, although, as previously noted, Good et al. (16) also report that a substantial proportion of patients exhibit symptoms of both disorders. In a recent study, Riskind et al. (25) describe revised versions of the Hamilton Rating Scales for depression and anxiety. Internal consistency analysis was used to revise these frequently used scales such that anxiety and depression are measured as discretely as possible. Overall, the distinction between depression and anxiety appears to be one area in which the issue of categorizing symptoms versus classifying individuals needs to be kept more clearly in mind. Analyses of symptom data typically support the hypothesis that depression and anxiety are separate, but correlated syndromes. Nonetheless, many individuals present with significant symptoms of both disorders.

Finally, internal consistency analysis was used by Zimmerman et al. (26) in the development of the Inventory to Diagnose Depression (IDD), a scale intended to identify cases of DSM-III major depressive episodes. Results suggest that the IDD adequately elicits information about the symptoms needed to operationalize the DSM-III criteria. No evidence is presented, however, to suggest that the IDD can be used to identify the subtypes of major depressive disorder suggested by DSM-III.

Overall, available evidence suggests substantial internal consistency for the DSM-III depressive disorders, with two qualifications. First, there is little to no evidence supporting the DSM-III subtypes of major depressive disorder. Second, it is not clear whether the various depressive disorders represent qualitatively different depressive syndromes or syndromes that differ only or primarily in severity.

Anxiety Disorders

Limited data exist concerning the internal consistency of anxiety disorders. The distinction between anxiety and depression was reviewed above and will not be repeated.

Two major studies have examined the internal consistency of all the major DSM-III anxiety disorders except posttraumatic stress disorder (PTSD). Cameron et al. (27) used internal consistency analysis to examine the distinctiveness of the DSM-III anxiety disorders. Their results indicated that obsessive-compulsive disorder is the most distinctive of the anxiety disorders, followed closely by simple and social phobias. In contrast, the boundaries among panic disorder, agoraphobia (with and without panic attacks), and generalized anxiety disorder (GAD) are very indistinct, calling their status as independent disorders into question. Barlow et al. (28) also examined the full spectrum of anxiety disorders (except PTSD), with the specific goal of determining whether GAD is a residual diagnosis or an independent syndrome. The results suggest that GAD is largely a residual diagnosis because patients diagnosed with other anxiety disorders almost always meet the criteria for GAD also. Nonetheless, the authors suggest that there may be two forms of GAD: a residual form representing the apprehensive expectations that accompany other anxiety disorders and a qualitatively different form of chronic worry that represents an independent syndrome.

Van Kampen et al. (29) performed an internal consistency study of PTSD. The DSM-III definition of PTSD was generally supported. More specifically, 11 of the 16 DSM-III PTSD symptoms exhibited excellent internal consistency and five items were more weakly related to the underlying construct. The authors also suggested the addition of one symptom to the PTSD diagnostic criteria: the perception that one's life lacks direction. Though methodologically sound, caution is needed in generalizing from this study because the sample was restricted to Viet Nam veterans.

Again, results of extant studies generally support the internal consistency of the DSM-III anxiety disorders. Not surprisingly, however, the DSM-III anxiety disorders differ in degree of distinctiveness and, in some cases, the boundaries between disorders are fuzzy rather than crisp.

Schizophrenic Disorders

Though relatively few studies focus on the internal consistency of DSM-III schizophrenic disorders, extant studies address some fascinating issues with regard to these mental disorders. Makanjuola and Adedapa (30) performed an internal consistency analysis to assess the robustness of the distinction between schizophrenia and schizophreniform disorder. These authors report that with the exception of symptom duration (which is the sole DSM-III criterion that distinguishes the two disorders), the symptom profiles of persons diagnosed as having active or residual schizophrenia do not differ from those of persons diagnosed as having schizophreniform disorder. They suggest that schizophrenia and schizophreniform are not distinct disorders and that duration reflects the rapidity with which treatment is sought rather than a criterion for differential diagnosis.

Solovay, Shenton, and Holzman (31,32) examined the role of thought disorders in three DSM-III diagnoses: manic episode, schizophrenia, and schizophreniform disorder. Their results indicate that thought disorder clearly distinguishes between manic episode and both schizophrenic disorders. Thought disorders did not distinguish between schizophrenia and schizophreniform, however.

Researchers and clinicians have long been cognizant of the substantial heterogeneity subsumed by the diagnosis of schizophrenia. This heterogeneity has led to interest in defining subtypes of schizophrenia. Though many early typologies of schizophrenic subtypes have now been dropped, DSM-III recognizes five types of schizophrenia. Interestingly, we have identified no internal consistency analyses that focus on the DSM-III schizophrenic subtypes. A number of authors, however, have recently attempted to define subtypes of schizophrenia on the basis of the distinction between positive (i.e., aberrant mental activity) and negative (i.e., deficiency in mental functioning) symptoms (e.g., 33,34). Two recent studies examine positive and negative schizophrenic symptoms using internal consistency analysis.

Liddle (35) used factor analysis to examine the structure of DSM-III schizophrenia symptoms. Three factors emerged from this analysis representing psychomotor poverty, disorganization, and reality distortion. Liddle points out that the first and third factors closely resemble clinical definitions of positive and negative schizophrenic symptoms. He also cautions, however, that the symptoms that load on the disorganization factor cannot be easily classified as positive or negative but represent core symptoms of schizophrenia. Liddle concludes that the positive-negative distinction is meaningful but is inadequate, by itself, for defining schizophrenic subtypes.

Opler et al. (36) used a cluster analysis of positive and negative schizophrenic symptoms to classify a sample of state hospital patients diagnosed as having chronic schizophrenia. Fifty-six percent of this sample could not be classified on the basis of positive and negative symptoms because they exhibited too few symptoms to permit reliable classification. The remainder of the patients could be clearly classified into two groups, the positive versus negative distinction appeared to account for group membership, and there was minimal overlap of positive and negative symptoms among these subgroups.

It is interesting to compare the results of these two studies. Liddle's study is based on categorization of symptoms; the study by Opler and associates is based on classification of individuals. Again we see that results based on symptoms are more clear cut than those based on patients. Both symptom syndromes and people are "fuzzy"—but people, it seems, are fuzzier.

Overall, current evidence permits few conclusions about the internal consistency of DSM-III schizophrenic disorders. At this point, the distinction between schizophrenia and schizophreniform disorder appears to rest on shaky empirical ground. Evidence also does not support a typology of schizophrenic subtypes, though that topic clearly merits additional effort.

Substance Use Disorders

DSM-III substance use disorders have received very limited attention in terms of internal consistency analysis. (A large number of investigators have used internal consistency analysis to examine patterns of alcohol use, but those studies are not based on DSM-III definitions of substance use disorders.) One recent study, however, provides an interesting internal consistency analysis of the concept of dependence as it is applied to substance abuse disorders in DSM-IIIR.

Kosten et al. (37) examined the concept of dependence in relation to the use of alcohol and six types of drugs. The results indicated that dependence is a unidimensional phenomenon that is equally meaningful regardless of the substance under consideration. The authors suggest that the concept of dependence as defined in DSM-IIIR is strongly supported.

Personality Disorders

DSM-III personality disorders have received substantial attention from investigators employing internal consistency analysis. Several studies are quite broad, examining the internal consistency of all 11 personality disorders defined by DSM-III. Other studies focus on one or two specific personality disorders.

Livesley examined the 11 DSM-III personality disorders using both the specific symptoms listed in DSM-III and associated behaviors (which he believes require less inference by clinicians). In his first study, in which the internal consistency analyses focused directly on the 11 personality disorders, the results supported the DSM-III diagnostic categories in that each personality disorder exhibited good internal consistency (15). Nonetheless, there also was substantial overlap among disorders. Compulsive and paranoid personality disorders were the most distinctive. Two clusters of other disorders exhibited substantial overlap: (a) schizoid, avoidant, and schizotypal personality disorders and (2) histrionic, narcissistic, antisocial, and borderline personality disorders. In a second study, Livesley and

Jackson (38) ignored the DSM-III diagnostic definitions and used factor analysis to examine the dimensional structure of the 11 personality disorders. Three factors emerged from this analysis. The first factor appeared to represent interpersonal and cognitive symptoms; symptoms of avoidant, passive-aggressive, schizoid, and paranoid personality disorders loaded heavily on this factor. Impulsive and antisocial symptoms comprised the second factor; symptoms of histrionic, narcissistic, and antisocial personality disorder loaded heavily on it. The third factor consisted of symptoms of compulsive disorder. Although Livesley identified considerable overlap among the diagnostic syndromes, he concludes that these data strongly support DSM-III.

Kass et al. (39) also used factor analysis to examine the dimensional structure of the 11 DSM-III personality disorders. Four factors were identified and they are similar to those reported by Livesley. The first factor consisted of symptoms of paranoid, schizoid, and schizotypal personality disorders. Symptoms of avoidant, dependent, and passive-aggressive personality disorders loaded heavily on the second factor. The third factor included symptoms of histrionic, narcissistic, antisocial, and borderline personality disorders. The fourth factor consisted of compulsive personality disorder symptoms. Again, in spite of evidence of considerable overlap among certain disorders, Kass et al. conclude that the DSM-III typology of personality disorders is supported.

A final example along these lines is a study by Widiger et al. (40). These authors also examined the dimensional structure of DSM-III personality disorders. Rather than factor analysis, however, they used multidimensional scaling techniques. Three dimensions emerged from this analysis. The authors suggest that one dimension represents social involvement, both actual patterns of sociability and the desire for social interaction. Persons with schizoid and paranoid disorders scored low on this dimension; those with dependent, avoidant, borderline, and histrionic disorders scored high. The second dimension represents assertiveness; persons with schizoid, passive-aggressive, avoidant, and dependent personality disorders scored low on this dimension and persons with narcissistic, histrionic, and antisocial personality disorders scored high on it. The third dimensions consisted of a continuum of internal anxious rumination (represented by paranoid, schizotypal, compulsive, and avoidant disorders) versus external acting out (represented by antisocial, passive-aggressive, schizoid, and borderline personality disorders). When the three dimensions are examined simultaneously, the 11 DSM-III personality disorders exhibit considerable independence.

Some studies have examined the internal consistency of a narrower range of DSM-III personality disorders. One illustration of this approach is McGlashan's examination of the distinction between schizotypal and borderline disorders (41). He found that both disorders are defined by configurations of unique symptoms, but that most symptoms of the two diagnoses overlap and do not discriminate between them. Another example is Edell's analysis of the Borderline Syndrome Index (BSI) (42). He found that the BSI discriminates among normals, early schizophrenics, and personality disorders. It failed to discriminate, however, among borderline, schizotypal, and mixed disorders.

One final issue with regard to personality disorders merits brief comment. Some investigators have expressed concern that masochistic personality disorder is not included in DSM-III. Kass et al. (43) recently performed an internal consistency analysis of the 11 DSM-III personality disorders and symptoms they believed to be characteristic of masochistic personality. The results suggest that masochistic personality is a distinct syndrome and, accordingly, the authors recommend that it be added to the DSM nomenclature.

Overall, extant research generally supports the internal consistency of DSM-III personality disorders though there is clearly overlap among them. In addition, there is some evidence that at least one additional disorder—masochistic personality—merits inclusion.

Organic Brain Syndromes

Organic brain syndromes have seldom been the subject of internal consistency analysis. This is perhaps understandable in light of the practical difficulties associated with measuring organic symptoms and the fact that DSM-III imposes etiological attributions on organic mental disorders that are not imposed on nonorganic mental disorders. Another complication is the fact that most studies of organic impairments do not use DSM-III criteria in making diagnoses or developing measuring instruments. Nonetheless, a very limited data base exists concerning the internal consistency of organic brain syndromes as defined by DSM-III.

One illustration of this type of research is a recent study by Naugle et al. (44), based on a sample of patients meeting the DSM-III criteria for dementia. A broad array of neuropsychological measures was obtained from patients and used in a cluster analysis to identify possible dementia subtypes. Five clusters were identified based on degree of decrement in visual-spatial and verbal skills. Correlational evidence suggested that the clusters are related to progression of the disease and demographic characteristics.

There is insufficient evidence to make even tentative conclusions about the internal consistency of DSM-III organic brain syndromes. Given the complexities noted above, however, it is not clear that internal consistency analysis is as meaningful for organic syndromes as for nonorganic diagnoses.

Summary

There is wide variation in the degree to which internal consistency analysis has been applied to various DSM-III disorders and diagnostic classes. For some disorders there is simply insufficient evidence to warrant conclusions. For those disorders with moderate to extensive evidence, however, the nosology of DSM-III has been largely supported—although there are exceptions (e.g., the distinction between schizophrenia and schizophreniform appears very shaky) and there is clearly considerable overlap among disorders. In addition, internal consistency analysis has been particularly useful for examining subtypes within diagnoses. In some cases (e.g., melancholic versus nonmelancholic depression), internal consistency analysis has failed to support DSM-III guidelines. In other cases, results from internal consistency analyses have been used to explore subtypes not recognized by DSM-III (e.g., positive and negative symptoms of schizophrenia). Another clear pattern across studies is the fuzziness of both symptom syndromes and people—particularly the latter.

Two issues should be kept in mind as evidence concerning the internal consistency of DSM-III disorders is reviewed. First, the methodological adequacy of extant studies varies considerably. Though space limitations preclude a methodological critique of extant studies, this issue should be acknowledged. Of particular importance is the degree to which samples vary in size, source of information, and heterogeneity. As several authors appropriately note (e.g., 35,40), the base rates of symptoms and disorders among sample members have especially strong effects on the results of internal consistency analyses. Consequently differences across studies often reflect compositional differences of samples rather than instability in the underlying phenomena of concern. Second, and obviously, the validity of DSM-III diagnoses cannot be determined solely on the basis of internal consistency. Extant research affirms, however, that internal consistency is one meaningful criterion by which the DSM-III nosological system can be evaluated.

GRADE OF MEMBERSHIP ANALYSIS: A NEW PROCEDURE FOR ASSESSING THE INTERNAL CONSISTENCY OF PSYCHIATRIC DISORDERS

In clinical research, our ability to portray realities—especially complex realities—is determined by a number of factors. One important factor is our ability to measure phenomena accurately; another is our ability to statistically model the relationships among measured indicators. In this section we describe a relatively new procedure—grade of membership analysis—that we have used with considerable success to examine the internal consistency of DSM-III disorders. A rationale for the procedure is presented first, followed by the general principles of grade of membership analysis and illustrative findings.

Rationale

As noted previously, the degree to which symptom overlap and correlations among diagnostic categories are viewed as problematic depends, in part, on whether diagnoses are conceptualized as "crisp" or "fuzzy" categories. In crisp classification systems, it is assumed that although an individual may exhibit more than one disorder, the diagnostic categories are empirically distinct and that individuals do or do not meet the criteria for each diagnostic category. Partial or mixed cases are not represented with the exception of residual or mixed categories. In contrast, a "fuzzy set" nosology differs from crisp set classification systems in two ways (45). First, a fuzzy set nosology does not assume that all diagnostic categories are discrete—classification relies on loose associations among definitional characteristics and the resulting diagnostic categories may have overlapping or fuzzy boundaries. Second, in a fuzzy set nosology individuals frequently exhibit more than one symptom profile and express the attributes of those profiles to varying degrees. In such a system, an individual may be a "partial case" and degree of caseness can be quantified, based on the similarity between the individual's symptom profile and that of a prototypical case. Fuzzy set nosological systems also may generate a greater number of diagnostic categories than crisp set nosologies because no inherent effort is made to maximize the differences among symptom syndromes.

Grade of Membership Analysis: General Principles

Grade of membership (GOM) analysis is a multivariate statistical procedure designed to identify and describe profiles of disease symptomatology. Unlike crisp clustering techniques such as factor and cluster analysis, GOM is designed to identify and test the statistical significance of fuzzy clustering tendencies among a set of variables. More specifically, GOM simultaneously identifies symptom profiles, called "pure types," and determines the degree to which an individual's symptomatic complaints fit these symptom profiles. Thus, the clustering of symptoms into profiles and the categorization of individuals across symptom profiles is accomplished simultaneously. The application of this procedure to medical and psychiatric diagnoses has been described in previous studies (45,46); consequently, only a brief description is presented here.

Variables can be used in GOM in two ways: as either "internal" or "external" variables. Internal variables are used to identify and define the pure types; in studies of diagnostic classification, symptoms typically comprise the internal variables. External variables do not affect the definitions of the pure types, but the associations between pure types and external variables are estimated. In nosological research, demographic variables, other personal characteristics, and independently generated diagnostic variables often are used as external variables. External variables are valuable for identifying correlates of symptom profiles and for examining the relationships between empirically derived pure types and diagnoses rendered by clinicians using standard nomenclatures.

The number of pure types that best describes the natural clustering of symptoms is established by likelihood ratio tests. The model's overall goodness of fit is tested by seeing if the change in the likelihood function associated with adding additional pure types is significant (the change in the likelihood function is approximately distributed as a χ^2 variable).

Two sets of coefficients are estimated by maximum likelihood statistical procedures. Lambda coefficients (i.e., λ_{kjl}s) are coefficients that describe the probability that a particular variable (i.e., a symptom) is associated with a particular pure type. The larger the lambda, the stronger the relationship between the symptom and the pure type. The other set of coefficients, the g_{ik}s, estimate the grades of membership of individuals for each pure type. Thus, the g_{ik}s quantify the "partial membership" of each individual in each pure type or the degree to which individuals exhibit the symptomatic complaints that characterize the pure type. Both lambdas and g_{ik}s range from 0-1. A lambda of 1.0 indicates that a given symptom is always associated with a given pure type. A g_{ik} of 1.0 indicates that an individual manifests all of the symptoms described by the pure types. (For a detailed description of the statistical basis of GOM, see 45,47).

The interface between GOM and two aspects of other forms of internal consistency analysis merits explicit note. First, evidence of fuzziness was noted in the previous review of the internal consistency of DSM-III diagnoses. In those studies, fuzziness was evidenced in several ways: (a) by results in which specific symptoms loaded on multiple factors rather than on a single symptom syndrome, (b) by correlations between symptoms intended to measure different syndromes, and (c) by difficulty in classifying individuals into diagnostic categories. Thus, in those studies, fuzziness was documented by the failures of discrete modeling. In contrast, GOM models the natural clustering of symptoms and quantifies individuals' degrees of membership on the pure types. Thus, using GOM, fuzziness is quantified rather than observed by lack of model fit.

Second, as noted previously, some investigators believe that mental disorders are discrete and that individuals either do or do not meet the criteria for those discrete syndromes. Advocates of this perspective would seek assurance that GOM can identify discrete diagnostic syndromes and assign individuals to a single pure type. GOM indeed has that capability. If a symptom is associated exclusively with a single pure type, that symptom will have a lambda of 1.0 on that pure type and lambdas of zero on all other pure types. Similarly, if an individual is described exactly by a single pure type, he or she will have a g_{ik} of 1.0 on that pure type and g_{ik}s of zero on all other pure types. Thus, GOM can identify either discrete or fuzzy relationships among symptoms and total or partial caseness among individuals.

GOM Applications

Duke University is one of five sites participating in the NIMH Epidemiologic Catchment Area (ECA) Program, a multisite collaborative research initiative. The purposes of the ECA program were to (a) estimate the prevalence and 1-year incidence of specific psychiatric disorders in five geographically and demographically diverse U.S. communities, (b) identify the treated and untreated prevalence of specific psychiatric disorders and factors associated with help-seeking for psychiatric problems, and (c) identify some of the social and environmental risk factors for the onset and maintenance of psychiatric disorders. As is typical of collaborative research programs, the research designs implemented at the five ECA sites included several common features: (a) use of stratified random sampling techniques to generate representative samples of approximately 3,000 community and 500 institutional residents age 18 and older from defined CMHC catchment areas, (b) a longitudinal design involving three interviews over a 1-year interval, and (c) use of the same instruments for measuring psychiatric disorders, health service utilization, and demographic characteristics of respondents. Psychiatric disorders were measured using the NIMH Diagnostic Interview Schedule (DIS), a highly structured diagnostic interview developed for use by lay interviewers and from which computer-based diagnoses can be generated for selected DSM-III disorders (48). The DIS elicits the elements required for DSM-III diagnoses, including the presence or absence of symptoms; their severity, frequency, and distribution over time; and whether or not they can be explained by physical illness, drug and/or alcohol use, or other psychiatric disorders.

The majority of our ECA publications have been based on DIS/DSM-III diagnoses and symptom counts as generated by the DIS scoring program. We also have used the DIS symptoms, however, as internal variables in GOM analyses that were used (a) to examine the internal consistency and natural clustering of three categories of symptoms, and (b) to examine the relationships between the resulting symptom profiles and DIS/DSM-III diagnoses. The three categories of symptoms examined include somatization symptoms, depression symptoms, and symptoms of antisocial personality and substance use disorders. Results of each analysis will be briefly described to illustrate the potential of GOM analysis in assessing the internal consistency of DSM-III diagnoses.

Somatization Symptoms

Our first GOM analysis examined the natural categorization of somatization and related symptoms in the Duke ECA sample. The paper resulting from this work represented the first publication of the use of GOM in the psychiatric literature (46). In this study, we compared the DIS/DSM-III categorization of somatization disorder to the natural symptom profiles (i.e., pure types) derived from a GOM analysis.

This analysis was based on all Duke ECA Wave I respondents with three or more lifetime symptoms of somatization disorder (N = 1,626). The internal variables used in the GOM analysis included all the somatization symptoms in the DIS, three depression symptoms expected to be related to somatization, one anxiety symptom (i.e., self-reports of nervousness), and one schizophrenia symptom. External variables examined in relation to the pure types included demographic characteristics, use of outpatient health services, and the DIS/DSM-III diagnosis of somatization disorder. Recall that external variables are not used in the definition of the pure types, but the associations between external variables and the pure types are estimated.

GOM analysis indicated that seven pure types best described the interrelationships among the somatic symptoms. Very few symptoms loaded on the first pure type, suggesting that individuals expressing this pure type are relatively asymptomatic. An asymptomatic pure type is expected in analyses based on a sample that includes respondents with relatively few symptoms. Pure Type II was defined primarily by menstrual symptoms (e.g, painful periods, irregular periods). This pure type was exhibited exclusively by females. Other external variables associated with this pure type included young age (18–30), white race, and high educational attainment. Pure Type III was defined largely by depressive symptoms found in the somatization section of the DIS as well as the three dysphoric symptoms from the DIS depression section. This pure type also was exhibited exclusively by women. Other external variables associated with this pure type included young age and white race. Pure Type IV comprised 12 symptoms—primarily symptoms of musculoskeletal pain associated with weakness and difficulty walking and four conversion symptoms. External variables related to this pure type included older age (51–70), black race, low levels of educational attainment, and high utilization of health services. In addition, this pure type was exclusively male.

The fifth pure type strongly resembled somatization disorder as defined by DSM-III. Twenty-four somatic symptoms loaded heavily, and sometimes exclusively, on this factor. External variables associated with this pure type included older age, black race, high levels of health care utilization, being unmarried, low levels of education, and rural residence. In addition, this pure type was exclusively female. The DIS/DSM-III diagnosis of somatization disorder also loaded exclusively on this pure type.

The sixth pure type was characterized by gastrointestinal symptoms, the schizophrenia symptom, and self-reports of nervousness. Examination of the external variables indicated that Pure Type VI was equally represented among men and women. Older, black, rural respondents, however, were strongly represented on this pure type. Pure Type VII was defined primarily by cardiac symptoms (e.g., chest pain, shortness of breath), but other somatic symptoms loaded heavily upon it also. External variables associated with this pure type included male sex, older age, low levels of education, being married, and high use of health services.

The g_{ik}s in this analysis tell us about the distribution of respondents across pure types. Recall that g_{ik}s range from 0–1, with 0 representing no grade of membership on the pure type and 1 indicating total membership. Interestingly, no respondent had a score of 1.0 on any of the pure types. Indeed, using a cutpoint of .501, only 52% of the sample had a predominant grade of membership on a single pure type. GOMSUMS refer to the summed grades of membership of all respondents on each of the pure types and is roughly equivalent to a prevalence estimate (45). The GOMSUMS ranged from 660 for the asymptomatic pure type to 50 for the type that closely resembled somatization disorder (Pure Type V). Thus, all respondents expressed multiple pure types, but the sample is not evenly distributed across them.

Overall, these results suggest that there are several subtypes of somatic symptoms. One pure type, however, was strongly representative of somatization disorder as defined by DSM-III, as evidenced by both the number and types of symptoms comprising the pure type and the fact that DIS/DSM-III somatization disorder was exclusively associated with that pure type. Moreover, examination of the external variables indicates that this pure type is associated with the demographic characteristics that would be expected on the basis of previous clinical and epidemiological studies of somatization disorder.

Depressive Symptoms

We also have applied GOM analysis to depressive and related symptoms as reported by Duke ECA respondents (49). This analysis was based on Duke ECA Wave II respondents reporting significant numbers of current (i.e., 6-month) depressive symptoms (N = 406). Internal variables for this analysis included all of the DIS depressive symptoms, all of the DIS mania symptoms, all of the DIS generalized anxiety disorder symptoms, measures of cognitive performance as measured by the Mini-Mental State Exam (50), one alcohol symptom reflecting excessive drinking, and several somatization and schizophrenia symptoms expected to be related to depressed affect. External variables examined included demographic characteristics and seven DIS diagnostic variables (i.e., major depression, dysthymia, alcohol abuse/dependence, generalized anxiety disorder, mild cognitive impairment, severe cognitive impairment, and somatization disorder).

Five pure types emerged from the GOM analysis. Pure Type I was a relatively asymptomatic pure type and none of the symptoms loaded heavily on it. Pure Type II was defined by symptoms of cognitive impairment. It is especially interesting that none of the depressive symptoms loaded on this pure type. Demographic variables were associated with this pure type in predictable ways. External variables highly associated with Pure Type II included old age, black race, low education, being widowed, and rural residence.

Pure Type III resembled classic major depressive or dysthymic disorder. Virtually all of the DIS depression symptoms loaded heavily on this pure type. Manic symptoms and anxiety for more than 1 month also were characteristic of this pure type. As expected, being female was strongly associated with Pure Type III. DIS/DSM-III diagnoses of major depression and dysthymia were strongly but not exclusively associated with this pure type; generalized anxiety disorder, however, was not associated with Pure Type III.

Pure Type IV was characterized by dysphoria preceding the menstrual cycle, lability of affect, weight gain, and somatic symptoms. This pure type appears to represent a premenstrual syndrome. This interpretation is buttressed by the fact that it is associated with young age and is exclusively expressed by females. Interestingly, this pure type was overrepresented among black respondents. In addition, the DIS/DSM-III diagnosis of major depression was strongly related to this pure type.

Pure Type V was defined by a mixture of depression and anxiety symptoms. Indeed, symptoms of generalized anxiety disorder loaded almost exclusively on this pure type. In addition, a number of depressive symptoms were associated with this pure type, though not as strongly as for Pure Type III. Examination of the external variables reveals that this pure type is expressed equally by males and females, that a DIS/DSM-III diagnosis of generalized anxiety disorder loads exclusively on this pure type, and that a DIS/DSM-III diagnosis of major depression also loads heavily on this type.

The g_{ik} distribution indicates that most respondents express multiple pure types. Seven percent of the sample had g_{ik}s of 1.0 on a single pure type, although 57% of this subgroup were perfectly described by the asymptomatic pure type. Using the cutpoint of .501, 89% of the sample was predominantly described by a single pure type. Again, however, 62% of this subgroup was predominantly described by the asymptomatic factor. GOMSUMS ranged from 197 for the asymptomatic pure type to 39 for Pure Type IV (premenstrual syndrome).

Thus, the pure types emerging from a GOM analysis of depressive and related symptoms suggest a pure type that is nearly identical to DSM-III major depression and dysthymia. Other pure types characterized by significant numbers of depressive symptoms and associated with a DIS/DSM-III diagnosis of major depression include a premenstrual syndrome and a mixed anxiety and depression syndrome. These results suggest meaningful subtypes of depression, but subtypes that differ from those described in DSM-III.

Acting Out Symptoms

A third GOM analysis was used to examine the natural categorization of "acting out" symptoms (51). The sample for this analysis consisted of 914 Duke ECA Wave I respondents who reported significant numbers of antisocial personality disorder symptoms. Internal variables in this analysis included all the DIS antisocial personality disorder symptoms (adult and child), alcohol and drug abuse/dependence symptoms from the DIS, and selected symptoms of depressive, anxiety, and somatization disorders. External variables included demographic characteristics and DIS/DSM-III diagnoses of antisocial personality disorder and substance abuse/dependence.

Seven pure types best described the relationships among the internal variables. As is typical in GOM analysis, the first pure type was relatively asymptomatic and will not be described further. Two pure types strongly resemble the DSM-III description of antisocial personality disorder. Pure Type II is defined by high levels of conduct disorder symptoms, extremely problematic employment histories, high rates of arrests and felonies, adult violence, and numerous alcohol and drug symptoms. Pure Type III also is characterized by numerous conduct disorder symptoms. In contrast to Pure Type II, however, Pure Type III is defined by relatively few adult antisocial symptoms, few alcohol and drug problems, but relatively high levels of Axis I symptoms, especially depression, anxiety, and somatic complaints. In terms of external variables, both pure types are exclusively male and are associated with being unmarried and having low levels of education. Interestingly, place of residence differs strongly across the two pure types. Pure Type II is associated almost exclusively with residence in prison, whereas Pure Type III is about evenly split between residence in the community and in a mental hospital. Both pure types are strongly associated with a DIS/DSM-III diagnosis of antisocial personality disorder. Pure Type II also is strongly associated with a diagnosis of drug abuse/dependence.

Pure Types IV and V are strongly associated with females and offer an interesting contrast to the prior two, exclusively male profiles. Pure Type IV is characterized by problems relating to marriage, interpersonal relationships, and employment. It is not characterized by symptoms of conduct disorder or of alcohol or drug use. Given the nature of the symptoms that define this pure type, we believe that it represents a borderline personality syndrome—though the DIS does not include all the DSM-III symptoms required for a diagnosis of borderline personality disorder. Pure Type V is primarily characterized by symptoms of depression. Neither alcohol and drug use nor conduct disorder symptoms load on this pure type. Pure Type IV is associated with black race, relatively low levels of education, and having never been married. Pure Type V, in contrast, is associated with white race, high levels of education, and low rates of marriage. In terms of DIS/DSM-III diagnoses, Pure Type IV is not related to any diagnostic variable in the analysis, probably reflecting the absence of a measure of borderline personality disorder. Pure Type V is associated only with a diagnosis of major depression.

The final pure types represent distinctive patterns of substance abuse, observed in the relative absence of antisocial behaviors. Pure Type VI is largely defined by symptoms of alcohol abuse and dependence as well as selected adult antisocial symptoms that are compatible with heavy drinking. Pure Type VII is characterized most strongly by symptoms of drug abuse, though interestingly, the experience of drug withdrawal is not characteristic of this pure type. Both of these pure types are predominantly male. Beyond that, however, there are clear demographic differences between them. The alcohol abuse syndrome is associated with middle-age, being married, low levels of education, and, especially, veteran status. The drug use syndrome is associated with young age and high levels of education. In terms of the diagnostic variables, Pure Type VI is strongly associated with a DIS/DSM-III diagnosis of alcohol abuse or dependence. Pure Type VII, in contrast, is not associated with any of the diagnostic measures, reflecting, we believe, the occasional and largely recreational nature of the drug use characteristic of this pure type.

Again, the g_{ik} distribution indicates that most respondents are distributed across multiple pure types. Thirty-two respondents (4%) had g_{ik}s of 1.0 on a single pure type, but 30 of them were perfectly described by the asymptomatic pure type. Using the cutpoint of .501, 60% of the sample loaded predominantly on a single pure type, but 59% of this subgroup was described by the asymptomatic pure type. GOMSUMS ranged from 332 for the asymptomatic pure type to 49 for the pure type that most closely resembled antisocial personality disorder (Pure Type II).

The three GOM analyses lead to similar conclusions. In each case, one or more pure types were identified that closely resembled a DSM-III diagnostic category. But additional pure types, which may represent subtypes not recognized by DSM-III, also emerged during analysis. In addition, "caseness" rather than all-or-none membership is the rule. The symptom profiles identified seem to be prototypes of psychiatric syndromes that are seldom fully expressed by respondents. One caution is necessary in interpreting these results, however. The sample was a predominantly community rather than a clinical sample. Consequently, (a) the pure types identified may largely represent milder forms of psychiatric disorder, and (b) the distributions of g_{ik}s may be skewed toward the asymptomatic and milder pure types. In this regard, in a recent GOM analysis of depressive symptoms in a clinical sample, we observed pure types similar to those described above and, though the g_{ik}s on symptomatic pure types were somewhat higher, a wide distribution across pure types was observed (52).

DSM-III AND INTERNAL CONSISTENCY ANALYSIS IN BROADER PERSPECTIVE

Our final comments will attempt to place DSM-III and internal consistency analysis into broader perspective. An effective method of approaching this aim is to examine one of the most common criticisms of DSM-III. Though a number of critiques of DSM-III could be noted, a recent article by Faust and Miner (53) serves as a useful point of departure. The title of this article, "The Empiricist and His New Clothes," conveys an immediate sense of their central thesis. In essence, Faust and Miner object to the DSM-III's goal of strict empiricism and take special exception to the statement by its developers that "DSM-III is atheoretical with regard to etiology . . . except for those disorders for which this is well established" (17, p. 7). Faust and Miner argue that progress is best made by moving from theory to fact rather than the reverse and fault DSM-III for placing primary emphasis on precise measurement and description rather than on concepts and theories.

Although Faust and Miner launch an interesting argument, we believe that it ultimately rests on a faulty foundation. DSM-III is largely atheoretical with regard to etiology perhaps, but it is not atheoretical. Indeed, we view DSM-III as a theory about the nature and characteristics of mental disorders—a theory that can be disaggregated into hundreds of specific hypotheses about particular psychiatric syndromes. It is not necessary, we would argue, to have a theory about causation in order to have a theory about the nature of phenomena. One can have theories about what constitutes intelligence, socioeconomic status, or charisma, for example, without first developing theories about the causes of those phenomena. The same is true for mental disorders.

Similarly, application of internal consistency analysis requires theoretical decisions throughout its implementation. The specific indicators included in any analysis, the statistical techniques used to model the relationships among indicators, and interpretation of results all require decisions based on theory or substantive knowledge of the phenomena under investigation. Investigators may not always explicate their theories, but they operate on them nonetheless.

Faust and Miner, as well as others who share their philosophical stance, might be well-advised to reread the classic article by Robins and Guze (1) that served as the springboard for this conference. That article lays out a series of steps that can be used to establish the diagnostic validity of psychiatric disorders. Robins and Guze explicitly note that the purpose of these steps is to provide a solid base for studies of etiology and treatment outcome. We agree with their stance that careful clinical description and validation of psychiatric diagnoses is a necessary component of such studies rather than a separate or contrary activity. Internal consistency analysis is one tool that can be used in this validation process. Indeed, we believe that internal consistency analysis could be used in a broader, more aggressive way than is characteristic of extant studies. Thus far, internal consistency analysis has been restricted to a phenomenological approach (i.e., in which indicators of mental disorders are restricted to symptoms). Other indicators— including biological markers, information concerning longitudinal course, and family history measures—could easily be added to internal consistency models. Such "expanded" internal consistency models might permit greater specificity and disaggregation than is possible using only symptomatic indicators.

ACKNOWLEDGMENT

This work was supported by cooperative agreement MH35386 and center grant MH40159 from the National Institute of Mental Health.

REFERENCES

1. Robins, E., Guze, S. B. (1970): Establishment of diagnostic validity in psychiatric illness: Its application to schizophrenia. *Amer J Psychiatry*, 126:983–987.
2. Nunnally, J. C. (1967): *Psychometric Theory*. McGraw-Hill, New York.
3. Cronbach, L. J. (1951): Coefficient alpha and the internal structure of tests. *Psychometrika*, 16: 297–334.
4. Kerlinger, F. N. (1973): *Foundations of behavioral research*, 2nd edition. Holt, Reinhart and Winston, New York.
5. Radloff, L. (1977): The CES-D scale: A self-report depression scale for research in the general population. *Applied Psychol Measurement*, 1:388–401.
6. Ross, C. E., and Mirowsky J. (1984): Components of depressed mood in married men and women. *Am J Epidemiol*, 119:997–1004.
7. Krause, N. (1987): Chronic financial strain, social support, and depressive symptoms among older adults. *Psychology and Aging*, 2:185–192.
8. Marradi, A. (1981): Factor analysis as an aid in the formation and refinement of empirically useful concepts. In: *Factor Analysis and Measurement in Sociological Research*, edited by D. J. Jackson and E. F. Borgotta, pp. 11–50. Sage, Beverly Hills.
9. Joreskog, K. G. (1966): Testing a simple structure hypothesis in factor analysis. *Psychometrika*, 31:165–178.
10. Burt, R. S. (1973): Confirmatory factor analysis and the theory construction process. *Sociological Methods and Research*, 3:131–190.

11. Schiffman, S., Reynolds, M. and Young, F. (1981): *Introduction to multidimensional scaling*. Academic Press, Orlando.
12. Duncan-Jones, P., Grayson, D. A., and Morgan, P. A. P. (1986): The utility of latent trait models in psychiatric epidemiology. *Psychol Med*, 16:391–405.
13. Wolfe, J. H. (1970): Pattern clustering by multivariate maximum likelihood. *Multivariate Behavioral Research*, 5:329–350.
14. Weber, A. C., and Scharfetter, C. (1984): The syndrome concept: History and statistical operationalizations. *Psychol Med*, 14:315–325.
15. Livesley, W. J. (1986): Trait and behavioral prototypes of personality disorder. *Am J Psychiatry*, 143:728–732.
16. Good, W. R., Vlachonikolis, I., Griffiths, P., Griffiths, R. A. (1987): The structure of depressive symptoms in the elderly. *Br J Psychiatry*, 150:463–470.
17. American Psychiatric Association. (1980): *Diagnostic and Statistical Manual of Mental Disorders*, 3rd edition. (DSM-III). American Psychiatric Association, Washington, D.C.
18. Fabrega, H., Mezzich, J. E., Mezzich, A. C., and Coffman, G. A. (1986): Descriptive validity of DSM-III depressions. *J Nerv Ment Dis*, 174:573–584.
19. Zimmerman, M., Coryell, W., and Pfohl B. (1986): Melancholic subtyping: A qualitative or quantitative distinction? *Am J Psychiatry*, 143:98–100.
20. Young, M. A., Scheftner, W. A., Klerman, G. L., Andreasen, N. C., and Hirschfeld, R. M. A. (1986): The endogenous sub-type of depression: A study of its internal construct validity. *Br J Psychiatry*, 148:257–267.
21. Davidson, J., and Turnbull, C. D. (1986): Diagnostic significance of vegetative symptoms in depression. *Br J Psychiatry*, 148:442–446.
22. Clark, D. C., Gibbons, R. D., Fawcett, J., Aagesen, C. A., and Sellers D. (1985): Unbiased criteria for severity of depression in alcoholic inpatients. *J Nerv Ment Dis*, 173:482–487.
23. Breslau, N., and Meltzer, H. Y. (1988): Validity of subtyping psychotic depression: Examination of phenomenology and demographic characteristics. *Am J Psychiatry*, 145:35–40.
24. Kendler, K. S., Heath, A. C., Martin, N. G., and Eaves, L. J. (1987): Symptoms of anxiety and symptoms of depression. *Arch Gen Psychiatry*, 44:451–457.
25. Riskind, J. H., Beck, A. T., Brown G., and Steer, R. A. (1987): Taking the measure of anxiety and depression. *J Nerv Ment Dis*, 175:474–479.
26. Zimmerman, M., Coryell, W., Corenthal, C., and Wilson S. (1986): A self-report scale to diagnose major depressive disorder. *Arch Gen Psychiatry*, 43:1076–1081.
27. Cameron, O. G., Thyer, B. A., Nesse, R. M., and Curtis, G. C. (1986): Symptom profiles of patients with DSM-III anxiety disorders. *Am J Psychiatry*, 143:1132–1137.
28. Barlow, D. H., Blanchard, E. B., Vermilyea, J. A., Vermilyea, B. B., and DiNardo, P. A. (1986): Generalized anxiety and generalized anxiety disorder: Description and reconceptualization. *Am J Psychiatry*, 143:40–44.
29. Van Kampen, M., Watson, C. G., Tilleskjor, C., Kucala, T., and Vassar P. (1986): The definition of posttraumatic stress disorder in alcoholic Vietnam veterans. *J Nerv Ment Dis*, 174:137–144.
30. Makanjuola, R. O., and Adedapa, S. A. (1987): The DSM-III concepts of schizophrenic disorder and schizophreniform disorder. *Br J Psychiatry*, 151:611–618.
31. Solovay, M. R., Shenton, M. E., and Holzman, P. S. (1987): Comparative studies of thought disorders: I. Mania and schizophrenia. *Arch Gen Psychiatry*, 44:13–20.
32. Shenton, M. E., Solovay, M. R., and Holzman, P. (1987): Comparative studies of thought disorders: II. Schizoaffective disorder. *Arch Gen Psychiatry*, 44:21–30.
33. Andreasen, N. C. (1982): Negative symptoms in schizophrenia: Definition and reliability. *Arch Gen Psychiatry*, 39:784–788.
34. Crow, T. J. (1980): Positive and negative schizophrenic symptoms and the role of dopamine. *Br J Psychiatry*, 137:383–386.
35. Liddle, P. F. (1987): The symptoms of chronic schizophrenia. *Br J Psychiatry*, 151:145–151.
36. Opler, L. A., Kay, S. R., Rosado, V., and Lindenmayer, J. (1984): Positive and negative syndromes in chronic schizophrenic inpatients. *J Nerv Ment Dis*, 172:317–325.
37. Kosten, T. R., Rounsaville, B. J., Babor, T. F., Spitzer, R. L., and Williams J. B. W. (1987): Substance-use disorders in DSM-III-R. *Br J Psychiatry*, 151:834–843.
38. Livesley, W. J., Jackson, D. N. (1986): The internal consistency and factorial structure of behaviors judged to be associated with DSM-III personality disorders. *Am J Psychiatry*, 143:1473–1474.

39. Kass, F., Skodol, A. E., Charles, E., Spitzer, R. L., and Williams, J. B. W. (1985): Scaled ratings of DSM-III personality disorders. *Am J Psychiatry*, 142:627–630.
40. Widiger, T. A., Truell, T. J., Hurt, S. W., Clarkin, J., and Frances A. (1987): A multidimensional scaling of DSM-III personality disorders. *Arch Gen Psychiatry*, 44:557–563.
41. McGlashan, T. H. (1987): Testing DSM-III symptom criteria for schizotypal and borderline personality disorders. *Arch Gen Psychiatry*, 44:143–148.
42. Edell, W. S. (1984): The Borderline Syndrome Index. *J Nerv Ment Dis*, 172:254–263.
43. Kass, F., MacKinnon, R. A., and Spitzer, R. L. (1986): Masochistic personality: An empirical study. *Am J Psychiatry*, 143:216–218.
44. Naugle, R. I., Cullum, C. M., Bigler, E. D., and Massman, P. J. (1985): Neuropsychological and computerized axial tomography volume characteristics of empirically derived dementia subgroups. *J Nerv Ment Dis*, 173:596–604.
45. Woodbury, M. A., and Manton, K. G. (1982): A new procedure for analysis of medical classification. *Methods Inf Med*, 21:210–220.
46. Swartz, M., Blazer, D., Woodbury, M., George, L., and Landerman, R. (1986): Somatization disorder in a U.S. southern community: Use of a new procedure for analysis of medical classification. *Psychol Med*, 16:595–609.
47. Woodbury, M. A., Clive, J., and Garson, A. (1978): Mathematical typology: A grade of membership technique for obtaining disease definition. *Comput Biomed Res*, 11:277–298.
48. Robins, L. N., Helzer, J. E., Croughan, J., and Ratcliff, K. S. (1981): National Institute of Mental Health Diagnostic Interview Schedule: Its history, characteristics, and validity. *Arch Gen Psychiatry*, 38:381–389.
49. Blazer, D. G., Swartz, M., Woodbury, M. A., Manton, D. G., Hughes, D., and George, L. K. (1988): Depressive symptoms and depressive diagnoses in a community population: Use of a new procedure for analysis of psychiatric classification. *Arch Gen Psychiatry*, 45:1078–1084).
50. Folstein, M. F., Folstein, S. E., and McHugh, P. (1975): "Mini-Mental State": A practical method for grading the cognitive state of patients for the clinician. *J Psychiatr Res*, 12:189–198.
51. Jordan, B. K., Swartz, M. S., George, L. K., Woodbury, M. A., and Blazer, D. G. Antisocial and related disorders in a southern community: An application of grade of membership analysis. *J Nerv Ment Dis*, (in press).
52. Blazer, D., Woodbury, M., Hughes, D. C., George, L. K., Manton, K. G., Bachar, J. R., and Fowler, N. A statistical analysis of the classification of depression in a mixed community and clinical sample. *J Affective Disorders* (in press).
53. Faust, D., and Miner, R. A. (1986): The empiricist and his new clothes: DSM-III in perspective. *Am J Psychiatry*, 143:962–967.

DISCUSSION

Dr. Zubin: I want to illustrate the problem of consistency by an anecdote that goes back to Kraepelin who at one time conducted a staff meeting at which a patient was declared to have dementia praecox. After they talked about it for a while, one of the staff members said, "All of you think he is a case of dementia praecox, but 5 years ago he was here, and we called him manic depressive." Kraepelin threw up his hands and exclaimed: "Oh, no, no, that is impossible. It didn't happen; it couldn't be." He dismissed the staff, turned to his assistant, and said, "You know and I know, that it is possible, but we cannot tell these young psychiatrists that!" It is a problem which goes back to the earliest distinctions between the most important two kinds of psychoses, and yet Kraepelin himself was fully aware of the fact that consistency is not really the most important thing to consider. You have got to consider the patient, and what you have to deal with first is whether or not a psychosis is present. Once that is decided, the course of the illness will go in one direction or another, depending upon the premorbid personality, the psychosocial factors involved, and many other incidental things. We must be aware of the fact that in nature we don't have consistency. We have approximations. We have to be ready to realize that there is no perfect schizophrenic, no perfect depressive. They approximate the kinds of things we have conceptualized, and to look for certainty where there is no certainty is a vain thing. Consistency is no evidence for validity.

Dr. George: I couldn't agree more.

Dr. Dohrenwend: There seem to be very few demographic correlates to patients grouped by your different types of symptomatology. Is that because you don't include them, or is it because mixed depression and anxiety relate differently to social class than do major depression and dysthymia?

Dr. George: In general the demographic factors were moderately related to the pure types. We typically included variables such as rural-urban residence, age, race, sex, social class, education, marital status, and presence or absence of children. Overall I view this area as one where an analogy is apt: is the glass half full or half empty? We do find strong demographic correlates, but not lots of them. We did find that low education or low SES in a broad sense tend to be more strongly related to the mixed syndrome of anxiety and depression than to the syndrome that looks similar to the DSM-III major depression. We also found a different sex ratio for the mixed anxiety and depression pure type than is described in the literature for depression. Overall, the associations were relatively strong, and they were usually related to age, sex, and occasionally to race and to socioeconomic status.

Dr. Klein: I didn't understand how you derived your pure types. Were they ever specified?

Dr. George: The pure types were not specified. The analysis does that. One enters a pool of symptoms or other indicators into the analysis, which is an iterative program that identifies what it calls pure types which you could think of as factors or dimensions. It will iterate a number of solutions. However, let me tell you where theory does enter into it. One has to carefully use theory in generating the item pool that will be put into the analysis. In general, what we put into the analyses were items that we expected to be interrelated, those that the DSM-III told us would make coherent syndromes. We usually found such a syndrome, but we also found variations on it.

Dr. Klein: The analysis you described sounded to me like some sort of cluster analysis. The outstanding thing about cluster analyses as applied to psychiatric data is that if you do two different analyses you end up with two different sets of clusters. How many analyses did it take before your clusters came out, those that looked a lot like DSM-III categories?

Dr. George: First of all, we do not keep the analysis going until it generates something that we like the looks of. It does that on its own. I am not the statistician in our group, but I do know some of the ways that this technique differs from factor analysis and from traditional cluster analysis. Traditional cluster analysis, even more than factor analysis, is a crisp classification technique. It attempts to put individuals or bits of data into one and only one cluster, and to maximize the differences between clusters, so that it highlights the strongest contrasts that the data is capable of producing. Grade of membership analysis is exactly the opposite. There is no attempt to highlight, to make contrasts particularly strong, and there is clearly no attempt to put pieces of data—either from individuals or from symptoms—into one and only one pure type. We look for loose associations.

Dr. Klein: Clustering procedures usually end up maximizing some measure of distance or of similarity. You say that you are not concerned about that, but how then do you end up with pure types?

Dr. George: This technique is different in the sense that it looks for as many loose associations that nonetheless meet the criteria for statistical significance as it can find. It tries to maximize associations.

Dr. Grove: In reading the grade of membership papers that have been written by your group, I have been puzzled by the nature of your interpretation of these g_{ik} coefficients. They look superficially as if they might be like probabilities, but it is specifically stated that they are not to be interpreted so. I am having difficulty understanding precisely what they are. In discrete classification systems one has some sense of what is meant by saying that somebody is in a certain category, whether that attribution is correct or incorrect. I am not clear what you think these g_{ik}'s mean. What does it mean to be a partial case of Huntington's chorea, for example?

Dr. George: I don't know anything about Huntington's chorea, but let me talk about depression. g_{ik}'s are grades of membership. They range from zero to one. A person who has a one is exactly described by a pure type. Therefore that person will have a g_{ik} of zero on every other pure type. For convenience we describe a person who has a g_{ik} greater than .5 on a particular pure type as "predominantly" expressed by that pure type. It just means that they are above the 50% mark.

Dr. Grove: Let me see if I understand you. Somebody who is a 1.0 on Huntington's chorea manifests all the symptoms of Huntington's chorea and no symptoms of any other types which are present in your analysis, and somebody who is 75/25 may manifest certain symptoms not typically seen with Huntington's chorea and seen with another syndrome, but not very many or very strongly. Would that be correct?

Dr. George: What you said is exactly right. This procedure, developed by Max Woodbury, was originally designed to look at physical illness, not psychiatric disorders. The prize that he won from the American Statistical Association for this procedure had to do with applications to physical illness. The original GOM applications were based on data from a tumor registry, looking at cancer patients where things ought to be fairly clear cut, since you can measure tumors, ascertain their size, their shape, their location, and so forth. Dr. Woodbury found that these tumor characteristics generated multiple pure types—not just one. There also was heterogeneity such that most individuals did not fall on just one pure type. Thus, you have to be aware of partial membership. My understanding is that in terms of treatment, it may be very different to treat somebody who has a g_{ik} of one on a particular pure type and a zero on everything else than to treat someone who has a g_{ik} of .6 on a pure type—their "primary" pure type or syndrome, if you will—but who also has a .35 on another pure type. Such a pattern could alter the way you consider that person clinically, what course and what treatment response one would expect. We are currently seeing if these pure types differ in terms of treatment response and longitudinal course.

Dr. Guze: I still am not fully clear about some issues. Let me give you a case and ask you how it would affect your analysis. Let us say that you had a patient who had panic disorder, but who also suffered from asthma. How would that combination affect your class of membership analysis?

Dr. George: Probably not at all, simply because one case wouldn't change the overall solution that much. If you had a bunch of those people, two pure types should emerge from the analysis. One pure type would be panic disorder; the other would be panic disorder plus the feature of asthma. We have seen this result in the depression and anxiety area. In community samples, where base prevalence rates are low, we frequently get a pure type for depression and a pure type for anxiety, and we have some individuals whose g_{ik}'s are, to make it simple, .5 on one, and .5 on the other. If you have a large enough sample, you then will get three pure types—a pure depression, a pure anxiety, and a mixed anxiety—depression. That one individual who, when you had only depression and anxiety pure types, was 50/50 on each, will load 1.0 on the combined pure type. If you have sufficient data, GOM will identify increasingly specific variants. This is the goal—to break down these patient groups into increasingly refined pure types.

The Validity of Psychiatric Diagnosis, edited by
Lee N. Robins and James E. Barrett.
Raven Press, Ltd., New York © 1989.

Quantitative and Qualitative Distinctions Between Psychiatric Disorders

*William M. Grove and **Nancy C. Andreasen

*Department of Psychiatry, University of Minnesota Medical School, Minneapolis, Minnesota 55455; and **Department of Psychiatry, University of Iowa College of Medicine, Iowa City, Iowa 52242

In their classic article, Robins and Guze (1) list an important step in validating psychiatric disorders: delimitation of the disorder from other disorders. They state that "it is necessary to specify exclusion criteria so that patients with other illnesses are not included in the group to be studied. These criteria should also permit exclusion of borderline cases and doubtful cases." (1, p. 984). We can adopt this suggestion as a point of departure. How do we carry it out?

OVERLAP BETWEEN DISORDERS

The phenomenological overlap of disorders can be considerable. For instance, 15% to 33% of depressives have panic attacks (2–4) and panic disorder patients very frequently develop, or give histories of, depression (5–6). Overlap also exists with respect to other aspects of mental disorders. For example, while typical schizophrenia leads to considerably more symptoms, social disability, and economic dependence than typical manic-depressive illness, perhaps 20% of schizophrenias appear to have a favorable outcome (7) while 5% to 20% of bipolar patients have chronic, debilitating illnesses (8). Treatment response differentiates schizophrenia from bipolar affective disorder, but lithium may sometimes be beneficial in the former (9) and clinical experience suggests that some bipolar patients need neuroleptic prophylaxis (10). With personality disorders, overlap in manifestations is even more pronounced (11).

One could proceed by assuming that two disorders, such as panic and depression, are distinct because their pure forms look different clinically, and they have different outcomes, different family backgrounds, and so on. Then the question becomes whether the disorders co-occur because they share risk factors or because one disorder is itself a risk factor for the other. If the former, what are the shared risk factors and what are the unshared ones? If the latter, what is the mechanism by which one disorder leads to the other? This is the primary-secondary approach used by investigators of a number of disorders, most prominently depression. However, this approach would seem to assume a fact not yet in evidence. We may not know that two disorders are really two and not one.

R. E. Kendell pointed out that the mere existence of significant or even strong differences between two groups of patients no more proves the existence of two disorders than demonstrating that tall and short men differ in weight establishes the existence of two species (12). Kendell's observation has two consequences. First, distinguishable syndromes are necessary but not sufficient to posit separate disorders, since one might say there is a "tall syndrome," the signs of which are wearing a big hat, having long fingers, and weighing a lot. Second, quantitative differences are also necessary but not sufficient. We need some criterion for concluding that quantitative differences are larger than obtainable from an arbitrary division of a continuum, and hence that they support a nosological distinction.

Other chapters in this volume address methods for demonstrating differences between patient groups as part of a program to validate a diagnosis. Without such a demonstration, diagnoses are mere speculations. However, we will concentrate on concepts and methods important to demonstrating that diagnostic distinctions are based in nature and are probably not arbitrary.

ETIOLOGIES, SYNDROMES, AND CLINICAL BOUNDARIES

In the authors' opinion, really satisfying distinctions between disorders are almost always etiological. Therefore, we have considered what kinds of relationships between etiologies and disorders suffice to create distinguishable disorders. Our criteria for calling disorders distinguishable are the existence of syndromes of intercorrelated signs and the existence of nonartifactual quantitative distinctions between groups.

When specific etiologies are categorical and very strongly affect the risk of disease, large quantitative differences between groups in symptoms or laboratory data may be obvious. Those forms of causality called necessary-and-sufficient, only necessary, and only sufficient will often lead to both syndromes and clear boundaries between disorders. However, if the influence of etiological factors on risk of disease is weaker than these, disorders may be much harder to distinguish.

Obviously, there is more than one way for clinical overlap to arise out of etiological differences. First, it may be that risk factors for two disorders are different, but presence of the respective risk factors does not strongly influence the probability of developing the respective disorders. Alternatively, it may be that different etiological factors strongly and differentially affect risks for two disorders, but clinical manifestations or even laboratory data do not sharply distinguish them.

We have examined the overlap question with respect to syndromes and the existence of large quantitative differences. It turns out that rather weak conditions suffice to create distinct syndromes. For example, if people arrive at a clinic through processes which implicitly or explicitly select for extremity on either of two graded traits, then in that clinic we will almost surely see two syndromes (one related to each trait), which will often have a negative correlation.

This is true even if the two causal factors at work are uncorrelated in the general population. For example, let us suppose, purely for illustrative purposes, that two independent traits, impulse control and testosterone level, both affect the risk of developing two "disorders," petty criminality and pedophilia. Both deficient impulse control and high testosterone can lead to petty crime or sexual acts with a child, but impulsivity is a more potent risk factor for engaging in petty crime and testosterone for engaging in pedophilic acts. Suppose impulsive individuals and those with excess testosterone are very likely to be sent to prison. Then commission of one petty crime will correlate with commission of another, sex acts will correlate with each other, and petty crime will correlate slightly negatively with pedophilia. If two disorders rarer than these are considered, then the correlation between these syndromes in prison populations will ordinarily be more strongly negative. Even though a causal situation like this suffices to generate two syndromes, it may be that so many patients have moderate levels of both syndromes that their distinctness will not be clear.

THRESHOLD ETIOLOGICAL ACTION AND BIMODALITY

In thinking about these issues, we have found a paper by Meehl (13) on quantitative meanings of "specific etiology" helpful. We borrow two models of specific etiology from him. First, we conjecture that the following may occur in psychopathology though we suppose it is rare. A factor varies in intensity in a population. Small amounts of this factor never cause illness, large amounts always do, and the risk rises quite precipitously at some intermediate level. Experimentally confirmed examples like this are lacking, but the "loss of control" phenomenon in alcoholism is sometimes spoken of in this way. Here, the illness is a relapse of alcoholism, and the agent with threshold effect is alcohol. Because the sequelae of loss of control will cluster together due to their common etiology, a syndrome will be apparent. But will two such disorders have a clear boundary?

It all depends on what one means by "clear." Suppose one stresses the "large quantitative difference" criterion for delimiting disorders and requires a bimodal distribution of disorder-discriminating scores. With this as criterion, it is hard to demonstrate boundaries for the threshold-causation situation. We explored this question numerically in order to see how strong the causal differences between disorders had to become before bimodality was evident.

We simulated a two etiological factor, two disorder model as described above for petty criminality and pedophilia. We assumed that two normally distributed causal factors, degree of impulse control and testosterone level, both contribute to the risks of petty crime and pedophilia. We assumed that indirect measures of these etiological factors were available. Finally, we assumed that the liability to

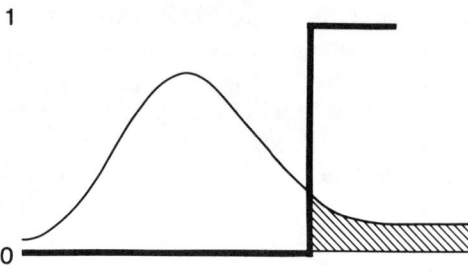

FIG. 1. Sharp threshold effect of specific etiology on risk.

develop a given disorder predicted a 10-symptom "syndrome" score for that disorder. Over a range of values for (a) the relationship between etiological factors and liabilities, (b) the relationships between etiological factors and indirect measures of etiologies, and (c) the relationships between liabilities and disorder-specific symptoms, we simulated 1,000 criminal samples. For each sample, we examined whether (a) the difference between indirect measures of our two causal factors and (b) the difference between our two "syndrome" scores yielded bimodal histograms.

Table 1 shows that it is not until (a) disorders become strongly differentially influenced by specific etiologies *and* (b) indirect measures of causes become quite valid that such measures show bimodality. Symptoms, too, have to be tightly tied to liabilities for bimodality to appear.

TABLE 1. *Presence of bimodality in sharp threshold risk model*

% Variance in variable due to antecedent		Bimodality present on indicator	
etiology→liability	liability→indicator	Etiological index	Symptom score
60	30		absent
60	50	absent	absent
60	75	absent	absent
60	90	absent	
60	95	absent	
75	30		absent
75	50	absent	absent
75	75	absent	absent
75	90	slight	
75	95	slight	
90	30		slight
90	50	absent	slight
90	75	slight	clear
90	90	mild	
90	95	clear	

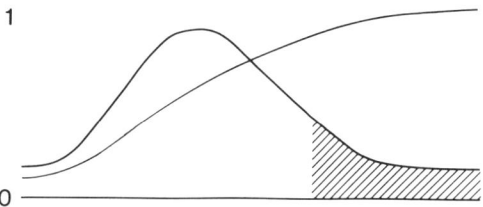

FIG. 2. Graduated effect of specific etiology on risk.

GRADUATED RISK, ETIOLOGICAL ACTION, AND BIMODALITY

We also considered a weaker form of specific etiology, one we think may aptly describe some mental disorders. Suppose that instead of a sharp threshold relation between liability and disease, there is a gradual risk increase with increasing liability (see Fig. 2), as in the polygenic threshold model. Suppose that two such disorders exist and have correlated etiological factors. This still produced two syndromes, but bimodality was never seen with "syndrome" scores or indirect causal measures when we tested for it using the same parameter values as in Table 1.

THE TROUBLE WITH BIMODALITY

Bimodality or the lack thereof has often been cited as evidence for or against the existence of subtypes of disorders or the existence of separate disorders. In the debate over the existence of endogenous depression, Kendell (14) argued that absent a replicable and real bimodal distribution on some syndrome measure, variations in the presentation of depressions could be attributed to a continuum. Using discriminant analysis of symptom and sign measures of depression, he found only a unimodal distribution of scores, and concluded that there were not two subtypes of depression. By contrast Sir Martin Roth and colleagues used bimodal distributions in Newcastle scale scores to argue for separate endogenous and neurotic depressions.

However, bimodality turns out to have major problems as a criterion for delimiting disorders. Here is a catalog of the difficulties. First, Murphy (15), Everitt (16), and Kendell (12) have observed that with moderate sample sizes, histograms can be drawn so as to make bimodality appear or disappear. Figures 3 and 4 show the distribution of the sum of six Schedule for Affective Disorders and Schizophrenia (SADS) anxiety items (worry, phobia, panic attacks, obsessions/compulsions, psychic and somatic anxiety) for 327 primary unipolar depressives from the NIMH Collaborative Depression Study—Clinical. Both figures show the same data, but plotted two ways; one figure appears to suggest a distinctly more anxious subgroup of depressives, the other appears to refute this suggestion.

Second, taking unrepresentative samples of the total population may falsely suggest or refute the validity of a distinction. Failure to observe very mild and

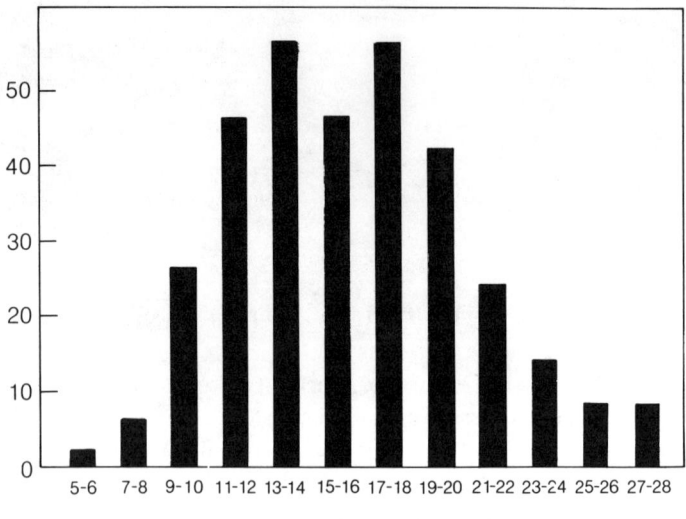

FIG. 3. Bimodal appearing histogram for anxiety summary score.

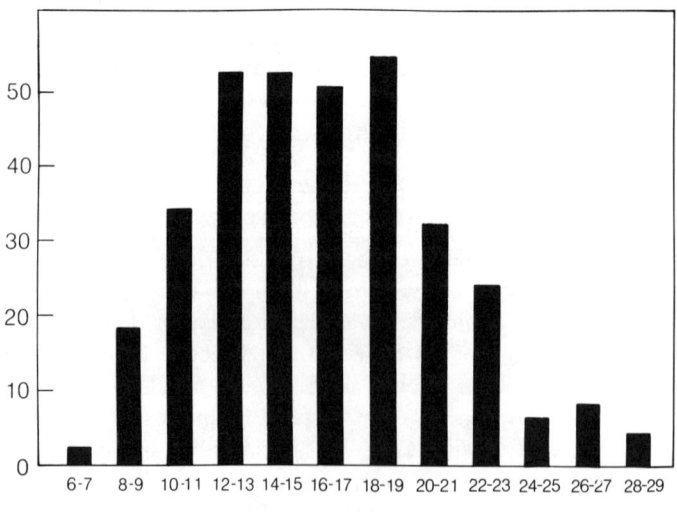

FIG. 4. Unimodal appearing histogram for anxiety summary score.

very extreme cases along a continuum could cause a distribution to look more concentrated in the middle than it really is, leading to a missed distinction between disorders (16). Failure to study "mixed" cases obviously makes differences between groups appear black and white, even though grays may truly predominate (14).

Third, observer biases may falsely suggest or refute a distinction. As Kendell (12) pointed out, analyses are often based on ratings made by skilled clinicians who may hold views which could influence their rating habits, potentially making such studies rather circular. He presented evidence that if one adhered to the two-type theory of depression it affected the distribution of ratings such as those often used to decide whether the two-type thesis was correct.

One might cure sampling problems by obtaining bigger samples, take care to study representative samples, and ameliorate bias problems by using raters who are naive to the clinical hypothesis or who do not hold strong positions on the matter. A fourth problem not so easily dealt with is that bimodality may not emerge for the simple reason that available measures do not discriminate disorders very well. Hope (18) pointed out that equimixed groups less than two standard deviations apart on a normally distributed variable yield a unimodal distribution. If within-group variances are too unequal, or if one group is much more common than the other, unimodal histograms will almost always be found even for mixed normal distributions (15). Unreliable measurements make bimodality hard to obtain for the same reason they make statistical significance of group differences harder to obtain: They make available measures less discriminating than would more reliable measures of the same phenomena. Because our given limited knowledge of many disorders in psychiatry, we may sometimes measure the wrong things (such as measuring effects of illness rather than proximal measures of etiology), and because the reliability of our measurements is often not high, failure to obtain bimodality may not be very probative.

THE BITANGENTIALITY CRITERION

Bitangentiality has been advanced as an alternative for deciding whether or not groups have been admixed. Bitangentiality consists of requiring that there be two distinct tangents to the distribution curve, of identical slope, on one side of the mode for unimodal distributions. (See Fig. 5.) Bitangentiality is considerably more sensitive to mixed disorders than is bimodality. Harris and Smith (19) showed that bitangentiality is manifested for group separations much smaller than required for bimodality. However, unitangentiality is still formally compatible with a two-disorder model since two distributions which are separated only modestly may together comprise a unitangential mixed distribution.

NUMERICAL TAXONOMY AS AN AID TO DELIMITATION

If bimodality and bitangentiality are both excessively stringent in their requirements for separating disorders, can one do better? We think one can, but not nec-

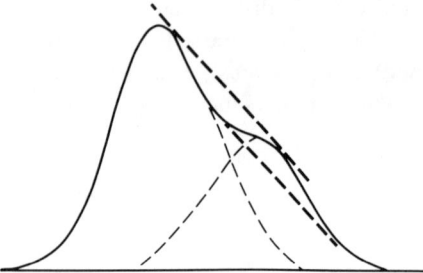

FIG. 5. A distribution showing bitangentiality.

essarily by much and not without risk. We have some experience with trying to delimit depressive subtypes using numerical taxonomy. The issues encountered in that work seem to be similar to those seen in other nosological controversies.

Numerical taxonomic methods have the virtue of moving perpetual arguments between lumpers and splitters to a more sophisticated and objective stage. Four methods have been recently applied to psychiatric disorder delimitation: regression nonlinearity, cluster analysis, multivariate normal mixture models, and latent class models.

Regression Nonlinearity

Kendell and Brockington (20) proposed this method; it is related to work by Meehl (21) on indicator covariances. Basically the method relies on the fact that pairs of variables which discriminate between disorders correlate due to two influences: within-group regression of one variable on the other, and between-group differences on the two variables. If two distinct disorders have been mixed and if the regression of one variable on the other is linear *within disorders*, then the regression of one variable on the other in the *mixed* group will be nonlinear, with maximum slope at the best dividing line between disorders. Kendell and Brockington took as one variable a symptom discriminant score for schizophrenia versus affective disorder, and as the other an outcome measurement, using several sets of data to try to discriminate schizophrenia from affective disorders. They were unable to demonstrate nonlinear regression of outcome on discriminant score. This could be due to two factors. First, they sampled only psychotic cases, not the entire range of affective disorder, thereby probably decreasing the apparent difference between these disorders and schizophrenia. Second, the method may not be very sensitive to differences between disorders. We have not systematically studied their method, but analytic work on a related problem is astonishing in the degree to which linear regression fits even grossly nonlinear data arising from mixing diagnostic groups (22).

Cluster Analysis

This is a whole family of methods which can be divided into three general classes: hierarchical agglomerative, partitioning, and divisive. Divisive methods are not much used and have certain undesirable properties, so we do not discuss them here. Hierarchical agglomerative methods such as Ward's method (the error sum of squares) start with N individuals, combining them according to maximum similarity (e.g., minimum within-group variance) and proceeding until everyone is in one cluster. It is up to the investigator to decide at what point of unification the clustering is most meaningful. Partitioning or K-means methods start with an initial assignment of individuals to K user-specified clusters, moving them from cluster to cluster to maximize within-cluster similarity. Similarity between patient profiles can be measured in various ways; lack of space prevents our discussing them.

Many investigators have used cluster analyses to subtype depression, almost always on symptom measures even though one could as well cluster patients on cortisol levels or family history or response to treatment. For example, we and our colleagues in the NIMH Collaborative Depression Study—Clinical have used partitioning versions of Ward's method to group patients based on symptom profiles on the SADS interview. In three analyses (23–25) on various subsets of patients from the pilot and main series, what replicated best was one cluster with prominent endogenous and especially vegetative symptoms, severe illness, meeting multiple criteria sets for endogenous depression, with a relatively guarded prognosis, and with a hint (but not strong evidence) of increased heritability of depression in families.

A very serious problem with cluster analyses is that the clusters developed may be artifactual. If one drops in homogeneous data one will get clusters just the same. We have dealt with this by computer simulation, finding certain statistics which seem to indicate whether clusters are merely arbitrary slices along continua. However, our simulation method is expensive and lacks statistical appeal. Bock (26) has recently published some theoretical work on significance tests for cluster analysis, but such tests are not implemented in widely used computer programs, and their empirical soundness has not yet been evaluated.

Multivariate Normal Mixture Analysis

These methods offer elegant and relatively powerful significance tests for mixture of disorders in clinical populations, yielding greater sensitivity than bimodality or bitangentiality criteria. In particular this method's sensitivity falls off more slowly than does bimodality's as the mixing proportion deviates from 50–50. This method has been applied to several psychiatric delimitation problems. Recently, Fawcett and colleagues (27) used it to resolve depressed patients' scores on the Pleasure Scale, dividing the patients into a normally hedonic and a severely anhedonic group.

It is a rule of thumb in statistics that high power is purchased at the cost of relatively strict mathematical assumptions. If the assumptions behind normal mixture analysis are violated, there is considerable risk of drawing boundaries where none exist. Everitt (28) has offered the following caveats based on his computer simulations: first, unless 10 times as many patients as variables are used, the test for mixture is unreliable. Second, power to detect mixture is no higher than that of bitangentiality or even bimodality unless 500 or more cases are analyzed.

Other authors raise additional problems. A skewed but unmixed distribution may be misread as a mixture of two normal distributions by mixture analysis (29). Statistical methods have been developed and implemented in the computer program SKUMIX to simultaneously take account of skewness and perform univariate normal mixture analysis. A method closely related to SKUMIX was recently applied by Cloninger and his Swedish adoption study colleagues to somatoform disorder subtypes in women (30). Two types of somatizers were found, and they were differentiated on familial background. Since the analysis safeguards against mistaking simple skewness in discriminant scores for mixture, one can say with much more than usual confidence that these two kinds of somatoform patients are not simply arbitrarily delimited.

Even SKUMIX-type analyses on large samples may not be completely free from statistical problems. If the variable being analyzed is a sum of dichotomous items and if these items are highly correlated (say, over .5), then mistaken inferences about the existence of discrete classes of individuals can occur (31). With such a scale, subjects tend to get many items wrong or many right, with fewer scores in the middle than would occur in a single normal distribution. Programs like SKUMIX may read this as evidence of mixture.

Fortunately, psychiatric questionnaire and interview items seldom have such high correlations. However, this kind of problem should not be dismissed too lightly. George and Elston (32) have recently suggested methods for removing skewness and kurtosis while estimating normal mixture model parameters, in the context of genetic analyses. These methods are too new for us to judge their usefulness in psychiatry.

Latent Class Analysis (LCA)

This is a family of mixture models for categorical data, e.g., symptoms recorded as present or absent. The most common LCA model postulates "local independence," i.e., syndromal cohesion results from mixing populations within which symptoms are independent. Another way of stating this is that the only cause of symptoms' tendency to co-occur is that all are indicators of whether or not one has a specific disorder. Young has used this method, treating schizophrenic symptoms as indicators of a dichotomous latent class (33) and concluding that the Taylor and Abrams (34) criteria for schizophrenia neatly describe a latent class with three symptom groups which are independent within schizophrenia: formal thought disorder, blunted affect, and first-rank symptoms. He and other Collaborative Study investigators also used LCA on depressive phenomenology, finding independent vegetative and anhedonic syndromes (35). The vegetative latent class agrees with the nuclear depressive group found in our cluster analysis of an overlapping Collaborative Study sample (25).

A METHODOLOGICAL MORAL

We have labored in the vineyards of disorder subtyping and delineation. Our numerical taxonomic analyses, and those of others, have not convinced everyone that there is a distinct endogenous, vegetative, or nuclear depressive subtype. Similarly, controversies now exist about the overlap between depression and anxiety and between positive and negative schizophrenia. These disputes may not subside when results of sophisticated analyses become known. Still, we do advocate the use of numerical taxonomic techniques in many cases. They help put nosological arguments on a more objective footing and at least force us to try to be clearer about concepts. They also have the potential to "carve nature at its joints" since there are conditions under which such analyses can discover a latent dichotomy, assign all patients correctly to groups, and tell us the strengths of sign-disorder relationships, all without *any* prior (let alone reasonably correct) assignment of patients to groups (21). Thus, taxonomic methods may help us find groups with powerful relationships to biological factors, where initial attempts to produce criteria-based divisions may have led to significant but perhaps not very strong relationships. However, and this is a big "however," this promise of numerical taxonomy has yet to be convincingly actualized in psychopathology (36).

In advocating numerical taxonomy as an approach to delimitation issues, we do not wish to be accused of practicing numerology. In psychopathology, we believe that precision will ultimately come from biology. It cannot be borrowed from mathematics. Choices of one numerical taxonomic method over another are probably less important than making smart choices of a few good discriminating measures. Nonetheless, in borderline cases (no pun intended), a more precise statistical analysis of phenomenological and other overlaps may often help clarify matters.

USING FAMILY SYNDROME ANALYSES TO AID DELIMITATION

Where would we seek more discriminating data, then? We could look at brain structure and regional brain activity, neuroendocrine tests, receptor density studies, and a number of other areas. We would argue, however, that genetic epidemiological studies offer an especially good opportunity to get to the etiological bottom of things. Ties to specific loci are about as powerful a form of evidence for disorder delimitation as one can get.

Such genetic studies show us how complicated boundary questions can be. It is remarkable how frequently such studies demonstrate that different syndromes can stem from the same genetic cause. In Tourette's syndrome, it would appear that presentations as varied as schizoidia, phobias, panic attacks, obsessions, compulsions, depression, mania, and perhaps attention deficit disorder may sometimes express the tic-prone genotype (37), though debate on this continues. In affective disorder, both Old Order Amish (38) and Jerusalem-based work (39) show that bipolar I, bipolar II, unipolar, schizoaffective, and cyclothymic affective syndromes are probably manifestations of the same genetic diatheses, whether caused by variation at loci on chromosomes 11 or X. In such studies the clinical boundaries must sometimes be redefined as data analysis proceeds.

Discoveries of such gene-behavior linkages become more likely as disorder phenotypes become better defined. We note that "better" does not mean "more narrowly," as the above examples illustrate. In genetic epidemiology, one cannot simply make restrictive definitions of disorders under the assumption that the narrowest definition will be the most transmissible. Missing a case can impair inferences about segregation or linkage as much as false positive diagnoses, though newer techniques such as multipoint linkage mapping can help in this regard. Cases with mild manifestations, "in-between" features, or atypical presentations may show continuities with typical cases in symptoms and in genetic linkage.

Generalizations of numerical taxonomy for family data are now being developed by a number of investigators. We believe these techniques will be important tools in better delimiting psychiatric disorders. They will facilitate understanding how clinical boundaries can be drawn across multiple syndrome dimensions in accordance with genetic transmission patterns.

REFERENCES

1. Robins, E., Guze, S. B. (1970): Establishment of diagnostic validity in psychiatric illness: Its application to schizophrenia. *Am J Psychiatry*, 126:983–987.
2. Woodruff, R. A., Murphy, G. E., and Herjanic, M. (1967): The natural history of affective disorders. I. Symptoms of 72 patients at the time of index hospital admission. *J Psychiatr Res*, 5:255–263.
3. Van Valkenburg, C., Winokur, G., Behar, D., and Lowry M. (1984): Depressed women with panic attacks. *J Clin Psychiatry*, 45:367–369.
4. Coryell, W., Endicott, J., Andreasen, N. C., et al. Depression and panic attacks: The significance of overlap as reflected in follow-up and family study data. *Am J Psychiatry (in press)*.
5. Brier, A., Charney, D. S., and Heninger, G. R. (1984): Major depression in patients with agoraphobia and panic disorder. *Arch Gen Psychiatry*, 41:1129–1135.
6. Dealey, R. S., Ishiki, D. M., Avery, D. H., Wilson, L. G., and Dunner, D. L. (1981): Secondary depression in anxiety disorders. *Compr Psychiatry*, 22:612–618.
7. Tsuang, M. T., Woolson, R. F., and Fleming, J. A. (1979): Long-term outcome of major psychoses: Schizophrenia and affective disorder compared with psychiatrically symptom-free surgical conditions. *Arch Gen Psychiatry*, 36:1295–1301.
8. Angst, J. Clinical course of affective disorders. In: *Depressive illness: Predictors of course and outcome*, edited by T. Helgason and R. Daly. Springer, Berlin *(in press)*.
9. Braden, W., Fink, E. B., Qualls, C. B., Ho, C. K., and Samuels, W. O. (1982): Lithium and chlorpromazine in psychotic inpatients. *Psychiatry Res*, 7:69–81.
10. Klein, D. F., Gittelman, R., Quitkin, F., and Rifkin, A. (1980): *Diagnosis and drug treatment of psychiatric disorders: Adults and children*, 2nd edition. Williams & Wilkins, Baltimore.
11. Gunderson, J. G., Siever, L. J., and Spaulding, E. (1983): The search for a schizotype: Crossing the border again. *Arch Gen Psychiatry*, 40:15–22.
12. Kendell, R. E. (1968): *The classification of depressive illness*. Oxford University Press, London.
13. Meehl, P. E. (1977): Specific etiology and other forms of strong influence: Some quantitative meanings. *J Med Philos*, 2:33–53.
14. Kendell, R. E. (1969): The continuum model of depressive illness. *Proc R Soc Med*, 69:335–339.
15. Murphy, E. A. (1964): One cause? Many causes? The argument from a bimodal distribution. *J Chronic Dis*, 17:301–324.

16. Guze, S. B. (1985): Diagnosis of psychiatric disorders. In: *Mental disorders: Alcohol- and drug-related problems. International perspectives on their diagnosis and classification.* (International Congress Series No. 669). Excerpta Medica, Hague, The Netherlands, pp. 191–194.
17. Everitt, B. A. (1981): Bimodality and the nature of depression. *Br J Psychiatry*, 138:336–339.
18. Hope, K. (1969): Review of R. E. Kendell (1968) "The Classification of Depressive Illness." *Br J Psychiatry*, 115:731–741.
19. Harris, H., and Smith, C. A. B. (1948): The sib-sib age of onset correlation among individuals suffering from a hereditary syndrome produced by more than one gene. *Ann Eugenics*, 14:309–318.
20. Kendell, R. E., and Brockington, I. F. (1979): The identification of disease entities and the relationship between schizophrenic and affective psychoses. *Br J Psychiatry*, 137:324–331.
21. Meehl, P. E. (1973): MAXCOV-HITMAX: A taxonomic search method for loose genetic syndromes. In: *Psychodiagnosis: Selected papers,* by P.E. Meehl. University of Minnesota Press, Minneapolis.
22. Grove, W. M. When is a diagnosis worth making? A statistical comparison of two prediction strategies. *(Submitted for publication.)*
23. Andreasen, N. C., Grove, W. M., and Maurer, R. (1980): Cluster analysis and the classification of depression. *Br J Psychiatry*, 137:256–265.
24. Andreasen, N. C., Grove, W. M. (1982): The classification of depression: Traditional versus mathematical approaches. *Am J Psychiatry*, 139:45–52.
25. Grove, W. M., Andreasen, N. C., Young, M., Endicott, J., Keller, M. B., Hirschfeld, R. M. A., and Reich, T. (1987): Isolation and characterization of a nuclear depressive syndrome. *Psychol Med*, 17:471–484.
26. Bock, H. H. (1985): On some significance tests in cluster analysis. *J Classification*, 2:77–108.
27. Fawcett, J., Clark, D. C., Scheftner, W. A., and Gibbons, R. D. (1983): Assessing anhedonia in psychiatric patients: The Pleasure Scale. *Arch Gen Psychiatry*, 40:79–84.
28. Everitt, B. S. (1981): A Monte Carlo investigation of the likelihood ratio test for the number of components in a mixture of normal distributions. *Multivariate Behavioral Res*, 16:171–180.
29. MacLean, C. J., Morton, N. E., Elston, R. C., and Yee S. (1976): Skewness in commingled distributions. *Biometrics*, 32:695–709.
30. Cloninger, C. R., Sigvardsson, S., von Knorring, A.-L., and Bohman, M. (1984): An adoption study of somatoform disorders. II. Identification of two discrete somatoform disorders. *Arch Gen Psychiatry*, 41:863–871.
31. Eaves, L. J. (1983): Errors of inference in the detection of major gene effects on psychological test scores. *Am J Hum Genet*, 35:1179–1189.
32. George, V. T., and Elston, R. C. (1987): Testing the association between polymorphic markers and quantitative traits in pedigrees. *Genet Epidemiol*, 4:193–201.
33. Young, M. A. (1983): Evaluating diagnostic criteria: A latent class paradigm. *J Psychiatr Res*, 17:285–296.
34. Taylor, M. A., and Abrams, R. (1978): The prevalence of schizophrenia: A reassessment using modern diagnostic criteria. *Am J Psychiatry*, 135:945–948.
35. Young, M. A., Scheftner, W. A., Klerman, G. L., Andreasen, N. C., and Hirschfeld, R. M. A. (1986): The endogenous subtype of depression: A study of its internal construct validity. *Br J Psychiatry*, 148:257–267.
36. Meehl, P. E. (1979): A funny thing happened to us on the way to the latent entities. *J Personality Assess*, 43:564–581.
37. Comings, D. E. (1987): A controlled study of Tourette Syndrome. VII. Summary: A common genetic disorder causing disinhibition of the limbic system. *Am J Hum Genet*, 41:839–866.
38. Egeland, J. A., Gerhard, D. S., Pauls, D. L., et al. (1987): Bipolar affective disorders linked to DNA markers on chromosome 11. *Nature*, 325:783–787.
39. Baron, M., Risch, N., Hamburger, R., et al. (1987): Genetic linkage between X-chromosome markers and bipolar affective illness. *Nature*, 326:289–292.

DISCUSSION

Dr. Robert Cloninger: Dr. Grove, I think you are excessively critical of the use of commingling or admixture analysis. We have recently developed extensions of SKUMIX in which we can simultaneously allow for both skewness and kurtosis. We have applied these methods in analysis of the somatiform disorder data from our Swedish adoptee sample, and they allowed us to pick out groups which were validated by distinct family background. Your objection was that by using indicators that were highly correlated with one another, you might get the appearance of two different disorders, which you regarded as an artifact. In fact, if you have a set of variables that are highly correlated with each other, that is the requirement that you expect when you have a syndrome. If you have multiple symptoms which are highly correlated with each other, that is the circumstance under which you get the appearance of bimodality.

You perhaps were saying that you want indicators that are independent of one another, but then I would maintain that you will never get the appearance of two different clinical groups. The conditions that you say would be ideal to satisfy the statistical conditions are the very conditions which make it uninteresting from a clinical nosological standpoint.

There is a more serious problem. We have applied these analytic methods to schizophrenia, somatiform disorders, and to some personality disorders, and we have demonstrated groups of patients that are relatively discrete. But that does not necessarily prove that underlying those groups there are not continuums. In fact, in all our analyses, whether examining anxiety states or depression, we have only relative separation. There has always been a fair amount of overlap.

Dr. Grove: Usually a good deal.

Dr. Cloninger: A good deal, and in interpreting our data on somatiform disorder and personality disorder, we found that underlying those relatively discrete subgroups appeared to be multiple dimensions of personality that were normally distributed. The real take-home message to me is not that we do not have methods to detect relatively discrete groups, but that with psychiatric disorders the groups are not totally discrete, and this finding may be consistent with extreme syndromes that develop superimposed on top of underlying dimensional variation. That is a difficult situation.

Dr. Grove: I tried to indicate how difficult I think it is.

Dr. Cloninger: But I think your criticism is misplaced by emphasizing the statistical problems of admixture and cluster analysis. The situation is not as bad as you depicted. For example, your criticism of plotting data to show evidence of admixture is really not appropriate. The way to evaluate that is to use computer programs that allow for the full data. The way you graphically display results is really incidental to the conclusion about whether or not there is bimodality.

Dr. Grove: I did it that way because that is how it was done in the English work on depression.

Dr. Cloninger: But that is not the current standard. Those methods, and a lot of the British work, in fact, have been subpar. They have not applied formal tests of commingling analysis, and they have not used replication samples. There has been other work, in which replication samples and proper statistical methods using maximum likelihood methods have been used, which came to quite clear conclusions. The problem is not with the methods themselves. I think we are seeing the beast for what it is. It is a complex beast with bumps. The disorders are not totally discrete.

Dr. Grove: That latter point is a conclusion with which I agree. With the measures we have now, we see a good deal of overlap. While I am not sure where you stand, I will tell you where I stand. I believe that there are really nice, discrete entities waiting to be discovered, with relatively clean etiologies, but the measures that we have today are too weak to make the relative discreteness of those disorders clear. Work on panic disorder is one place where data seem to show an ever-clearer separation of a disorder from the matrix from which it was originally defined. I didn't think I was being as critical of SKUMIX as you felt. If you have methods of taking care of kurtosis as your modified SKUMIX method does, then you have methods of dealing with some of the potential problems.

Dr. Craig Nelson: A simpler way to look at the question, and I think this is what you were getting at in your emphasis on whether we have adequate measures, is whether the symptoms that we measure are really directly related to the illness. I think many of us would conclude that they are not, that they are approximations. As long as we are trying to analyze approximations our categories will be fuzzy; our distributions will not show points of rarity, and so forth.

A more interesting problem relates to the fact that it is extremely difficult to link up genetic underpinnings or neurochemistry with behavior. For example, we know genetic control has to do with intracellular events. From that we might get to neurotransmitter or neurochemical events. Then there is a set of physiologic systems related to how the dopamine system works. We are still a long way from behavior. It is not clear whether the disorder is mediated at intracellular levels, at physiologic levels, or at behavioral levels. The interesting statistical or conceptual question is: how do we determine at what level we should be looking?

Dr. Grove: There I agree with Jean Endicott's phrase, "Let a thousand flowers bloom." Look at all the kinds of things that you have for taking apart disorders, whether symptom variables or something else. There is nothing the matter with looking at symptoms. That is how we get started. One would also look at course and outcome variables, and at laboratory data. You look at the whole thing. You could feed all of these into analyses such as the Grade of Membership analysis, or admixture analyses, and see what you come up with. Sometimes you come up with some striking evidence for discreteness. Let me give you one example because it is such a gorgeous one. Siegel et al. published a paper this year in *Archives* on a P50 inhibition paradigm for auditory-evoked potentials. In that article there is a graph which shows P50 inhibition data, and in that graph there is a hole the size of a Mack truck in the middle of that distribution. Basically, everybody is piled up at one end or the other. It thus appears that P50 inhibition is something you would very much want to include in studies of the familial aggregation of schizophrenia and related disorders, since that is the sample in which this distributional phenomenon was observed. So, in some cases there may be laboratory findings of this sort. In other cases, the laboratory data may be no more than weak correlates of the etiological factors. It is purely an empirical question.

Dr. Zubin: When I entered this field it was all qualitative. There were no measures. There were no quantitative approaches applied to psychopathology. With the help of my colleagues, we finally developed systematic structured interviews. We developed measures, psychophysiological measures, behavioral measures, and so on. I took great pride in it, and I think we made some advances. However, I think we have gone too far. From our patients we gather material which is still very qualitative. We try to measure it in a better way, but it is still basically qualitative. Trying to quantify qualitative material is a problem, it is like trying to develop the science of ichthyology out of fishermen's lore or astronomy out of a sea captain's knowledge. We may not be ready to do this yet, even though I back you fully in attempts at doing it. But perhaps it is premature, and we should not push quantification too far.

Psychiatric Diagnosis in the Age of Molecular Genetics

*J. Gelernter and **E. S. Gershon

*Department of Psychiatry, Yale University School of Medicine,
New Haven, Connecticut 06511; and
**National Institute of Mental Health, Clinical Neurogenetics Branch,
Bethesda, Maryland 20892
Presented at Annual Meeting of American Psychopathological Association, New York City, March 3, 1988, Revised July, 1988.

I. INTRODUCTION

The study of the role of genetics in diagnosis has historically been through epidemiologic family studies. The finding of coaggregation in suitable classes of relatives, that is, finding that a diagnosis is familial, was seen as a validator of a diagnostic categorization (1). (Of course, a valid diagnostic category could be nonfamilial as well, such as toxic psychosis; coaggregation is only one of several possible validators.) Coaggregation has been very valuable in demonstrating through twin and adoption studies that several classes of illness are most likely inherited. Coaggregation in various family study designs has also demonstrated that there are larger diagnostic groupings, that is, spectra of diagnoses, which are found together in families. These may be termed "meta-diagnostic groups." This implies that several clinical diagnoses may share the same genetic predisposition, an implication which has been demonstrated in at least one linkage marker study in psychiatry (see below).

Genetics has taken on a new importance in diagnosis with the advent of positive linkage findings in bipolar disorder, and with the improvements in gene mapping through applications of molecular genetics. If it is known that a single gene variant on chromosome 11 predisposes some individuals to manic-depressive illness, but that other cases have no predisposing gene at that location, it must be concluded that there are at least two separate genetic etiologies for manic-depressive illness, and that diagnosis is now more precise if it distinguishes the separate etiologies.

Conceivably, several or all forms of manic-depressive illness will be directly diagnosable in individuals, using molecular methods, in the not-too-distant future. It might then be appropriate to define diagnoses such as "11p affective disorder," and to refer by this term to a disorder which has a specific and known etiology, and which requires treatment appropriate to that etiology. The distinction between bipolar and unipolar illness might then be relegated to a subclassification of the major diagnostic category, a fifth or sixth digit in the DSM-X, as it were, with a place in diagnosis like the specific kind of end-organ failure seen in a case of diabetes.

The purpose of this chapter is to assess where we are now in relation to the use of molecular genetics in diagnosis, starting with the data on coaggregation of diagnoses, and to discuss recent findings and new methods which might lead to use of molecular genetics as a laboratory component of psychiatric diagnosis. When we incorporate genetic data in diagnosis, we take a step toward genotypic diagnoses and away from phenotypic diagnosis, and thus also toward the possibility of making diagnoses more exact and therefore more useful. In this chapter we will discuss how the goal of genotypic diagnosis is being approached.

II. DIAGNOSTIC GROUPS BASED ON FAMILIAL AGGREGATION

The great number of epidemiologic family studies that have been performed in the past decades allow the construction of a coaggregation map (Fig. 1) as a visual display of the overlap of diagnoses in families. Several elements of the map have been thoroughly reviewed elsewhere, and can be touched on briefly here, but other aggregation studies will need review to justify their map placement. From the perspective of progress toward molecular genetics-based diagnosis, this map can be seen as a first approximation for use in pedigree linkage analyses, where

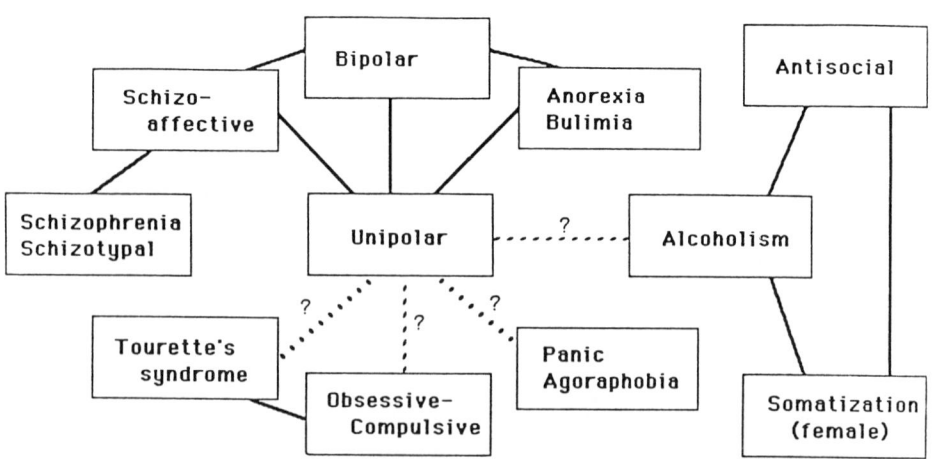

FIG. 1. A scheme of disorders which coaggregate in family studies. Disorders in the same box coaggregate strongly in either direction (starting with either one as proband). Boxes connected by solid lines have consistent data for coaggregation in one or the other direction, or coaggregate with other disorders which do not coaggregate with each other. Dashed lines with question marks have insufficient family study data to draw an unequivocal conclusion. For discussion of alcoholism-somatization-sociopathy relationship see Cloninger et al (100) and Gilligan, et al. (101). For discussion of other disorders, see text.

each individual must be classified as affected or unaffected. We consider at first two types of disorders in which the major coaggregation studies are relatively recent, Tourette's syndrome (TC) and panic disorder.

A. Tourette's Syndrome and Obsessive-Compulsive Disorder

Tourette's syndrome (TS) is a disorder with psychiatric and neurological manifestations which has its onset in childhood and which exhibits a male predominance. There is considerable epidemiological evidence to support the characterization of TS as a genetic disease, such as reports of familial TS (2) and segregation analyses (Table 1).

Historically, TS has been considered different from other psychiatric illnesses because its motor components are so clear. TS and chronic multiple tics (CMT) share some symptoms, and according to family study and twin study data, occur together in families (3–8). It is also established that obsessive-compulsive symptoms (OCD) frequently occur in patients with TS and in their relatives (9,10). The connection between TS and OCD in family members was, however, established after the initial broadening of the diagnosis with the demonstration of the TS-multiple tics relationship. In a key study, Pauls et al. (11) compared incidence of OCD in family members of TS patients with and without OCD themselves. They found that the 50% of their TS probands who had OCD themselves had the same prevalences of OCD, TS, and multiple tics in their family members as did the 50% without OC symptoms. The TS-OCD relationship has also been confirmed elsewhere (12).

The standing of attention deficit disorder (ADD) with respect to TS remains unclear, with data presented both favoring and opposing its inclusion on the TS spectrum (13–15). This refinement in the understanding of the diagnosis has al-

TABLE 1. *Family studies of coaggregation of Tourette's syndrome*

Authors	Probands	Relatives with disorder (%)				
		TS	CMT	OCD	TS+OCD	ADD
Montgomery et al., 1982	Tourette's	7	17	17		
Pauls et al., 1986	Tourette's without OCD	4.4	11.1	13.3	4.4	
	Tourette's with OCD	6.9	15.5	12.1	5.2	
	Tourette's (all)	5.8	13.6	12.6	4.9	
	Tourette's without ADD	11	20			2
	Tourette's with ADD	10	17			17

OCD = obsessive-compulsive disorder, ADD = attention-deficit disorder, TS = Tourette's syndrome, CMT = chronic multiple tics.

lowed the application of sophisticated genetic analyses. An analysis using a narrow (TS and multiple tics) illness definition (16–17) could not rule out multifactorial-polygenic transmission. Baron et al. (18), however, found the family data consistent with single major locus (SML) inheritance, using TS or chronic tics as the illness definition. They estimated a gene frequency of 0.003, and they had to allow for a majority of phenocopies among affected individuals. This model also provided for the requirement for higher genetic loading in females. In their data, Baron et al. found that relatives of female patients were at higher risk for TS than relatives of male patients (as did Kidd et al. [19]). Some other SML formulations have yielded simpler results, without having to hypothesize the presence of so many phenocopies. Genetic studies using complex segregation analysis have been consistent with the hypothesis that TS is inherited as an SML (20-21).

Pauls and Leckman (22), by including OCD patients as affected in their analysis, concluded that TS is most likely transmitted as an SML dominant. Taking a broad definition of illness, including TS, CMT, and OCD, they conclude that most people with a TS gene do express it, with higher penetrance in males (1.00) than in females (0.71). They estimate the gene frequency to be 0.006, using this illness definition. This model is consistent with a low proportion (10%) of phenocopies in the affected population; it favors the inclusion of OCD in a broader (meta-diagnostic) category with TS.

B. Anxiety Disorders

Panic disorder (PD) and generalized anxiety disorder (GAD) are common disorders with prevalences of 0.4 to 3.1% and 2.5 to 6.4%, respectively (23). Segregation analyses of family studies have shown that panic disorder is consistent with SML dominant inheritance (24–25), and there have been encouraging preliminary findings in a linkage study using classic genetic markers (discussed below). Generalized anxiety disorder, on the other hand, does not seem to have as prominent a genetic component as panic disorder from twin data evidence (26–27) and family data (28–29), and to the extent that it is familial, it coaggregates separately from PD. Relatives of agoraphobic patients have agoraphobia and PD, but not GAD (Table 2). This suggests that panic and agoraphobia have a shared familial basis, but GAD is distinct from them.

The relationships of generalized and panic anxiety to other disorders have proven complex. They could be distinct genetic entities, or either could be secondary to or otherwise related to other disorders such as depression or alcoholism (30). Some data (31–32) suggest that a common vulnerability may underlie major depression and anxiety disorders in some patients. Presence of an anxiety disorder in relatives may help identify a subtype of affective disorder, suggesting that in contrast to the DSM-III criteria, episodes of anxiety disorder should be diagnosed even if they are concurrent with an episode of major depression (33–34).

It has been suggested that PD is related to mitral valve prolapse, but family

TABLE 2. *Family studies and family history studies of panic disorder (PD) and generalized anxiety disorder*

Authors	Type of Study	Probands	Relatives with disorder (%)			
			PD	UP	GAD	EtOH
Noyes et al., 1978 (96)	FHS	PD	18	5		6
		Controls		3	4	4
Pauls et al., 1979 (24)	FHS	PD	9.5	1.1		1.4
		Controls (2° relatives)	1.4	1.1		2.4
Leckman et al., 1983 (33)	FS	UP+PD	3.8	19.6	10.5	21.1
		UP+GAD	0.4	19.8	9.1	10.7
		UP	2.1	10.7	6.2	8.9
		Controls	0	5.6	4.0	7.9
Harris et al., 1983 (28)	FS	PD	20.5	6.5	9.9	
		Agora.	7.7		5.1	17.6
		Controls	4.2		5.3	5.4
Crowe et al., 1983 (29)	FS	PD	17.3	4.0	4.8	6.1
		Controls	1.8	4.6	3.6	3.8
Noyes et al., 1987, 1986 (97,99)	FS	PD	14.9	4.1	5.4	6.6
		Agora.	7.0	4.7	3.9	12.9
		GAD	4.1	7.3	19.5	6.5
		Controls	3.5	7.1	3.5	4.4
Coryell et al., 1988 (98)	FS	PD+UP	6.7	24.4	13.3	20.0
		UP+PAs	1.2	39.0	10.4	18.9
		UP−PAs (1° relatives)	1.2	29.9	6.3	13.0

FS = family study, FHS = family history study, PA = panic attack, EtOH = alcoholism, PD = panic disorder, GAD = generalized anxiety disorder, UP = unipolar, Agora. = agoraphobia.

studies do not confirm this, because the disorders aggregate separately (35), and because when relatives assessed through PD patients with and without mitral valve prolapse were compared, the risks for PD in the groups were similar (36).

Pedigree analysis led Pauls et al. (37) to suggest that panic disorder is inherited as a dominant with about 75% penetrance; Crowe et al. (38) proposed that it is transmitted by a dominant gene with a frequency of about 0.05, partially penetrant, with penetrance greater in females than in males.

C. Bipolar Affective Disorder

Bipolar affective disorder is the only psychiatric disorder with demonstrated genetic heterogeneity based on linkage studies, as discussed below. The linkage data demonstrate that bipolar and unipolar illness can be caused by the same disease gene, but do not settle the more general epidemiologic controversy about whether or not unipolar and bipolar disorders are generally distinct illnesses (39–44, for review see 40.) Some have found increases of bipolar disorder itself only in relatives of bipolars (39, 41, 42), others in relatives of UPs as well (43–44).

Adoption study (45) evidence supports, in the biological parents of adopted away bipolars, excesses of bipolar affective disorder, unipolar depression, schizoaffective disorder, and cyclothymia, significant when taken together but not separately. Bipolar affective disorder also was associated in families with schizoaffective disorder, bipolar II disorder, and unipolar depression, in a large family study (46). An excess of cyclothymic personality also was found in these families, but there was no excess risk for minor depression or depressive personality. This is consistent with a single gene's possibly causing less severe illnesses, including unipolar depression as well as bipolar disorder. Family study evidence (41) also supports excesses of affective disorders and anxiety disorders in family members of bipolar and unipolar probands. Bipolar probands' relatives also had increased incidence of cyclothymia and hypomania. Neither of these family studies found an excess of alcoholism in relatives.

Klerman et al. (47), for unipolar depression, and Gershon et al. (48), for bipolar affective disorder, have suggested that there has been an increase in affective disorder in succeeding birth cohorts, a finding which cannot be explained without invoking nongenetic influences. First degree relatives born in succeeding decades were found to have greater risk for affective disorders (47). The effect is greater in families of patients than in families of controls, suggesting an interaction of familial-genetic with environmental causes.

It appears that there is considerable genetic overlap across the spectrum of affective disorders. The position of schizoaffective disorder in the spectrum is more difficult to pinpoint; there is an excess of schizoaffective disorder in both bipolar and schizophrenic families, and whether it represents a more severe form of either or both disorders, or a combination of them, cannot be answered yet.

D. Schizophrenia

Schizophrenics are inconsistent not only in their symptoms and response to treatment, but also in biological measures, with the schizophrenic population typically distinguished from a control population by increased variance on measures relating to neurotransmitter function (49–50). This extensive clinical heterogeneity need not point to genetic heterogeneity. For example, if this variation were genetically based, it would be expected that schizophrenic siblings would share particular clinical characteristics of illness, as they would presumably have the same genetic form of the disorder, but this was not seen except for affective symptoms (51).

Adoption studies have been consistent with generally present genetic component(s) in the etiology of schizophrenia (52–54). Family studies of schizophrenia suggest that the illnesses coaggregating with it are quite variable, including schizoaffective disorder, paranoid disorder, and atypical psychosis (55–57), and "schizoid-schizotypal" personality disorder (57), but generally no increased risk of bipolar or unipolar affective disorder or alcoholism. In one study (57) there was no increased incidence of paranoid disorder in relatives.

It has been reported that the relatives of more affective schizoaffectives (SA-A) resembled the relatives of bipolars, whereas relatives of more schizophrenic schizoaffective (SA-S) probands resembled schizophrenic probands' relatives (58), but not all investigators agree (46, 59). According to another study, there is also high risk for schizophrenia spectrum illness and affective disorders in family members of schizoaffectives (61). The relationship between schizoaffective disorder and schizophrenia remains unresolved.

Although most studies find no excess of affective disorder in relatives of schizophrenics, we (59) did find increased rates of bipolar affective disorder in relatives of schizoaffectives with chronic psychosis (SA-S) and increased rates of unipolar disorder in relatives of schizophrenics. Ours is also the most recent study, and the excess of affective disorders seen in this study might be related to the cohort effect widely observed, that is, the trend for later born generations to have higher rates of affective disorders.

Chromosomal abnormalities have occasionally been found to be associated with schizophrenia-like illnesses. Presence of an X chromosome with a fragile site (for review see [62]) is associated with mental retardation, especially in males who are hemizygous (that is, who have only one X chromosome). Reiss et al. (63) studied 35 female fragile X carriers (that is, heterozygotes with one fragile X) and found more psychiatric abnormality in that group than in a control group, including schizotypal features, intermittent depressive disorder, and chronic affective disorder. Bassett et al. (64) described an unbalanced translocation involving chromosome 5 in two schizophrenics in a single family (these patients are therefore triploid with respect to the genes on the part of the chromosome involved in the translocation). It is difficult as yet to gauge the significance of this finding: it has generated great interest in searching for related linkage markers in schizophrenia pedigrees.

The findings associating schizophrenia-like disorders with a chromosomal translocation and with fragile X are important in their implication that at least some schizophrenic illness is related to a localized genetic abnormality.

III. GENETIC MARKERS IN DIAGNOSIS

For analysis of genetic transmission or linkage, relatives who have a different psychiatric diagnosis from the patient's present a problem, similar to the problem of Type I and Type II errors in statistical analysis. If they are considered unaffected or unclassified when they in fact share the same genetic basis as the patient, the power of the analysis is reduced. If they are considered affected when in fact they do not share a genetic basis, the analysis may be erroneous. A widely used approach to this problem is to use the meta-diagnostic groupings described above to decide whom to consider affected and unaffected. A second strategy, if there is a linkage or association, would be to consider as affected all persons who share a marker and therefore have a high probability of having the disease gene, and redefine the diagnostic grouping accordingly.

A. Linkage Markers

A linkage implies that the chromosomal area of the marker must contain a disease susceptibility locus in pedigrees for which linkage has been demonstrated ("linked pedigrees"). One can expect that linkage will eventually lead to the identification of the disease gene itself. We discuss here the significance of linkage and its particular current implications regarding psychiatric illnesses, including diagnostic implications, in instances where a linkage has been reported.

Bipolar affective disorder may be a harbinger of what may eventually be found in several psychiatric disorders. There is evidence through chromosomal linkage markers that at least a portion of affective disorders are inherited through a single gene with a known location, as reviewed elsewhere (65–66). The evidence is strong that such a locus exists on chromosome 11p (short arm of chromosome 11) in an Amish pedigree, with a LOD score exceeding 3 under several groups of assumptions (67). At a recent metting, we reported a Jewish family possibly consistent with the same inheritance (68). Joffe et al. (69) have reported a Canadian family where thalassemia (a mutation of the globin gene in the same region of 11p) may be linked to affective disorder. These fragmentary data suggest that the 11p disorder may not be unique to the Amish. There are a considerable number of published pedigrees in which linkage of affective disorder to the X-chromosome region for color blindness has been reported (70–71). Although the evidence for this linkage is strong (Baron et al. reported a LOD score of 9.17 [70]), we have never been able to confirm it (72–73), which may perhaps be ascribed to linkage heterogeneity. Linkage of affective disorder to HLA has also been reported, principally in the work of Weitkamp et al. (74), but there are methodological issues that have been raised about the analysis on which the claim was made (75) and later evidence from the investigators does not appear to support this linkage (76).

We may conclude from linkage studies that transmission of BPD can be mediated by a single gene. It seems that the 11p form of bipolar disorder is not a common one outside the Amish (77–78). It also appears that most bipolar families do not show linkage to one of the known markers. If other psychiatric disorders are similarly heterogeneous, we may expect other disease loci to be identified through linkage to psychiatric disorders, even when segregation analysis of the pattern of inheritance seems to be unpromising, as with schizophrenia. (Note added in proof: Until recently, studies reported so far for schizophrenia have been negative or equivocal [79]. However, there has been a recent demonstration of linkage of schizophrenia to a susceptibility locus on chromosome 5 [80].) This is the region of chromosome 5 with the translocation associated with schizophrenia, discussed above.

Crowe et al. (81) tested a variety of classical genetic markers for linkage in 26 families with multiple cases of panic disorder. For one marker, alpha-haptoglobin, a LOD score of 2.27 was obtained; this is not significant, but clearly the chromosomal area (16q22) merits further study in panic pedigrees.

B. Research Based on Linkages

Perhaps the greatest potential value of linkage markers is for research on identification of the actual disease mutation. A finding of linkage provides information about the whereabouts of the disease gene, at least in the specific pedigrees where the linkage can be demonstrated. Association methods, discussed below, may prove to be a good way to further narrow down possible candidate genes (82).

Another research use of linkage is to study the correlates of diagnosis. Since each linkage presumably represents a different disease mutation, one would expect that differences may be found in course and treatment response between forms of a disorder that have different linkages.

C. The Clinical Value of Linkage Markers

The existence of valid linkages implies separate etiologies in pedigrees with and without a particular linkage, but it provides a precise genetic diagnosis only for individuals in a linked pedigree. Even in such pedigrees, the recombination fraction presents a limit on the precision of genetic diagnosis. Furthermore, decisions on treatment for patients within a linked pedigree may continue to depend on traditional methods until enough patients with the linked form of disease are available to determine if they also have distinct treatment responses.

What, then, is the present clinical utility of linkage markers within a pedigree? An emerging clinical use of linkage markers in genetic diagnosis is the prediction of risk in linked pedigrees. New accuracy is introduced into genetic counseling by linkage information, better than that based on overall morbid risk to relatives of probands with the illness.

D. Disease Mutation and Linkage Disequilibrium

The ability to directly detect the disease mutation (where the presence of a mutation is deduced from linkage) would, of course, constitute a major scientific advance over a linkage marker in several respects. For diagnostic purposes, this ability would offer a precise genetic diagnosis in individuals without investigating their pedigrees.

How can the disease mutation be found, once a linkage is identified, bearing in mind that there is demonstrated genetic heterogeneity in manic-depressive illness and that it may exist in other psychiatric diseases as well? Where a linkage marker exists, any one of the numerous genes in the region of linkage might contain the disease mutation. Any gene which unequivocally recombines with illness (that is, is not transmitted to all ill individuals in a linked pedigree) is not the disease gene. It is possible that the disease gene might manifest certain physical properties that would make it distinguishable from the other genes in the region, such as an insertion or a deletion. It is also possible that the disease mutation itself is recognized by an RFLP in such a way as to make it distinguishable from the wild type (nondisease) gene. If an association of a particular RFLP with illness is found, then it is possible that this RFLP identifies the disease mutation itself. Even if this is not the case, the locus recognized must be close to the disease gene in molecular terms, and it could identify a region that must contain it, and which then could be studied by other means in the hope of confirming the presence of a causative gene.

E. Power of Association Markers in Diagnosis

If an association marker exists, due to linkage disequilibrium or other causes, how might it enhance specificity of diagnosis? Narcolepsy provides a model system. In separate studies in Japan and in Canada, 100% of patients with narcolepsy were found to have HLA antigen DR2, which was present in 22% of controls in Canada and 34% of controls in Japan (83–85). How might such an association be of diagnostic value? Clearly the HLA type is not required to diagnose narcolepsy, nor can it subdivide patients into etiologic groups. But there are disorders of excessive sleep (DES) which do not meet the full diagnostic requirements for narcolepsy, and which are found in excess in relatives of narcoleptics (86). In Honda's paper (83), 16 of 34 independently sampled essential hypersomnia (EHS) patients had DR2. What is the likelihood that a patient with EHS and DR2 has the same genetic disorder as narcoleptics?

The desired probability can be computed using Bayesian analysis. The assumptions are as follows: the prior probability that an EHS patient shares the genetic basis with narcolepsy is arbitrarily set at 50%. The desired probability is the probability of shared genetic basis with narcolepsy (N) conditional on a patient having DR2 [p(N|DR2)].

$$p(N|DR2) = \frac{p(DR2|N)p(N)}{p(DR2|N)p(N) + p(DR2|notN)p(notN)}$$

From the observed Japanese association data, we know that $p(DR2|N) = 1.0$ and $p(DR2|notN) = 0.34$. Since we have assumed a prior probability of N of 50% [p(N)] for the population in question,

$$p(N|DR2) = \frac{(1)(0.5)}{(1)(0.5) + (0.34)(0.5)} = 0.75$$

That is, when you select among EHS patients for those with DR2, you increase the proportion sharing the narcolepsy gene from the prior probability of 50% to the posterior probability of 75%, which gives more power to studies trying to detect physiological or pharmacological similarities between narcolepsy and narcolepsy-related EHS. On the other hand, even with this selection, 25% of the individuals with DR2 and EHS do not have a form of EHS related to narcolepsy, so that although the diagnostic specificity is improved it is not complete.

If there were a stronger population association for these disorders than HLA type DR2, the diagnostic specificity would improve. This would be an allele which is as frequent in narcoleptics as DR2, but much less frequent in the general population. Such an allele might be found by intensive investigation of the adjacent genetic code at very short distances from the DR locus, searching for association markers. With this kind of power, molecular genetic laboratory contribution to clinical diagnosis, and to research on treatment, can be considerable. Even with the current association of DR2 and disorders of excessive sleep, at least in the Japanese population, it becomes proper to subdiagnose and counsel according to genotype.

IV. CYTOGENETIC DIAGNOSTIC MARKERS

The political and ideological controversy over the validity of the increased rate of criminal convictions in XYY men has gone on since the phenomenon was first reported by Jacobs (87). However, the weight of evidence from several countries, particularly from the prospective Danish study of Witkin et al. (88), is that the association is valid; in Denmark that study found the rate of having a felony conviction by age 26 is 41.7% for XYY, vs. 9.3% for XY males ($p<0.01$) and 18.8% for XXY males. In the same data, the rate of XYY in adult males was 0.3%, and the rate of XXY was 0.4%. Although most of the XYY people who are convicted of anything are convicted of minor offenses, there is a considerable overrepresentation of these men among persons convicted for serious crimes as well (89).

Despite the strength of the association of XYY and criminal convictions, the cytogenetic determination is of no clear utility in clinical diagnosis of adult behavior problems, since XYY is such a rare condition and criminal convictions or antisocial personality are common in the population and present no nosological problems.

Perhaps of more eventual importance is the opportunity the XYY karyotype offers to study the development of antisocial and other behaviors associated with it. To consider this, we must briefly review what is known about the clinical and biological manifestations of XYY. Although antisocial adult behavior is the best known abnormal outcome, and apparently the most common one, this aneuploidy has been associated in the literature with cases of psychosis (90), infantile autism (91), and gross cerebral malformations in aborted fetuses (92–94).

We may conclude that there is a behavioral disorder and possibly a neurodevelopmental disorder variably produced by the presence of XYY karyotype, that it generally may not be associated with reduced intelligence, and that very little is known about the specific biological defect. To go further, a more sophisticated genetic research strategy may be needed. Perhaps one may draw an appropriate analogy from Down syndrome, which is usually but not always a duplication of chromosome 21, and from the recent findings on XX males and XY females (95). In these instances, although a host of biological events occur which are usually associated with an entire chromosome being present, there is in fact a small region on the chromosome which produces the phenomenon of interest (in this case, determination of sex) when present (or when present in extra gene dosage).

How might this locus be found for the XYY behavioral syndrome? Perhaps by study of non-XYY individuals with similar behavioral manifestations. One research strategy would be to look for regions of duplicated Y chromosome or on other chromosomes, using *in-situ* hybridization with Y-chromosome DNA probes. The individuals to study would be tall males present in the same institutions in which XYYs are most heavily overrepresented, namely penal institutions. An XX male in such a setting would be of particular interest.

V. DISCUSSION

A. Genetic Diagnosis

Genetic findings have begun to lead to a reconceptualization of diagnoses in psychiatry in two disparate directions; toward meta-diagnoses based on epidemiological coaggregation of diagnoses in families, and toward diagnoses based on demonstrated single genes or inherited risk factors. Both types of progress lead away from diagnosis based purely on clinical symptoms and life history.

In the classical sense, "diagnosis" has referred to the output of an algorithmic process using as input a patient's personal and family history, physical findings, and results of laboratory tests and diagnostic tests. Subjectivity is a particular problem for accurate psychiatric diagnosis, where verbal communication, as opposed to direct observation, has always played the most important role. Psychiatric diagnosis has historically been equivocal; it has depended for its exactness on multiple behavioral observations and reports from as many individuals as possible, and on structured interviews. If a patient decides not to report a psychiatric symptom and is consistent about it, there is no way that it can be uncovered. Psychiatric diagnosis is therefore not only inexorably phenotypic, it also must depend to a great extent on the memory and good faith of the subject, whose judgment and ability to report his experiences may be impaired by the very illness under study. This imperfect diagnostic conclusion may still help to predict some of the patient's future symptoms and course, but understanding the true categorization of signs and symptoms, that is, discovering the correct set of diagnostic algorithms, is a central problem.

Family studies have led to improved understanding of psychiatric diagnosis, and can lead to further improvements. We are only just starting to understand the spectrum of symptoms that can aggregate with Tourette's syndrome. We are just beginning to understand differences in family members' risk for unipolar depression based on the symptoms of the proband. We can subcategorize some bipolar pedigrees on the basis of linkages, but we cannot distinguish them on clinical grounds at all.

Eventually, more particular behaviors may be related to particular specific genetic defects. When this process approaches completion, there will be such a thing as genotypic diagnosis which will retrospectively clarify the phenotypic diagnostic process.

Future Applications in Psychiatric Diagnosis

Applications of genetically influenced or genotypic diagnosis may be anticipated. We would expect it to become acceptable to report results on treatment or etiology in which the results depend on persons being grouped together into such a category as schizophrenia spectrum, or Tourette's OCD spectrum, and not subdivided further. (It is possible that knowing a patient's symptoms will still be more important in determining treatment than knowing the etiology of his form of illness, as is sometimes the case now with syndromes such as congestive heart failure.) One is virtually forced to diagnose broad spectra of disorders when dealing with linkage studies of pedigrees, because the crucial distinction is the binary one of affected or unaffected, and considerable information may be lost by leaving ill individuals uncategorized.

The reports of valid linkage markers in certain pedigrees with psychiatric disorders should eventually lead to two additional developments in diagnosis: diagnosis defined by etiology and direct diagnosis of a genetic disorder in individuals, independent of family history or pedigree linkage data.

A finding of linkage implies that there is a causative gene within the linkage region. In a linked pedigree, it would be appropriate to diagnose 11p affective disorder, for example. Further research will clarify whether there is any advantage in drawing this distinction in therapeutic decisions, life course, prevention, or epidemiologic risk factor studies. But there is already one area in which this distinction is clearly an important one: in performing genetic counseling. Particularly when the presenting question is whether a particular person is at increased risk, linkage data is far superior to our current empirical risk figures.

Once the gene defect within a linkage region is discovered, or a complete association of illness with one allele is identified, dependence on pedigree information is eliminated; direct diagnosis based on detection of the defect in an individual becomes possible. This is now possible in only a few unusual instances in psychiatry, but there is hope that it will become more generally available in the coming decades, leading to new precision in the diagnostic algorithms of psychiatry.

ACKNOWLEDGMENTS

Bayesian analysis was performed by Dr. Lynn Goldin of the NIMH.

REFERENCES

1. Robins, E., and Guze, S. (1970): Establishment of diagnostic validity in psychiatric illness: Its application to schizophrenia. *Amer J Psychiat*, 126:937–987.
2. Kurlan, R., Behr, J., Medved, L., Shoulson, I., Pauls, D., Kidd, J. R, and Kidd, K. K. (1986): Familial Tourette's syndrome: Report of a large pedigree and potential for linkage analysis. *Neurology*, 36:772–776.
3. Kidd, K. K., Prusoff, B. A., and Cohen, D. J. (1980): Familial pattern of Gilles de la Tourette syndrome. *Arch Gen Psychiatry*, 37:1336–1339.
4. Pauls, D. L., Cohen, D. J., Heimbuch, R., Detlor, J., and Kidd, K. K. (1981): Familial pattern and transmission of Gilles de la Tourette syndrome and multiple tics. *Arch Gen Psychiatry*, 38:1091-1093.
5. Nee, L. E., Polinsky, R. J., and Ebert, M. H. (1982): Tourette Syndrome: Clinical and family studies. In: *Gilles de la Tourette Syndrome*, edited by A. J. Friedhoff, and T. N. Chase, pp. 291–295. Raven Press, New York.
6. Kondo, K., and Nomura, Y. (1982): Tourette syndrome in Japan: Etiologic considerations based on associated factors and familial clustering. In: *Gilles de la Tourette Syndrome*, edited by A. J. Friedhoff and T. N. Chase. Raven Press, New York.
7. Price, R. A., Leckman, J. F., Pauls, D. L., Cohen, D. J., and Kidd, K. K. (1986): Gilles de la Tourette's syndrome: Tics and central nervous system stimulants in twins and nontwins. *Neurology*, 36:232–237.
8. Price, R. A., Kidd, D. K., Cohen, D. J., Pauls, D. L., and Leckman, J. F. (1985): A twin study of Tourette syndrome. *Arch Gen Psychiatry*, 42:815–820.
9. Nee, L. E., Caine, E. D., Polinsky, R. J., Eldridge, R., and Ebert, M. M. (1980): Gilles de la Tourette Syndrome: Clinical and family study of 50 cases. *Ann Neurol*, 7:41–49.
10. Montgomery, M. A., Clayton, P. J., and Friedhoff, A. J. (1982): Psychiatric illness in Tourette syndrome patients and first-degree relatives. In: *Gilles de la Tourette Syndrome*, edited by A. J. Friedhoff and T. N. Chase, pp. 335–339. Raven Press, New York.
11. Pauls, D. L., Towbin, K. E., Leckman, J. F., Zahner, G. E. P., and Cohen, D. J. (1986): Gilles de la Tourette's syndrome and obsessive-compulsive disorder. *Arch Gen Psychiatry*, 43: 1180–1182.
12. Comings, D. E., and Comings, B. G. (1987): Hereditary agoraphobia and obsessive-compulsive behavior in relatives of patients with Gilles de la Tourette's syndrome. *Brit. J. Psychiatry*, 151:195–199.
13. Pauls, D. L., Hurst, C. R., Kruger, S. D., Leckman, J. F., Kidd, K. K., and Cohen, Dr. J. (1986): Gilles de la Tourette's syndrome and attention deficit disorder with hyperactivity. *Arch Gen Psychiatry*, 43:1177–1179.
14. Comings, D. E., and Comings, B. G. (1987): A controlled study of Tourette Syndrome. I. Attention-deficit disorder, learning disorders, and school problems. *Am J Hum Genet*, 41:701–741.
15. Pauls, D. L., Leckman, J. F., Towbin, K. E., Zahner, G. E. P., and Cohen D. J. (1986): A possible genetic relationship exists between Tourette's syndrome and obsessive-compulsive disorder. *Psychopharmacology Bulletin*, 22:730–733.
16. Kidd, K. K.,, and Pauls, D. L. (1982): Genetic hypotheses for Tourette syndrome. In: *Gilles de la Tourette Syndrome*, edited by A. J. Friedhoff, and T. N. Chase, pp. 243–249. Raven Press, New York.
17. Pauls, D. L., Cohen, D. J., Heimbuch, R., Phil, M., Detlor, J., and Kidd, K. K. (1981): Familial pattern and transmission of Gilles de la Tourette syndrome and multiple tics. *Arch Gen Psychiatry*, 38:1091–1093.
18. Baron, M., Shapiro, E., Shapiro, A., and Rainer, J. D. (1981): Genetic analysis of Tourette syndrome suggesting major gene effect. *Am J Hum Genet*, 33:767–775.

19. Kidd, K. K., Prusoff, B. A., and Cohen, D. J (1980): Familial pattern of Gilles de la Tourette syndrome. *Arch Gen Psychiatry*, 37:1336–1339.
20. Comings, D. E., Comings, B. G., Devor, E. J., and Cloninger, C. R. (1984): Detection of major gene for Gilles de la Tourette syndrome. *Am J Hum Genet*, 36:586–600.
21. Devor, E. J. (1984): Complex segregation analysis of Gilles de la Tourette syndrome. Further evidence for a major locus mode of transmission. *Am J Hum Genet*, 36:704–709.
22. Pauls, D. L., and Leckman, J. F. (1986): The inheritance of Gilles de la Tourette's syndrome and associated behaviors. *New England Journal Medicine*, 315:993–997.
23. Weissman, M M., and Merikangas, K. R. (1986): The epidemiology of anxiety and panic disorders: An update. *J Clin Psychiatry*, 47:Suppl:11–17.
24. Pauls, D. L., Noyes, R., and Crowe, R. R. (1979): The familial prevalence in second-degree relatives of patients with anxiety neurosis (panic disorder). *J Affective Disorders*, 1:279–285.
25. Pauls, D. L., Crowe, R. R., and Noyes, R. (1979): Distribution of ancestral secondary cases in anxiety neurosis (Panic disorder). *J Affective Disorders*, 1:287–290.
26. Torgersen, S. (1983): Genetic factors in anxiety disorders. *Arch Gen Psychiatry*, 40:1085–1089.
27. Kendler, K. S., Heath, A. C., Martin, N. G., and Eaves, L. J. (1987): Symptoms of anxiety and symptoms of depression. *Arch Surg*, 122:451–457.
28. Harris, E. L., Noyes, R., Crowe, R. R., and Chaudhry, D. R. (1983): Family study of agoraphobia. Report of a pilot study. *Arch Gen Psychiatry*, 40:1061–1064.
29. Crowe, R. R., Noyes, R., Pauls, D. L., and Slymen, D. (1983): A family study of panic disorder. *Arch Gen Psychiatry*, 40:1065–1069.
30. Munjack, D. J., and Moss, H. B. (1981): Affective disorder and alcoholism in families of agoraphobics. *Arch Gen Psychiatry*, 38:869–871.
31. Leckman, J. F., Weissman, M. M., Merikangas, K. R., Pauls, D. L., and Prusoff, B. A. (1983): Panic disorder and major depression. *Arch Gen Psychiatry*, 40:1055–1060.
32. Breier, A., Charney, D. S., and Heninger, G. R. (1984): Major depression in patients with agoraphobia and panic disorder. *Arch Gen Psychiatry*, 41:1129–1135.
33. Leckman, J. F., Merikangas, K. R., Pauls, D. L., Prusoff, B. A., and Weissman, M. M. (1983): Anxiety disorders and depression: Contradictions between family study data and DSM-III conventions. *Am J Psychiatry*, 140:880–882.
34. Leckman, J. F., Weissman, M. M, Merikangas, K. R., Pauls, D. L., Prusoff, B. A., and Kidd, K. K. (1985): Major degression and panic disorder: A family study perspective. *Psychopharmacology Bulletin*, 21:No. 3, 543–545.
35. Crowe, R. R., Gaffney, G., and Kerber, R. (1982): Panic attacks in families of patients with mitral valve prolapse. *J Affective Disorders*, 4:121–125.
36. Crowe, R. R., Pauls, D. L., Slymen, D. J., and Noyes, R. (1980): A family study of anxiety neurosis. *Arch Gen Psychiatry*, 47:77–79.
37. Pauls, D. L., Bucher, K. D., Crowe, R. R., and Noyes, R. (1980): A genetic study of panic disorder pedigrees. *Am J Hum Genet*, 32:639–644.
38. Crowe, R. R., Noyes, R., Pauls, D. L., and Slymen, D. (1983): A family study of panic disorder. *Arch Gen Psychiatry*, 40:1065–1069.
39. Perris, C. (1966): A study of bipolar (manic-depressive) and unipolar recurrent depressive psychoses. *Acta Psychiatrica Scandinavica*, 42:15–44.
40. Goldin, L. R., and Gershon, E. S. (1988): The genetic epidemiology of major depressive illness. In: *Review of Psychiatry*. American Psychiatric Press, Washington, D. C., 7:148–169.
41. Weissman, M. M., Gershon, E. S., Kidd, K. K., et al. (1984): Psychiatric disorders in the relatives of probands with affective disorders: The Yale University-National Institute of Mental Health collaborative study. *Arch Gen Psychiatry*, 41:13–21.
42. Rice, J., Reich, T., Andreasen, N. C., Endicott, J., Van Eerdewegh, M., Fishman, R., Hirschfeld, R. M. A., and Klerman, G. L. (1987): The familial transmission of bipolar illness. *Arch Gen Psychiatry*, 44:441–447.
43. Winokur, G., Tsuang, M. T., and Crowe, R. R. (1982): The Iowa 500: Affective disorder in relatives of manic and depressed patients. *Am J Psychiatry*, 139:2, 209–212.
44. Stancer, H. C., Persad, E., Wagener, D. K., and Jorna, T. (1987): Evidence for homogeneity of major depression and bipolar affective disorder. *J Psychiat Res*, 21:37–53.
45. Mendlewicz, J., and Rainer, J. D. (1977): Adoption study supporting genetic transmission in manic-depressive illness. *Nature*, 268:327–329.
46. Gershon, E. S., Hamovit, J., Guroff, J. J., Dibble, E., Leckman, J. F., Sceery, W., Targum, S. D., Nurnberger, J. I., Goldin, L. R., and Bunney, W. E. Jr. (1982): A family study of schizoaf-

fective, bipolar I, bipolar II, unipolar, and normal control probands. *Arch Gen Psychiatry*, 39: 1157–1167.
47. Klerman, G. L., Lavori, P. W., Rice, J., Reich, T., Endicott, J., Andreasen, N. C., Keller, M. B., and Hirschfeld, M. A. (1985): Birth-cohort trends in rates of major depressive disorder among relatives of patients with affective disorder. *Arch Gen Psychiatry*, 42:689–693.
48. Gershon, E. S., Hamovit, J. H., Guroff, J. J., and Nurnberger, J. I., Jr. (1987): Birth cohort changes in manic and depressive disorders in relatives of bipolar and schizoaffective patients. *Arch Gen Psychiat*, 44:314–319.
49. van Kammen, D. P., and Gelernter J. (1987): Biochemical instability in schizophrenia I: The norepinephrine system. In: *Psychopharmacology, The Third Generation of Progress*, edited by H. Y. Meltzer, pp. 745–752. Raven Press, New York.
50. van Kammen, D. P., and Gelernter, J. (1987): Biochemical instability in schizophrenia II: The serotonin and gamma-Aminobutyric acid systems. In: *Psychopharmacology, The Third Generation of Progress*, edited by H. Y. Meltzer, pp. 753–758. Raven Press, New York.
51. DeLisi, L. E., Goldin, L. R., Maxwell, M. E., Kazuba, D. M., and Gershon, E. S. (1987): Clinical features of illness in siblings with schizophrenia or schizoaffective disorder. *Arch Gen Psychiatry*, 44:891–896.
52. Kety, S. S., Rosenthal, D., Wender, P. H, and Schulsinger, F. (1967): The types and prevalence of mental illness in the biological and adoptive families of adopted schizophrenics. In: *The Transmission of Schizophrenia*, edited by D., Rosenthal, and S. S. Kety, pp. 345–362. Pergamon Press, London.
53. Heston, L. L. (1966): Psychiatric disorders in foster home reared children of schizophrenic mothers. *Brit J Psychiat*, 112:819–825.
54. Tienari, P., Lahti, I., Sorri, A., Naarala, M., Moring, J., Wahberg, K.-E., and Wynne, L. C. (1987): The Finnish adoptive family study of schizophrenia. *J Psychiat Res*, 21:No. 4, 437–445.
55. Guze, S. B., Cloninger, R., Martin, R. L., and Clayton, P. J. (1983): A follow-up and family study of schizophrenia. *Arch Gen Psychiatry*, 40:1273–1276.
56. Kendler, K. S., Gruenberg, A. M., and Tsuang, M. T. (1985): Psychiatric illness in first-degree relatives of schizophrenic and surgical control patients. *Arch Gen Psychiatry*, 42:770–779.
57. Kendler, K. S., Masterson, C. C., and Davis, K. L. (1985): Psychiatric illness in first-degree relatives of patients with paranoid psychosis, schizophrenia and medical illness. *British J Psychiatry*, 147:524–531.
58. Baron, M., Gruen, R., Asnis, L., and Kane, J. (1982): Schizoaffective illness, schizophrenia and affective disorders: Morbidity risk and genetic transmission. *Acta Psychiat Scand*, 65:253–262.
59. Gershon, E. S., DeLisi, L. E., Maxwell, M. E., Nurnberger, J. I., Jr., Hamovit, J., Schreiber, J., Dauphinais, D., Dingman, C. W. II, and Guroff, J. J. (1988): A controlled family study of chronic psychoses: Schizophrenia and schizo-affective disorder. *Arch Gen Psychiatry*, 45:328–336.
60. Deleted in page proofs.
61. Angst, J., Felder, W., Lohmeyer, B. (1979): Schizoaffective disorders, Results of a genetic investigation. I. *J Affective disorders*, 1:139–153.
62. Brown, W. T., Jenkins, E. C., Cross, A. A. C., Chan, C. B., Wisiewski, K., Cohen, I. L., and Miezejeski, C. M. (1987): Genetics and expression of fragile X syndrome. *Upsala J Med Sci*, 44:137–154.
63. Reiss, A. L., Hagerman, R. J., Vinogradov, S., Abrams, M., and King, R. J. (1988): Psychiatric disability in female carriers of the fragile X chromosome. *Arch Gen Psychiatry*, 45:25–30.
64. Basset, A., McGillivary, B., Jones, B., and Pantzar, J. T. (1988): Partial trisomy chromosome 5 congregating with schizophrenia. *Lancet*, I (8589): 799–801.
65. Gershon, E. S. Single locus markers in affective disorders, In: *New Directions in Affective Disorders*, edited by S. Gershon and B. Lerer. Springer-Verlag, New York (*in press*).
66. Gershon, E. S., Merril, C. R., Goldin, L. R., DeLisi, L. E., Berrettini, W. H., and Nurnberger, J. I., Jr. (1987): The role of molecular genetics in psychiatry. *Biol Psychiatry*, 22:1388–1405.
67. Egeland, J. A., Gerhard, D. S., Pauls, D. L., Sussex, J. N., Kidd, K. K., Allen, C. R., Hostetter, A. M., and Housman, D. E. (1987): Bipolar affective disorders linked to DNA markers on chromosome 11. *Nature*, 325:783–787.
68. Detera-Wadleigh, S. D., deMiguel, C., Berretini, W. H., Bonner, T. I., Hoehe, M., Lentes, U.,

Gelernter, J., Gejman, P., and Gershon, E. S. (1987): Molecular genetic studies on familial and sporadic Alzheimer disease. Abstract, 26th Annual Meeting American College of Neuropsychopharmacology, December 7–11, 1987.
69. Joffe, R. T., Horvath, Z., and Tarvydas, I. (1986): Bipolar affective disorder and thalassemia minor (letter). *Am J Psychiatry*, 143:933.
70. Baron, M., Risch, N., Hamburger, R., Mandel, B., Kushner, S., Newman, M., Drumer, D., and Belmaker, R. H. (1987): Genetic linkage between X-chromosome markers and bipolar affective illness. *Nature*, 326:289–292.
71. Mendlewicz, J., Simon, P., Sevy, S., Charon, F., Brocas, H., Legras, S., Vassart, G. (1987): Polymorphic DNA marker on X chromosome and manic depression. Lancet, I (8544):1230–1232.
72. Gelernter, J. E., Gejman, P. V., Detera-Wadleigh, S. D., Goldin, L. R., Berrettini, W. H., and Gershon, E. S. Restriction fragment length polymorphisms (RFLPs) show no linkage of bipolar affective disorder to the x-chromosome color blindness region in three pedigrees. Poster, 26th Annual Meeting American College of Neuropsychopharmacology, December 7–11, 1987.
73. Gershon, E. S., Targum, S. D., Matthysse, S., and Bunney, W. E., Jr. (1979): Color blindness not closely linked to bipolar illness. Report of a new pedigree series. *Arch Gen Psychiatry*, 36:1423–1430.
74. Weitkamp, L. R., Stancer, H. C., Persad, E., Flood, C., and Guttormsen, S. (1981): Depressive disorders and HLA: A gene on chromosome 6 that can affect behavior. *New England Journal of Medicine*, 305:1301–1306.
75. Goldin, L. R., Clerget-Darpoux, F., and Gershon, E. S. (1982): Relationship of HLA to major affective disorder not supported. *Psychiatry Research*, 7:29–45.
76. Price, R. A. Affective disorder not linked to HLA. Genetic Analysis Workshop V, *Genetic Epidemiology* (in press).
77. Detera-Wadleigh, S. D., Berrettini, W. H., Goldin, L. R., Boorman, D., Anderson, S., and Gershon, E. S. (1987): Close linkage of c-Harvey-ras-1 and the insulin gene to affective disorder is ruled out in three North American pedigrees, *Nature*, 325:806–808.
78. Hodgkinson, S., Sherrington, R., Gurling H., Marchbanks, R., Reeders, S., Mallet, J., McInnis, M., Petursson, H., and Brynojolfsson, J. (1987): Molecular genetic evidence for heterogeneity in manic depression. *Nature*, 325:805–806.
79. Goldin, L. R., DeLisi, L. E., and Gershon, E. S. (1987): Genetic aspects to the biology of schizophrenia. In: *Handbook of Schizophrenia*, Vol. 2, edited by F. A. Henn and L. E. DeLisi, pp. 467–487.
80. Sherrington, R., Brynjolsson, J., Petursson, H., et al. (1988): Localization of a susceptibility locus for schizophrenia on chromosome 5. *Nature*, 336:164–167.
81. Crowe, R. R., Noyes, R., Jr., Wilson, A. F., Elston, R. C., and Ward, L. J. (1987): A linkage study of panic disorder. *Arch Gen Psychiatry*, 444:933–937.
82. Bodmer, W. F. (1986): Human genetics: The molecular challenge. Cold Spring Harbor Symposia on Quantitative Biology, Cold Spring Harbor Laboratory, 51:1–13.
83. Honda, Y., Juji, T., Matsuki, S., Naohara, T., Sataka, M., Inoko, H., Someya, T., Harada, S., and Doi, Y. (1986): LHA-DR2 and Dw2 in narcolepsy and in other disorders of excessive somnolence without cataplexy. *Sleep*, 9:133–142.
84. Billiard, M., Seignalet, J., Besset, A., and Cadihac, J. (1986): HLA-DR2 and narcolepsy. *Sleep*, 9:149–152.
85. Poirier, G., Montplasisr, J., Decary, F., Momege, D., and Lebrun, A. (1986): HLA antigens in narcolepsy and idiopathic central nervous system hypersomnolence. *Sleep*, 9:153–158.
86. Leckman, J. F., and Gershon, E. S. (1976): A genetic model of narcolepsy. *Br J Psychiatry*, 128:276–279.
87. Jacobs, P. A., Brunton, M., Melville, M. M., Brittain, R. P., McClermont, W. F. (1965): Aggressive behavior, mental subnormality, and the XYY male. *Nature*, 208:1351–1352.
88. Witkin, H. A., Mednick, S. A., Schulsinger, F., Bakkestrom, E., Christiansen, K. O., Goodenough, D. R., Hirschhorn, K., Lundsteen, C. Owen, D. R., Philip, J., Rubin, D. B., and Stocking, M. (1976): Criminality in XYY and XXY men. *Science*, 193:547–554.
89. Schroder, J., de la Chapelle, A., Hakola, P., and Virkkunen, M. (1981): The frequency of XYY and XXY men among criminal offenders. *Acta Psychiatr Scand*, 63:272–276.
90. Dorus, E., Dorus, W., and Telfer, M. A. (1977): Paranoid schizophrenia in a 47, XYY male. *Am J Psychiatry*, 134:No. 6, 687–689.

91. Gillberg, C., Winnergard, I., and Wahlstrom, J. (1984): The sex chromosomes—one key to autism? An XYY case of infantile autism. *Appl Res Men Retard*, 5:353–360.
92. Austin, G. E., and Sparks, R. S. (1980): Abnormal cerebral cortical convolutions in an XYY fetus. *Hum Genet*, 56:173–175.
93. Brun, A., and Gustavson, K. H. (1982): Abnormal cerebral cortical convolutions in an XYY fetus. *Hum Genet*, 60:298.
94. Brun, A., and Gustavson, K. H. (1972): Cerebral malformations in the XYY syndrome. *Acta Pathol Microbiol Scand*, 80:627–633.
95. Simpson, E., Chandler, P., Goulmy, E., Disteche, C. M., et al. (1987): Separation of the genetic loci for the H-Y antigen and for testis determination on human Y chromosome. *Nature*, 326: 876–878.
96. Noyes, R., Clancy, J., Crowe, R., Hoenk, P. K., and Slymen, D. J. (1978): The familial prevalence of anxiety neurosis. *Arch Gen Psychiatry*, 35:1057–1059.
97. Noyes, R., Jr., Clarkson, C., Crowe, R. R., Yates, W. R., and McChesney, M. (1987): A family study of generalized anxiety disorder. *Am J Psychiatry*, 144:1019–1024.
98. Coryell, W., Endicott, J., Andreasen, N. C., Keller, M. B., Clayton, P. J., Hirschfeld, M. A., Scheftner, W. A., and Winokur, G. (1988): Depression and panic attacks: The significance of overlap as reflected in follow-up and family study data. *Am J Psychiatry*, 145:293–300.
99. Noyes, R., Crowe, R. R., Harris, E. L., Hamra, B. J., McChesney, C. M., and Chaudhry, D. R. (1986): Relationship between panic disorder and agoraphobia. *Arch Gen Psychiatry*, 43:227–232.
100. Cloninger, C. R., vonKnorring, A. L., Sigvardsson, S., and Bohman, M. (1986): Symptom patterns and causes of somatization in men: II. Genetic and environmental independence from somatization in women. *Genet Epidemiol*, 3(3):171–185.
101. Gilligan, S. B., Reich, T., and Cloninger, C. R. (1987): Etiologic heterogeneity in alcoholism. *Genet Epidemiol*, 4(6):395–414.

DISCUSSION

Dr. Arthur Shapiro: In both your material and that presented by Dr. Grove, patients with Tourette's syndrome (TS) and/or their families were characterized as having obsessive-compulsive symptoms (OCS) or disorder (OCD), diverse behavior problems, and other psychopathology. Although much of the published literature can be cited as supporting this association, careful scrutiny of the literature indicates that the evidence is predominantly anecdotal and uncontrolled. Many clinical reports have concluded that psychopathology is not associated with TS or with the families of patients with TS. Two of our controlled studies concluded that OCS and OCD are not associated with TS, and two others concluded that behavior problems and psychopathology in patients with TS were not greater than expected in the population.

Our conclusion from our studies and our review of the literature is that TS is a "thing in itself" and is not associated with other primary psychologic characteristics.[1] We thus disagree with the statement in DSM-III-R, under "Associated features" for TS, that "In clinical samples, other mental disorders are frequently associated with Tourette's disorder."

Dr. Gershon: The points that you made really have to be answered by aggregation studies, not by whether or not the patient also has obsessive-compulsive disorder.

Dr. Klein: You quoted Leckman and Weissman as showing that when depressed probands had panic attacks, the incidence of depression and panic attacks went up. We went at it from the other direction and found exactly the same thing. We studied panic disorder probands; if at any time in their life they were depressed, the incidence of panic attacks, panic disorder, and depression went up. It leads me to speculate that perhaps this is not comor-

---

[1]Shapiro, A. K., Shapiro, E., Young, J. G., Feinburg, T. E. (1987): *Gilles de la Tourette Syndrome*, 2nd edition. Raven Press, New York.

bidity but rather syndromal complexity. The patients who have both panic disorder and depression may actually have a more homogeneous condition than people who have only panic attacks or who have only depression. Simple diagnoses may be contaminated by phenocopies. It is harder to have a phenocopy for a very complex clinical syndrome.

Dr. Gershon: That is what aggregation is for, an answer applied to both your point and Dr. Shapiro's. It doesn't matter so much whether you see two diseases in the patients, for the reasons you both mentioned. What matters is what do you see in the relatives. If you find unipolar depression without panic is more frequent in the relatives of patients with panic, it tells you something. If you find obsessive-compulsive disorder in excess in the relatives of Tourette's syndrome patients without obsessive symptoms, it tells you something.

Dr. Arthur Falek: In bipolar manic depressive illness, molecular genetic studies have shown two different chromosomes to be involved, causing speculation about heterogeneity of that disorder. Could you comment about heterogeneity and schizophrenia as you see it?

Dr. Gershon: If the possible linkage that I showed you is a true linkage, then it has to be a different form of schizophrenia than is most often seen. Most often the families don't hang together enough to do large linkage studies, and there is a lot of affective disorder in them. I would be amazed if there were not genetic heterogeneity in schizophrenia, since there appears to be genetic heterogeneity in all the other behavioral disorders that have been mapped.

The Validity of Psychiatric Diagnosis, edited by
Lee N. Robins and James E. Barrett.
Raven Press, Ltd., New York © 1989.

Linkage Markers and Validation of Psychiatric Nosology: Toward an Etiologic Classification of Psychiatric Disorders

Richard D. Todd and Theodore Reich

Department of Psychiatry, McDonnell Center for Studies of Higher Brain Function, Washington University School of Medicine, and The Jewish Hospital, St. Louis, Missouri 63110

We believe that a valid classification is an essential step in science. In medicine, and hence in psychiatry, classification is diagnosis.

Eli Robins and Samuel B. Guze, 1970 (1)

INTRODUCTION

The ultimate goal of nosology in medicine is to identify specific syndromes or disorders which lead to specific treatments. Classification of psychiatric disorders, however, is primarily based on the history of illness and the clustering of signs and symptoms. Few diagnoses are based on known etiologies. To be sure, 30 years of family and outcome studies have lead to improvements in psychiatric nosology and have validated many diagnostic distinctions. For example, mania and schizophrenia, though often clinically similar, can be distinguished by family and natural history. In general, current psychiatric nosology is a collection of more or less distinct syndromes rather than a grouping of diseases or disorders of known etiology.

What the eventual basis for psychiatric classification will be is still an open question. In time there will be a nosology based on major etiological factors but the extent to which these factors will be environmental, genetic, or both, is unknown. Whether future etiologic classification schemes will be simpler or more complex is also unknown. Different psychiatric diagnoses may turn out to have a common etiological basis, which will reduce their status to subtypes of a primary disorder. An historical example is syphilis. What appeared to be a variety of disorders was due to the involvement of varying organs in different individuals with a single infectious agent. In contrast, the clinical diagnosis of pneumonia (fever, productive cough, elevated white count) has now expanded into several hundred etiologically specific diseases. Family studies have suggested that some psychiatric illnesses are subtypes of a primary disorder. For example, many studies have found that bipolar I, bipolar II, and recurrent unipolar depression cluster in families (2-4). Other studies have suggested that schizophrenia, schizotypal personality disorder, and schizoaffective disorder form a spectrum of presentations of the same illness (5-7). In contrast, dementia can now be divided into a number of clearly independent illnesses (8).

Linkage studies of familial psychiatric illnesses can directly address these nosological issues. In theory, the linkage approach can determine if a disorder is or is not the consequence of genetic variation at a single locus of major effect. If linkage between a disorder and a particular gene is found, then other disorders in the same family, or the same disorder in other families, can be tested for linkage to the same locus. In this manner, linkage studies can establish the validity of a particular classification.

In this chapter we will review the nature of linkage markers, general linkage approaches, and uses of linkage information. We will discuss how linkage approaches can validate psychiatric nosology and how current limits to linkage studies may be minimized.

THE NATURE OF LINKAGE MARKERS

In searching for an etiology-based nosology in psychiatry, a modified version of Robert Koch's postulates (9) for determining the etiologic relationship between a microorganism and a disease serves as a useful guide; the agent must be observed in every case of the illness, the agent must be isolated in pure form, and the agent must induce the illness in susceptible individuals. Psychiatric etiologic agents could be genes, infectious organisms, chemicals, psychosocial stresses, life events, etc. All of these potential agents could be isolated or identified in pure form and shown to be necessary, if not sufficient, to precipitate an illness in susceptible individuals. Most psychiatric studies of potential agents, often called risk factor studies and biological marker studies, are correlative in nature and have identified general, nonspecific risk or protective factors (such as intelligence, sex, social class, and cortisol suppression) as derived correlative measures.

Studies searching for genetic linkages are also correlative. However, once established, a linkage marker is not correlative in nature, but is an indirect, physical measure of cause. The linkage marker co-occurs with the genetic disorder because their two associated genes are close together on the same chromosome. If the genomic locus for a marker is some distance from the disease's locus, the marker may not be present in every affected individual in a family, due to recombination. In contrast to other types of risk or biological markers, therefore, the physical distance between a linkage marker and the disease locus is predicted by their degree of association. Linkage studies, then, offer a fundamentally different type of information from other psychiatric nosology studies. When the genomic locus of the marker is close to the genomic locus of the disease, the linkage marker identifies a necessary, if not sufficient, condition for development of the illness. In addition, if a distant (unlinked) marker is found to be linked to the same illness in another family, then the illness can be immediately divided into two diseases. In this sense linkage markers are specific, causal factors. To be sure, other unlinked forms of an illness may exist, even in the same pedigree. These other forms of illness are known to be fundamentally different from the disease of the index case since with a high probability they were not caused by the same genetic defect.

GENERAL METHODS OF LINKAGE STUDIES

The central observation of a linkage study is the cosegregation of the linkage marker with the trait or phenotype of interest. For studies on psychiatric nosology, the phenotype of interest is usually the diagnosis. The linkage marker could be any distinguishable form of an enzyme, protein, blood group antigen, etc. All that is required is that two or more forms of the marker exist so that the investigator can determine which parent contributed a particular form of the marker to the offspring, making the mating informative with respect to a given marker.

Two major advances in human genetics in the last 10 years have greatly increased the power of linkage studies. First, it was found that restriction enzymes (enzymes which cut DNA at specific sequences) occasionally produced different sizes of DNA fragments from the same area of genomic DNA for different individuals (10,11). These restriction fragment length polymorphisms (RFLPs) are due to individual differences in DNA sequence. All of the offspring of a mating will have one maternal and one paternal form of an RFLP. By annealing small radioactive segments of a given DNA sequence (DNA probes) to genomic DNA cut with restriction enzymes, differences between individuals for a specific locus can be conveniently measured. RFLPs for a DNA probe are the equivalent of alleles at a genetic locus. By studying parents and offspring, one can determine which parent contributed a given form of an RFLP (which allele) to each child.

The second major recent advance was beginning construction of human genetic linkage maps by the use of DNA probes which recognized many RFLPs (polymorphic DNA probes) (12). The use of highly polymorphic probes increases the chances of determining which parent contributed a particular form of an RFLP. The first reasonably complete human linkage maps constructed with DNA probes were published in 1987 (13,14). Now DNA probes of known chromosomal location can be tested for linkage with any disorder. When sufficient polymorphic DNA probes are available to cover the entire genome, an exhaustive screening for linkage will be possible for any familial disorder.

EXAMPLES OF LINKAGE STUDIES

Using the incomplete linkage map, there have already been notable successes in mapping the locations of some disorders with a Mendelian pattern of inheritance.

These have included the mapping of the autosomal dominant Huntington's disease (15) and adult polycystic kidney disease (16), the autosomal recessive cystic fibrosis (17–19), and the X-linked recessive Duchenne's muscular dystrophy (20). The extension of the human genetic linkage map over the next few years will allow the analysis of more complex genetic traits and disorders (21).

Two psychiatric disorders have also been successfully mapped by linkage studies. A familial form of early onset dementia of the Alzheimer's type has been linked to a marker on the long arm of chromosome 21 (22). The location is distinct from the loci for Down Syndrome (22) and for the A4 amyloid protein gene (23,24).

The second psychiatric disorder which has been mapped is bipolar illness. In contrast to other mapped disorders, familial bipolar illness has been linked to two distinct loci. In the Old Order Amish, bipolar disorder cosegregates with markers on the short arm of chromosome 11 (11p15-pter region; [25][1]). In several Scandanavian (26), Israeli (27), and North American (28) families, bipolar illness maps to the long arm of the X chromosome (X q27 region). However, in several Icelandic (29) and North American (30) families no linkage was found with either chromosome location. Whether or not other loci will be linked to bipolar illness and which locus will be identified as that of the major form of familial bipolar illness are current topics of active research.

LINKAGE MARKERS AND GENE IDENTIFICATION

The identification of a linkage marker for a psychiatric illness is a major accomplishment. This is the first step in isolating and characterizing the gene product which is a necessary, if not sufficient, ingredient in the development of the disorder. The presence of a linkage marker also increases the power of a variety of studies even before the gene is actually identified or characterized. As we will discuss below, some of these studies directly address nosological issues.

The demonstration of linkage between a marker of known chromosomal location and a disorder means that the two are close together in terms of recombination distance (usually expressed in units of morgans or centimorgans). Since recombination is a rare event, two loci about 1 million base pairs apart have about a 1% chance of recombining per generation. Physically, therefore, a linked marker and the disease locus may be thousands or millions of base pairs apart (usually expressed in terms of kilobases). Demonstration of linkage, then, narrows the number of possible genes from about 100,000 to a few hundred (31).

---

[1]Locations on chromosomes are designated by a three part code: first the number or letter of the chromosome (1–22, X, or Y); second, which arm of a given chromosome (p = short, q = long), and finally by the band number of a chromosome arm. The third part of the code may also designate the position as being at the tip or terminal of a chromosome arm by the abbreviation "ter." The uncertainty in an assignment is indicated by giving the band range. Hence for bipolar illness in the Old Order Amish, the location lies in the short (p) arm of chromosome 11 between band 15 and the tip of the arm, that is, 11 p15-pter.

Progress from demonstration of linkage to isolating the disease gene has been slow in most linked disorders. The rewards of identifying the actual genetic defect, however, make such gene isolation studies worthwhile. When identified, the functions of normal and abnormal gene products can be determined by DNA sequencing and biochemical studies. Knowing the disease gene function will identify the metabolic or neural pathways involved in developing the disorder and could guide studies of the neuroanatomy, the imaging, and the biochemistry of the disorder. Identification of the abnormal gene may lead to specific new treatments such as gene replacement or cofactor modulation. Knowledge of an involved pathway may also suggest novel therapeutic manipulations to overcome or circumvent a defect that blocks a particular pathway.

Results from linkage studies of familial illness may also be applicable to seemingly sporadic illness (i.e., illness when no family members are affected). To identify a linkage marker, the marker and the disease locus must be associated together more frequently than expected by chance (i.e., in genetic disequilibrium). Such associations may be due to founder effects in genetically isolated populations such as the Amish, who have restricted gene pools secondary to their cultural marriage restrictions, which limits their matings to the descendents of a very small band of individuals who migrated together to the United States. A disease gene in such an isolated population may also be an important cause of the same illness in the general population, but it may not be linked to the same marker due to recombination in a larger gene pool. Establishing very closely linked markers to the disease gene (less than 1 centimorgan away) or identifying the disease gene itself allows the detection of the defective gene in the general population as well. Such tests are available for α-antitrypsin deficiency and Huntington's disease.

Gene-based diagnostic tests may allow early detection of at-risk groups in the population at large. The identification of particular defective or abnormal genes could also lead to a gene-based classification system. Presently bipolar illness can be divided into three diseases: X q27 linked, 11 p15-pter linked, and non X q27, non 11 p15-pter linked. In the near future, we can expect the reclassification of bipolar illness into at least these three designations of gene-linked illnesses.

DIRECT USES OF LINKAGE MARKERS

In addition to being a first step in gene identification, a marker can be directly used in a variety of studies. As discussed below, these include studies of phenotypic variation, incomplete penetrance, disease heterogeneity, high risk and protective factor studies, and natural history.

A. Nosology, Phenotypic Variation, and Disease Heterogeneity

Psychiatric investigators frequently talk about distinct illnesses whose multiple etiologies all happen to affect some "final common pathway" and so produce a unitary clinical picture. The determination of different chromosomal locations for linkage with a disorder in different families directly confirms that such a clinical picture has a heterogeneity of causation. As discussed above, a minimum of three familial forms of bipolar illness have been documented. This is reminiscent of the division of pneumonia into a variety of disorders. If such etiologic heterogeneity is common among current psychiatric diagnoses, a shift to an etiology-based nosology will mean a marked increase in the number of disease categories.

Based on family studies and underlying theories of causation, investigators have also grouped together dissimilar clinical presentations. Different clinical pictures are assumed to be phenotypic variations of the same disorder. For example, schizophrenia, schizotypal personality disorder, and schizoaffective disorder are thought to be phenotypic variations of a schizophrenia spectrum disorder (5-7). Tourette's syndrome, multiple chronic motor tics, and obsessive-compulsive disorder have also been thought to be different manifestations of the same underlying defect (32). The demonstration of linkage of these different clinical descriptions to the same locus would answer this question directly. For example, in the Old Order Amish, bipolar I disorder is linked to chromosome 11 p15-pter (25). The inclusion of cases of bipolar II and unipolar major depression increases the significance of the linkage. This demonstrates that all three diagnoses in this family are linked to the same site and are phenotypic variations of the same genetic disorder. This also demonstrates that there are genetically caused forms of bipolar II and major depressive illness. If such etiologic clusterings are common among current diagnoses, an etiology-based nosology will have fewer diagnostic categories than the current one.

B. Explaining Penetrance

Even when best modelled by Mendelian inheritance patterns, familial psychiatric disorders do not display complete penetrance. For example, the penetrance of the autosomal dominant gene for bipolar illness in the Old Order Amish population is about 0.63 at age 30 and above (25). If a linkage marker is known for a disorder, then factors which modify penetrance can be directly studied. Unaffected individuals beyond the age of risk who possess the linkage marker represent a truly nonpenetrant population for study. Study of this population avoids some of the problems inherent in studies requiring a search for discordant identical twins.

C. Identifying Risk and Protective Factors

Of perhaps greater potential impact, the discovery of a linkage marker greatly increases the power of studies of environmental risk and protective factors. Branches of families can be unequivocally identified as being at high or very low genetic risk, as can children within a branch with some affected members. An example of the increased power is shown in Fig. 1. A portion of a large midwestern pedigree is displayed in which the transmission of bipolar illness is best modelled as autosomal dominant with approximately 0.6 penetrance and for which the inferred genetic and phenotypic risks are shown for each individual without knowledge of a linkage marker (Fig. 1A). Generations I and II are elderly and beyond the age of risk. The father in Generation I is an obligate nonpenetrant carrier. His genetic risk is 1 and his phenotypic risk is 0. The two affected siblings in Generation II obviously have genetic and phenotypic risks of 1. The unaffected siblings of generation II had a genetic risk at birth of 0.5. Once these unaffected siblings are also beyond the age of risk, the chance each has of being a nonpenetrant carrier is 0.2 [0.5 × (1 − 0.6]. The offspring of the affected siblings of Generation II who are entering the age of risk have an a priori 0.5 genetic risk and a 0.3 phenotypic risk [0.5 × 0.6]. Some of these offspring of an unaffected sibling of generation II are already affected. This makes the unaffected parent an obligate carrier and changes his genetic risk to 1.0. The unaffected offspring of the unaffected siblings of Generation II, in contrast, have a 0.1 genetic risk and a 0.06 phenotypic risk. These calculations show that in generation III genetic and phenotypic risks vary fivefold for currently unaffected offspring. For generation IV the variation is tenfold.

In the high risk group, the rate of expression of the disease, which is the end point of measurement, is at most only 0.3. A linkage marker improves the risk ratios for the high and low risk groups. If a linkage marker very close to the actual disease gene were available for this family, then the genetic risks for the high and low risk groups would be approximately 1 and 0, respectively. The phenotypic risks for the high and low risk groups would be about 0.6 and 0, respectively. Differences between the groups in both the a priori risks and the outcome measures are increased. In addition, as shown in the hypothetical marker distribution in Figure 1B, both false positive and false negative members of risk groups would be eliminated. In this hypothetical example of a risk study design with a linkage marker, the discrimination between groups is increased, the expected end point measurement is doubled in magnitude in the high risk group, and false positive and negative cases are identified. Once a linkage marker is established, high risk groups can be identified for study in genetic terms, rather than by parental diagnosis. The risk of living with a psychiatrically ill parent, then, can be compared to that of living with a parent who is a carrier of the gene, and with a parent who does not have the gene. Thus, comparisons of children at high or very low genetic risk can be controlled for parent genotype and phenotype. Prodromal symptoms, environmental variables, family variables, family atmosphere measurements, etc. can be compared on more homogeneous study groups. Factors which delay or prevent phenotypic expression can be studied prospectively. In this fashion, linkage studies can enhance environmental studies by controlling for genotype.

Using linkage approaches may allow the classification of many psychiatric disorders on a major effect or etiologic basis. Linkage markers may also further elaborate the contents of our nosology by increasing the power of studies to identify effects which influence penetrance, age of onset, phenotypic expression, etc. In

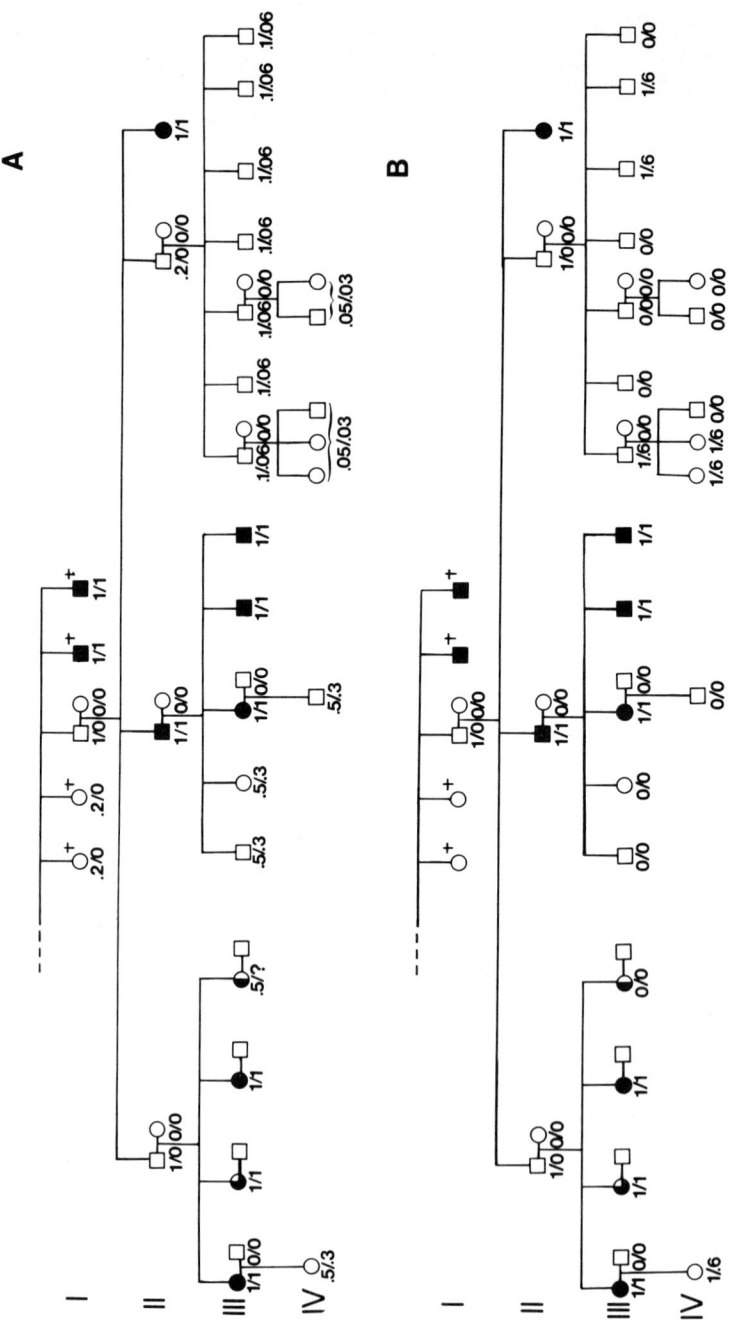

such a fashion the necessary *and* sufficient conditions for developing certain psychiatric illnesses may one day be defined.

CURRENT LIMITATIONS AND NEW DIRECTIONS FOR LINKAGE STUDIES

The ultimate importance of linkage studies to psychiatric nosology depends on the extent to which genes of major specific effect cause psychiatric disorders. Since the observation that a disorder is familial does not necessarily mean it has a genetic cause, it is difficult to estimate what proportion of familial disorders is genetic. Nor does nonfamilial occurrence of an illness prove that it does not have genetic causes. The majority of cases of many metabolic disorders which have low reproductive fitness, e.g., Lesch-Nyhan syndrome, are due to new mutations in genes (33,34). The genetic basis of these cases could not be determined by linkage studies. In addition to these general limitations, there are a variety of practical problems which need to be addressed.

First, the analytic power of current linkage algorithms depends on the assumed genetic model of disease transmission, on the sampling strategy by which families are selected, and on family size (35). All of the successful linkage studies based on DNA probes have relied on a Mendelian model of inheritance in large multi-generation pedigrees of rare disorders. For many psychiatric disorders, such large families with affected members have not been identified. In addition, many psychiatric disorders may follow complex transmission patterns where several loci are important (polygenic models); for other disorders, genes may have minor effects compared with environment. To some extent the pedigree size problem can be overcome by using smaller families with special disease incidence patterns such as affected sib-pairs (36) or increased genetic risk because of cousin-cousin matings (37). Simulation studies suggest methods for dealing with the issues of choice of genetic model, penetrance, and recombination (35,38,39).

For common syndromes, the extended pedigree approach may break down due to the presence in the same kindred of two or more clinically similar, but genetic-

---

FIG. 1. Effect of linkage on assignment of risk. A and B show the same portion of a large pedigree in which the segregation of bipolar illness follows an autosomal dominant form of transmission with about 0.6 penetrance. In A the genetic and phenotypic risks for developing bipolar illness inferred from the transmission model are shown (risk of having the genotype/risk of displaying the genotype). Generations I and II are beyond the age of risk. Generation III is entering the age of risk and generation IV has not reached the age of risk. In B are shown the hypothetical results when a closely associated linkage marker is known. Since the marker is closely linked, the recombination fraction between the marker and disease locus is low and the genetic risks are approximately 1 or 0 for presence and absence of the marker, respectively. The phenotypic risks are, therefore, approximately 0.6 or 0, respectively. Key: Squares = males. Circles = females. Filled symbols = bipolar I. Three-quarter filled symbols = bipolar II. Half filled symbols = major depression. Open symbols = no affective disorder. Crosses = deceased.

ally distinct disorders. In this situation, studying smaller families with several affected individuals may be advantageous. Preliminary results indicate that mapping recessive or near recessive loci can be achieved with great power if inbred pedigrees can be studied. Accordingly, endogamous populations such as the Amish will be very useful, as will be the offspring of cousin marriages. New methods for the study of complex quantitative traits are also being developed so that major genes will be detectable which determine continuous characteristics such as personality scores or neurophysiological measurements. To the extent that major genes which determine such continuous characteristics play a role in the etiology of psychiatric disorders, these advances may lead to improvements in our understanding of the nosology of psychiatric illnesses.

Analytic methods are being improved to allow the simultaneous use of multiple markers to characterize disease loci (35), resulting in increased power for the detection of genes which cause psychiatric illness. Since the limiting factor in many linkage studies is the ascertainment of pedigrees with sufficient numbers of affected subjects, increases in power may greatly expand the range of linkage analysis. The simultaneous study of multiple marker loci may also make resolution of etiologic heterogeneity within a single pedigree possible since several diseases segregating within a single kindred might be separable by association with different markers.

The most powerful method for the detection of genetic linkage requires specification of the mode of transmission of the phenotype. Unfortunately, the mode of transmission of many psychiatric phenotypes is certainly complex, and not well understood. Further, etiologic heterogeneity within existing diagnostic categories makes specification of the mode of transmission extremely difficult. In addition, assortative mating, variable age of onset, sex effects, and secular trends complicate the picture. Model free methods are being developed which do not require specification of the mode of transmission (36,42). These methods use affected individuals only, in whom it can be safely assumed that the gene was fully penetrant. Currently, affected sib-pairs or sib-trios are used. These approaches are being generalized to include other classes of affected relatives, with a concomitant increase in power.

Of great practical concern is the enormous labor and time involved in screening the entire genome for linkage with a given disorder. Most current successes in linkage can be attributed to good luck or to the presence of a cytological chromosomal abnormality which suggested where to look for linkage. For example, efforts to localize familial Alzheimer's dementia were focused on chromosome 21 by the observation that trisomy 21 (Down syndrome) patients frequently developed Alzheimer's disease-like pathology at an early age (40,41). The routine, systematic screening of the genome for linkage to different disorders will require the development of automated or semi-automated laboratory procedures to decrease cost and time requirements. It is to be hoped that technologies planned for use in sequencing the human genome will be applicable to linkage studies, as well.

Identifying highly informative polymorphic DNA probes which span the human genome is a necessity for linkage studies in all kinds of genetically caused illnesses. Once established, the same 500 to 3,000 DNA probes could be used in the study of disorders of many types. Several laboratories are actively pursuing this goal and batteries of DNA probes will become available over the next few years.

In contrast, the problem of defining the phenotype of interest is unique to each field. The polymorphisms of DNA markers are readily distinguished. Marker measurement, then, has high sensitivity and specificity. The same is not always true of psychiatric diagnosis. Unfortunately, the accuracy and reliability of defining the phenotype will greatly affect the power to detect linkage. Lack of diagnostic stability, sensitivity, and specificity all decrease the likelihood of establishing linkage. New methods of estimating diagnostic sensitivity by using symptom stability data (43) may reduce, but are not likely to solve, these problems.

In summary, linkage approaches offer the opportunity of classifying psychiatric disorders by etiology if there are genes of major, specific effect. Once linkage is established for a disorder, studies addressing a variety of issues such as etiologic heterogeneity, penetrance, and modifying factors are increased in power. The establishment of a linkage marker is also the first step in the identification of the abnormal gene. Such identification may lead to new specific treatments and early detection of high risk groups.

ACKNOWLEDGMENTS

The authors wish to thank Drs. Karen O'Malley and Keith E. Isenberg for a critical reading of the manuscript and Mrs. Jeanette A. Sharif and Ms. Judith Hunt for secretarial assistance. This work was supported by grants MH31302, MH25430, MH43028, MH40841, and by the John D. and Catherine T. MacArthur Foundation.

REFERENCES

1. Robins, E., Guze, S. B. (1970): Establishment of diagnostic validity in psychiatric diagnosis: Its application to schizophrenia. *Amer J Psychiatry*, 126:983–987.
2. Gershon, E. S., Hamovit, J., Guroff, J., et al. (1982): A family study of schizoaffective, bipolar I, bipolar II, unipolar and normal control probands. *Arch Gen Psychiatry*, 39:1157–1167.
3. Coryell, W., Endicott, J., Andreasen, N., and Keller, M. (1985): Bipolar I, bipolar II and nonbipolar major depression among the relatives of affectively ill probands. *Am J Psychiatry*, 42:817–821.
4. Tsuang, M. T., Faraone, S. V., and Fleming, J. A. (1985): Familial transmission of affective disorders. Is there evidence supporting the distinction between unipolar and bipolar disorders? *Br J Psychiat*, 146:268–271.
5. Kety, S. S., Rosenthal, D., Wender, P. H., and Schulsinger, F. (1976): Studies based on a total sample of adopted individuals and their relatives: Why they were necessary, what they demonstrated and failed to demonstrate. *Schizophr Bull*, 2:413–428.
6. Kendler, K. S., Gruenberg, A. M., and Strauss, J. S. (1981): An independent analysis of the Copenhagen sample of the Danish adoption study of schizophrenia, II: the relationship between schizotypal personality disorder and schizophrenia. *Arch Gen Psychiat*, 38:982–984.
7. Kendler, K. S., and Gruenberg, A. M. (1984): An independent analysis of the Danish Adoption

Study of schizophrenia VI: The relationship between psychiatric disorders as defined by DSM-III in the relatives and adoptees. *Arch Gen Psychiatry*, 41:555–564.
8. American Psychiatric Association. (1987): *Diagnostic and Statistical Manual of Mental Disorders*, 3rd ed., revised American Psychiatric Association, Washington, D.C., p. 5.
9. Davis, B. D., Dulbecco, R., Eisen, H. N., Ginsberg, H. S., Wood, W. B., and McCarty, M. (1973): *Microbiology*, 2nd ed. Harper and Row, Maryland. pp. 8–9.
10. Kan, Y. and Dozy, A. (1978): Antenatal diagnosis of sickle-cell anaemia by DNA analysis of amniotic-fluid cells. *Lancet*, 2:910–912.
11. Wyman, A., and White, R. (1980): A highly polymorphic locus in human DNA. *Proc Nat Acad Sci USA*, 77:6754–6758.
12. Botstein, D., White, R. L., Skolnick, M., and Davis, R. W. (1980): Construction of a genetic linkage map using restriction fragment length polymorphisms. *Am J Hum Genet*, 32:314–331.
13. White, R., Lalouel, J. M., O'Connell, P., et al. (1987): *Linkage Maps of Human Chromosomes*. Howard Hughes Medical Institute Report, Salt Lake City, Utah.
14. Donis-Keller, H., Green, P., and Helms, C., et al. (1987): A genetic linkage map of the human genome. *Cell*, 51:319–337.
15. Gusella, J. F., Wexler, N. S., Conneally, P. M., et al. (1983): A polymorphic DNA marker genetically linked to Huntington's disease. *Nature*, 306:234–238.
16. Reeders, S. T., Breuning, M. H., Davies, K. E., et al. (1985): A highly polymorphic DNA marker linked to adult polycystic kidney disease on chromosome 16. *Nature*, 317:542–544.
17. Tsui, L. C., Buchwald, M., Barker, D., et al. (1985): Cystic fibrosis locus defined by a genetically linked polymorphic DNA marker. *Science*, 230:1054–1057.
18. Wainwright, B. J., Scambler, P. J., Schmidtke, J., et al. (1985): Localization of cystic fibrosis locus to human chromosome 7cen-q22. *Nature*, 318:384–386.
19. White, R., Woodward, S., Leppert, M., et al. (1985): A closely linked genetic marker for cystic fibrosis. *Nature*, 318:382–384.
20. Davies, K. E., Pearson, P. L., Harper, P. S., et al. (1983): Linkage analysis of two cloned sequences flanking the Duchenne muscular dystrophy locus on the short arm of the human X chromosome. *Nucl Acids Res*, 11:2303–2312.
21. Lander, E. S., and Botstein, D. (1986): Mapping complex genetic traits in humans: New strategies using a complete RFLP linkage map. *Cold Spring Harbor Symp Quant Biol*, 51:49–62.
22. St. George-Hyslop, P. H., Tanzi, R. E., Polinsky, R. J., et al. (1987): The genetic defect causing familial Alzheimer's disease maps on chromosome 21. *Science*, 235:885–890.
23. Van Broeckhoven, C., Genthe, A. M., Vandenberghe, A., et al. (1987): Failure of familial Alzheimer's disease to segregate with the A4-amyloid gene in several European families. *Nature*, 329:153–155.
24. Tanzi, R. E., St. George-Hyslop, P. H., Haines, J. L., et al. (1987): The genetic defect in Alzheimer's disease is not tightly linked to the amyloid β-protein gene. *Nature*, 329:156–157.
25. Egeland, J. A., Gerhard, D. S., Pauls, D. L., et al. (1987): Bipolar affective disorder linked to DNA markers on chromosome 11. *Nature*, 325:783–787.
26. Mendlewicz, J., Sevy, S., Brocas, et al. (1987): Polymorphic DNA marker on X-chromosome and manic depression. *Lancet*, I:1230–1232.
27. Baron, M., Rish, N., Hamburger, R., et al. (1987): Genetic linkage between X-chromosome markers and bipolar affective illness. *Nature*, 326:289–292.
28. Reich, T., Clayton, P., Winokur, G. (1969): Family history studies: V. The genetics of mania. *Am J Psychiat*, 125:1358–1369.
29. Hodgkinson, S., Sherrington, R., Gurling, H., et al. (1987): Molecular genetic evidence of heterogeneity in manic depression. *Nature*, 325:805–806.
30. Detera-Wadleigh, S. D., Berrettini, W. H., Goldin, L. R., Boorman, D., Anderson, S., and Gershon, E. S. (1987): Close linkage of C-Harvey-*ras*-I and the insulin gene to affective disorder is ruled out in three North American pedigrees. *Nature*, 325:806–808.
31. White, R., and Lalouel, J. M. (1987): Chromosome mapping with DNA markers. *Scientific American*, 258:40–48.
32. Pauls, D. L., Towbin, K. E., Leckman, J. F., Zahner, G. E. P., and Cohen, D. J. (1986): Gilles de la Tourette's syndrome and obsessive-compulsive disorder. *Arch Gen Psychiatry*, 43:1180–1182.
33. Haldane, J. B. S. (1935): The rate of spontaneous mutation in a human gene. *J Genet*, 31:317–326.
34. Yang, T. P., Patel, P. I., Chinault, A. C., et al. (1984). Molecular evidence for new mutation at the *hprt* locus in Lesch-Nyhan patients. *Nature*, 310:412–414.

35. Spence, M. A. (1987): Genetic linkage: Sampling issues and multipoint mapping. *J Psychiat Res*, 4:631–638.
36. Suarez, B. K., Rice, J., and Reich, T. (1978): The generalized sib pair IBD distribution: Its use in the detection of linkage. *Ann Hum Genet. Lond*, 42:87–94.
37. Lander, E. S., and Botstein, D. (1987): Homozygosity mapping: A way to map human recessive traits with the DNA of inbred children. *Science*, 236:1567–1570.
38. Goldin, L. R., Cox, N. J., Pauls, D. L., Gershon, E. S., and Kidd, K. K. (1984): The detection of major loci by segregation and linkage analysis: A simulation study. *Genet Epidemiol*, 1:285–296.
39. Gershon, E. S., and Goldin, L. R. (1987): The outlook for linkage research in psychiatric disorders. *J Psychiat Res*, 21:541–550.
40. Ropper, A. H., and Williams, R. S. (1980): Relationship between plaques, tangles, and dementia in Down syndrome. *Neurology*, 30:639–644.
41. Price, D. L., Whitehouse, P. J., Struble, R. G., et al. (1982): Alzheimer's disease and Down syndrome. *Ann NY Acad Sci*, 396:145–164.
42. Weeks, D. E., and Lange, K. (1988): The affected-pedigree-member method of linkage analysis. *Am J Hum Genet*, 42:315–326.
43. Rice, J. P., Endicott, J., Knesevich, M., and Rochberg, N. (1987): The estimation of diagnostic sensitivity using stability data: An application to major depression disorder. *J Psychiat Res*, 21:337–345.

DISCUSSION

Dr. Ray DePaulo: I want to underline your point about the importance of accurate phenotype definition in genetic linkage studies. I would emphasize that the misidentification of a family member as genotypically affected when he or she is not is more damaging (to the LOD score) than the misidentification of a family member as genotypically unaffected when they are affected. Thus, for linkage studies we need to use conservative diagnostic criteria and procedures, that is: (a) screening for environmentally caused cases or phenocopies; (b) direct interviews by trained clinicians; and (c) initial classification of uncertain phenotypes as unaffected, to avoid false positive diagnosis.

The opposite error, calling a phenotype unaffected when it is associated with the affected genotype, is much less of a problem and one we expect to encounter since most genetic disorders have less than complete penetrance.

Dr. Todd: I agree with that.

Dr. Rapoport: Can you comment on the messy data with respect to attention deficit disorder? The data seem to suggest that it is related to almost every other disorder.

Dr. Todd: I agree that ADD is really a quagmire. Attention deficit disorder has been associated with oppositional disorder, conduct disorder, and Tourette's syndrome. I also think that ADD is a diagnosis that has had considerable diagnostic confusion in its application to particular studies. It is another example of where a lack of systematic collection of data, and a systematic application of diagnostic schemes, whatever you choose them to be, have really done us a disservice.

The Validity of Psychiatric Diagnosis, edited by
Lee N. Robins and James E. Barrett.
Raven Press, Ltd., New York © 1989.

Laboratory Studies and Validity of Psychiatric Diagnosis: Has There Been Progress?

David J. Kupfer and Michael E. Thase

Department of Psychiatry, University of Pittsburgh School of Medicine, Western Psychiatric Institute and Clinic, Pittsburgh, Pennsylvania 15213

INTRODUCTION

Laboratory studies play an important role in most areas of contemporary medical practice. In this chapter we will consider the current role of laboratory studies in the validation of psychiatric diagnoses. This topic has been one of considerable interest in psychiatry over the past several decades and has emerged in concert with other developments in our field which may be viewed as increasing the medical orientation of psychiatric practice.

Historically, the availability of laboratory testing has been associated with major advances in all areas of medicine. One needs to look no further than the advent of microbiological or pathological technical capabilities to appreciate the obvious impact on the assessment and treatment of various infectious and surgical conditions. A natural desire to achieve similar breakthroughs for the most serious mental disorders has long stimulated research in these areas. Indeed, some of the most striking medical advances in the 20th century have involved the clarification of the etiology of organic mental syndromes formerly treated in psychiatric facilities, including general paresis of the insane (GPI) and behavioral syndromes associated with pellagra. Paradoxically, once the etiology of these conditions was identified, they generally ceased to be considered within psychiatry's domain.

As Akiskal (1) has noted, the relatively simplistic (unicausal) nature of such conditions unfortunately may have been detrimental to the study of the majority of psychiatric disorders, in the sense that investigators have searched for a single factor (i.e., infectious agent, a dietary deficiency, or any enzymatic disturbance) which is *the* cause of the psychiatric illness. Over the past few decades, however, it has become increasingly clear that a majority of the major psychiatric disorders will prove to have a multifactorial pathogenesis (e.g., see Eisdorfer et al. [2]).

In the absence of straightforward "single cause-single illness" relationships for many of the major psychiatric disorders, researchers nevertheless have sought techniques to provide more objective and reliable assessment of the patients they treat and the conditions they suffer from. Initially, there was considerable enthusiasm that such greater objectivity could come from various psychological tests. For example, the introduction of projective tests, such as the Rorshach test, was thought to provide an analogue to laboratory testing. Indeed, the Rorshach ink blot test was referred to as the x-ray of the mind (3). Despite such enthusiasm, however, further studies demonstrated that projective psychological testing offered little additional reliability of assessment and, without reliability, the validity of the testing procedure cannot be established (3). Perhaps hidden within such pursuit of psychological tests for diagnosis of the major psychiatric disorders was the unspoken assumption that such conditions were of a "functional" nature and could not be meaningfully studied through biological paradigms.

Major research advances beginning in the 1950s and continuing to the present have refocused interest on the role of biological factors in a number of the major psychiatric disorders. These developments include the introduction of a number of effective psychopharmacological agents, refinement of methods for family history and genetic studies, and the development of progressively more sensitive laboratory methods to assess molecular and neurophysiological processes. The advent of effective pharmacological treatments and promising methods to assess the neurobiological substrates of the major psychiatric disorders further fostered renewed interest in the reliability and validity of psychiatric diagnosis. Indeed, the whole notion of the diagnostic use of laboratory testing methods is dependent upon the existence of reliable clinical diagnosis (4). It is accurate to state that prior to 1970, psychiatric diagnosis of most of the major disorders was, at best, not very reliable (3,5). This major problem is being slowly rectified, beginning with the pioneering studies of the psychiatric research group at Washington University. Such efforts have led to development of the criteria of Feighner et al. (6), the first edition of the Research Diagnostic Criteria (7), the third edition of the American Psychiatric Association's Diagnostic and Statistical Manual (DSM-III) (8), and, most recently, a revised edition of DSM-III (9).

Through the application of such systematic approaches, for the first time, psychiatric diagnoses of several major conditions can be made with a level of reliability comparable to that for many standard medical diagnoses. Such accurately defined conditions include schizophrenia, senile dementia, bipolar affective disorder, major depression, antisocial personality disorder, and panic disorder (5,10). The reliability (and hence, validity) of yet other conditions, such as generalized anxiety disorder, dysthymic disorder, and borderline personality disorder, are less robust but certainly are subject to ongoing investigation. Nevertheless, many major psychiatric disorders can now be assessed clinically with fair to high inter-rater and test-retest reliability (for example, KAPPA coefficients ranging from 0.5 to 0.8) (8), thus providing a more solid foundation for studies employing laboratory parameters.

The particular line of investigation of psychiatric conditions discussed in this volume was originally proposed by Robins and Guze (11) and includes five phases of inquiry: clinical description, laboratory studies, delimitation from other disorders, follow-up study, and family study. Robins and Guze noted a number of scientific advantages for the laboratory phase of study, including objectivity, reliability, precision, and reproducibility of findings. They also were well aware of the necessary caveats of this line of investigation, particularly that the clinical syndrome under study must be well-defined and the laboratory method must be well established and reliable. Particular laboratory areas of interest suggested by these authors included neurochemical, neurophysiological, radiological, and anatomical (biopsy and autopsy). Developments within the past 20 years have broadened the neurochemical area to include studies of neuroendocrine parameters and potential genetic markers. In the next sections of this chapter we will consider: (a) the conceptual basis for the use of laboratory tests in relation to psychiatric diagnosis; (b) the methodological and statistical basis for such assessments; and (c) a brief summary of results reflecting the current state-of-the-art laboratory assessment using two salient examples, major depression and primary degenerative dementia of the Alzheimer type.

CONCEPTUAL ISSUES

Laboratory methods may serve three essential purposes in psychiatric diagnosis: (a) to rule out or to confirm a primary medical pathogenesis for a psychiatric syndrome; (b) as a specific laboratory test to confirm psychiatric diagnosis; and (c) for research on biological processes. The first purpose, which is useful in contemporary differential diagnosis, is both well established and should be a standardized section of every patient's initial assessment. Relevant examples include assessment of thyroid function in a patient with depression, screening for unreported illicit drug use in a patient with a recent onset of psychosis, and cardiovascular evaluation in a patient suffering from severe anxiety. Although such evaluations often are negative in psychiatric patients, failure to perform basic, relevant medical evaluations can easily lead to a failure to correctly diagnose the patient. For example, approximately 15% of new admissions to our own tertiary-care clinical research inpatient unit have a significant unrecognized medical syndrome underlying the presenting diagnosis of affective disorder (12). Consideration of such underlying and/or associated medical illnesses within the differential diagnostic assessment is a hallmark of the medical basis of psychiatry and may help differentiate, at practical and conceptual levels, psychiatric assessment from other forms of behavioral or psychosocial evaluation.

A second major purpose of laboratory methods is to provide relatively accurate laboratory tests to rule out and/or confirm diagnoses of the major psychiatric syndromes. Development of such tests often is a goal of research on the biological disturbances of psychiatric disorders. Such reliable and valid tests could be used for: (a) screening new cases; (b) differential diagnosis; or (c) confirmation of presumed clinical diagnosis. While much research in this area is ongoing, it is our opinion that *no* such standard laboratory tests for routine screening or differential diagnosis are yet available for the principal psychiatric conditions of schizophrenia, the affective disorders, or the anxiety disorders. The research strategy described below suggests a number of steps necessary to develop such laboratory "markers" which, when proven reliable and valid, can be evaluated as tests for clinical diagnostic purposes in psychiatric settings. Once the accuracy of a laboratory parameter is established in research settings, its value as a diagnostic indicator must be further evaluated, both in terms of generalizability and cost-effectiveness.

The third purpose, namely research on biological processes related to the major psychiatric syndromes, is most pertinent to the current status of the field of laboratory studies. Simply put, we still need to know much more about the pathogenesis and pathophysiology of the major psychiatric disorders. As noted above, such research also is a prerequisite for development of meaningful laboratory diagnostic tests. We propose that the biological variable being measured must meet two criteria: (a) it must clearly differentiate the criterion psychopathological group from a relevantly matched healthy control group; and (b) it must distinguish the criterion group from other unrelated psychopathologic conditions. For example, a pertinent research finding on the biology of schizophrenia not only should be able to distinguish individuals with a diagnosis of schizophrenia from age- and sex-matched normal controls, it must also differentiate schizophrenics from individuals with nonpsychotic depression or anxiety states. It is important to keep in mind that most currently psychopathologic classifications are based on description of clinical *syndromes*, not distinct and fully articulated disease states. Therefore, studies of biological factors in various diagnostic groupings should be conducted with an "eye open" to the possibility that smaller subsets of patients within a clinical diagnostic condition may manifest an abnormality not present in the majority of cases. Thus, evaluation of sampling distributions for subgroups of outliers may be quite useful, even though the group mean for the criterion condition may not differ significantly from that of the relevant control groups (13).

We have reviewed elsewhere (14) a number of factors that may compromise the reliable and valid assessment of biological factors in psychiatric conditions. To briefly summarize, such factors include unreliable clinical diagnosis, the contribution of extraneous variables (age, sex, weight loss, menstrual status, or time of day), the nonspecific effects of stress or hospitalization, the direct biological effects of medication, treatment or withdrawal from drugs or alcohol, the confounding effects of intercurrent medical illness, and inaccuracy or unreliability of the biological test parameters being utilized. Given such a wide array of factors which may adversely affect the results of biologic research, it is not surprising that so many false leads and unreplicated findings exist in our field. Suggested solutions to these problems include emphasis of research on conditions for which operationalized, descriptive diagnostic criteria (based on standardized interviews and collateral sources of information) are available, study of carefully matched patients and normal control groups, provision of relatively long medication-free washout periods, careful and definitive medical and neurological evaluations and exclusion of cases with potentially confounding medical conditions prior to research participation, documentation of intra- and inter-assay reliability of the biological parameter being studied, and interlaboratory collaboration and comparisons of laboratory methods whenever possible (14).

We would expect that during the development of a given area of biologic research, sufficient evidence will emerge in time so that a laboratory finding can be evaluated as a diagnostic test. Thus, a logical circularity exists in the sense that an abnormality which is considered to help validate the independence or uniqueness of the psychiatric diagnosis may then be considered for routine clinical use to confirm the diagnosis. In our opinion, such a circular strategy is not problematic when the biological parameter has been exhaustively studied in a variety of research settings *and* when it has first been determined to discriminate the criterion condition from both normal controls and other psychopathologic conditions. We consider this strategy to be no more circular than the notion that the demonstration of the pneumococcus in sputum samples of some patients (but not others) helps establish the validity of pneumococcal pneumonia from other types of lower respiratory infection, and the use of sputum samples either confirms or rules out a clinical diagnosis of pneumococcal pneumonia. Logical circularity does prove problematic, however, when the value of a biologic parameter is asserted before sufficient evidence is available to show clearly that it regularly occurs in the criterion group more often than in other psychopathological groups. Examples of this problem may include the overzealous clinical application of the dexamethasone suppression test following promising early findings (see, for example, the discussion by Carroll [15]) or use of nocturnal penile tumescence studies as the "gold standard" for assessment of presumably irreversible organic erectile dysfunction (e.g., Thase et al. [16]).

Following the precise demonstration that a laboratory abnormality is found in a significant portion of individuals with a given diagnosis *but not* in a substantial proportion of normal controls or patients in other psychopathologic groups, it must be considered whether the abnormality exists as part of the etiopathogenesis of a condition or whether the abnormality reflects a correlate or epiphenomenon of having the condition. An example of the latter might be a biologic abnormality which is caused directly by weight loss rather than reflecting an underlying physiologic process of the depression that causes the weight loss. Research directly controlling for the possible intervening variable (i.e., using normal dieters as a control group) is instrumental in clarifying the significance of epiphenomenal effects (17,18). Abnormalities which prove to be of etiopathological significance obviously will have greater relevance in the ultimate understanding of the psychiatric condition being studied. Nevertheless, study of epiphenomenal variables still may lead to relevant advances in knowledge and, if the phenomenon is sufficiently frequent in the index condition but not in other conditions, may have practical utility as a laboratory test.

STATISTICAL CONCERNS

A primary consideration in the evaluation of biological abnormalities in psychiatric conditions is, as noted above, the reliability of the clinical diagnosis of the condition being studied. We perseverate on this issue because of its importance; the validity of a laboratory method is constrained by the reliability of the clinical diagnosis of the patients being studied. For the foreseeable future, the "gold standard" then must continue to be clinical diagnosis. And, while we seek laboratory evidence to improve the objectivity and reliability of our assessments, our research efforts in the interim are no more meaningful than the reliability of current clinical diagnosis allows. From this standpoint, the term "gold standard" is indeed misleading since clinical diagnoses of all medical conditions are fallible.

Other statistical concerns pertinent to development of laboratory parameters for psychiatric study include sampling techniques and the choice of analytic methods to assess potential differences between groups. With respect to sampling concerns, clinical diagnosis must be determined absolutely independent of knowledge of the laboratory parameter being studied. Otherwise the investigation is biased in favor of finding a significant relationship, which may not prove to be valid in the long run.

Tests selected for statistical assessment of laboratory differences between conditions should, of course, be appropriate to the data available. For example, biologic variables often are not normally distributed; hence, statistical comparisons utilizing tests which require normal distribution of data should not be performed. Appropriate transformation techniques and nonparametric techniques are available for use in those cases. This approach would be useful in comparisons of laboratory test results within the various subtype groupings of major depression, comparing patients with a given subtype diagnosis (e.g., psychotic depression) with those with other subforms of depression.

Diagnostic performance frequently is summarized using the following descriptive terms: sensitivity, specificity, and predictive value (19). Such values have utility in communicating the ability of a given laboratory parameter to correctly identify true cases and to rule out cases without the index condition, as well as reflecting the proportion of cases with an abnormal test value who have the index condition and the proportion of cases with negative test results who do not have the index condition. It should be appreciated, however, that these values are not constant and are dependent on a number of factors, including the sample, the comparison group being studied, and the accuracy of the clinical diagnosis and laboratory procedures being evaluated (20). Further, these statistics are influenced by the prevalence of the index condition (e.g., schizophrenia or endogenous depression) within the population under study. Another frequently used statistical technique is the weighted KAPPA coefficient, although KAPPA is more appropriate for measuring reliability than validity.

CONSIDERATION OF TWO SALIENT EXAMPLES

The proliferation of laboratory investigations of the major mental disorders during the past decade has been striking, and a comprehensive review of this area would be the appropriate subject of a volume (or two) rather than a chapter! We have accordingly focused our discussion on two important and common neuropsychiatric conditions, major depression and primary degenerative dementia (Alzheimer's disease). These conditions are reliably diagnosed, yet their etiologies remain uncertain and essential aspects of their pathophysiologies have not yet been identified. Moreover, since primary degenerative dementia (PDD) has a demonstrable microscopic neuropathology (and depression does not), it serves as a useful point of comparison about the strengths and limitations of laboratory methods circa 1988.

Major Depression

The clinical diagnosis of the major affective disorders is made with a relatively high degree of reliability (6-10), thus meeting a basic requirement for valid laboratory study. Moreover, since the major affective disorders are characterized by a variety of disturbances in physiological functioning (including sleep, motor activity, appetite, and libido), the pursuit of studies of potential biologic mechanisms is conceptually appealing. Such interest is fueled further by the genetic association in several forms of the major affective disorders, particularly bipolar affective disorder and early-onset forms of major depression (21). Finally, evidence of the efficacy of various forms of somatic treatment for the major affective disorders strengthens the intuitive and conceptual evidence for the role of biological factors in these conditions. In the following paragraphs we will briefly consider the laboratory evidence for validation of the diagnosis of major depression, following the suggested parameters of Robins and Guze (11).

Autopsy Results

Studies of postmortem brain specimens by gross anatomical and microscopic methods in individuals who have died during or following an episode of major depression have failed to yield any specific evidence to support the validity of this diagnostic grouping (Table 1). More recently, investigators have applied neurochemical methods to the study of material obtained at autopsy. Such studies are limited by a variety of methodological factors, including medication exposure, the cause of death, and the length of time between death and laboratory study. Preliminary evidence does suggest reduced serotonergic function in the brains of recently deceased depressed individuals, including reduced levels of 5-hydroxyindoleacetic acid (22), decreased number of imipramine binding sites (23) and increased serotonin (5HT-2) binding activity (24), and increased beta-adrenergic binding activity

TABLE 1. *Laboratory evidence of validity of major depression*

A. Autopsy Methods
  1. Lack of gross and microscopic evidence
  2. Neurochemical studies
    a) Reduced IMI-binding sites
    b) Increased $5HT_2$-binding activity
    c) Increased Beta-adrenergic binding activity
    d) Link to suicide
B. Radiologic methods
  1. Lack of specific anatomical findings
  2. PET findings
    —Specific vs. nonspecific
    —Comparison vs. schizophrenia
C. Neurophysiological correlates
  1. Waking EEG
    a) Spectral analysis
    b) BEAM
    c) Evoked potentials
  2. Sleep EEG
    a) Depressed vs. normal
    b) Depressed vs. other psychopathological states
    c) Depressed vs. remitted
    d) Treatment correlates
  3. Motor activity measures
    a) Depression vs. mania
    b) Facial EMG
  4. Electrodermal activity
    a) Depression vs. other states
    b) Depression vs. remission
    c) Relationship to suicide
D. Neuroendocrine studies
  1. HPA axis
    a) Hypercortisolemia
    b) DST nonsuppression
    c) CRF, ACTH
    d) Relative specificity—other states
    e) Clinical subgroups
  2. Thyroid axis
    a) TRH-stimulation test
    b) Relative specificity
    c) Depression vs. remission
  3. Other parameters
E. Neurochemical studies
  1. Diminished MHPG
  2. Diminished 5-HIAA
  3. Increased adrenergic output
  4. Serotonin binding sites
  5. Muscarinic probes
  6. Clinical correlates
  7. Specificity
F. Clinical boundaries
  1. Dysthymic disorder
  2. Personality disorders
  3. Anxiety disorders
  4. Schizoaffective disorder
  5. Eating disorders

(24). These findings are of keen interest since comparable observations have been made in studies of living individuals with affective disorders (22) and because these variables are affected by antidepressant treatment. The most compelling evidence for such differences at autopsy comes from the brains of depressed individuals who have completed suicide by violent means (22,23). Determining whether these neurochemical findings are more related to depression than to suicidality will require further investigations in this methodologically difficult area.

Radiographic Findings

To date, the lack of any gross or anatomical lesion present at autopsy in the brains of individuals with a diagnosis of major depression has been paralleled by a lack of positive findings by radiologic methods which permit *in vivo* assessment of brain structure in living individuals with affective disorder. Of course, methods such as skull x-rays, computed tomography (CT), and nuclear magnetic resonance (NMR) imaging can prove invaluable in the differential diagnosis of organic affective syndromes secondary to brain trauma, tumors, or other cerebral pathology. Also, such studies have shown promise in assessing the prognosis of individuals with an affective disorder. For example, there is evidence that cortical atrophy (a nonspecific finding detected by either CT or NMR scans) is associated with poorer outcome and increased mortality in older depressed individuals (25).

Recently, the development of the positron emission tomography (PET) method has been of considerable interest, since this form of brain imaging permits both structural and functional assessments (Table 1). Several studies of individuals suffering from depression suggest altered cerebral metabolic activity (26,27). One particularly interesting finding is the increased nondominant hemispheric cerebral glucose metabolism in some depressed individuals as compared to normal controls or patients with schizophrenia (27). However, decreased frontal glucose metabolism has been found in both schizophrenia and affective disorders (26-28). Thus, there are data from PET studies which suggest both the validity of depression and that it includes nonspecific disturbances. Investigations employing the PET scan have yet to be done in substantial numbers of depressed outpatients, a crucial group, since less severely depressed patients constitute the largest group of individuals suffering from mood disorders. Longitudinal study of depressed individuals during *and* following treatment also will be essential, as will the study of bipolar patients in depressed, remitted, and manic states.

Electroencephalographic Studies

Among potential neurophysiological correlates of mood disorder, waking electroencephalograms (EEG) have received extensive study (Table 1). Routine waking EEG studies are useful to rule out cerebral pathology which may cause an organic affective syndrome. More advanced technology permits studies employing spectral analysis, evoked potential, and, more recently, brain electrical activity mapping (BEAM) methods (29). Some topographical studies have shown abnormal lateralization of waking EEG rhythms in depression (30,31). Although these findings have not been consistently replicated (29), they are consonant with the preliminary evidence from subgroups of depressed patients studied with PET scans noted above and are pertinent to theories of nondominant hemispheric lateralization in depression (32). Research employing computer-assisted methods to determine average EEG response amplitude suggests an approximate 25% reduction in average amplitude in depression (reviewed in Kupfer and Reynolds [29]). However, one relatively large and well-done study employing this method found little discrimination between manic and schizophrenic individuals or between nonpsychotic depressives and personality-disordered controls (33). No specific pattern of altered evoked-potentials associated with depression has emerged, although there is evidence that differences in P_{100} (i.e., "augmenter" vs. "reducer" patterns) may discriminate between bipolar and unipolar depressions (34), and increased latency and decreased amplitude of P_{300} may be related to cognitive or information processing difficulties in severely depressed inpatients (35).

All-night recordings of EEG rhythms during sleep initially were utilized to document the characteristic sleep disturbances of depressed individuals (4); however, the correlations between clinical ratings of sleep disturbances and EEG recordings are less robust than one would hope, and EEG sleep variables such as sleep latency, amount of wakefulness, and slow-wave sleep time do not substantially discriminate between depressed individuals and those suffering from other major psychiatric disorders (4). Therefore, we now consider these indicators to be relatively nonspecific. Available evidence indicates that sleep continuity disturbances normalize upon recovery from depression, whereas diminished slow sleep may persist for months following recovery (36).

Greater evidence of specific EEG sleep disturbances has emerged with respect to rapid eye movement sleep variables, such as the latency to the onset of the first REM sleep (REM latency) and the "density" of the first REM (4,36). For example, abnormally diminished REM latency (i.e., less than 60 minutes for younger patients or less than 40 minutes for patients over the age of 50) is found in between 50-90% of various samples of depressed patients, but in fewer than 20% of normal controls (4,36). Further, the combination of two REM variables, such as REM latency and REM density, may heighten discrimination between depressed patients and other comparison groups (37). Shortened REM latency has received other forms of external validation as a useful marker of major depression, at least of depressions of a more severe or autonomous nature, in family history studies (38) and in longitudinal studies of subsyndromal cases (39), drug treatment response (40,41), patients showing poor response to intensive inpatient milieu treatment (42) or to cognitive therapy (43), and risk of relapse (44). Antidepressant pharmacotherapy prolongs REM latency and reduces REM sleep time. Withdrawal from medication after recovery is followed by a return of shortened REM latency even in the absence of depressive symptoms (36). Underlying pathophysiological mechanisms linking aberrant REM sleep with other biological disturbances in depression also have been proposed (4,36).

Shortened REM latency would be a more valuable marker of major depression were not similarly reduced values found in other clinical populations, including patients with obsessive compulsive disorder (45), schizophrenia (46), mania (47), borderline personality disorder (48), and narcolepsy (49), as well as in relatively large numbers of healthy older individuals (50), and were it consistently found in prepubertal depressions, but it is not (14). Its appearance in mania is no problem, since mania and depression are both part of bipolar disorder (4). While the association with other disorders is not uniform (a recent study of younger, never-medicated schizophrenic patients failed to document significant REM sleep disturbances [51]), several of these conditions in which it appears have been linked to the boundary of an affective disorder spectrum (36). The interaction of aging and EEG sleep is well described and should be taken into account in a detailed way in any investigation employing older subjects (50).

Given their less than perfect sensitivity or specificity, REM sleep abnormalities may prove to be biological phenomena which help to validate the existence of depression as a disorder but do not prove useful as a straightforward laboratory test of depression. Further, the expense and inconvenience of EEG sleep studies might mitigate against their routine clinical use even if their diagnostic accuracy was substantial.

Motor Activity Measures

Other neurophysiologic techniques which have been employed in the study of depressed individuals include motor activity measures (52), facial electromyographic recording (53), electrodermal activity (54), and measurement of smooth pursuit eye movement activity (55). Depressed individuals often have served as a psychopathologic control group for the study of eye movement activity in schizophrenia. Such studies show that depressed individuals do *not* have the frequency or severity of smooth pursuit eye movement disorder that schizophrenic patients do (55), and that they do not differ from normals on this variable.

Motor activity studies generally have been found to support the distinction between agitated and retarded depressions, although such findings do not directly validate the existence of depression as a unique entity (14). Preliminary evidence from several groups does suggest a pattern of diminished electrodermal activity in depression that is distinct from observations in schizophrenia, most patients with anxiety disorders, and normal controls (54,56,57). This pattern is related most clearly to the presence of psychomotor agitation or psychomotor retardation, a cardinal feature of significant depression, and appears to persist in remission. In one study, the pattern of diminished electrodermal responsivity was present in very mild and chronic depressions as well as in more severe states (57).

Neuroendocrine Studies

Intensive study of a variety of neuroendocrine parameters in affective disorders has taken place over the past two decades (see Table 1). These studies have been of key importance, primarily because of the close interrelationship between the limbic system and mechanisms of neuroendocrine regulation involving the hypothalamus and pituitary gland.

Perhaps the best studied neuroendocrine axis has been the hypothalamic-pituitary-adrenal cortex (HPA) axis. Study of this area was fostered by initial observations of hypercortisolemia in depressed patients, as well as of a high frequency of affective syndromes in individuals with Cushing's disease. At this time, it is reasonable to conclude that a significant subset of severely depressed patients will show one or more abnormalities of the HPA axis. Commonly, such abnormalities will include hypercortisolemia and/or failure to suppress cortisol levels following administration of 1 or 2 mg dexamethasone (58). In most studies, the rates of test abnormality in depression are substantially higher than those seen in normal controls and are generally higher than rates seen in other psychopathologic populations (58-60). The significance of these findings in establishing the existence of objective biological correlates in depressive syndromes should not be underestimated, although attempts to develop routine clinical diagnostic tests based on these findings, such as the dexamethasone suppression test (DST), have not proved of immediate practical benefit (60). Nevertheless, simply from the heuristic value of the research fostered in this area, the widespread interest in the DST has been quite important (see Chapter 14).

Large and detailed studies of HPA parameters are now available from a number of research centers. These studies indicate that assessments are relatively reliable over a short period of time and that the abnormality (i.e., hypercortisolemia or dexamethasone nonsuppression) is relatively state dependent (58-60). That is, effective treatment of the affective syndrome results in resolution of the abnormality in a high proportion of cases. Preliminary evidence suggests that when recovery following treatment occurs without normalization of these parameters, there may be a high risk of clinical relapse (61,62). A number of studies have attempted to relate HPA abnormalities, particularly dexamethasone nonsuppression, to response to particular somatic treatments (see Yerevanian [63]). Results of such studies have been inconsistent and, therefore, cannot be viewed as adding information concerning the validity of depressive disorder diagnoses. However, patients with dexamethasone nonsuppression may be less likely to respond to placebo interventions, suggesting that they may have depressions which require biological treatment (64). This important finding supports the validity of at least one biologically defined subgroup of depressed patients.

Studies of HPA parameters in other psychopathologic groups, including patients with obsessive compulsive disorder, schizophrenia, and mania, have yielded somewhat inconsistent findings but overall suggest an intermediate proportion of abnormal cases (59,60). These results indicate that HPA abnormalities are not absolutely specific to depression and that HPA function may be related to stress, in addition to some more particular relationship with depression. Depressed patients who are DST nonsuppressors are especially likely to show evidence of EEG sleep disturbance, particularly shortened REM latency (14).

Within the clinical subgroups of depression, there are relatively consistent relationships of dexamethasone nonsuppression and, to a lesser extent, of hypercortisolemia with clinical severity, weight loss, the presence of agitation and/or anxiety, and the presence of psychotic features (59,60). Thus, the particular behavioral dimension of depression associated with dexamethasone nonsuppression or hypercortisolemia may relate to a more global construct such as severity or central nervous system arousal. Interestingly, harsh dieting with significant (5 to 10 kg) weight loss or alcoholic withdrawal states may induce a transient mimicking of this phenomenon (60).

A second neuroendocrine area which has received extensive study involves regulation of the thyroid axis. Clinical evidence of a high incidence of depression in individuals with thyroid disease sparked clinical curiosity about this relationship. While there is no specific alteration in the amount of thyroid hormone in individuals with depression, acute depressive states often are associated with a transient increase in thyroid hormone level which does not exceed the normal range (65). There is speculation that increased thyroid activity may be a partial compensation for some other biologic process ongoing in depression (66).

One dynamic test of thyroid function which has received extensive study is the thyroid releasing hormone (TRH) stimulation test (65,67). Abnormally blunted pituitary response to TRH stimulation has been consistently observed in a significant minority (20 to 40%) of depressed individuals. This abnormality is not related to coarse thyroid pathology and often does not normalize immediately following acute treatment. Blunted TRH stimulation test responses unfortunately are not specific to depression, but are also observed in relatively high frequency in schizophrenia (68) and in alcoholism (69). This observation again suggests a commonality between a biological process in several psychopathologic states, with perhaps an increased liability for this abnormality in depression. Studies following somatic treatment have provided some preliminary evidence of high risk for relapse in individuals with blunted TRH stimulation test results, both in depression and schizophrenia (70).

Other neuroendocrine parameters which have received less extensive study include regulation of growth hormone secretion, prolactin regulation, and the pineal hormone melatonin (see Thase et al. [14]). Evidence of disturbances in each of these parameters or systems in depression has been reported, adding to the overall weight of evidence that depression is associated with a variety of neuroendocrine disturbances. But none of these findings has been consistently replicated or is robust enough at this point to directly support the validity of depression.

Neurochemical Studies

Neurochemical studies of affective disorders are of special historical importance, since catecholamines and serotonin metabolites were the first biologic parameters to be investigated in a consistent and methodical way (Table 1). The initial hypothesis was that diminished levels of norepinephrine or serotonin in the brain were central to the etiology of depression (71-73). Indeed, demonstration that tricyclic antidepressants and monoamine oxidase inhibitors had significant effects on these systems and that other agents which depleted monoaminergic activity, such as reserpine, could induce depression strengthened the intuitive appeal of studying these monoamines. Unfortunately, the methodologic difficulty of such studies was manifold. One analogy offered was that evaluating peripheral levels of excretion of monoamine metabolites is much like a detective's evaluating the garbage of a suspect in order to obtain clues!

The initial hypothesis of a simple reduction in brain norepinephrine or serotonin in depression has not been confirmed. However, subgroups of depressed patients do show diminished monoamine metabolites, such as low levels of excretion of urinary 3-methoxy, 4-hydroxy phenelethyleneglycol (MHPG) (74) or diminished cerebrospinal levels of 5-hydroxyindoleacetic acid (5-HIAA) (75). Moreover, these low values have been associated with increased responsivity to the antidepressants imipramine and amitriptyline (74,75). Such findings suggest that depression is heterogeneous and they therefore throw doubts on the validity of the depression diagnosis.

More recently, considerable evidence has emerged that significant depressive syndromes, particularly those which lead to inpatient hospitalization, are associated with increased adrenergic output (76-78). Also, the clinical effect of antidepressant treatment appears to be down-regulation of this system when it is in "overdrive" (79,80). Studies involving correlational methods have linked this overdrive state with parameters such as agitation, psychic distress, and increased HPA activity (77,81-83). Whether or not such an overdrive state is related to an attempt to respond homeostatically to some initial deficit state remains a speculation.

Other neurochemical studies have focused on the relationship between two additional brain neurotransmitters, dopamine and acetylcholine. The significance to the mood disorders of dopamine, which historically had been linked more closely to the etiology of schizophrenia, is slowly being appreciated. Indeed, the relationship of dopamine with psychomotor activity in depression and mania is increasingly being studied (81,84). Investigation of acetylcholine has been hampered by the very ubiquitous nature of this tiny molecule. Nevertheless, new methods employing various probes and challenges have shown promise, such as the use of muscarinic agonists and antagonists to probe or challenge physiologic systems (85-87). An excellent example of this model involves the use of arecoline infusions to induce the onset of rapid eye movement sleep episodes (87). It appears that depressed individuals, both during an episode and when in remission, show unique sensitivity to arecoline infusions. Further study in appropriately matched psychopathologic controls is necessary in order to consider these findings of substantial importance to the validation of mood disorder diagnoses.

Clinical Boundaries

A final area of clinical significance concerning the use of laboratory parameters in validating mood disorder diagnoses specifically deals with what had been referred to as the "boundary" conditions related to affective disorders (Table 1). In current practice, these conditions include dysthymic disorder, various personality disorders (with borderline personality disorder being the most pertinent), anxiety states, schizoaffective disorder, and eating disorders. Each of these conditions has been linked to the mood disorders spectrum on the basis of multiple variables, including treatment response and family history, and such linkage has been supported by documentation of higher than expected (in comparison to normal controls) rates of biologic test abnormality. Major investigations of these areas often have employed the DST, TRH stimulation test, or EEG sleep studies, and in rare cases some combination of these parameters. An interesting example is the contrast between obsessive-compulsive disorder (45,88) and more chronic, low-grade generalized anxiety disorders (89,90), where obsessive-compulsive disorder appears to show greater liability to the correlates of depression than do the generalized anxious states. Because of the risk of applying circular logic discussed earlier, however, we would caution that our knowledge of biological processes in more clear-cut cases of depression is sufficiently limited at this point that all hypotheses concerning the boundary zone conditions should remain open and subject to the results of further study.

Depression Summary

In summary, there is now substantial evidence of a variety of disturbances of neurophysiological, neuroendocrine, and neurochemical processes in depression. Taken together, the weight of these findings indeed supports the conclusion that depression can be validly distinguished from both other key psychopathologic states (most particularly schizophrenia) and from normality. Nevertheless, the evidence does not indicate that depression should be viewed, biologically, as a unitary process or as an illness with one cause and one pathophysiology. If these biologic studies are applied to test the "one cause-one pathogenesis" hypothesis, such a hypothesis would be rejected. In its place, we advocate a heterogeneity hypothesis, and suggest that efforts focused on detailed studies of clinical phenomenology, treatment response, longitudinal course, and biologic processes continue. We know that key clinical correlates of selected biologic disturbances include suicidality (particularly of a violent and extreme nature), psychomotor disturbances, particular forms of sleep disturbance, and the presence of psychosis. Thus, subtypes of mood disorder from the clinical sphere may be associated with subgroups with various abnormalities from the biological sphere. That this overlap between clinical subtypes and biological subgroups is not perfect should not be surprising.

Primary Degenerative Dementia

As mentioned earlier, we selected primary degenerative dementia (PDD) as a counterpoint for discussion largely because a distinct neuropathology has been known for this condition for over 80 years (91). It is also a condition that is, in terms of lifetime expected prevalence, roughly comparable to major depression and is associated with profound morbidity and mortality (92). Like depression, extensive biologic investigation has been directed toward improving clinical diagnosis, gaining better knowledge of the pathophysiology, and development of more effective treatment. Although Alzheimer's disease was recognized as a specific entity long before categorical definitions of major depression, we are further ahead with depression in terms of developing effective treatments. This is true in part because depression tends to be episodic and its symptoms are reversible, whereas Alzheimer's disease is progressive and associated with clinical and neuropathological deterioration.

Autopsy Studies

As demonstrated by autopsy findings, the neuropathology of Alzheimer's disease includes generalized cortical atrophy and, at a microscopic level, neuronal loss, neuritic plaques in the grey matter, perivascular amyloid deposits, and neurofibrillary tangles (e.g., see Katzman [92]). The structure of the amyloid protein found in the senile plaques is identical to that found in the perivascular deposits. The interest in this structure has heightened over the past few years following the identification of the precise molecular structure of brain amyloid polypeptide (93). Despite the relatively characteristic nature of this pathology, only within the past two decades has Alzheimer's disease been recognized as the major cause of what used to be referred to as senility. In earlier generations, what we now know as PDD or Alzheimer's disease often was thought to be due to cerebrovascular disease (92).

The clinical syndrome of PDD is documented with relatively good clinical reliability (KAPPA values of approximately 0.6 [8] and test/retest reliabilities on the order of 80% [94]). Similarly, a clinical diagnosis of PDD is supported at autopsy between 80 to 90% of the time. Thus, PDD can serve as a clinical model of a neuropsychiatric syndrome with relatively good clinical diagnostic precision and relatively accurate laboratory detection at postmortem. A major clinical challenge is introduced by the comorbidity of PDD with other potential illnesses; an extensive laboratory battery is necessary to rule out the multiple other causes of dementia which are potentially reversible. It is indeed a tragedy when a presumptive clinical diagnosis of Alzheimer's disease leads to therapeutic inaction. Other clinical diagnostic problems include the differentiation of PDD from the cognitive impairment (pseudodementia) of depression in the elderly. A final area of concern to the pathologist is the need for accurate threshold and severity criteria in order to distinguish between the early phases of dementia and changes due to normal aging, since a few senile plaques and neurofibrillary tangles are commonly seen in the brains of apparently normal aged individuals (92).

Radiologic Methods

Radiologic methods have served importantly in clinical research to visualize *in vivo* possible early signs of PDD. Unfortunately, while cortical atrophy is a hallmark pathological finding of Alzheimer's disease, it is not so specific that CT or NMR findings can be used with a high degree of diagnostic confidence (95,96); too many false-positive cases are detected. Positron emission tomography scans appear to have great promise (97); however, the necessary normative studies in healthy aged individuals are only now underway. It remains to be seen whether more molecular applications of the NMR and PET technology of membrane and receptor phenomenon (98) will be of particular value.

Neurophysiology

Neurophysiology parameters considerably studied have included waking EEG rhythms, which generally document a reduction of main amplitude and a generalized slowing of dominant EEG rhythms (99,100). But again, the specificity of such findings has not been sufficient to make EEG assessments the definitive diagnostic test for Alzheimer's disease. Studies involving evoked potentials have documented slowing of the P_{300} response in Alzheimer's disease as they have in depression, and such studies show promise for practical application (101). Nevertheless, it is unclear at this point if the evoked potential methodology can discriminate between mild early dementia and depression in an elderly individual. Further, the range of normal variation in the healthy aged on this parameter is not yet well known.

EEG sleep studies have shown some differences between demented and depressed individuals, with dementia characterized by less marked shortening of REM sleep latency and a greater proportion of indeterminate stage sleep (49, 50,102). The critical issue here is whether these differences could be used to discriminate cases with dementia alone from cases of dementia plus depression, given the high incidence of depression in the early phase of primary degenerative dementia (102).

Neurochemical Studies

Neurochemical studies have amply documented the reduction of cholinergic neurons in the brains of demented individuals, particularly in the hippocampal areas (103-105). In addition, there appear to be reductions in noradrenergic and dopaminergic systems (103,104). The frustrations of interpreting neurochemical research are amply documented by these investigations since substantial deficits found at postmortem have yet to be measured precisely and practically *in vivo*. Various neuroendocrine parameters, such as dexamethasone nonsuppression, are abnormal in some cases of Alzheimer's and multi-infarct dementia (106), but less frequently than in depressions. Studies of neuroendocrine markers linked to circadian rhythms have helped to document the clinical observation of altered sleep/wake cycles in senile dementia (106).

New and exciting methods of locating gene markers are now being applied in the investigation of Alzheimer's disease. The most dramatic example of the promise of this methodology can be seen in the identification of the gene which codes for the amyloid polypeptide on chromosome #21 (107,108). Identification of the molecular sequence of amyloid polypeptide in the early 1980s, coupled with the finding of an association between Alzheimer's disease and Down syndrome (109), steered investigators to focus on chromosome #21 as the site of a possibly abnormal gene. In the relatively short time that has followed identification of the amyloid polypeptide, the gene coding for the precursor of the amyloid polypeptide was located in the Q-21 region of the long arm of chromosome #21 (107,108), and genetic linkage studies found a defect in the chromosomal region adjacent to #21 Q-21 in individuals with a clearly familial type of Alzheimer's disease (110). The first hypothesis directly related to the etiology of Alzheimer's disease was that the amyloid gene was duplicated in all individuals with PDD, as it is duplicated in all individuals with the trisomic form of Down syndrome (109). Unfortunately, this hypothesis has not been supported in either sporadic or familial forms of PDD (111-113). Nevertheless, the localization of a suspected area of high likelihood for an aberrant genetic finding will allow other potential markers to be tested. One candidate has been suggested by the finding of an apparently genetically mediated trait controlling membrane fluidity (114). Therefore, it is likely that location of the gene responsible for Alzheimer's disease will soon be known.

Dementia Summary

This brief review of the laboratory methods used in the study of Alzheimer's disease highlights a number of different parameters showing evidence of abnormalities. But even with abundant laboratory evidence for the validity of Alzheimer's disease, laboratory studies are not precise and accurate enough to provide a definitive laboratory test to be used on living patients. At present, the major clinical value of laboratory methods is to rule out other possible causes of dementia, very much like the major current clinical role of laboratory testing for depression. Laboratory studies (CT, NMR, EEG evoked potential, waking EEG, and so forth) have only a *relative* sensitivity and specificity, despite the clear-cut neuropathology. As mentioned above, it seems likely that molecular genetic mechanisms may shortly allow a more specific laboratory test, although the possibility that clinical heterogeneity is related to specific biochemical and/or genetic forms of PDD will need to be addressed in detail (115,116).

SUMMARY

In this chapter we have reviewed many of the historical, conceptual, and statistical issues related to the use of laboratory methods to validate neuropsychiatric diagnosis. Our review of two pertinent clinical examples, major depression and primary degenerative dementia, was conducted to emphasize the promise and importance of these studies as well as the pitfalls and difficulties encountered in performing them. There certainly are substantial grounds for optimism regarding the outcome of future studies. However, at this time, no basis exists for biological or laboratory chauvinism, particularly in the area of major depression. Integrative studies in the future, including those employing the simultaneous assessment of family history, treatment response, early adverse psychosocial experiences, current life stress, and personality style will undoubtedly be of considerable value in understanding the clinical and biological heterogeneity not only of major depression, but also of a majority of the other major neuropsychiatric syndromes. This may be less the case in Alzheimer's disease. A faith that laboratory tests will be the most important component of future studies may be of value in establishing a movement and in ensuring its initial success, but in the long run, investigators have to take a multidimensional or a multifactorial perspective in order to understand complex clinical phenomena.

ACKNOWLEDGMENTS

This work was supported in part by National Institute of Mental Health grants MH-24652, MH-30915, MH-41884, and a grant from the John D. and Catherine T. MacArthur Foundation Research Network on the Psychobiology of Depression.

REFERENCES

1. Akiskal, H. S. (1978): Introduction: Biological prediction in psychiatry. In: *Psychiatric Diagnosis: Exploration of Biological Predictors*, edited by H. S. Akiskal and W. L. Webb, pp. 1–8. Spectrum, New York.
2. Eisdorfer, C., Cohen, D., Kleinman, A., and Maxim, P. (1981): *Models for Clinical Psychopathology*. Spectrum, New York.

3. Mischel, W. (1968): *Personality and Assessment*. John Wiley & Sons, New York.
4. Kupfer, D. J., and Thase, M. E. (1987): Validity of major depression: A psychobiological perspective. In: *Diagnosis and Classification in Psychiatry: A Critical Appraisal of DSM-III*, edited by G. L. Tischler, pp. 32–60. Cambridge University Press, New York.
5. Matarazzo, J. D. (1983): The reliability of psychiatric and psychological diagnosis. *Clin Psychol Rev*, 3:103–145.
6. Feighner, J. P., Robins, E., Guze, S. B., Woodruff, R. A., Winokur, G., and Munoz, R. (1972): Diagnostic criteria for use in psychiatric research. *Arch Gen Psychiatry*, 26:57–63.
7. Spitzer, R. L., Endicott, J., and Robins, E. (1978): Research diagnostic criteria. *Arch Gen Psychiatry*, 34:773–782.
8. American Psychiatric Association. (1980): *Diagnostic and Statistical Manual of Mental Disorders*, 3rd edition. American Psychiatric Association, Washington, D.C.
9. American Psychiatric Association. (1987): *Diagnostic and Statistical Manual of Mental Disorders*, 3rd edition revised. American Psychiatric Association, Washington, D.C.
10. Spitzer, R. L., Fleiss, J. L., and Endicott, J. (1978): Problems of classification: Reliability and validity. In: *Psychopharmacology: A Generation of Progress*, edited by M. A. Lipton, A. DiMascio, and K. F. Killam, pp. 857–869. Raven Press, New York.
11. Robins, E., and Guze, S. B. (1970): Establishment of diagnostic validity in psychiatric illness: Its application to schizophrenia. *Am J Psychiatry*, 126:107–111.
12. Kupfer, D. J., and Spiker, D. G. (1981): Refractory depression: Prediction of nonresponse by clinical indicators. *J Clin Psychiatry*, 42:307–312.
13. Buchsbaum, M. S., and Rieder, R. O. (1979): Biological heterogeneity and psychiatric research. *Arch Gen Psychiatry*, 36:1163–1169.
14. Thase, M. E., Frank, E., and Kupfer, D. J. (1985): Biological processes in major depression. In: Beckham, E. E., Leber, W. R., eds., Homewood: Dorsey Press, pp. 816–913.
15. Carroll, B. J. (1985): Dexamethasone suppression test: A review of contemporary confusion. *J Clin Psychiatry*, 46:13–24.
16. Thase, M. E., Reynolds, C. F., Glanz, L. M., Jennings, J. R., Sewitch, D. E., and Kupfer, D. J. (1987): Nocturnal penile tumescence in depressed men. *Am J Psychiatry*, 144:89–92.
17. Edelstein, C. K., Roy-Byrne, P., Fawzy, F. I., and Dornfeld, L. (1983): Effects of weight loss on the dexamethasone suppression test. *Am J Psychiatry*, 140:338–341.
18. Mullen, P. E., Linsell, C. R., and Parker D. (1986): Influence of sleep disruption and calorie restriction in biological markers for depression. *Lancet*, 2:1051–1055.
19. Galen, R. S., and Gambino, S. R. (1975): *Beyond Normality: The Predictive Value and Efficiency of Medical Diagnoses*. John Wiley & Sons, New York.
20. Kraemer, H. C. (1987): The methodological and statistical evaluation of medical tests: The dexamethasone suppression test in psychiatry. *Psychoneuroendocrinology*, 12:411–427.
21. Blehar, M. C., Weissman, M. M., Gershon, E. S., and Hirschfeld, R. M. A. (1988): Family and genetic studies of affective disorders. *Arch Gen Psychiatry*, 45:289–292.
22. Van Praag, H. M. (1982): Neurotransmitters and CNS disease: Depression. *Lancet*, 2:1259–1264.
23. Stanley, M., Vigilio, J., and Gershon, S. (1982): Tritiated imipramine binding sites are decreased in the frontal cortex of suicides. *Science*, 216:1337–1339.
24. Mann, J. J., Stanley, M., McBride, P. A., and McEwen, B. S. (1986): Increased serotonin$_2$ and B-adrenergic receptor binding in the frontal cortices of suicide victims. *Arch Gen Psychiatry*, 43:954–959.
25. Jacoby, R. J., and Levy, R. (1980): Computed tomography in the elderly: 3. Affective disorder. *Br J Psychiatry*, 136:270–275.
26. Baxter, L. R., Phelps, M. E., Mazziotta, J. C., et al. (1985): Cerebral metabolic rates for glucose in mood disorders. *Arch Gen Psychiatry*, 42:441–447.
27. Buchsbaum, M. S., DeLisi, L. E., Holcomb, H. H., et al. (1984): Anteroposterior gradients in cerebral glucose use in schizophrenia and affective disorder. *Arch Gen Psychiatry*, 41:1159–1166.
28. Buchsbaum, M. S., Ingvar, D. H., Kessler, R., et al. (1982): Cerebral glucography with positron tomography: Use in normal subjects and in patients with schizophrenia. *Arch Gen Psychiatry*, 39:251–259.
29. Kupfer, D. J., and Reynolds, C. F. (1983): Neurophysiologic studies of depression: State of the art. In: *The Origins of Depression: Current Concepts and Approaches*, edited by J. Angst, pp. 235–252. Springer-Verlag, New York.

30. Schaeffer, C. E., Davidson, R. J., and Saron C. (1983): Frontal and parietal electroencephalogram asymmetry in depressed and nondepressed subjects. *Biol Psychiatry*, 18:753–762.
31. Flor-Henry, P., and Koles, Z. J. (1980): EEG studies in depression, mania and normals: Evidence for partial shifts of laterality in the affective psychoses. *Biol Psychiatry*, 4:21–43.
32. Flor-Henry, P. (1979): On certain aspects of the localization of the cerebral systems regulating and determining emotion. *Biol Psychiatry*, 14:677–698.
33. Shagass, C., Amadeo, M., and Overton, D. A. (1974): Eye tracking performance in psychiatric patients. *Biol Psychiatry*, 9:245–260.
34. Buchsbaum, M. S. (1975): Average evoked response augmenting/reducing in schizophrenia and affective disorders. In: *The biology of major psychoses: A comparative analysis*, edited by D. X. Freedman, pp. 129–142. Raven Press, New York.
35. Pfefferbaum, A., Wenegrat, B. G., Ford, J. M., Roth, W. T., and Kopell, B. S. (1984): Clinical application of the P3 component of event related potentials. II. Dementia, depression and schizophrenia. *Electroencephalogr Clin Neurophysiol*, 59:104–124.
36. Thase, M. E., Kupfer, D. J. (1987): Current status of EEG sleep in the assessment and treatment of depression. In: *Advances in Human Psychopharmacology*, vol. IV, edited by G. D. Burrows and J. S. Werry, pp. 93–148. JAI Press, Greenwich, CT.
37. Feinberg, M., Gillin, J. C., Carroll, B. J., Greden, J. P., and Zis, A. P. (1982): EEG studies of sleep in the diagnosis of depression. *Biol Psychiatry*, 17:305–316.
38. Akiskal, H. S. (1981): Subaffective disorders: Dysthymic, cyclothymic, and bipolar II disorders in the "borderline" realm. *Psychiatr Clin North Am*, 4:25–46.
39. Rush, A. J., Erman, M. K., and Schlesser, M. A., et al. (1985): Alprazolam versus amitriptyline in depressions with reduced REM latencies. *Arch Gen Psychiatry*, 42:1154–1159.
40. Rush, A. J., Giles, D. E., Roffwarg, H. P., et al. Predicting response to tricyclic medication in depressed outpatients. *Biol Psychiatry* (in press).
41. Coble, P. A., Kupfer, D. J., Spiker, D. G., Neil, J. F., and McPartland, R. J. (1979): EEG sleep in primary depression: A longitudinal placebo study. *J Affective Disord*, 1:131–138.
42. Thase, M. E., Kupfer, D. J. (1987): Characteristics of treatment-resistant depression. In: *Treating Resistant Depression*, edited by J. Zohar and R. H. Belmaker, pp. 23–45. PMA Publishing Corporation, Great Neck, New York.
43. Giles, D. E., Jarrett, R. B., Roffwarg, H. P., and Rush, A. J. (1987): Reduced rapid eye movement latency: A predictor of recurrence in depression. *Neuropsychopharmacology*, 1:33–49.
44. Giles, D. E., Biggs, M. M., Rush, A. J., and Roffwarg, H. P. (1987): Risk factors in families of unipolar depression. I. Psychiatric illness and reduced REM latency. *J Affective Disord*, 14:51–59.
45. Insel, T. R., Gillin, J. C., Moore, A., Mendelson, W. B., Loewenstein, R. J., and Murphy, D. L. (1982): The sleep of patients with obsessive-compulsive disorder. *Arch Gen Psychiatry*, 39:1372–1377.
46. Zarcone, V. P., Benson, K. L., and Berger, P. A. (1987): Abnormal rapid eye movement latencies in schizophrenia. *Arch Gen Psychiatry*, 44:45–48.
47. Hudson, J. I., Lipinski, J. F., Frankenburg, F. R., Grochocinski, V. J., and Kupfer, D. J. (1988): Electroencephalographic sleep in mania. *Arch Gen Psychiatry*, 45:267–273.
48. McNamara, E., Reynolds, C. F., and Soloff, P. H., et al. (1984): Electroencephalographic sleep evaluation of depression in borderline patients. *Am J Psychiatry*, 141:182–186.
49. Reynolds, C. F., Christiansen, C. L., Taska, L. S., Coble, P. A., and Kupfer, D. J. (1983): Sleep in narcolepsy and depression. Does it all look alike? *J Nerv Ment Dis*, 171:290–295.
50. Reynolds, C. F., Spiker, D. G., Hanin, I., and Kupfer, D. J. (1983): Electroencephalographic sleep, aging, and psychopathology: New data and state of the art. *Biol Psychiatry*, 18:139–155.
51. Ganguli, R., Reynolds, C. F., and Kupfer, D. J. (1987): Electroencephalographic sleep in young, never medicated schizophrenics. *Arch Gen Psychiatry*, 44:36–44.
52. Greden, J. F., and Carroll, B. J. (1981): Psychomotor function in affective disorders: An overview of new monitoring techniques. *Am J Psychiatry*, 11:1441–1448.
53. Greden, J. F., Genero, N., Price, H. L., Feinberg, M., and Levine M. (1986): Facial electromyography in depression. *Arch Gen Psychiatry*, 43:269–274.
54. Iacono, W. B., Lykken, D. T., Peloquin, L. J., Lumry, A. E., Valentine, R. H., and Tuason, V. B. (1983): Electrodermal activity in euthymic unipolar and bipolar affective disorders: A possible marker for depression. *Arch Gen Psychiatry*, 40:557–565.

55. Iacono, W. G., Peloquin, L. J., Lumry, A. E., Valentine, R. H., Tuason, V. B. (1982): Eye tracking in patients with unipolar and bipolar affective disorders in remission. *J Abnorm Psychol*, 91:35–44.
56. Storrie, M. C., Doerr, H. O., and Johnson, M. H. (1981): Skin conductance characteristics of depressed subjects before and after therapeutic intervention. *J Nerv Ment Dis*, 69:176–179.
57. Ward, N. G., Doerr, H. O., and Storrie, M. C. (1983): Skin conductance: A potentially sensitive test for depression. *Psychiatry Res*, 10:295–302.
58. Carroll, B. J. (1982): The dexamethasone suppression test for melancholia. *Br J Psychiatry*, 140:292–304.
59. Arana, G. W., Baldessarini, R. J., and Ornsteen, M. (1985): The dexamethasone suppression test for diagnosis and prognosis in psychiatry. *Arch Gen Psychiatry*, 42:1193–1204.
60. APA Task Force on Laboratory Tests in Psychiatry. (1987): The dexamethasone suppression test: An overview of its current status in psychiatry. *Am J Psychiatry*, 144:1253–1262.
61. Greden, J. F., Kronfol, Z., and Gardner, R., et al. (1981): Dexamethasone suppression test and selection of antidepressant medications. *J Affective Disord*, 3:389–396.
62. Greden, J. F., Gardner, R., King, D., Grunhaus, L., Carroll, B. J., and Kronfol, Z. (1983): Dexamethasone suppression test in antidepressant treatment of melancholia. *Arch Gen Psychiatry*, 40:493–500.
63. Yerevanian, B. I., Olafsdottir, H., and Milanese, E., et al. (1983): Normalization of the dexamethasone suppression test at discharge from hospital: Its prognostic value. *J Affective Disord*, 5:191–197.
64. Brown, W. A., Shrivastava, R., and Arato, M. (1987): Pretreatment pituitary- adrenocortical status and placebo response in depression. *Psychopharmacol Bull*, 23:155–159.
65. Prange, A. J., Loosen, P. T., Wilson, I. C., and Lipton, M. A. (1984): The therapeutic use of hormones of the thyroid axis in depression. In: *Neurobiology of Mood Disorders*, edited by R. M. Post and J. C. Ballenger, pp. 311–322. Williams & Wilkins, Baltimore.
66. Whybrow, P. C., and Prange, A. J. (1981): A hypothesis of thyroid catecholamine-receptor interaction. *Arch Gen Psychiatry*, 38:106–113.
67. Kirkegaard, C. (1981): The thyrotropin response to thyrotropin-releasing hormone in endogenous depression. *Psychoneuroendocrinology*, 6:189–212.
68. Langer, G., Aschauer, H., Koinig, G., Resch, F., and Schonbeck G. (1983): The TSH response to TRH: A possible predictor of outcome in antidepressant and neuroleptic treatment. *Prog Neuropsychopharmacol Biol Psychiatry*, 7:335–342.
69. Loosen, P. T., Wilson, I. C., Dew, B., and Tipermas A. (1983): Thyrotropin-releasing hormone (TRH) in abstinent alcoholic men. *Am J Psychiatry*, 140:1145–1149.
70. Krog-Meyer, I., Kirkegaard, C., and Kijne, B., et al. (1984): Prediction of relapse with the TRH test and prophylactic amitriptyline in 39 patients with endogenous depression. *Am J Psychiatry*, 141:945–948.
71. Bunney, W. E., Jr., and Davis, J. M. (1965): Norepinephrine and depressive reactions: A review. *Arch Gen Psychiatry*, 13:483–494.
72. Schildkraut, J. J. (1965): The catecholamine hypothesis of affective disorder: A review of supporting evidence. *Am J Psychiatry*, 122:509–522.
73. Murphy, D. L., Campbell, I., and Costa, J. L. (1978): Current status of the indoleamine hypothesis of the affective disorders. In: *Psychopharmacology: A Generation of Progress*, edited by M. A. Lipton, A. DiMascio, and K. F. Killam, pp. 1235–1247. Raven Press, New York.
74. Schildkraut, J. J. (1982): The biochemical discrimination of subtypes of depressive disorders: An outline of our studies on norepinephrine metabolism and psychoactive drugs in the endogenous depressions since 1967. *Pharmacopsychiatry*, 15:121–127.
75. Van Praag, H. M. (1980): Central monoamine metabolism in depressions. I. Serotonin and related compounds. *Compr Psychiatry*, 21:30–43.
76. Linnoila, M., Karoum, F., and Potter, W. Z. (1982): High correlation of norepinephrine and its major metabolite excretion rates. *Arch Gen Psychiatry*, 39:521–523.
77. Jimerson, D. C., Insel, T. R., Reus, V. I., and Kopin I. (1983): Increased plasma MHPG in dexamethasone-resistant depressed patients. *Arch Gen Psychiatry*, 40:173–176.
78. Koslow, S. H., Maas, J. W., Bowden, C. L., Davis, J. M., Hanin, I., and Javaid, J. (1983): CSF and urinary biogenic amines and metabolites in depression and mania. *Arch Gen Psychiatry*, 40:999–1010.
79. Linnoila, M., Karoum, F., Calil, H. M., Kopin, I. J., and Potter, W. Z. (1982): Alteration of

norepinephrine metabolism with desipramine and zimelidine in depressed patients. *Arch Gen Psychiatry*, 39:1025–1028.
80. Golden, R. N., Markey, S. P., Risby, E. D., Rudorfer, M. V., Cowdry, R. W., Potter, W. Z. (1988): Antidepressants reduce whole-body norepinephrine turnover while enhancing 6-hydroxymelatonin output. *Arch Gen Psychiatry*, 45:145–149.
81. Redmond, D. E., Katz, M. M., Maas, J. W., Swann, A., Casper, R., and Davis, J. M. (1986): Cerebrospinal fluid amine metabolites: Relationships with behavioral measurements in depressed, manic, and healthy control subjects. *Arch Gen Psychiatry*, 43:938–947.
82. Barnes, R. F., Veith, R. C., Borson, S., Vershey, J., Raskind, M. A., and Halter, J. B. (1983): High levels of plasma catecholamines in dexamethasone-resistant depressed patients. *Am J Psychiatry*, 140:1623–1625.
83. Stokes, P. E., Fraser, A., and Casper R. (1981): Unexpected neuroendocrine relationships. *Psychopharmacol Bull*, 17:72–75.
84. Linnoila, M., Karoum, F., and Potter, W. Z. (1983): Effects of antidepressant treatments on dopamine turnover in depressed patients. *Arch Gen Psychiatry*, 40:1015–1017.
85. Carroll, B. J., Greden, J. F., Haskett, R., et al. (1980): Neurotransmitter studies of neuroendocrine pathology in depression. *Acta Psychiatr Scand [Suppl]*, 280:183–200.
86. Sitaram, N., Moore, A. M., and Gillin, J. C. (1979): Scopolamine-induced muscarinic supersensitivity in normal man. *Psychiatry Res*, 1:9–16.
87. Sitaram, N., Nurnberger, J. I., Gershon, E. S., and Gillin, J. C. (1982): Cholinergic regulation of mood and REM sleep: Potential model and marker of vulnerability to affective disorders. *Am J Psychiatry*, 139:571–576.
88. Insel, T. R., Kalin, N. H., Guttmacher, L. B., Cohen, R. M., and Murphy, D. L. (1982): The dexamethasone suppression test in patients with primary depressive-compulsive disorder. *Psychiatry Res*, 6:153–160.
89. Reynolds, C. F., Shaw, D. F., Newton, T. F., Coble, P. A., and Kupfer, D. J. (1983): EEG sleep in outpatients with generalized anxiety: A preliminary comparison with depressed outpatients. *Psychiatry Res*, 8:81–89.
90. Akiskal, H. S., and Cassano, G. B. (1983): The impact of therapeutic advances in widening the nosologic boundaries of affective disorders: Clinical and research implications. *Pharmacopsychiatry*, 16:111–118.
91. Alzheimer, A. (1907): Uber eine eigenartig Erkrankung der Hirnrinde. *Allegemeine Zeitschrift fur Psychiatrie und Psychisch Gerichtliche Medizine*, 64:146–148.
92. Katzman, R. (1986): Alzheimer's disease. *N Engl J Med*, 314:964–973.
93. Glenner, G. G., and Wong, C. W. (1984): Alzheimer's disease and Down's syndrome: Sharing of a unique cerebrovascular amyloid protein. *Biochem Biophys Res Commun*, 122:1131–1135.
94. Silverman, J. M., Breitner, J. C. S., Mohs, R. C., and Davis, K. L. (1986): Reliability of the family history method in genetic studies of Alzheimer's disease and related dementias. *Am J Psychiatry*, 143:1279–1282.
95. Jacoby, R., and Levy, R. (1980): CT scanning and the investigation of dementia: A review. *J R Soc Med*, 73:366–369.
96. Council on Scientific Affairs Report of the Panel on Magnetic Resonance Imaging. (1988): Magnetic resonance imaging of the central nervous system. *JAMA*, 259:1211–1222.
97. Cutler, N. R. (1984): Brain imaging: Aging and dementia. *Ann Intern Med*, 101:355–369.
98. Sedvall, G., Farde, L., Persson, A., and Wiesel, F. A. (1986): Imaging of neurotransmitter receptors in the living human brain. *Arch Gen Psychiatry*, 43:995–1005.
99. Wilson, W. P., Musella, L., and Short, M. J. (1977): The electroencephalogram in dementia. In: *Dementia*, 2nd edition edited by C. E. Wells, pp. 205–222. Davis, Philadelphia.
100. Prinz, P. N., Peskind, E. R., Vitaliano, P. P., et al. (1982): Changes in the sleep and waking EEGs of nondemented and demented elderly subjects. *J Am Geriatr Soc*, 30:86–93.
101. Blackwood, D. H. R., St. Clair, D. M., Blackburn, I. M., and Tyrer, G. M. B. (1987): Cognitive brain potentials and psychological deficits in Alzheimer's dementia and Korsakoff's amnestic syndrome. *Psychol Med*, 17:349–358.
102. Reynolds, C. F., Kupfer, D. J., Houck, P. R., et al. (1988): Reliable discrimination of elderly depressed and demented patients by electroencephalographic sleep data. *Arch Gen Psychiatry*, 45:258–264.
103. Bondareff, W., Mountjoy, C. Q., and Roth, M. (1982): Loss of neurons of origin of the adrener-

gic projection to cerebral cortex (nucleus locus ceruleus) in senile dementia. *Neurology*, 32:164–168.
104. Gottfries, C. C., Adolfsson, R., Aquilonius, S. M., et al. (1983): Biochemical studies of early-onset changes in dementia disorders of Alzheimer's type (AD/SDAT). *Neurobiol Aging*, 4:261–271.
105. Coyle, J. T., Price, D. L., and Delong, M. R. (1983): Alzheimer's disease: A disorder of cortical cholinergic innervation. *Science*, 219:1184–1189.
106. Raskind, M., Peskind, E., Rivard, M. F., Veith, R., and Barnes, R. (1982): Dexamethasone suppression test and cortisol circadian rhythm in primary degenerative dementia. *Am J Psychiatry*, 139:1468–1471.
107. Goldgaber, D., Lerman, M. I., McBride, O. W., Saffiotti, V., Gajdusek, D. C. (1987): Characterization and chromosomal localization of a cDNA encoding brain amyloid of Alzheimer's disease. *Science*, 235:877–880.
108. Robakis, N. K., Wisniewski, H. M., Jenkins, E. C., et al. (1987): Chromosome 21q21 sublocalization of gene encoding beta-amyloid peptide in cerebral vessels and neuritic (senile) plaques of people with Alzheimer disease and Down syndrome. *Lancet*, 1:384–385.
109. Thase, M. E. The relationship between Down syndrome and Alzheimer's disease. In: *Psychobiology of Down syndrome*, edited by L. Nadel. Bradford/M.I.T. Press, Boston. (in press).
110. Saint George-Hyslop, P. H., Tanzi, R. E., Polinsky, R. J., et al. (1987): The genetic defect causing familial Alzheimer's disease maps on chromosome 21. *Science*, 235:885–888.
111. Podlisny, M. B., Lee, G., and Selkoe, D. J. (1987): Gene dosage of the amyloid beta protein precursor in Alzheimer's disease. *Science*, 238:669–671.
112. Saint George-Hyslop, P. H., Tanzi, R. E., Polinsky, R. J., et al. (1987): Absence of duplication of chromosome 21 genes in familial and sporadic Alzheimer's disease. *Science*, 238:664–666.
113. Tanzi, R. E., Bird, E. D., Latt, S. A., and Neve R. L. (1987): The amyloid beta protein gene is not duplicated in brains from patients with Alzheimer's disease. *Science*, 238:666–669.
114. Zubenko, G. S. (1986): Hippocampal membrane alteration in Alzheimer's disease. *Brain Res*, 385:115–121.
115. Bondareff, W., Mountjoy, C. Q., Roth, M., Rossor, M. N., Iverson, L. L., and Reynolds, G. P. (1987): Age and histopathologic heterogeneity in Alzheimer's disease. *Arch Gen Psychiatry*, 44:412–417.
116. Mayeux, R., Stern, Y., and Spanton, S. (1985): Heterogeneity in dementia of the Alzheimer type: Evidence of subgroups. *Neurology*, 35:453–461.

DISCUSSION

Dr. Stokes: You mentioned site differences, which is an extremely important point that needs more attention, as was emphasized in the 1984 GAP report. For example, there are research centers where the patients have been hospitalized for 5 or 6 weeks off drugs. They are a very different population than newly admitted individuals who have the same diagnosis at admission but who require some active intervention relatively quickly. You have also underscored very nicely the problem of differences in biological findings when one studies individuals in the course of a particular illness, as you did in your recurrent depression studies, versus studying them at the time of original identification of their illness. Length of time in a particular study is important. Lastly, concerning your point about whether biological tests are effective diagnostic aids at this time, I don't think we are at a point where we can use them to change our diagnosis, in terms of our research or our treatment plan, but they are useful as a confirmatory measure for our clinical diagnostic classification and acumen.

Dr. Kupfer: I question your last point on the issue of confirmatory measures. I think that we need to establish some appropriate operational criteria. Certainly I totally agree with your points about site differences and where a patient is in a particular episode. We have not paid enough attention to these two issues.

Dr. Schildkraut: Following up on what was just said, I think we all agree site differences are terribly important, but there is a site that we in academia very often overlook because we really don't have access to it. Patients with depressive disorders who are treated in nonpsychiatric settings—in general medical settings by office practitioners—often may respond to relatively low doses of antidepressant drugs. These patients never reach psychiatric referral. They may be the sorts of patients who were seen in psychiatric studies 20 or 25 years ago but who no longer present to psychiatrists, let alone to secondary and tertiary referral research centers. I think that is a population terribly worth re-examining. The problems of how to do it and how to get into the sites where these patients are located are quite formidable.

One brief question—how do the findings on manic patients differ from those on patients with near sleep deprivation?

Dr. Kupfer: The REM density changes in the sleep of manic patients are not seen in sleep deprivation, although some subjects show shortened REM latency.

Dr. John DeFigueiredo: In your studies comparing geriatric depression with early Alzheimer's, what methods and criteria did you use to establish early Alzheimer's?

Dr. Kupfer: We have a specialized unit to assess patients. We use the NINCDS criteria for possible dementia of the Alzheimer type which were published 4 years ago. Our patients have usually been followed for 18 months to 2 years.

Dr. Rose: Has there been any progress in utilizing laboratory markers to define the boundaries of psychiatric disorders? How specific are markers derived from laboratory studies? For example, bipolar disorders do not appear to differ from unipolar disorders in terms of REM latency.

Dr. Kupfer: We have not made as much progress as we probably could have with respect to examining boundary conditions and issues of sensitivity. I emphasize that it is really appropriate for those of us working in specific areas to pool our data sets, despite all the problems mentioned about differences between sites, and attempt to see what we can learn. Despite the many, many studies in the literature on various kinds of laboratory indicators, correlates, and markers, most of us have not paid sufficient attention to validity issues, the topic of this conference. We need to examine our data without necessarily doing new studies.

The Validity of Psychiatric Diagnosis, edited by
Lee N. Robins and James E. Barrett.
Raven Press, Ltd., New York © 1989.

The Pharmacological Validation of Psychiatric Diagnosis

Donald F. Klein

New York State Psychiatric Institute, New York, New York 10032

The vexing problem is that we do not, in general, know the etiology or pathophysiology necessary for the development of a psychiatric disorder. One could take a purely descriptive or syndromatological approach, eschew etiological speculations, and simply advance the belief that certain combinations of manifest symptoms, associated with particular demographic characteristics such as race and sex, age of onset, and certain precipitating factors, etc., define a clinical picture worth attending to.

The problem with this approach is that indefinitely many syndromes can be imaginatively stipulated. The belief that computer analyses, via clustering techniques, will carve nature at her joints has not lived up to early hopes, and there are good, logical reasons to believe that such techniques will only occasionally work (1). We need validity criteria to decide which syndromes are likely to reflect relatively uniform pathophysiologies and, hopefully, etiologies.

Robins and Guze (2) emphasize the need for clear-cut inclusion and exclusion criteria (reliability requirements), the desirability of consistent, reliable, laboratory findings, and the utility of family studies (validators). With regard to follow-up studies, they state that marked differences in outcome, "such as between complete recovery and chronic illness, suggest that the group is not homogeneous. . . . The same illness may have a variable prognosis, but until we know more about the fundamental nature of the common psychiatric illnesses, marked differences in outcome should be regarded as a challenge to the validity of the original diagnosis." Therefore, they suggest that the difference between poor and good prognosis schizophrenia "is not simply a matter of severity of illness, but that the two groups represent different illnesses."

I. PHARMACOLOGICAL DISSECTION

We extend their views and deal with distinctive pharmacological treatment responses as syndromal validators. If a particular syndrome reflects a distinctive underlying pathophysiology, then one should be able to specify effective and ineffective treatments, syndromal aspects which are targets for particular therapies, and even the propensity for particular toxicities. The study of secondary and tertiary effects of treatments that initially affect a particular syndromal component may allow us to develop hypotheses about the course of syndromal development.

An emphasis on underlying pathophysiology as reflected in follow-up naturally leads to a concern with premorbid course. If something has gone wrong with regulatory mechanisms, this may be most apparent prior to the complexity of the full-blown syndrome. This leads to the possibility that "premorbid" course may be a powerful predictor of the pattern of pharmacological reactivity. Robins and Guze do not emphasize this point, although it is certainly compatible with their approach.

Why are we concerned about clinical improvement and clinical toxicity brought about by psychotropic drugs? Is there really any difference between the application of psychotropic drugs for clinical purposes and simply studying their differential psychophysiological effects? For instance, why not look to see if atropine affects the pupils differently in different diagnostic groups?

The reason we emphasize clinical improvement and toxicity is because major psychotropic drug effects are not congeries of many different discrete effects, but are normalizing. The antidepressants, antipsychotics and lithium have little effect on normal human beings. It is their interaction with a deranged pathophysiology that results in their striking effects. Therefore, a differential medication response cuts close to the illness's basic pathophysiological derangement rather than reflecting some epiphenomenon. The following discussion offers examples of differential pharmacological responses as validators.

A. Heterogeneity of Schizophrenia

Early clinical experience with chlorpromazine in acute schizophrenia indicated a subgroup for whom antipsychotic effects were only moderate (3). In this group, development of an extrapyramidal bradykinetic syndrome (zombie appearance) was common despite the use of antiparkinson medications. Although this subgroup did not differ from other schizophrenias in their current symptomatology, their histories indicated these schizophrenics were isolated, aloof, gauche, and asocial during childhood. When schizophrenics were rated using the Premorbid Asocial Scale (PAS) (4), the entire group showed a clear bimodal distribution with the asocials restricted to the poorer mode. Kendell (5 and this volume) emphasizes bimodality as useful for establishing nosological classes. This is an example where developmental history provides such a distinction, although symptomatic expression does not. Follow-up (6) showed that this subgroup of patients with poor childhood functioning had uniformly poor outcomes consistent with the frequent report that poor premorbid schizophrenics deteriorate. During a placebo controlled trial of chlorpromazine plus procyclidine, Klein and Rosen (7) showed that schizophrenics rated as asocial prior to the drug trial developed a toxic reaction to the drug marked by inaudible speech, emotional unresponsivity, overinhibited behavior, etc. This did not occur within the nonasocial group. Conversely, the benefits of chlorpromazine with regard to irrelevant speech, incoherent speech, anxiety, overtalkativeness, uninhibited behavior, frequent mood swings, ideas of influence, and feelings of sinfulness were significantly greater among nonasocial than asocial patients. Further validating the distinction between asocial and nonasocial schizophrenia was (8) the high incidence of neurological soft signs in the asocial group but not in other schizophrenics, when examined blindly in a drug-free state.

These results of our study of chlorpromazine effects are in harmony with Robins and Guze's suggestion that poor and good prognosis schizophrenia are different disorders. Therefore, we support Robins and Guze, both biologically and substantively. Interestingly, this well established distinction between poor and good premorbid schizophrenics has not been reflected in either DSM-III or DSM-IIIR. Given the support from pharmacological treatment, follow-up, CAT scan, neurological examinations, and possibly genetics (9), this nosological distinction should be reviewed by the DSM-IV committee.

We have found that imipramine caused acute psychotic disorganization in some schizophrenics. Such exacerbation of symptoms was almost entirely limited to the childhood asocial group and did not occur in schizoaffective patients (10).

The bradykinetic syndrome produced by chlorpromazine plus procyclidine in the asocial schizophrenics is of interest because it is known that patients with brain damage are particularly sensitive to the pharmacological production of extrapyramidal syndromes. The possibility that the asocial subgroup has brain damage is congruent with findings of neurological dysfunction and dilated ventricles in childhood asocial schizophrenics (11).

One could speculate that the relative ease of parkinsonian induction in these patients argues against a hyperdopaminergic overdrive. Both excited manics and schizoaffectives, on the other hand, show remarkably little antipsychotic induced parkinsonism when receiving antipsychotic drugs during their psychotic exacerbation.

II. PSYCHOPHARMACOLOGICAL SIMILARITIES

Demonstrations of behavioral differences in drug effects on asocial and nonasocial schizophrenics allowed for the discovery of distinct pathophysiologies. However it is far more difficult to draw conclusions about common pathophysiologies from behavioral *similarities* in drug effect. Drugs have multiple effects; because a drug benefits two different groups does not necessarily affirm that this is due to a common pathophysiological amelioration. That the anti-depressant imipramine is effective in enuresis does not necessarily imply that the children are depressed, although it does raise the question.

The same issue arises on noting that imipramine benefits both panic disorder and depression. Does this mean they have a common pathophysiology? Other commonalities, e.g., response to ECT, sleep patterns, family history, response to panicogens, differential symptomatology, etc., need to be found as well before an affirmative response is convincing.

III. CO-MORBIDITY, SYNDROMAL COMPLEXITY AND SEVERITY

The co-occurrence of Syndrome A with Syndrome B if A also occurs alone is usually referred to as comorbidity. The symptomatic similarity between A, when it stands alone and when it occurs with B, is usually assumed to indicate that A is correctly perceived as a single disorder. However, given that the etiologies of A and AB are unknown, it is also possible that the A which stands alone resembles but is not the same as the A which co-occurs with B. This "comorbidity" challenges us to see if the two A's differ developmentally, therapeutically, genetically or physiologically, even when they appear symptomatically similar.

As we have discussed elsewhere (12), there are several situations in which pharmacologic dissection can elucidate comorbid relationships. Let us examine the example of drug response in individuals with syndrome A vs. those with syndrome AB. To simplify our discussion we will index the A that stands alone as A_s and the A aspect of the complex AB as A_c.

Does A_s equal A_c?
What is the relationship of A_c to B_c?

Let us assume that the two syndromes are treated with the same drug and that if improvement during drug treatment is shown, appropriate placebo-controlled trials show that this is indeed due to specific drug effect.

If, then, in these trials, A_s does not respond to drug treatment in the same fashion as A_c, this would be preliminary evidence of a real distinction between these similar syndromes.

Yet suppose that A_s gets better and A_c does not. Here it is possible that A_c is simply a more severe form of A_s, as indicated by its forming part of a more complex syndrome. Therefore, the difference in the drug responsivity of A_s and A_c may be due to context and severity rather than to a qualitative distinction, just as the fever of a mild pneumonia would more likely respond to aspirin than the fever of a severe pneumonia. As an example, antidepressants have been reported to be ineffective with delusional depression, but effective for the less severe form, melancholia. The relative lack of efficacy of tricyclics for the delusional syndrome may simply be due to its greater severity. Delusional depression may respond to a higher dose of tricyclics than has been used in the trials that report relative inefficacy (13).

It should be noted that this is a heuristic rather than a clinical discussion. It is possible that the joint use of antipsychotics and antidepressants is the sensible clinical approach to delusional depression, although it has not been unequivocally demonstrated. Our nosological point is that one must be more cautious about using its lesser response rate to justify dissecting psychotic depression from melancholia, in view of its greater severity.

Differential drug response is more suggestive of distinct disorders when medication benefits A_c but not A_s, since we assume that A_s is less severe than A_c and should therefore be easier to treat. We will call this a disordinal interaction.

Therefore, if spontaneous panics associated with agoraphobia respond to imipramine, but situationally bound panic associated with simple phobia does not, one suspects that these two forms of panic are qualitatively different and may, on closer inspection, be found to differ descriptively, prognostically, genetically, etc., as well.

Other information may be gained from the effects of treatment on the respective components of a complex syndrome. For instance, if the drug causes A_c to remit while B_c remains severe well beyond A_c's remission, one would suspect that A_c did not have a maintaining role for B_c. If, on the other hand, once A_c subsides, B_c slowly begins to subside, one might suspect that A_c had been maintaining B_c. An example of this pattern is found when panic and agoraphobia co-occur. Treatment with imipramine typically has an immediate effect on the panic attacks (A_c), followed by a secondary delayed effect on agoraphobic avoidance (B_c).

Conversely if B_c shows a temporary improvement but relapses on treatment cessation, while A_c remains unaffected throughout, and if A_c anteceded B_c, one might hypothesize that A_c incited and maintained B_c. The therapy is seen as having helped one of A_c's effects without changing the underlying disorder. An illustration here may be the beneficial effects of exposure therapy on the phobic component of agoraphobia with panic attacks but not on the panic attack component, given that the panic attacks preceded the agoraphobia (14).

A. Discovering Dependencies Between Symptoms Within a Syndrome

Differential drug effects on particular symptoms of a syndrome can suggest causal connections between them. For instance, all antipsychotic medications are also antihallucinatory. This suggests that a common factor is responsible for both effects. This evidence for some common roots coupled with the observation that while delusions can occur without auditory hallucinations, the reverse is virtually never seen, suggests the possibility that auditory hallucinations may require a particular type of delusional misinterpretation. This is substantiated by other psychopathological features such as the common report by schizophrenics that they are hearing their own thoughts (*Denklautenwerden*), or the report of the recovering schizophrenic that his hallucinations have turned into sick ego alien thoughts (indistinguishable from obsessions). In other words, auditory hallucinations may be delusional misinterpretations of thoughts unrecognized as one's own. Therefore they are believed to be somehow either directly inserted (thought insertion) or the result of hearing an external voice (perceptual misattribution).

It has been reported that mouth opening (15) will stop auditory hallucinations. Clinical experience is convincing that this (and chewing gum) often works. How can we integrate this finding? Perhaps the auditory hallucination requires the delusional misinterpretation of subvocal speech, which is then disrupted by oral activity. With the remission of the delusional state, these perceptions become more realistically interpreted as obsessive thoughts.

IV. PHARMACOLOGICAL RESPONSES IN THE MAJOR DISORDERS

A. Pseudoneurotic Schizophrenia

Pseudoneurotic schizophrenia is a term that has dropped out of fashion. It was an ill-defined category of patients with multiple neurotic complaints (pan neurosis) that did not respond to psychotherapy. If it were the case that neurotics in general respond to psychotherapy, there might be some merit in making this distinction. However, the reasoning behind allying these patients to schizophrenia was less plain, since they rarely were delusional, hallucinated, or manifested thought disorder. Various clinicians claimed, however, to be able to detect a soft thought disorder.

In our trial with this group, imipramine proved globally superior to chlorpromazine, which was not different from placebo (16,17). In another trial in this group (18), it was found that MAO inhibitors were also efficacious. Since pseudoneurotic schizophrenics are considerably more severe than ordinary neurotics, their distinction on the basis of a lack of benefit of psychotherapy may simply reflect the severity effect. The pharmacological data, however, show benefits from "antidepressants." This is not much help since antidepressants benefit a wide range of anxious and depressed patients. It is probably a good thing that this category has suffered atrophy from disuse.

B. Anxiety Disorders

Our initial finding on using imipramine to treat panic disorder was that imipramine ablated spontaneous panic attacks without immediately lessening the severe generalized anxiety. This led to the hypothesis that imipramine effects are restricted to patients who manifest spontaneous panic attacks, and therefore should be ineffective in simple phobia and generalized anxiety disorder. Our trial (19) indicated that indeed simple phobics did not respond to imipramine, but phobic patients with spontaneous panic attacks did. However, whether panic disorder differs qualitatively or only quantitatively from generalized anxiety disorder is a still debated issue. If it were shown that imipramine was an effective agent against generalized anxiety, this would cast doubt on the qualitative distinction between panic and chronic anxiety.

Almost all studies which have attempted to assess the antianxiety effects of imipramine or to contrast them with those of the benzodiazepines (BZD) have included a mixture of anxious, depressed, and phobic patients. This makes it impossible to determine if imipramine is effective against anxiety because any improvement as compared with placebo may be attributable to its well known antidepressant and antipanic effects.

As we have discussed elsewhere (12,20), the most convincing evidence for a distinct anxiolytic effect of imipramine, unrelated to its antipanic effect, comes from the 1986 study by Kahn et al. (21) in which the antigeneralized anxiety effects of imipramine, chlordiazepoxide, and placebo were compared in nondepressed anxious outpatients. Unfortunately panic disorder patients and patients with both agoraphobia and panic attacks had not been prospectively excluded. Therefore, though a significant imipramine antianxiety effect was found, it is not possible to assess to what extent this was due to the drug's antipanic action.

Kahn et al. attempted to address this issue post hoc by reanalyzing their data after excluding 35 patients with panic and phobia from their 242-patient sample. However, one wonders whether this small proportion (14%) excluded captured all cases of panic disorder (22,23). Severe cases of panic disorder, in which panic is masked by chronic high levels of anticipatory anxiety, and cases in whom the attacks were too infrequent or too mild to meet diagnostic criteria might have been missed using these retrospective methods.

Kahn et al. also undertook a multiple regression analysis in an attempt to show that imipramine's antianxiety effects were independent of its antipanic effects. However, this analysis depends on the reliability of the assessments of panic and generalized anxiety. Since the panic assessments were retrospective, their reliability must be considered questionable. This compromises the overall result. Kahn et al. agree that replication is necessary.

To sum up, the argument that panic disorder with agoraphobia and simple phobia are distinct diagnoses is supported by imipramine's beneficial effects on the former and its lack of benefit in the latter. Imipramine trials have not yet settled the question of the distinction between panic and generalized anxiety disorder; a better designed prospective study will be needed. Benzodiazepines have been shown to benefit spontaneous panic attacks in outpatients, but not in hospitalized patients. As noted above, the greater success of a treatment in the milder form of a disorder is not a strong argument for subdividing the disorder. Instead, it suggests that the more severe form may require more vigorous treatment. This seems the case for panic attacks when there is no accompanying agoraphobia. Cognitive-behavioral psychotherapy (24) has been shown to benefit such mildly affected patients, although the benefit was not as marked in patients with panic disorder and agoraphobia.

This raises the interesting possibility that spontaneous panics themselves might be subdivided into a severe form regularly accompanied by phobic developments, which require antidepressants for their amelioration, and a milder uncomplicated form that is responsive to both benzodiazepines and psychotherapy.

In the treatment of severe spontaneous panic attacks with imipramine, the patients frequently go through a phase during which panic attacks start to develop but suddenly cease without full expression. The patient helplessly awaits the full development of the attack and is surprised to see it go away. Such a clinical phenomenon is not consistent with a purely cognitive theory of panic attacks that relies upon a patient's apprehension of danger.

Conceivably some spontaneous panic attacks consist of two stages. The first stage is a waxing of the general level of chronic anxiety that may be ameliorable by cognitive techniques and benzodiazepines. The second severe, peaking stage may consist of a runaway positive feedback loop that requires antidepressants to normalize. On quite other grounds, we have suggested previously that antidepressants work by converting pathological positive feedback loops back to stabilizing negative feedback loops (1,25).

1. Social Phobia

Social phobia is a common disorder associated with considerable morbidity (26,27). Until recently effective treatments were not available for most patients.

The 1980 DSM-III (28) defined the central feature of social phobia as persistent and irrational fear of humiliation while being observed by others in the course of certain activities. Common social phobic fears include speaking, eating, or writing in public, talking to strangers, attending social occasions such as parties, or speaking with authority figures. Either avoidance or endurance with dread of one or more situations of this type was required for a diagnosis. The DSM-III definition described most sufferers as having only one or two fears.

In the course of two open medication trials with social phobics, Liebowitz et al. (29) and Gorman et al. (30) observed two types of socially anxious patients. The first were individuals who conformed closely to the DSM-III description. Each had discrete fears of a few situations in which they were convinced that they would be humiliated or shamed if observed by others. Typical fears were of speaking, writing, or eating in public. Despite their phobias, these patients usually had normal interpersonal relationships. Most were married and/or had active social lives. They enjoyed and were relaxed in contact with others provided they were not faced with their specific phobic situations.

In contrast, a second group of patients presented with pervasive avoidance of, or severe anxiety during, most activities involving social interaction. This subgroup also feared humiliation, but their fears included a wide range of interpersonal encounters. Most had few friends and severely restricted or nonexistent romantic lives. Some had no contact with individuals outside of their immediate family.

The discrete social phobics may be considered to have a simple form of social phobia and the generalized social phobics a severe or complex form.

Liebowitz is currently comparing characteristics of these two subcategories of patients in a double-blind controlled trial of phenelzine, atenolol, and placebo

(31). To date, 56 patients have completed the acute 8-week treatment trial. Twenty of the completers have been randomized to placebo, 18 to atenolol, and 18 to phenelzine. Forty-one of the 56 completers were classified as having generalized social anxiety. The remaining 15 met criteria for the discrete subtype.

Among the generalized social phobics, 79% (11/14) responded well to phenelzine, 15% (2/15) to atenolol, and 21% (3/14) to placebo ($p < .001$). Phenelzine was significantly more effective than both atenolol ($p = .001$) and placebo ($p = .003$). Placebo and atenolol did not differ significantly from each other.

Among the 15 discrete social phobics, only one out of four (25%) responded well to phenelzine, three out of five (60%) to atenolol, and two out of six (33%) to placebo. These results were not statistically significant because of the small sample size. However, they do suggest a disordinal pattern of phenelzine response, in that phenelzine was more effective in the more severe group, i.e., the generalized social anxiety patients. Despite small numbers, this difference showed a trend toward significance (Fisher exact test, two-tailed, $p = .08$). Within the atenolol group, 15% (2/13) of those with generalized social anxiety responded vs 60% (3/5) of those with discrete social phobia (Fisher exact test, two-tailed, $p = .10$). The atenolol pattern (if eventually definitive) is compatible with either a quantitative or qualitative distinction.

B. Depression

In Quitkin et al.'s review (32), it was pointed out that the evidence for MAOI efficacy in nonendogenous depression was quite strong, while the evidence in endogenous depressions was still unclear. At least one well-designed trial showed no benefit from MAO inhibitors in hospitalized endogenous patients (33). These pharmacological findings are consistent with a severity gradient. However, there were surprising reports of imipramine failing to benefit nonendogenous atypical depressions. Since atypical depressions are especially mild, this would be a disordinal result.

Our group has defined atypical depression as a mood reactive depression. That is, these people can be cheered up temporarily if good things happen, but they then slump back into low mood. This depressive pattern is often accompanied by signs of hypersomnia, hyperphagia, sensitivity to rejection, and a feeling of leaden paralysis.

Drug trials in these atypical depressions have demonstrated the superiority of phenelzine to imipramine (34,35). Therefore it is clear that the nonendogenous atypical group has a biological reactivity quite different from the endogenous groups. This is also corroborated by the fact that many atypical symptoms are not simply different from but the opposite of the endogenous vegetative symptoms, e.g., hypersomnia vs insomnia, hyperphagia vs anorexia, mood reactivity vs autonomous mood disturbance.

C. Personality Disorders

There have been few clinical trials where different types of personality disorder were randomized to different drugs. Our initial studies were on a group who suffered from an extremely labile mood that was both overreactive and autonomous. That is, these patients would overreact to disappointments, but also would have mood shifts for no apparent reason several times a day. We differentiated these emotionally unstable types from a histrionic type. The histrionic patients craved attention, sought the center of attention, and could maintain a positive mood under conditions of social applause. Akiskal refers to the emotionally unstable patients as cyclothymic (36). Others might consider them borderline personality disorders.

A distinction between these two personality types was supported by the finding that chlorpromazine benefited only the emotionally unstable group. In fact, the histrionic group showed substantial behavioral toxicity from chlorpromazine. Despite its benefits, most of the unstable group dislike chlorpromazine because they felt it deadened them, but they did not react with the confusional or withdrawn states that the histrionic personalities often did.

The pharmacological reactivity of emotionally unstable personality disorders was supported by their positive response to lithium in a placebo-controlled crossover trial (37), suggesting that this "personality disorder" might be a chronic affective disorder. This hypothesis was supported by our follow-up studies (38,39), when we found a substantial proportion developed major depressive episodes.

CONCLUSION

In many instances pharmacologic dissection serves only to generate hypotheses that a given diagnosis is actually a complex of more than one diagnosis or that two phenomenologically dissimilar diagnoses are actually one. However, in the special case where a disordinal interaction is observed between severity of subtype and drug response, therapeutic outcome may strongly suggest the existence of qualitative distinctions between syndromes.

We have presented this survey to indicate the utility of pharmacological dissection and to clarify some of its nosological implications. Unfortunately, the necessary multidrug cross-diagnostic comparison is rare. The vast majority of clinical trials are as narrowly limited in diagnosis as possible, making cross-diagnosis comparisons impossible. Further, these trials are usually restricted to one active agent and placebo.

Trials that use at least two active agents plus placebo do have the potential for dissecting diagnostic categories, as was shown by work on atypical depression and social phobia. More recently Soloff et al. (40) have fruitfully used amitriptyline, haloperidol, and placebo to investigate borderline personality disorder, a disorder thought by many to be heterogeneous (41). It is regrettable that such studies are infrequent, since their heuristic payoff may be considerable. Further, if a diagnostic subgrouping is discerned by pharmacological dissection, there is the immediate benefit of the delineation of a specific treatment for this newly defined diagnostic group.

ACKNOWLEDGMENTS

The author wishes to thank Hilary M. Klein and Lee N. Robins for their editorial assistance.

This work was supported in part by U.S. Public Health Service grants MH-33422 and MH-37592.

REFERENCES

1. Klein, D. F., Gittelman, R., Quitkin, F., and Rifkin, A. (1980): *Diagnosis and drug treatment of psychiatric disorders: Adults and children.* 2nd edition. Williams and Wilkins, Baltimore.
2. Robins, E., and Guze, S. B. (1970): Establishment of diagnostic validity in psychiatric illness: Its application to schizophrenia. *Am J Psychiat,* 126:983–987.
3. Klein, D. F., and Fink, M. (1962): Behavioral reaction patterns with phenothiazines. *Arch Gen Psychiat,* 7:449–459.
4. Gittelman-Klein, R., and Klein, D. F. (1969): Premorbid asocial adjustment and prognosis in schizophrenia. *J Psychiat Res,* 7:35–53.
5. Kendell, R. E. (1975): *The role of diagnosis in psychiatry.* Blackwell Scientific Publications.
6. Pollack, M., Levenstein, S., and Klein, D. F. (1968): The three year post-hospital follow-up of adolescent and adult schizophrenics. *Am J Orthopsychiat,* 38:94–109.
7. Klein, D. F., and Rosen, B. (1973): Premorbid asocial adjustment and response to phenothiazine treatment among schizophrenic inpatients. *Arch Gen Psychiat,* 29:480–485.
8. Quitkin, F. M., Klein, D. F. (1969): Two behavioral syndromes in young adults related to possible minimal brain dysfunction. *J Psych Res,* 7:131–142.
9. Quitkin, F., Rifkin, A., Tsuang, M. et al. (1980): Can schizophrenia with premorbid asociality be genetically distinguished from the other forms of schizophrenia? *Psych Res* 2:99–105.
10. Pollack, M., Klein, D. F., Millner, A., Blumberg, A. G., and Fink, M. (1964): Imipramine-induced behavioral disorganization in schizophrenic patients: Physiological and psychological correlates. *Recent Adv Biol Psych,* 7:53–61.
11. Weinberger, D. R., Cannon-Spoor, E., Potkin, S. V., Wyatt, R. J. (1980): Poor premorbid adjustment and CT scan abnormalities in chronic schizophrenia. *Am J Psychiat,* 137:1410–1413.
12. Fyer, A. J., Liebowitz, M. R., and Klein, D. F. (1988): Co-morbidity, syndromal complexity and treatment trials. In *Co-morbidity in anxiety and depression,* edited by Maser, J. D., and Cloninger, C. R. American Psychiatric Press (in press).
13. Quitkin, F., Rifkin, A., and Klein, D. F. (1978): Imipramine response in deluded depressive patients. *Amer J Psych,* 135:806–811.
14. Klein, D. F., Ross, D. C., and Cohen, P. (1987): Panic and avoidance in agoraphobia: Application of PATH analysis to treatment studies. *Arch Gen Psychiat,* 44:377–385.
15. Bick, P. A., and Kinsbourne, M. (1987): Auditory hallucinations and subvocal speech in schizophrenic patients. *Amer J Psychiat,* 144:222–225.
16. Klein, D. F. (1967): Importance of psychiatric diagnosis in prediction of clinical drug effects. *Arch Gen Psychiat,* 16:118–126.
17. Klein, D. F. (1968): Psychiatric diagnosis and a typology of clinical drug effects. *Psychopharmacologia,* 13:359–386.
18. Hedberg, D. L., and Glueck, B. C. (1967): Drug combinations in schizophrenia. In International Congress Series No. 129, Washington, D.C.
19. Zitrin, C. M., Klein, D. F., Woerner, M. G., and Ross, D. C. (1983): Treatment of phobias I. Comparison of imipramine hydrochloride and placebo. *Arch Gen Psychiat,* 40:125–138.
20. Klein, D. F., and Klein, H. K. (1988, forthcoming): The definition and psychopharmacology of

spontaneous panic and phobia: A critical review I. In: *The Psychopharmacology of Anxiety*, edited by P. Tyrer, Oxford University Press.
21. Kahn, R. J., McNair, D. M., Lipman, R. S., Covi, L., Rickels, K., Downing, R., Fisher, S., and Frankenthaler, L. M. (1986): Imipramine and chlordiazepoxide in depressive and anxiety disorders II. Efficacy in anxious outpatients. *Arch Gen Psychiat*, 43:79–85.
22. Barlow, D. H., et al. (1985): The dimensions of anxiety disorders. In: *Anxiety and the anxiety disorders*, edited by Tuma, A. H., and Maser, J. D. Lawrence Erlbaum Associates, Hillsdale, New Jersey.
23. Boyd, J. H. et al. (1986): Use of mental health service for the treatment of panic disorder. *Am J Psychiat*, 143:1569–1574.
24. Clark, D. M., Salkovskis, P. M., Gelder, M., Koehler, M. M., Anastasiades, P., Hackmann, A., Middleton, H., and Jeavons, A. (1988): *Tests of a cognitive theory of panic in panic and phobias II*, edited by Hand, I., and Wittchen, H. U. New York: Springer-Verlag, (*in press*).
25. Klein, D. F. (1987): Cybernetics, activation and drug effects (*in press*).
26. Liebowitz, M. R., Gorman, J. M., Fyer, A. J., and Klein, D. F. (1983). Social phobia: Review of a neglected anxiety disorder. *Arch Gen Psychiat*, 40:139–145.
27. Aimes, P., Gelder, M., Shaw, P. (1983): Social phobia: A comparative clinical study. *Br J Psychiat*, 142:174–179.
28. American Psychiatric Association (1980): *Diagnostic and statistical manual of mental disorders*, 3rd edition, American Psychiatric Association, Washington, D.C.
29. Liebowitz, M. R., Fyer, A. J., Gorman, J., et al. (1986): Phenelzine in social phobia. *J Clin Psychiat*, 43:613–614.
30. Gorman, J., Liebowitz, M. R., Fyer, A. J., and Klein, D. F. (1985): Treatment of social phobia with atenolol. *J Clin Psychopharm*, 5:298–301.
31. Liebowitz, M. R., Gorman, J. M., Fyer, A. J., et al. (1987): Pharmacotherapy of social phobia: A placebo controlled comparison of phenelzine and atenolol. *J Clin Psychiat* (*in press*).
32. Quitkin, F., Rifkin, A., Klein, D. F. (1979): Monoamine oxidatse inhibitors: A review of antidepressant effectiveness. *Arch Gen Psychiat*, 135:749–760.
33. British Medical Research Council (BMRC). (1965): Clinical trial of the treatment of depressive illness. *Br Med J*, 1:881–886.
34. Liebowitz, M. R., Quitkin, F. M., Stewart, J. W., McGrath, P., Harrison, W., Rabkin, J., Tricamo, E., Markowitz, J. S. and Klein, D. F. (1984): Phenelzine versus imipramine in atypical depression: A preliminary report. *Arch Gen Psychiat*, 41:669–677.
35. Liebowitz, M. R., Quitkin, F. M., Stewart, J. W., McGrath, P. J., Harrison, W. M., Markowitz, J. S., Rabkin, J. G., Tricamo, E., Goetz, D. M., Klein, D. F. (1987): Antidepressant specificity in atypical depression. *Arch Gen Psychiat*. (*in press*).
36. Akiskal, H. S. (1981): Subaffective disorders: Dysthymic, cyclothymic, and bipolar II disorders in the "borderline" realm. *Psychiatr Clin North Am*, 4:25–46.
37. Rifkin, A., Quitkin, F., Carrillo, C., Blumberg, A. G., and Klein, D. F. (1972): Lithium carbonate in emotionally unstable character disorders. *Arch Gen Psychiat*, 27:519–523.
38. Rifkin, A., Levitan, S. J., Galewski, J., Klein, D. F. (1972): Emotionally unstable character disorder: A follow-up study I: Description of patients and outcome. *Biol Psych*, 4:65–79.
39. Rifkin, A., Levitan, S. J., Galewski, J., Klein, D. F. (1972): Emotionally unstable character disorder: A follow-up study II: Prediction of outcome. *Biol Psych*, 4:81–88.
40. Soloff, P. H., George, A., Nathan, R. S., Schulz, P. M., Ulrich, R. F., Perel, J. M. (1986): Progress in pharmacotherapy of borderline disorders. A double-blind study of amitriptyline, haloperidol and placebo. *Arch Gen Psychiat*, 43:691–697.
41. Klein, D. F. (1977): Psychopharmacological treatment and delineation of borderline disorders. In *Borderline Personality Disorders: The Concept, the Syndrome, the Patient*, edited by Hartocollis, P. pp. 365–383. International Universities Press, Inc.

DISCUSSION

Dr. Patrick Shrout: Would you comment on the use of response to treatment for the development of categories, in contrast to the validation of categories. In my experience, it is common for researchers to try to explain heterogeneous responses to treatment by fishing through the data until they find some variable that seems to differentiate responders from nonresponders. Even though the variable was not initially hypothesized to be related to outcome, the researchers often conduct statistical tests of the associations, and, if one is significant, publish it as though it were a confirmatory result. Such misrepresentation will result in an excess number of Type I errors in the literature. I believe it would be far better to report exploratory results without p values, and let others test them in new samples. Could you comment on this issue, and suggest mechanisms for clearly identifying exploratory studies and results?

Dr. Klein: I think the distinction is a crucial one. Our experience with our childhood asocial schizophrenics was actually confirmatory rather than exploratory because in the pilot trial we had noticed the particular antipsychotic effect, had done the ratings for premorbid asociality prior to the trial, and had made a specific prediction. So that was truly a confirmatory trial.

Some of the material I reported was not confirmatory, but was exploratory. I had the most fun and learned the most from the exploratory work, and I think that it is an economic catastrophe that the drug houses are not interested in Phase II studies. Phase II studies are where you learn the range of efficacy, the kind of patients who respond, the kind of doses to use, and when you expect to get into trouble. All this is viewed by drug houses as a nuisance that should be gotten through as fast as possible. The drug houses want to move on to the double-blind study because that is what is going to convince the FDA to get the drug on the market. You see a lot of absolutely terrible double-blind studies on that basis, because they have done insufficient Phase II work.

Convincing journals to accept work labeled as exploratory is also difficult, although there are well known psychiatric journals that publish exploratory work, such as *Biological Psychiatry*. Journals like *Archives of General Psychiatry* won't touch exploratory work, so you know what you are going to be reading when you turn to these different journals.

Dr. Rapoport: Obsessive-compulsive disorder has been a uniquely differentially responsive syndrome to two or three drugs that are selective in their effects on serotonin. All these antiobsessional drugs are also good antidepressants. How do you conceptualize this finding?

Dr. Klein: I have a design comment about this. By and large, we do either open trials or parallel group double-blind design. If you are looking for a subgroup that is especially relevant to treatment, and you are dealing with a chronic condition like obsessive-compulsive disorder, then in all likelihood you are going to have a high relapse rate following drug discontinuation. An underused design is the drug discontinuation, double-blind, placebo-controlled design. In this design you enter all appropriate subjects into an open trial. You are able to determine those people who apparently respond and those who apparently don't respond. Of the apparent responders, once they have stabilized, you randomize them into either drug continuation or placebo. That is a powerful design because the ones who fail on placebo were the real drug responders. Their characteristics are central to the definition of the drug/placebo difference.

As for why a particular drug works for obsessive-compulsive disorder in comparison to another antidepressant which does not, who knows? The fact that other serotonin-active drugs, like Fluoxetine and Fluvoxamine, seem to be particularly effective for this disorder is certainly stimulating.

Dr. Zubin: It seems to me that your approach is similar to that quote I uttered earlier: "Throw away all diagnoses, and simply call disorders by the name of the particular drug that is efficacious." In order to avoid the possibility that 10 years from now these drugs may not be used anymore, it would be well to study them while they still work, to try to find out what it is about the people who respond that differentiates them from those who don't respond. That not only holds true for drugs; it holds true for psychotherapy and for such psychophysiological measures as the orienting response. Why do some people respond and some don't? The notion you proposed, to give these drugs to a random population, is an excellent one, but we should not expect too much from this procedure beyond finding out whether they do or do not work.

Dr. Klein: I would like to find out why they work. One point I should have made is that the outstanding thing about psychotropic drugs is that they do so little to normal people. Since that is true, it is likely that the psychotropic drugs exert their beneficial effect by some interaction with a deranged control mechanism. So whatever those drugs are doing is close to the illness. If you randomize people by different ways of orienting or by whether their pupils enlarge in response to eye drops, you might find differences between groups, but the probability is pretty high that those are simple epiphenomena having nothing to do with the illness.

Dr. Glassman: A comment on the delusional depression issue. From a scientific point of view, I agree with you when you say that nobody has really tested what high doses of tricyclic antidepressant, such as 500 or 750 mg of Tofranil, would do in psychotic depressions. As a scientific point, we just simply don't know the answer. What worries me about that statement from a clinician's point of view is the fact that combined therapy works in a very dependable way, and in a significantly different way, than standard antidepressant treatment. When you bring up theoretical issues, it is easy to confuse the clinician. I think the clinician should stay with what is proven and not play around with what is theoretical.

Dr. Klein: I don't disagree. I was talking about the use of pharmacological dissection as a procedure for seeing whether certain conditions are really different from each other. The argument that psychotic depression is a different illness from regular depression depends upon the supposed bad effects of the tricyclics in that group. I was really not arguing about the practicalities of treatment.

Dr. John Straumanis: Concerning the differences between psychotic and nonpsychotic depressives, one way of getting a handle on the problem would be to use the PET scan to look at the D_2 receptors. Should the delusional depressives show an excess of D_2 receptors compared to nondelusional depressives, then this would strengthen the rationale for treating them with antidopamine (antipsychotic) drugs in addition to antidepressants.

Dr. Klein: I emphatically am not an expert in the D_2 receptor area, but I have recently read a manuscript by Arvid Carlsson in which he points out that the D_2 finding is entirely dependent on a very complicated mathematical model. We should reserve judgment about the role of D_2 receptors.

The Validity of Psychiatric Diagnosis, edited by
Lee N. Robins and James E. Barrett.
Raven Press, Ltd., New York © 1989.

Validating Affective Personality Types

Hagop S. Akiskal

Department of Psychiatry, College of Medicine, University of Tennessee, Memphis, Tennessee 38163

The past decade has witnessed a renaissance of systematic research on personality disorders. This is in part due to new theoretical constructs deriving from neurobiology and genetics (18), but what has helped clinical studies most is the formulation of operational diagnostic criteria for the axis II disorders in DSM-III. These include the "eccentric," "dramatic," and "anxious" clusters of personality disorders. Despite the existence of an extensive classical literature (30,31,43) on affective personalities, they have received relatively little attention from the research community during the past decade. This neglect is in part due to DSM-III conventions, which recognized cyclothymic and dysthymic types only in their symptomatic forms classed under affective disorders; by contrast, schizotypal and related conditions were classified in the personality disorders (Axis II) section. In DSM-III-R (11), whereas the contrast between schizotypal and schizophrenic disorders is highlighted, dysthymic and cyclothymic disorders are further blurred with mood disorders in the "not otherwise specified" (formerly atypical depressive and atypical bipolar) categories. As a consequence, the lifelong or trait nature of cyclothymic and dysthymic disorders is not sufficiently appreciated, leading to much confusion regarding trait-state issues in mood disorders. This means that in practice, most individuals who develop depressive and/or manic episodes are being tagged with characterologic diagnoses other than those pertaining to classic descriptions of the affective temperaments.

Applying the Robins-Guze validating strategy (40) to delineate the personality border of affective disorders was one of the major research efforts at the University of Tennessee Mood Clinic. This chapter summarizes such efforts undertaken in Memphis (3,7,9,10) and those in collaborative investigations with Professor Cassano at the University of Pisa, Italy (15); our work has also benefited from the clinical observations and formulations of Kukopulos and his colleagues (32). In evaluating this combined U.S.-Italian work in the context of other trends in the research literature, this chapter evaluates the validity of individual affective personality types for inclusion into DSM-IV and ICD-10.

In this presentation, the term "temperament" is reserved for constitutionally determined traits, "character" denotes acquired traits, and "personality" is used in a more general descriptive sense subsuming both constitutionally and acquired attributes. Because our research has generally supported the conceptualization of the affective personalities as *formes frustes* of the major affective disorders, we prefer the term "temperament" when describing cyclothymic, hyperthymic, and dysthymic disorders.

THE CYCLOTHYMIC TEMPERAMENT

At the University of Tennessee Mood Clinic we have evaluated a large number of patients who were impulsive, erratic, and volatile, but who had never met the duration and syndromal criteria for manic-depressive illness (7). They sought help primarily because of repeated romantic or conjugal failure in the context of social and interpersonal disturbances such as episodic promiscuity, geographic instability, dilettantism in academic and professional pursuits, uneven work record, and an episodic pattern of alcohol and drug abuse that alternated between sedatives and stimulants.

These probands exhibited, at various times, many of the behavioral features of depression and hypomania. They alternated between short (typically, a few days) and irregular cycles of drive and lethargy; euthymic periods were relatively uncommon. Decreased need for sleep was followed by slothful hypersomnolence, creative spurts by intellectual aridity, arrogant and naive overconfidence by sudden and unexplained lowering of self-esteem, hedonistic pursuits by apathetic withdrawal, and people-seeking by self-isolation; in general, passionate involvement in things gave way to a sudden loss of *joie de vivre*. Some patients used terms like "high" and "low" in describing their humor, which alternated between irritability or nervous moods and emotional quietude, or rapidly went from explosive angry outbursts to guilty self-recriminations. Although we observed some premenstrual clustering of these behaviors, they also occurred at other phases of the menstrual cycle. A large number of patients in our sample denied subjective mood changes; their main complaints revolved around disruptions in love life or work brought about by unpredictable shifts in psychomotor activity. In other cyclothymics, irritable and choleric moods predominated, leading to a clinical picture characterized by dysphoric restlessness, impulsivity, obstructiveness, and hypercritical and complaining attitudes (9) often (mis)diagnosed as borderline personality. That the tempestuous biographies of such individuals represent the sequelae of bipolar swings is suggested by data from a recent study (27) showing that the cyclothymic offspring of bipolar patients have far greater disruption in their social lives than do their noncyclothymic siblings.

The bipolar origin of the personality disturbances reviewed above was validated in our study (7) by the biphasic nature of their clinical manifestations, the even sex ratio, and, when compared with personality disorders of a nonaffective type, an excess of full-blown depressive and hypomanic/manic episodes during prospective follow-up; as many as a third of these episodes occurred during treatment with tricyclic antidepressants (TCAs). Further, the types and rates of psychiatric disorders in their families were essentially identical to those of controls with classic bipolar illness. These findings were replicated by Depue and associates in a series of meticulously conducted studies (19) in a nonclinical population.

To summarize, these data suggest the existence of symptomatologically attenuated cyclothymic forms of bipolar illness manifested in a tempestuous life-style that creates interpersonal havoc. Labelling such behavior "borderline" is misleading, unless "borderline" were used as an adjective to qualify bipolar psychosis (5).

THE HYPERTHYMIC TEMPERAMENT

Lifelong hypomanic adjustment is so useful in work- and activity-oriented societies that it is rarely considered to represent a form of psychopathology. The drive and self-assured entrepreneurial attitude characteristic of hypomanic individuals often places them in leadership roles where their less desirable uninhibited and meddlesome traits are tolerated. Although their intensity tends to drive others away, their exuberance and outgoing behavior are counterbalancing assets. Impaired judgment in social, sexual, and financial spheres often irritate, alienate, or hurt their loved ones and associates, as well as jeopardize their own welfare and financial assets; lack of insight and hypertrophied use of denial prevents them from seeking psychiatric help even when these behaviors lead to personal disasters. They appear in psychiatric settings only when the development of explosive mania or paralyzing depressions force their loved ones to take action on their behalf. Although described in both the Kraepelinian (30,43) and the psychoanalytic (2) literature, the hypomanic personality type does not appear in DSM-III-R (11). Research in our Center (3) has led to an operationalization of such a personality profile (Table 1) based, in part, on Schneider's descriptions (43). As the term "hypomanic" is often used in a symptomatologic sense, we prefer the designation "hyperthymic" for the trait condition.

TABLE 1. *The hyperthymic temperament**

- Indeterminate early onset (<21 years)
- Habitual short sleeper, including weekends (<6 hours of sleep)
- High energy level
- At least 5 of the following traits:
    1) Irritable, cheerful, overoptimistic, or exuberant
    2) Overconfident, self-assured, boastful, bombastic, or grandiose
    3) Full of plans, improvident, or impulsive
    4) Overtalkative
    5) Warm, people-seeking, and extroverted
    6) Overinvolved and meddlesome
    7) Uninhibited, stimulus-seeking, or promiscuous

*Modified from Akiskal and Mallya (9)

It is of theoretical significance that the extroverted, ambitious, and driven person with an inordinate capacity for work—Sjobring's "substable" profile (36) for the bipolar personality—overlaps considerably with the duty-bound and work-addicted "anancastic" (compulsive) personality (11). Recent empirical support for this affinity of hyperthymic and anancastic personalities has come from the demonstration of a significant excess of obsessionality in the offspring of bipolars (26). The "typus melancholicus" described by Tellenbach (45) as the characterologic constellation in persons predisposed to melancholic episodes also overlaps to some extent with the hyperthymic adjustment described above. These hyperthymic individuals are extremely dedicated to work and find little time for leisure; their "dynamism," however, appears artificial, and is usually considered an overcompensated "defense" against depressive tendencies (16); indeed, they sometimes abuse stimulant drugs either to enhance their hypomania or to combat transient states of "fatigue" (actually depression, but that term, considered a sign of personal weakness, is almost never used in self-descriptions by hyperthymic individuals).

These affinities between hyperthymic and depressive personality types find further support in sleep studies (3). In the Sleep Disorders Center affiliated with our Mood Clinic, 12 work-addicted individuals with chronic hypomanic tendencies have been observed during the past decade. Nearly all were highly energetic and successful people in leadership positions or in lucrative businesses who, over the years, had typically needed only 4–5 hours of sleep nightly. However, they had been intermittently bothered by "nervous energy" and inability to sleep. Now, in late middle age, they found alcohol no longer effective in putting them to sleep. These patients vigorously denied depressive and other psychiatric symptoms. Yet their REM latencies and related sleep abnormalities—except for duration of sleep—were similar to those of primary dysthymic subjects.

The Pittsburgh group (33) has shown shortening of REM latency to be a marker of primary depressive illness; in our sleep laboratory (8), we found this marker in many subjects who had never experienced major affective episodes. This raises the possibility that shortened REM latency may represent a trait abnormality that is present between as well as during depressive episodes. In line with this suggestion is a prospective study by Rush et al. (42) that reported shortened REM latency during asymptomatic post-recovery (drug-free) phases of depressive illness. Our finding of an abnormally shortened REM latency in hypomanic individuals may seem paradoxical. However, the drive and work habits of these individuals suggest that their adjustment is brittle and may have an underlying depressive component, as confirmed by a recent study of Cassano and associates (15) showing high rates of major depressive breakdown not only in those with depressive temperament, but also in those with hyperthymic temperament. A higher frequency of brief depressive episodes in hyperthymic subjects than controls has also been found in a study by Eckblad and Chapman (21).

That bipolar illness might arise from hyperthymic or related temperamental substrates is supported by some, but not all studies. Perris (38) reported that the extraversion/neuroticism ratio is higher in bipolars than unipolars. However, Hirschfeld et al. (24) failed to show unipolar-bipolar personality differences when they examined symptomatically recovered patients. Likewise, preliminary analysis of the Zurich prospective study by Angst failed to show any personality disturbances predictive of bipolar breakdowns (Clayton, personal communication, September 1987). Other studies have shown recovered bipolars to be entirely nonneurotic (20). One can either conclude that the premorbid adjustment of bipolar illness is normal or that the temperamental disturbance in this illness consists of denial of negative affective arousal and, possibly, avoidance of introspection. The latter interpretation is in line with our findings on hyperthymic and cyclothymic subjects who, despite considerable psychomotor disturbances and social dissonance, downplayed subjective distress. The hypomanic's denial of negative affects has also been commented on by others (2).

In conclusion, although hyperthymic personality is often expressed in highly adaptive extraverted traits, denial of distress and personal limitations, and an enormous capacity for work, there also appears to be an unstable adjustment. It is this very instability that leads to interpersonal losses, unusually intense work habits, and stimulant abuse (any of which may lead to sleep reduction), factors known to precede the onset of depressive and manic episodes (4,47).

THE DEPRESSIVE TEMPERAMENT

Cyclothymic and hyperthymic temperaments appears to have relevance for the cyclic forms of mood disorder. In unipolar depressive disorders, psychoanalytic formulations (17) have focused on dependency and obsessionalism. More recent cognitive formulations (1,29) have emphasized negative attributional styles. Both of these formulations failed to find major support in the NIMH collaborative study by Hirschfeld et al. (23), who reported obsessionalism, dependency, and negative self-attributions to be largely state-dependent; only introversion and lack of social adroitness emerged as distinct attributes of recovered depressives. Such data tend to favor Lewinsohn's model (34), which emphasizes the inadequacy of the behavioral repertoire of the depressive in the service of social reinforcement. All of these viewpoints, whether exploratory or based on systematic enquiries, have the methodologic limitation of being retrospective reconstructions of the premorbid characteristics of already depressed subjects. A prospective European study conducted on an epidemiologic sample (37) concluded that these deficits might be secondary to an "asthenic" disposition characterized by introversion and a tendency to easily give up. However, this study, as well as Perris' cross-sectional observations (38), suggests considerable overlap in the personalities of those prone to depressive and anxiety states.

We explored the temperamental foundations of depressive illness in 65 probands who reported they have "always" (at least since puberty) had depressive tendencies (10,41). In clinical parlance, such individuals are often considered "characterologic depressives" in whom dysphoric mood, low self-esteem, and pessimism are so deeply ingrained that they appear to be part of the personality structure. These characterologically expressed affective disturbances were until recently generally considered resistant to treatment. The disappointing results with pharmacotherapy can perhaps be ascribed to the tendency to overlook these patients' social deficits; psychotherapy on the other hand, appears impotent in reversing the temperamentally based inertia characteristic of these patients. In this heterogeneous universe of characterologic depressives, we could distinguish two groups on the basis of their response to treatment by a combination of behavioral modalities such as social skills training and vigorous sequential trials of several TCAs and/or lithium carbonate. Those who responded to this strategy—approximately a third of the sample—were hypothesized to represent an attenuated or "subaffective dysthymic" disorder in view of family history (often bipolar), superimposed major depressive episodes, and hypomanic responses to TCAs. The equal sex ratio observed was also in keeping with these bipolar tendencies. It is noteworthy that even when not in a depressive episode, these patients had the shortened REM latency characteristic of primary depressive states. By contrast, the nonresponsive group had normal REM latency, familial alcoholism, and high rates of parental loss early in life, and were classified as having a "character-spectrum" disorder. This nonresponsive group had lifelong instability, punctuated by transient nonmelancholic depressive episodes.*

The "subaffective" hypothesis of the origin of some dysthymic personality disturbances has been independently supported by positive response to imipramine in a study by Kocsis et al. (28). The subaffective dysthymic versus character-spectrum distinction was supported by Hauri and Sateia (22) who replicated the abnormal sleep EEG findings in dysthymic probands who conformed to the subaffective dysthymic pattern described above, and by Rihmer (39, in press), who has observed familial, developmental, and personality differences as well as pharmacologic response patterns similar to those of our initial report; in addition, he has shown that the subaffective dysthymic, unlike the character-spectrum patient, will often show positive responses to sleep deprivation.

The studies reviewed here argue in favor of the subaffective dysthymic pattern as one type of depressive personality. These individuals, who are introverted, obsessional, self-sacrificing, brooding, guilt-ridden, gloomy, self-denigrating, anhedonic, lethargic, and who tend to oversleep, appear to be suffering from an attenuated but lifelong form of melancholia. In collaborative work with the University of Pisa (16), we found that these dysthymic individuals were characterized by inability to enjoy leisure and overdedication to work that requires selfless devotion and much attention to detail. However, this stable adjustment in the vocational sphere was not paralleled in social adjustment. The somber personalities and in-

---

*Although Winokur and associates (49) have used the term "depression spectrum disorder" for this group, their own data underscore the characterologic—rather than the affective—nature of the illness. Like Winokur's sample, our character-spectrum subgroup was predominantly female.

tense attachment needs of these individuals may drive others away. Such interpersonal losses then cause them to sink into lower depths of black humor. Recent prospective observations have shown their vulnerability to depressive breakdowns, leading to the "double depressive" pattern, i.e., major depressive episodes superimposed on a dysthymic substrate (25). The personality attributes of these dysthymic subjects are reminiscent of the depressive personality described by Schneider (43) and Kretschmer (31) and, to some extent, of the psychoanalytic construct of "masochistic" personality (13,44).

Table 2 provides criteria for the depressive personality based on classical descriptions as modified by the case material examined at our Mood Clinic and in Pisa, Italy. We use the term "depressive" rather than "dysthymic" for this personality disorder, because the latter term is reserved in DSM-III-R (11) for a more symptomatic Axis I disorder. McCullough (35), too, has emphasized the trait aspect of the disorder, which he equates with acquired character pathology. Our data instead support a subaffective temperament. Although habitually introverted, depressive personalities may, for brief periods of time, appear extraverted and driven. These extraverted tendencies reach the threshold of clinical hypomania when the patient is treated with antidepressant medication. Table 3 compares the respective rates of major depressive, spontaneous hypomanic (or manic), and TCA-mobilized hypomanic episodes in subaffective dysthymic subjects with those of cyclothymic and nonaffective personality disorder controls. Rates of TCA-hypomania are comparable in the depressive and cyclothymic groups and significantly higher than in nonaffective personality controls. Only the cyclothymics had spontaneous manic episodes. These results lead us to conclude that the subaffective depressive personality is a less penetrant form of cyclothymic disorder, representing a subtle expression of central affective dysregulation that is manifest predominantly in phasic "minidepressions" which form part of the habitual self of the individual. It is also likely that a continuum exists between the depressive person-

TABLE 2. *The depressive temperament**

- Indeterminate early onset (<21 years)
- Habitually long sleeper (>9 hours of sleep)
- Psychomotor inertia which is typically worse in the a.m.
- At least five of the following traits:
  1) Gloomy, pessimistic, humorless, or incapable of fun
  2) Quiet, passive, and indecisive
  3) Skeptical, hypercritical, or complaining
  4) Brooding and given to worry
  5) Conscientious or self-disciplining
  6) Self-critical, self-reproaching, and self-derogatory
  7) Preoccupied with inadequacy, failure, and negative events to the point of morbid enjoyment of one's failures

*Modified from Akiskal and Mallya (9)

TABLE 3. *Affective episodes (in percentages) in cyclothymic, subaffective dysthymic and personality disorder controls during 1–4 years of follow-up**

	Type of personality disorder		
	Cyclothymic (N=46)	Subaffective dysthymic (N=20)	Nonaffective (N=50)
Major depression**	24	55	4
Tricyclic-hypomania**	35	33	0
Hypomania/mania (spontaneous)**	22	0	0

*Summarized from Akiskal et al. (7,10)
**Except for absence of spontaneous hypomania, dysthymics—like cyclothymics—had significantly high rates of affective episodes compared with controls (p<.02).

ality as conceptualized here, the epidemiologically derived construct of brief recurrent depression (12) and the DSM-III-R dysthymia of the early onset type.

RELEVANCE FOR DSM-IV AND ICD-10

The hyperthymic and depressive types presented in Tables 1 and 2 are defined by their habitual traits rather than by state-dependent symptomatologic clusters. The two represent opposite poles in energy level and sleep requirements. Cyclothymes alternate between these two poles on a frequent basis. In both clinical (7) and population studies (19), the depressive type has greater prevalence, followed by the cyclothymic, with the hyperthymic being the least frequent. There is an irritable variant of the cyclothymic temperament (9), not as well validated as the other affective types, which represents the temperamental analogue of bipolar mixed states, i.e., a simultaneous mixture of the hyperthymic and the depressive types. Persons with irritable temperament are habitually hyperactive, they often complain of insomnia (rather than simply needing little sleep), and their mood is depressed, irritable, or choleric. They are often described as habitually "hyperactively depressed" and "ready to jump on the slightest occasion." Table 4 summarizes proposed operational criteria in need of further study.

Except for some affinity between the cyclothymic (especially irritable) and borderline personalities, and that between obsessive-compulsive, depressive, and hyperthymic personalities, the affective temperaments described in this chapter have their equivalents in neither DSM-III-R (11) nor the proposed ICD-10 (50). However, the depressive temperament does overlap with masochistic personality. The latter term implies a questionable sexual etiology. Its formulation as a "self-defeating" personality disorder in an appendix of DSM-III-R (11,48) emphasizes aspects of the disorder which are not present in all depressive personalities. Furthermore, sacrificing the self for the welfare of others is not synonymous with self-defeating behavior. For all these reasons, we prefer the more descriptive term "depressive personality."

TABLE 4. *Toward an operational definition of the irritable temperament**

- Indeterminate early onset (<21 years)
- Frequent insomnia
- Lifelong history of dysphoric restlessness
- At least 5 of the following traits:
  1) Moody—irritable and choleric
  2) Intense emotionality to such a degree that even normally pleasurable activities are often unendurable
  3) Tendency to focus on the negative side of things
  4) Hypercritical and complaining
  5) Ill-humored joking
  6) Obtrusive
  7) Impulsive

*Modified from Akiskal and Mallya (9)

In all of the affective types, the description of the various behavioral traits forming part of the "habitual self" does not imply that these manifestations are present on a constant basis. Typically these manifestations are intermittent, rather than continuous (10,12). The affective personality types described here belong on Axis II because their affective dysregulation is woven into the habitual self, probably on a lifelong basis with origin typically in childhood or adolescence. Yet a case can also be made for maintaining cyclothymia and dysthymia on Axis I for persons with later onset and greater severity of symptoms. Ultimately, consensus needs to develop on general principles to guide assigning lifelong disorders to Axis I or II.

TOWARD CONSTRUCT VALIDITY

The findings reviewed in this chapter support the classic position that views affective personalities as the precursors of clinical episodes in recurrent mood disorders. Recent data from three different sources further suggest that these personalities represent the earliest clinically observable phenotypic expressions of an underlying genetic diathesis for primary mood disorders.

1. Bertlesen et al. (14) have reported that "discordant" members for strict manic-depressive illness in monozygotic pairs in about a third of cases tend to exhibit many of these affective temperamental disturbances.
2. In a recent University of Tennessee study (6), we found high rates of dysthymic, hyperthymic, and cyclothymic personality in the teenaged and, particularly, prepubertal offspring of adult bipolar patients.
3. Furthermore, our studies (3) have revealed as much classic bipolar family history in patients with subaffective dysthymic, hyperthymic, and cyclothymic disorders as in hospitalized bipolar patients.

All affective personalities appear to be at high risk both for depressive episodes and for hypomania—especially when exposed to TCAs (9,32,46). It is also of considerable interest that bipolar I (characterized by mania) is more likely to arise from a depressive temperament, whereas bipolar II (characterized by recurrent retarded depressions, plus hypomanic symptoms) is more likely to arise from the hyperthymic temperament (15). This reversal from a given temperament to its "opposite" affective episode might represent one of the most fundamental characteristics of bipolarity.

As proposed elsewhere (4), the affective personalities might represent an intermediate stage between remote (hereditary and developmental) factors and precipitating stressors. The premorbid affective instability might itself trigger stressors such as separations, substance abuse, and sleep deprivation, all of which have been found on occasion to precede major affective breakdowns. The predisposing affective instability of these personalities appears rooted in midbrain dysregulation, as indicated by their sharing with full-blown depressions a shortened REM latency and related circadian abnormalities. This sleep abnormality appears a trait marker of vulnerability, and not merely a nonspecific reaction to stress or a correlate of anxiety, since patients with lifelong anxiousness or neuroticism do not display these circadian abnormalities in REM sleep (8). Overall, the sleep findings in affective personalities suggest the possibility that neurophysiologic abnormalities might precede—and thus underlie—the full-blown affective episodes.

A next step in establishing the validity of the proposed affective personality disorders would be a prospective follow-up study of their course. In particular, such research should address the mystery of why in a pedigree with recurrent mood disorders one often finds behaviorally "opposite" temperamental disorders such as the hyperthymic and the depressive.

REFERENCES

1. Abramson, L Y., Metalsky, G. I., and Alloy, L. B. In: *Social Cognition and Clinical Psychology: A Synthesis,* edited by L. Y. Abramson. Guilford, New York *(in press).*
2. Akhtar, S. (1988): *Integrative Psychiatry,* 6:37–52.
3. Akiskal, H. S. (1984): *Integrative Psychiatry,* 2:83–88.
4. Akiskal, H. S. (1986): *Psychopharmacol. Bull.,* 22:579–586.
5. Akiskal, H. S., Chen, S. E., Davis, G. C., Puzantian, V. R., Kashgarian, M., and Bolinger, J. M. (1985): *J. Clin. Psychiatry,* 46:41–48.
6. Akiskal, H. S., Downs, J., Jordan, P., Watson, S., Daugherty, D., and Pruitt, D. B. (1985): *Arch. Gen. Psychiatry,* 42:996–1003.
7. Akiskal, H. S., Khani, M. K., and Scott-Strauss, A. (1979): *Psychiatr. Clin. North Am.,* 2:527–554.
8. Akiskal, H. S., Lemmi, H., Dickson, H., King, D., Yerevanian, B. I., and VanValkenburg, C. (1984): *J. Affective Disord.,* 6:287–295.
9. Akiskal, H. S. and Mallya, G. (1987): *Psychopharmacol, Bull.,* 23:68–73.
10. Akiskal, H. S., Rosenthal, T. L., Haykal, R. F., Lemmi, H., Rosenthal, R. H., and Scott-Strauss, A. (1980): *Arch. Gen. Psychiatry,* 37:777–783.
11. American Psychiatric Association (1987): *Diagnostic and Statistical Manual of Mental Disorders,* 3rd edition, revised. Washington, D.C.
12. Angst, J. and Dobler-Mikola, A. (1985): *European Archives of Psychiatry and Neurological Sciences,* 234:408–416.

13. Asch, S. (1988): In: *Psychiatry,* Vol. 1, Chapter 27, edited by R. Michels and J. O. Cavenar. J. B. Lippincott, Philadelphia.
14. Bertlesen, A., Harvald, B., and Hauge, M. (1977): *Br. J. Psychiatry,* 130:338–351.
15. Cassano, G. B., Musetti, L., Perugi, G., Mignani, V., Soriani, A., McNair, D. M., and Akiskal, H. S. (1987): In: *Diagnostic et Traitement de la Depression,* edited by K. Biziére and S. Simon, pp. 91–125. Sanofi Recherche, Montpellier.
16. Cassano, G. B., Pergui, G., Maremmani, I., and Akiskal, H. S. In: *Dysthymic Disorder,* edited by S. Burton and H. S. Akiskal. Gaskell, Royal College of Psychiatrists, London *(in press).*
17. Chodoff, P. (1972): *Arch. Gen. Psychiatry,* 27:666–673.
18. Cloninger, C. R. (1986): *Psychiatric Developments,* 4:167–226.
19. Depue, R. A., Slater, J. F., Wolfstetter-Kausch, H., Klein, D., Goplerud, E., and Farr, D. (1981): *J. Abnorm. Psychol.,* 90:S381–437.
20. MacVane, J. R., Lange, J. D., Brown, W. A. (1978): *Arch. Gen. Psychiatry,* 35:1351–1354.
21. Eckblad, M., and Chapman, L. J. (1986): *J. Abnorm. Psychol.,* 95:214–222.
22. Hauri, P., and Sateia, M. J. (1984): *Sleep Res.,* 13:119.
23. Hirschfeld, R. M., Klerman, G., Clayton, P., and Keller, M. (1983): *Arch. Gen. Psychiatry,* 40:993–998.
24. Hirschfeld, R. M. A., Klerman, G. L., Keller, M. B., Andreasen, N. C., and Clayton, P. J. (1986): *J. Affective Disord.,* 11:81–89.
25. Keller, M. B., Lavori, P. W., Endicott, J., Coryell, W., and Klerman, G. L. (1983): *Am. J. Psychiatry,* 140:689–694.
26. Klein, D., and Depue, R. A. (1985): *J. Abnorm. Psycol.* 94:291–297
27. Klein, D., Depue, R., and Slater, J. (1985): *J. Abnorm. Psychol.* 94:115–127.
28. Kocsis, J. H., Frances, A. J., and Mann, J. J. (1985): *Psychopharmacol. Bull.,* 21:698–700.
29. Kovacs, M. and Beck, A. T (1978): *Am. J. Psychiatry,* 135:525–533.
30. Kraepelin, E. (1921): *Manic-depressive Insanity and Paranoia.* Livingstone, Edinburgh.
31. Kretschmer, E. (1936): *Physique and Character* (E. Miller, Trans.) Kegan Paul, Trench, Trubner and Co., Ltd., London.
32. Kukopulos, A., Caliari, B., Tundo, A., Minnai, G., Floris, G., Reginaldi, D., and Tondo, L. (1983): *Compr. Psychiatry,* 24:249–258.
33. Kupfer, D. J., and Thase, M. D. (1983): *Psychiatr. Clin. North Am.,* 6:3–21.
34. Lewinsohn, P. M. (1974): In: *The Psychology of Depression: Contemporary Theory and Research,* edited by R. J. Freidman and M. M. Katz. Halstead, New York.
35. McCullough, J. P. *J. Nerv. Ment. Dis. (in press)*
36. Nyman, G. D. (1956): *Acta Psychiatr. Scand.,* 107:1–94.
37. Nystrom, S., and Lindegard, B. (1975): *Acta Psychiatr. Scand.,* 51:69–76.
38. Perris, C. (1971): *Acta Psychiatr. Scand.,* Suppl. 194:83–91.
39. Rihmer, Z. In: *Dysthymic Disorder,* edited by S. Burton and H. S. Akiskal, Gaskell, Royal College of Psychiatrists, London *(in press).*
40. Robins, E., and Guze, S. B. (1970): *Am. J. Psychiatry,* 126:983–987.
41. Rosenthal, T. L., Akiskal, H. S., Scott-Strauss, A., Rosenthal, R. H., and David, M. (198): *J. Affective Disord.,* 3:183–192.
42. Rush, A. J., Erman, M. K., and Giles, D. E. (1986): *Arch. Gen. Psychiatry,* 43:878–884.
43. Schneider, K. (1958): *Psychopathic Personalities* (M. W. Hamiton, trans.). Cassell, Ltd., London.
44. Simons, R. C. (1987): *J. Am. Psychoanal. Assoc.,* 35:583–608.
45. Telenbach, H. (1980): *Melancholia* (E. Eng., Trans.). Duquesne University Press, Pittsburgh.
46. Wehr, T. A., and Goodwin, F. K. (1987): *Am. J. Psychiatry,* 144:1403–1411.
47. Wehr, T. A., Sack, D. A., and Rosenthal, N. E. (1987): *Am. J. Psychiatry,* 144:201–204.
48. Widiger, T. A., Frances, A., Spitzer, R. L., and Williams, J. B. W. (1988): *Am. J. Psychiatry,* 145:786–795.
49. Winokur, G. (1979): *Arch. Gen Psychiatry,* 36:47–57.
50. World Health organization (1988): *ICD-10 Draft.* WHO, Geneva.

The Validity of Psychiatric Diagnosis, edited by
Lee N. Robins and James E. Barrett.
Raven Press, Ltd., New York © 1989.

Diagnostic Validity and Laboratory Studies: Rules of the Game

Bernard J. Carroll

*Department of Psychiatry, Duke University Medical Center,
Durham, North Carolina 27710*

Laboratory measures properly were included by Robins and Guze (1) among the desirable approaches to diagnostic validity in psychiatric disorders. In some areas such as depression encouraging progress has occurred, and one may be cautiously optimistic today that the biological heterogeneity revealed by some laboratory measures will prove important in future classifications of depressive disorders.

The significance of recent laboratory measures in depression is a controversial topic. Modest and reasonable proposals for the dexamethasone suppression test (DST) and sleep electroencephalogram (EEG) became exaggerated; methodological, conceptual, and interpretive caveats were ignored; and some clinicians adopted these tests uncritically with the enthusiasm of magical, absolutist thinking. Such phenomena are not new in the sociology of medicine. A similar reaction occurred when Paul Ehrlich introduced arsphenamine for the treatment of syphilis (recall the distorted exaggeration about a "magic bullet"); when hydrocortisone became available in the late 1940s (Oliver Sacks [2] has remarked that some medical conferences at that time resembled revivalist meetings more than scientific discussions); and after l-DOPA was introduced for parkinsonism in the late 1960s (2). Later, a critical counterreaction occurred, more concerned with the distortions and secondary claims than with the original proposals. Negative reviews, sometimes flawed in accuracy and scholarship (3), focused so much on the question of absolute specificity that the potential value of such measures in the subclassification of depression became a secondary issue. This trend doubtless was related to the concurrent deemphasis in DSM-III of the distinction between endogenous and other depressions.

An unfortunate consequence of such positive and negative absolutist thinking has been a tendency to hold laboratory measures to a higher standard than other external validators of diagnosis. As is clear in many of the chapters in this volume, inconsistent results among studies of genetics or natural history or treatment response are at least as common as in studies of laboratory measures. Indeed, these other proposed external validators rarely have been subjected to the stringent analyses of conditional probability that are the norm for laboratory measures.

Rather than hold laboratory measures to an unrealistic standard of perfection, a preferable approach would be to study their documented performance in the same way as clinical symptoms and other external validators, so that we take advantage of the incremental information they provide.

The eventual goal of discovering laboratory measures for validation remains important, but we are not yet within sight of such measures that can stand alone as etiologically relevant. The current tests all are surrogate measures (4) rather than pathognomonic indicators of the primary disease process (as are the vast majority of laboratory tests in the rest of medicine). Even though we have no "absolutely" reliable clinical tests in psychiatry, nevertheless, as Guze and others have emphasized, a less than perfect laboratory measure still may be useful. In other words, laboratory measures used within defined clinical contexts can offer important information for many research and clinical questions. The purpose of this review is to survey the potential of laboratory measures in the validation of diagnoses of major depression and its subtypes. In this chapter there will be emphasized methodologic issues that both biologic and nonbiologic investigators must keep in mind if they would fully appreciate what laboratory measures can offer. These issues are subsumed in 10 "rules of the game" fundamental to future research in depression, and that can be generalized to other diagnostic questions.

Rule 1: Only an iterative process can establish the value of laboratory measures. This rule applies also to all the other external validators proposed by Robins and Guze. By the iterative process of alternately regarding the clinical diagnosis as the independent, then the dependent variable in relation to other data, our nosology can be refined. Investigators unable to adopt this iterative approach will not progress beyond our unsatisfactory current syndromal nosologies that are based solely on clinical signs and symptoms.

Rule 2: No biologic measure can in principle do better than the clinical independent variable against which it is compared. This rule is a simple point of logic. It follows that if the "gold standard" clinical diagnosis is flawed, then the interpretation of laboratory measures will be compromised. In other words, laboratory measures can never "outperform" clinical diagnoses; they can only look worse. How much worse they might *appear* to be is illustrated in the next two rules.

Rule 3: Diagnostic reliability affects the apparent performance of a laboratory measure. Any proposed external validator necessarily will appear weaker than it really is when there is significant unreliability in the assignment of clinical diagnoses to patients. Nonbiologic investigators too readily overlook the widely documented unreliability of diagnoses of major depression and its subtypes when evaluating proposed laboratory measures such as the DST or sleep EEG. In Fig. 1, the degradation of apparent sensitivity and specificity of an external validator is illustrated in relation to the Kappa coefficient of diagnostic concordance. The figure illustrates a laboratory measure that is 65% sensitive and 95% specific under conditions of perfect agreement and accuracy for the assignment of clinical diagnoses. The *apparent* sensitivity and specificity then will be considerably lower un-

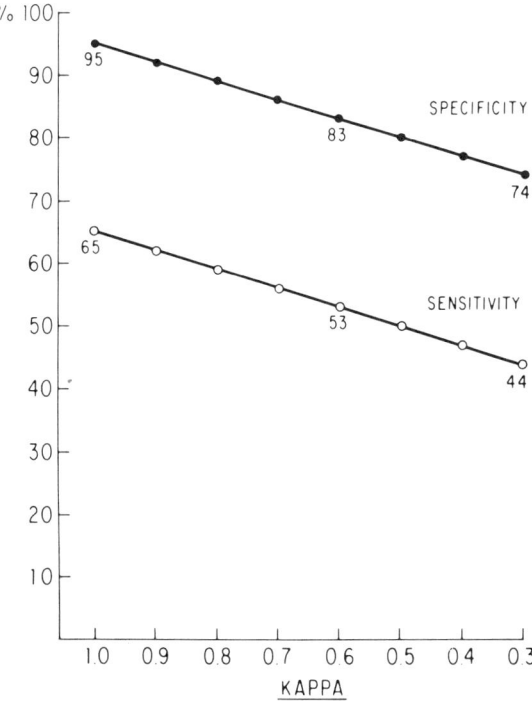

FIG. 1. Influence of diagnostic reliability on apparent sensitivity of a diagnostic test. Diagnostic reliability is indicated by Cohen's Kappa coefficient of diagnostic concordance (abscissa). A true sensitivity of 65% and a true specificity of 95% are assumed under conditions of perfect agreement and accuracy in assigning the clinical diagnoses (K = 1.0). Subsequent calculations assume (a) two observers make the diagnoses; (b) a binary diagnostic decision (e.g., endogenous/nonendogenous) is required; and (c) diagnostic disagreements (and inaccuracies) are distributed symmetrically at each K value below 1.0.

der real life conditions. For example, even in research units (5) the expected Kappa values are only about 0.6 when two clinicians independently assess the usual mix of psychiatric patients to diagnose major depression or separate endogenous depressive subtypes from non-endogenous depressions. The apparent sensitivity of the laboratory measure then would be 53% rather than 65% and its apparent specificity would be 83% rather than 95%. The apparent loss of specificity will appear most troubling to uneducated observers, even though this apparently poor performance has nothing to do with inherent problems of the laboratory measure, but rather is entirely predictable from the known unreliability of the clinical diagnoses. Indeed, given what we know about the actual unreliability of diagnoses of depression with current criteria, one would have to predict that no laboratory measure (or other external validator) could consistently appear highly specific when studied so widely as the DST or sleep EEG measures have been. Consequently, opinions about the lack of diagnostic utility of such measures (3,6) must be viewed with caution. Such caution will be even more in order when the diagnostic criteria are applied by unskilled personnel, or when the comparison groups selected are nosologically insecure, such as patients with schizoaffective disorder, atypical psychosis, schizophreniform disorder, and dysphoric borderline personality disorder. For these disorders, the established diagnostic reliability coefficients are even lower than for cases of major depression and its subtypes.

Rule 4: Diagnostic validity will affect the apparent performance of a laboratory measure. Whenever a diagnostic laboratory measure is proposed, its apparent performance in replication studies doubtless will be affected to the extent to which the diagnostic criteria used in the subsequent studies differ from those used in the original study. In the case of the DST, for example, the diagnostic guidelines specified (7) were based on the ICD-8 glossary and the ICD-9-CM (8,9). These diagnostic guidelines follow the historical European, Kraepelinian concepts of manic depressive illness and melancholia. Using these guidelines, we obtained good results with the DST for the diagnosis of melancholia (7,10). I should emphasize that the primary application we proposed for the DST was in the differential diagnosis of melancholic (endogenous) from nonendogenous depression. The separation of melancholic depression from various other "boundary" conditions is a separate issue which our own data did not address systematically (7,10).

Other groups using other criteria have had variable success in replicating our reported performance of the DST in the differential diagnosis of depressive subtypes. To put this matter in perspective, however, similar variability has been found in studies examining such a basic issue as the antidepressant efficacy of imipramine. At least one-third of the controlled studies of that question fail to confirm the superiority of imipramine over placebo treatment for depressed patients (11), yet nobody seriously believes that imipramine is not an effective antidepressant drug. Negative reports about the DST and other laboratory measures should be viewed in this light. The reasons for failure by some centers to replicate the diagnostic performance of the DST are similar to the reasons for negative reports about the specific antidepressant efficacy of imipramine. Chief among these reasons will be the validity of the clinical population of "depressed" patients and of the diagnostic criteria by which they were selected. A recent study illustrates very well the effect of varying diagnostic criteria on the apparent performance of the DST (12).

In this study, 66 inpatients with a clear depressive syndrome were studied using a 1.5 mg dose DST and with the requirement that the 0800h plasma dexamethasone concentration be above a threshold value of 200 ng/dL. The performance of the DST in the differential diagnosis of endogenous and nonendogenous subtypes then was evaluated with several sets of proposed diagnostic criteria, three of which are illustrated in Table 1. The best agreement between DST results and diagnostic classification of endogenous/nonendogenous depression was obtained using the ICD-9 guidelines. A somewhat lower but encouraging agreement was obtained using the Newcastle I Diagnostic Index (13), which is not surprising, as this index represents an attempt to operationalize the ICD diagnostic approach.

TABLE 1. *DST and endogenous classification*

Dx System	N ED	Sensitivity %	Specificity %	PV + 50 %
ICD 9	42	45	96	92
Newcastle I	31	48	86	77
DSM III	26	35	73	56

Influence of three alternative diagnostic systems on the apparent performance of the DST in 66 depressed inpatients (12). N ED denotes the number of cases classified as endogenous (or melancholic) by each diagnostic system.

PV + 50 denotes predictive value of an abnormal test result for the diagnosis of endogenous depression assuming a standardized 50% prevalence rate for this diagnosis.

The DSM-III criteria, however, applied to the *same patients* showed a much lower agreement with the laboratory measure, especially as reflected by the reduced apparent specificity. The predictive value of an abnormal test result ranged from 92% with ICD-9 to only 56% (virtually no better than chance) with DSM-III.

These results, which are quite similar to others reported in the literature, have several important implications. First, they confirm what we already know, namely, that the alternative classifications for endogenous/nonendogenous depression are not equivalent. The number of patients classified as endogenous ranged from a high of 42 with ICD-9 to a low of 26 with DSM-III. *Being not equivalent, these classifications are unlikely to be equally valid.* Second, such data do not encourage one to persist with the use of DSM-III criteria in the search for laboratory validators of diagnosis. Third, in reviewing these data, it is important to retain an open mind on the diagnostic alternatives. One could say that ICD-9 is not on trial in this comparison so much as DSM-III is on trial. ICD-9 is generally regarded in the U.S. as inferior to DSM-III because the ICD-9 diagnostic guidelines for depression are not "operationalized". Nevertheless, the ICD-9 approach is in direct continuity with the astute, intuitive, and imaginative insight of Kraepelin (14), whereas DSM-III depressive diagnoses derive from a different tradition that has yet to stand the tests of time and of data. In other words, we have here a classical tension between diagnostic validity and diagnostic reliability, as reviewed by Blashfield in this volume (15). At the very least, these data suggest that a pluri-diagnostic approach should be maintained in future studies of laboratory measures. The example illustrated in Table I strongly suggests that the laboratory measure, by revealing a dimension of biological heterogeneity, is telling us something important about the validity of the alternative classification systems. Nonbiologic investigators would do well to pay attention to this message. Indeed, recalling Rule 1, one could propose that the validity and homogeneity of a clinical diagnostic entity will be related to the frequency of abnormal biologic markers in that category (7). In other words, laboratory measures may help us choose among alternative symptom-based classification systems. A further illustration of this principle is shown in Table 2 where the endogenous/nonendogenous classification

TABLE 2. *DST with two classification systems (N = 137)*

N		Sensitivity %	Specificity %
95	Melancholia (Michigan ICD Dx)	59	98
42	Nonendogenous		
120	Primary MDD (Washington U Criteria)	43	71
17	Secondary MDD		

Influence of two alternative classification systems on the apparent performance of the DST in 137 depressed patients (Carroll, B.J., Feinberg, M., and Greden, J.F., unpublished data).

based on our ICD-derived guidelines (7) is compared with the primary/secondary classification of the Washington University group (16). Here again, the laboratory measure agreed much better with the endogenous/nonendogenous than with the primary/secondary classification system. Thase and colleagues recently have found a similarly stronger association of the REM sleep abnormalities with RDC endogenous/nonendogenous than with primary/secondary diagnostic subtypes of depression (17), thus confirming the original finding of Rush (18).

Rule 5: Any candidate laboratory measure must be evaluated by the standard approaches of face validity, construct validity, and predictive validity. Evidence of *face validity* will include acceptable sensitivity, high specificity, a high predictive value derived from the first two measures, and a probability gradient for sensitivity that parallels the clinical probability or certainty of the diagnosis.

Construct validation of an episode-related laboratory measure can come from many directions. The sum of converging evidence of this type will reflect the likely validity of the laboratory measure. Some of the construct validation approaches used with the DST as a marker of endogenous depression, for example, are: (a) it should revert to normal on full recovery from the episode; (b) a gradual reduction in the severity of the laboratory abnormality may be seen as clinical improvement occurs; (c) the abnormality should be consistently present in recurrent episodes of illness; (d) the laboratory disturbance may reappear before the clinical symptoms of a new episode of illness; (e) the extent of abnormality in the laboratory measure may be related to the clinical severity of illness; (f) an association between the laboratory disturbance and a family history of the disorder may be present; (g) a high frequency of abnormality is expected in subjects who proceed to treatment with ECT, the most biologic treatment for depression; (h) an association between the laboratory measure and the most serious complication of depression, namely suicide, may be found; (i) the laboratory disturbance should reflect disturbed function within the limbic areas of the brain that are believed responsible for the clinical manifestations of the depressive disorder.

Predictive validation also can be assessed in several ways. A valid laboratory marker should predict response to treatments. This will involve the evaluation not only of response to antidepressant drug treatment in patients with and without the marker present, but also the prediction of response to alternative treatments such as placebo and psychotherapy. This aspect is discussed below at greater length. Another approach is to study the predictive value of the laboratory marker for relapse in patients during follow-up. Considerable evidence of this type now exists for both the DST and the REM sleep abnormalities of depressed patients (19,20). In the case of the DST, patients who appear to have recovered but in whom the neuroendocrine marker still is present when they leave inpatient treatment have a high rate of relapse and suicide during follow-up periods of 6 months; the REM sleep abnormalities appear to be more of a "trait" marker in that they are persistently abnormal in recovered patients after all drug treatment is withdrawn and the finding of a short REM latency likewise predicts early relapse.

A third approach to predictive validity involves the follow-up study of patients initially considered to have "false positive" laboratory abnormalities. In a recent study of the DST, for example (21), five such results were obtained among 36 inpatients with depressive features who were considered not to meet diagnostic criteria for DSM-III major depressive disorder. The apparent specificity of the test, therefore, was 86%. Four of these five "false-positive-DST" patients had unstable clinical diagnoses, which changed to major depression on short-term follow-up: (i) adjustment disorder with depressed mood to major depression (symptoms of only 1 week duration when first evaluated); (ii) adjustment disorder with depressed mood to major depression with psychosis (readmitted 2 weeks after discharge); (iii) brief reactive psychosis to bipolar major depression with psychosis (readmitted for mania and responded to lithium): and (iv) schizophrenia to bipolar disorder. From a longitudinal clinical perspective, the investigators concluded that the initial cross-sectional diagnoses were misleading and that the patients had suffered from undiagnosed major depression at the time of first admission. The laboratory data would be consistent with this interpretation. Viewed in the light of the revised diagnoses on follow-up, the revised specificity of the DST in this study then would be 97% rather than 86%. Additional studies of this type are needed.

Rule 6: Functional laboratory measures will be more informative than baseline biologic measures. This rule comes from both theory and recent experience. From a theoretical perspective, baseline measures generally will reveal less marked deviations from normal than will functional measures. Baseline measures may be apparently "normal" because of adaptive neurobiologic compensation in the disease state. Functional measures that are designed to reveal the response capacity and regulatory integrity of a neurobiologic system would be expected to reveal stronger evidence of dysregulation. This principle is well seen in the hypothalamo-pituitary-adrenal (HPA) axis of depressed patients. Baseline measures of plasma cortisol generally are normal or only mildly elevated and are of no value in distinguishing the endogenous from the nonendogenous subtype of major depression (10). With dexamethasone administration, however, HPA disinhibition is more clearly seen and the two subtypes are better separated. A recent sleep EEG study illustrates this same principle (22). In this study, a short REM latency criterion of 40 minutes was associated with a sensitivity of 38% and a specificity of 89% for the discrimination of endogenous from nonendogenous major depression. In the same patients, the shortening of latency to the second REM period under the influence of arecoline discriminated the two groups at the same level of specificity but with sensitivity now increased from 38% to 75%.

Rule 7: Combinations of laboratory markers will be more useful than individual markers. The logic of this rule is the same as the logic of diagnostic algorithms that use combinations of clinical features rather than individual signs or symptoms, e.g., DSM-III criteria for major depression. There now is a considerable literature on the use of multiple markers, either in series or in parallel, for the separation of subtypes of depression. These early studies all rely on the principle that at least one laboratory abnormality is required for the identification of the endogenous subtype. Using this approach, the sensitivity observed is considerably increased above that obtained with a single marker, and the specificity is affected only slightly (23). As has always been the case with individual markers, however, diagnostic importance attaches only to the finding of an abnormal test result. Normal test results are uninformative.

In a recent extension of the combined marker approach, Feinberg and Carroll (24) have proposed a research strategy that promises also to increase the diagnostic significance of *normal* laboratory results in depressed patients. This study involved both the DST and the sleep EEG. For the latter, a discriminant function (DF) was derived using the variables REM latency and REM density. Sleep DF values less than one were strongly associated with the endogenous subtype while sleep DF values greater than two were strongly associated with the nonendogenous subtype. Patients with intermediate sleep DF values were considered unclassified. When these data were combined with DST results, a research category of "biological depression" was defined by a positive DST with a sleep DF value less than one. Similarly, a research category of "nonbiological depression" was defined by a normal DST result and a sleep DF value greater than two. This approach permitted the new biological/nonbiological classification of 40% of a group of 119 depressed patients. The laboratory-defined category biological depression agreed in 94% of the cases with the clinical subtype of endogenous depression; more importantly, the laboratory-defined category of nonbiologic depression agreed in 90% of the cases with the clinical subtyping of nonendogenous depression. This research strategy deserves to be pursued in future studies despite the limitation that many patients will be unclassified. From the clinical direction a similarly restrictive approach has been taken by Checkley (25) who recommends the study of patients on the two extremes of the Newcastle index for endogenous/nonendogenous depression in the development of laboratory markers, while leaving to a second stage the assessment of the markers' performance in the substantial group with intermediate Newcastle scale scores.

Rule 8: Laboratory measures do not have to stand alone but can be added to clinical features in diagnostic algorithms. Gillespie emphasized long ago that "no one sign will serve as a touchstone for diagnosis, or prognosis, or as a therapeutic indication" in the subtyping of depressed patients (26). The same is true for laboratory measures like the DST. When laboratory measures are compared with clinical features for their discriminative value, however, their performance is robust. To illustrate this point, Table 3 displays the diagnostic performance of three classical vegetative symptoms used in all clinical algorithms for depression. This study involved the comparison of 41 patients with major depression (23 of whom had chronic pain complaints) and 33 patients with chronic pain disorder, none of whom were considered to have associated major depression. The setting of a chronic pain unit is highly relevant clinically for the diagnosis of depression. In this setting the predictive values of these venerable clinical features for depression ranged from 70% to 80%. The symptom of diurnal mood variation had the highest predictive value but also the lowest sensitivity. In these same patients the DST performed with an observed specificity of 100% and a sensitivity of 40%. Thus, the observed predictive value of the DST in this population was 100%. Even assuming that eventually some false positive DST results would occur at, say, a 5% or even at a 10% rate, then, as illustrated in the lower portion of Table 3, the predictive value of the abnormal DST result still would be at least as high as that of the best clinical symptom and with considerably higher sensitivity. Such data are highly relevant to the construction of new diagnostic algorithms for DSM-IV subtypes of depression. Obviously, in this process data on the actual discriminating value of the clinical signs and symptoms will be desirable, in addition to knowledge of the performance of the laboratory measures.

Such data that do exist are unimpressive. For example, Davidson (27) has reported predictive values lower than 65% for the same symptoms discussed above in the differentiation of endogenous from nonendogenous depression by the Newcastle index. The same author (28) reports a predictive value of 82% for the DST in similar patients classified by the Newcastle index. Thus, such a laboratory measure could be included in the next generation of diagnostic algorithms to

TABLE 3. *Discriminative value of clinical features and DST in depression—chronic pain study*

	Sensitivity %	Specificity %	PV + 50 %
Early waking	78	67	70
Weight loss	63	79	75
Diurnal variation	24	94	80
DST (observed)	40	100	100
DST (projected)	40	95	89
DST (projected)	40	90	80

Diagnostic performance of three typical symptoms and DST in 74 patients with major depression (41) or chronic pain syndrome (33) (see text).

PV+50 denotes predictive value of the presence of the symptom or of an abnormal DST result, respectively, for the diagnosis of major depression assuming a standardized 50% prevalence rate for this diagnosis.

(Krishnan, K.R.R., Davidson, J.R.T., and France, R.D., unpublished data, Duke University Medical Center.)

strengthen the discrimination achieved with clinical features alone. This approach would serve the further useful purpose of reminding clinicians that laboratory data like DST results must be evaluated within specified clinical contexts.

Rule 9: Laboratory measures convey information to enable revision of the probability of clinical diagnoses and this information value will not be the same for every case. This rule derives from a frequently neglected principle that has been emphasized elsewhere: laboratory measures can best be interpreted in clinical context (29,30). Diagnoses, after all, are only probability statements, and those unable to think in probability terms about the diagnosis of an individual case tend not to understand this rule. A recent example from neurology will illustrate the principles involved.

Goodin and Aminoff (31) discuss the diagnostic value of the interictal EEG in the diagnosis of epilepsy. Recordings were obtained from 764 patients diagnosed epileptic and 948 patients eventually diagnosed nonepileptic. Paroxysmal spike-and-sharp-wave discharge patterns were sought in the EEG recordings. The sensitivity obtained was 52% and the specificity reported was 96%. In this illustration some important parallels between epilepsy and depression are pertinent. Epilepsy is a clinical diagnosis just as depression is a clinical diagnosis. The EEG is a laboratory aid for making the diagnosis of epilepsy but, as neurologists are fond of

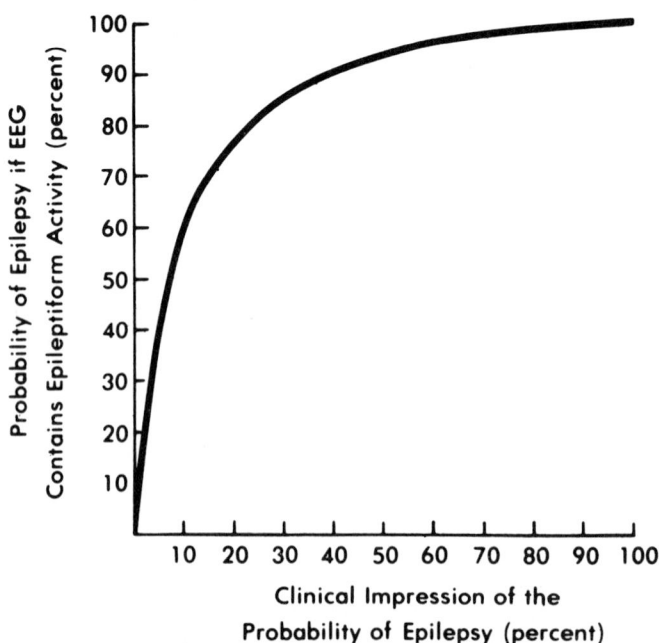

FIG. 2. Interaction between prior probability of epilepsy based on clinical history and examination (abscissa) and posterior probability of epilepsy when the EEG is abnormal (ordinate), based on the data of Goodin and Aminoff (31) (see text). Reproduced with permission.

saying, "there is no such thing as an epileptic neuron" and the diagnosis will not be made without supporting clinical features, regardless of the observed EEG patterns. This accounts for the low but palpable (4%) false positive rate reported in the study. The modest sensitivity of the EEG (52%) is consistent with the well-known neurological tenet that a negative EEG study does not by itself rule out the diagnosis epilepsy. All these qualifications about the EEG in epilepsy apply equally to the use of the DST or sleep EEG measures as laboratory aids in the diagnosis of endogenous depression.

Regarding the individualized information value of the laboratory studies, Fig. 2 illustrates such an analysis for the EEG, based on the observed sensitivity and specificity data. The abscissa denotes the probability of the diagnosis based on the clinical history and physical examination. This prior probability ranges from 0 to 100%. The ordinate denotes the *revised* probability of the diagnosis epilepsy based on the finding of an abnormal EEG study. This posterior probability also ranges from 0 to 100%. The interaction between prior and posterior probabilities clearly reveals the individualized information value of an abnormal EEG result. Where the prior probability already is high, say 90%, then the revised probability for the patient based on a positive EEG study rises to 99%. In this context the EEG study essentially confirms the clinical impression. Where the prior probability is in the mid range, say 50%, the revised probability for that patient based on a positive EEG study is increased to 90%. In this context, clinically different from the first, the laboratory measure serves as a powerful diagnostic aid. In yet a third clinical context, however, where the prior probability is low, say 2%, then the revised probability of the diagnosis epilepsy still is low at about 20% even if an abnormal EEG study is reported. Precisely the same principles will apply to the use of laboratory measures for diagnoses of depression or depressive subtypes. Further elaboration of these principles of context-based clinical decision analysis (as opposed to population-based predictive value analysis) has been presented recently by Krishnan et al. (32).

A related point concerns the context-based interpretation of specificity data for laboratory measures. A common error among reviewers of laboratory measures in psychiatry is to present unweighted average estimates of specificity in accordance with the early predictive value model of laboratory test interpretation. These unweighted average estimates of test specificity ignore the probabilities of nondepressive diagnoses for a given case. For example, the high positive DST rates observed in advanced Alzheimer's disease are not clinically relevant to the interpretation of the test result in a young patient who clearly is not demented. In other words, as discussed by Krishnan et al. (32), the prior probabilities of possible differential diagnoses for a given case are just as important as the prior probability of endogenous depression for the interpretation of a DST result. This issue of context and common sense brings to mind Marvin Minsky's comment about the same issue in the field of artificial intelligence and expert systems programming. As he pointed out, when one enters a room one might expect to see chairs, tables, and lamps, but not a battleship! Similarly, when one is evaluating a 30-year-old male teetotaler with depressive symptoms, certain differential diagnoses will be important but not Alzheimer's disease, alcohol withdrawal, or postpartum psychosis! Unweighted estimates of test specificity ignore such issues of clinical context and to that extent can lead to absurd reasoning (3).

Rule 10: Treatment response studies of the validity of laboratory measures are important but they must be controlled studies. Although Robins and Guze (1) did not emphasize specific response to treatment as a validating criterion for diagnosis, such studies increasingly are recognized as important. To be of any value for validation, however, these studies must be adequately controlled. Reviewers of the DST in relation to treatment response have overlooked this elementary principle (e.g., ref. 3). A compilation of uncontrolled studies of the DST in relation to response to antidepressant drug treatment suggests that there is no difference in rate of response whether the pretreatment DST result of a depressed patient is abnormal or normal. Three placebo-controlled studies (33,34,35), on the other hand, reveal that depressed patients with abnormal DST results uniformly fail to respond to placebo whereas 50% of those with normal DST results do respond (Table 4). One study (36) disagrees with the three just mentioned. Previously reported data from the same author (37,38) were consistent with those in Table 4, however, and the differences between this author's original and later reports need to be resolved.

A study of this question in 61 inpatients revealed that the placebo-corrected rate of specific response to antidepressant drugs was 69% among patients with an abnormal DST but less than 15% among those with normal DST results (35). This perspective from controlled clinical trials illustrates the potential importance of laboratory measures not only for validation of diagnoses but also for treatment. In the same vein, a preliminary report by Rush (39) suggests that patients with two abnormal laboratory measures, DST and sleep EEG, fail to respond to cognitive psychotherapy of their major depression whereas patients with normal values on both laboratory measures have a high rate of response to cognitive psychotherapy. Additional systematic studies of this area are needed.

TABLE 4. *DST and response to placebo*

Author (ref)	IP/OP	Abnormal DST Responders/nonresponders	Normal DST Responders/nonresponders
Shrivastava 1985 (33)	OP	0/9	10/12
Peselow, 1985 (34)	OP	0/7	7/5
Peselow, 1986 (35)	IP	0/5	7/5
TOTAL		0/21	24/22

Response to placebo of depressed patients according to pre-treatment DST result.
OP = outpatient study, IP = inpatient study.

CONCLUSION

In conclusion, the need for validation of clinical diagnoses of depression still is the major problem for research studies and clinical practice in this disorder. Referred to elsewhere (40) is the disturbing fact that current "operational" diagnostic criteria can yield groups of "major depressed" patients in whom it is impossible to demonstrate the therapeutic superiority of imipramine over placebo treatment! Also discussed (41) are the serious problems thereby created for the development of new antidepressant drugs as well as for other kinds of research studies. Clearly, there has been a significant shift in our diagnostic criteria and clinical nosology of depression beginning with the Washington University criteria in 1972 (16) and continuing through the Research Diagnostic Criteria and then DSM-III. Intense skepticism about this shift prevails among investigators who, like myself, came into the field of depression research through clinical psychopharmacology and biologic studies. It is to us very disconcerting that we cannot depend on the new diagnostic criteria and clinical nosologies reliably to identify depressed patients who will respond specifically to imipramine. After all, the antidepressant efficacy of imipramine was established in the first place using the "old fashioned" diagnostic systems of ICD-8 and DSM-II.

This need for the validation of clinical samples in research studies of depression cannot be overstated. When patients are recruited solely on the basis of "operationally defined" clinical signs and symptoms, *the acknowledged heterogeneity of the major depression syndrome is left uncontrolled*. These considerations return us to the iterative nature of our research task as outlined in Rule 1 above. From a scientific perspective, the crucial need is to obtain convergent evidence of the validity of the research population for the study of *any* question in the field of depression. From this perspective it may be pointless to spend time and research funds on family studies, or epidemiologic surveys, or natural history projects, or risk factor studies, and so forth unless we go beyond our unsatisfactory syndromal clinical criteria for case ascertainment and patient recruitment. In other words, real progress likely will not occur until a serious attempt is made to *triangulate* on the validity of the diagnoses. Practically speaking, this triangulation is not easily achieved. The ideal approach today would be to include a placebo-controlled treatment element in the research design so that the true relationship between the other variables of interest will be revealed. The example given above of the DST in relation to antidepressant drug treatment illustrates this point perfectly.

Laboratory measures may at some point in the future represent a more practical approach to this need for validation of research diagnoses. At the very least they will reveal additional dimensions of heterogeneity, some of which may prove to be strongly related to the deep nosologic structure of the syndrome major depression.

For the short term, the data reviewed above tell us that some laboratory measures already available outperform individual signs and symptoms for the endogenous/nonendogenous distinction. If the next generation of diagnostic algorithms are to be data-driven, as would be desirable, then the case for including the DST and sleep EEG along with selected clinical features (Rule 8) can be advocated strongly. The logic of this proposal is already seen in DSM-III-R, where two putative external validators, natural history and previous response to treatment, were added (without the benefit of data) to clinical symptoms in the diagnostic algorithm for melancholia (42).

Traditionalists will object that this proposal is too radical, that it presupposes too much about the significance of the laboratory measures. Shifts in paradigm predictably evoke such responses. Besides, the alternative is for us to continue to presuppose too much about the significance of demonstrably nonspecific and unreliable clinical signs and symptoms. That is not an encouraging prospect.

REFERENCES

1. Robins, E., Guze, S. B. (1970): Establishment of diagnostic validity in psychiatric illness: Its application to schizophrenia. *Amer J Psychiatry*, 126:983–987.
2. Sacks, O. (1973): *Awakenings*. Duckworth, London.
3. Arana, G. W., Baldessarini, R. J., and Ornsteen M. (1985): The dexamethasone suppression test for diagnosis and prognosis in psychiatry. *Arch Gen Psychiatry*, 42:1193–1204.
4. Feinstein, A. R. (1977): On the sensitivity, specificity and discrimination of diagnostic tests. In: *Clinical Biostatistics*. Mosby, St. Louis.
5. Bech, P., Gjerris, A., Andersen, J., et al. (1983): The melancholia scale and the Newcastle scales: Item-combinations and inter-observer reliability. *Brit J Psychiatry*, 143:58–63.
6. Berger, M., Pirke, K. M., Doerr, P., Krieg, J. C., and von Zerssen, D. (1984): The limited utility of the dexamethasone suppression test for the diagnostic process in psychiatry. *Brit J Psychiatry*, 145:372–382.
7. Carroll, B. J., Feinberg, M., Greden, J. F., Haskett, R., James, N. McI., Steiner, M., and Tarika, J. (1980): Diagnosis of endogenous depression: Comparison of clinical, research and neuroendocrine criteria. *J Affective Disorders*, 2:177–194.
8. World Health Organization. (1974): *Glossary of Mental Disorders and Guide to Their Classification for Use in Conjunction with the International Classification of Diseases, 8th Revision*. World Health Organization, Geneva.
9. Commission on Professional and Hospital Activities. (1978): *The International Classification of Disease, 9th Revision, Clinical Modification*. Commission on Professional and Hospital Activities, Ann Arbor.
10. Carroll, B. J., Feinberg, M., Greden, J., et al. (1981): A specific laboratory test for the diagnosis of melancholia: Standardization, validation and clinical utility. *Arch Gen Psychiatry*, 38:15–22.
11. Morris, J. B., and Beck, A. T. (1974): The efficacy of antidepressant drugs. *Arch Gen Psychiatry*, 30:667–674.
12. Philipp, J., Maier, W., and Holsboer F. (1986): Psychopathological correlates of plasma cortisol after dexamethasone suppression: A polydiagnostic approach. *Psychoneuroendocrinology*, 11:499–507.
13. Carney, M. W. P., Roth, M., and Garside, R. F. (1965): The diagnosis of depressive syndromes and the prediction of ECT response. *Brit J Psychiatry*, 111:639–645.
14. Kraepelin, E. (1921): *Manic depressive insanity and paranoia* (trans. by M. Barclay). Livingstone, Edinburgh.
15. Blashfield, R. K. (1989): Alternative taxonomic models for psychiatric classification. In: *The Validity of Psychiatric Diagnosis*, edited by Lee N. Robins and James Barrett. Raven Press, New York. pp. 19–34.
16. Feighner, J. P., Robins, E., Guze, S. B., Woodruff, R. A., Winokur, G., and Munoz, R. (1972): Diagnostic criteria for use in psychiatric research. *Arch Gen Psychiatry*, 26:57–63.
17. Thase, M. E., Kupfer, D. J., and Spiker, D. G. (1984): Electroencephalographic sleep in secondary depression: A revisit. *Biological Psychiatry*, 19:805–814.

18. Rush, A. J., Giles, D. E., Roffwarg, H. P., and Parker, C. R. (1982): Sleep EEG and dexamethasone suppression test findings in outpatients with unipolar major depressive disorders. *Biological Psychiatry*, 17:327–341.
19. APA Task Force on Laboratory Tests in Psychiatry. (1987): The dexamethasone suppression test: An overview of its current status in psychiatry. *Amer J Psychiatry*, 144:1253–1262.
20. Rush, A. J., Erman, M. K., Giles, D. E., Schlesser, M. A., Carpenter, G., Vasavada, N., and Roffwarg, H. P. (1986): Polysomnographic findings in recently drug-free and clinically remitted depressed patients. *Arch Gen Psychiatry*, 43:878–884.
21. Evans, D. L., and Nemeroff, C. B. (1987): The clinical use of the dexamethasone suppression test in DSM III affective disorders: Correlation with the severe depressive subtypes of melancholia and psychosis. *J Psychiatric Research*, 21:185–194.
22. Jones, D., Kelwala, S., Bell, J., Dube, S., Jackson, E., and Sitaram, N. (1985): Cholinergic REM sleep induction response correlation with endogenous major depressive subtype. *Psychiatry Research*, 14:99–110.
23. Feinberg, M., and Carroll, B. J. (1983): Biological markers for endogenous depression in series and parallel. *Biological Psychiatry*, 19:3–11.
24. Feinberg, M., and Carroll, B. J. Biological and nonbiological depression. *Biol Psychiatry*, (*in press*).
25. Checkley, S. A. (1979): Corticosteroid and growth hormone response to methylamphetamine in depressive illness. *Psychological Medicine*, 9:107–115.
26. Gillespie, R. D. (1929): The clinical differentiation of types of depression. *Guy's Hospital Reports*, 79:306–344
27. Davidson, J., Turnbull, C. D. (1986): Diagnostic significance of vegetative symptoms in depression. *Brit J Psychiatry*, 148:442–446.
28. Davidson, J. R. T., Lipper, S., Zung, W. W. K., Strickland, R., Krishnan, K. R. R., and Mahorney, S. (1984): Validation of four definitions of melancholia by the dexamethasone suppression test. *Amer J Psychiatry*, 141:1220–1223.
29. Carroll, B. J. (1980): Implications of biological research for the diagnosis of depression. In: *New Advances in the Diagnosis and Treatment of Depressive Illnesses*, edited by J. Mendlewicz, pp. 85–107. Elsevier, Amsterdam.
30. Carroll, B. J. (1985): Dexamethasone suppression test: A review of contemporary confusion. *J Clin Psychiatry*, 46 [2, Sec 2]:13–24
31. Goodin, D. S., Aminoff, M. J. (1984): Does the interictal EEG have a role in the diagnosis of epilepsy? *Lancet*, 1:837–839.
32. Krishnan, K. R. R., Davidson, J. R. T., Rayasam, K., Tanas, K. S., Shope, F. S., and Pelton, S. (1987): Diagnostic utility of the dexamethasone suppression test. *Biological Psychiatry*, 22: 618–628.
33. Shrivastava, R. K., Schwimmer, R., Brown, W. A., et al. (1985): DST predicts poor placebo response in depression. *American Psychiatric Association Scientific Proceedings* 1985; New Research Abstract 94.
34. Peselow, E. D., Stanley, M., and Fieve, R. R. (1985): Plasma cortisol and clinical response to antidepressants and placebo in depressed outpatients. *Scientific Proceedings of the American College of Neuropsychopharmacology* 124.
35. Peselow, E. D., Lautin, A., Wolkin, A., et al. (1986): The dexamethasone suppression test and response to placebo. *J Clin Psychopharm*, 6:286–291.
36. Georgotas, A., Stokes, P., McCue, R. E., et al. (1986): The usefulness of DST in predicting response to antidepressants: A placebo-controlled study. *J. Affective Disorders*, 11:21–28.
37. Georgotas, A., Stokes, P., Cooper, T., et al. (1983): Dexamethasone suppression in the elderly: Diagnostic and treatment implications. *Society of Biological Psychiatry*, 35.
38. Georgotas, A., Stokes, P. E., Krakowski, M., Fanelli, C., and Cooper, T. (1984): Hypothalamic-pituitary-adrenocortical function in geriatric depression: Diagnostic and treatment implications. *Biological Psychiatry*, 19:685–693.
39. Rush, A. J. (1984): A phase II study of cognitive therapy of depression. In: *Psychotherapy Research: Where Are We and Where Should We Go?* edited by J. B. W. Williams and R. L. Spitzer, pp. 216–233. Guilford Press, New York.
40. Carroll, B. J. (1984): Problems with diagnostic criteria for depression. *J Clin Psychiatry*, 45 [7 Sec 2]:14–18.
41. Carroll, B. J. (1983): Neurobiologic dimensions of depression and mania. In: *The Origins of Depression: Current Concepts and Approaches*, edited by J. Angst, pp. 163–186. Springer Verlag, Berlin.

42. American Psychiatric Association. (1987): *Diagnostic and Statistical Manual of Mental Disorders*, 3rd edition, revised. American Psychiatric Association, Washington, D.C., p. 224.

DISCUSSION

Dr. Larry Siever: When we evaluated depressed patients during a 2-week drug-free interval in the hospital to determine if their depresssion persisted off medication, two patterns emerged during this period. Patients identified as primarily depressed on admission do not generally improve clinically during this period. Patients with a primary diagnosis of personality disorder with a secondary depression generally remit very rapidly, within about 3 or 4 days. These patients had satisfied RDC criteria for depression, although not usually the melancholic subtype. From 60% to 70% of the primary depressives did not suppress on the dexamethasone suppression test after 2 weeks in the hospital. The personality disorder group with secondary depression had a nonsuppression rate of about 10%, and half of those nonsuppressors included the infrequent personality disorder patients with persistent depression in the hospital.

Dr. Carroll: I would add that if this is what you see in an inpatient setting, imagine the problems of attempting to establish clinical validity in an outpatient setting, where you do not have the luxury of milieu control and careful observation.

Dr. Zubin: Historically the American Psychopathological Association has shown itself to be different from most other groups in the field of psychopathology by having a rather wide scope, including not only the biological, but also the psychosocial and the behavioral. Today's discussion is unfortunately limited to only one disorder, namely depression, and limited also to only one or two types of laboratory research, namely sleep patterns and dexamethasone suppression. I would like to make a pitch for other things that have been left out, and indicate why I believe that the biological and the psychosocial techniques differ. The biological variables we talk about have primarily been wired in through evolution. The psychosocial variables came much later, when culture took over. Cultural transmission is not as efficacious, not as direct, and not as built-in as the biological, and yet it represents a very basic underpinning of total behavior, including biological behavior.

Culture does not maintain its persistence as well as biology, yet there must be underlying variables by which we may eventually be able to capture the essence of cultural transmission.

Dr. Carroll: You are right to point out that there are other areas and other disorders that could have been discussed. David (Kupfer) and I restricted our focus to affective illness and to the sleep and DST measures because that is where the data are right now. It is much better to talk about general principles, I think, using illustrations from real data than from much less developed areas.

Dr. Ellen Frank: I also support the emphasis on psychosocial variables, in addition to biological variables, in attempts to validate our diagnostic schemes. But I would urge that they be looked at simultaneously in the same patients in controlled trials, because I think we will only understand the impact of psychosocial variables if we understand how they relate to and act upon biological systems.

Dr. Carroll: Your comment underlines that, as a scientific objective, the ideal design is to gather data simultaneously on all the levels that we have been discussing, and certainly to avoid examining just two levels. You need three levels for a triangulation, as I call it, on the validity of the disorders being studied.

Dr. McHugh: I want to return to something that is crucial and embedded in the Robins and Guze idea about laboratory tests. If any laboratory test is going to be important in validating a construct, then it should be a measure of some crucial integrative function that is in some way vitally involved in the organism and its disorders. Laboratory tests have to demonstrate and reveal to us what the integrative purposes for the organism these particular functions play. The question is what do we know now about adrenal steroids, their controls, and their responsibilities in the organism under a variety of conditions, that we can propose to make them such a useful marker for depression as you have demonstrated. The same question should be directed to sleep studies: what is the role in biology of REM sleep, its structure, its latency, and its place in the integration of the organism. If we knew that, we would not only appreciate why it is disrupted in endogenous depression, but we would also be directed toward a clearer knowledge of the disorder itself. Surely, in our hopes for the future, we expect from markers not just a better phenomenology, but an understanding of the relationship of laboratory measurements to the construct of the condition itself.

Dr. Carroll: I agree that is a desirable objective. You asked an old and very important question, although, frankly, we don't know enough to get to that level of construct validity at this point.

The Validity of Psychiatric Diagnosis, edited by
Lee N. Robins and James E. Barrett.
Raven Press, Ltd., New York © 1989.

The Implications of Cross-National Research for Diagnostic Validity

*John E. Helzer, and **Glorisa Canino

*Department of Psychiatry, Washington University School of Medicine, St. Louis, Missouri 63110; and **Department of Psychiatry, University of Puerto Rico School of Medicine and the Mental Health Secretariat of Puerto Rico, San Juan, Puerto Rico 00936

In order to test the cross-national appropriateness and perceived utility of the DSM-III illness definitions, we analyzed questionnaire responses from 140 clinicians in 24 countries. Despite the fact that most were required to use some other nomenclature for record keeping and/or clinical work, most preferred the illness definitions provided in DSM-III. An examination by diagnosis showed that 80% or more of all respondents felt that the definitions for the 12 major illnesses examined were appropriate in their own cultural context.

We next used population survey data obtained using the Diagnostic Interview Schedule (DIS) to examine the relative prevalence of individual psychiatric disorders, the symptomatic expression of illness, and illness risk factors across countries.

We conclude by suggesting that the similarities we find across widely divergent cultures can be interpreted as evidence for the validity of the DSM-III definitions of illness.

INTRODUCTION

Cross-national comparisons of the occurrence and manifestations of psychiatric disorder as a means of testing the validity of diagnostic classifications has long been of interest. Kraepelin alluded to this in his 1904 paper, "Vergleichende (Comparative) Psychiatrie" (1) and in his subsequent textbook outlining the scientific basis for psychiatry (2). It is certainly relevant to the issue of validity to see if psychiatric taxonomies developed in one part of the world are useful in classifying the psychopathology in other cultural regions, and how consistent illness expression is between cultures.

This is not to say that it would be appropriate to simply equate cross-national consistency with validity. For example, it seems likely that societal context influences the occurrence of at least some psychiatric disorders, just as dietary habits are likely to have an impact on rates of atherosclerosis. For example, in the case of substance use disorders, availability has an obvious influence on frequency of use, social stigma likely influences propensity toward use and intoxication, and social context may govern the likelihood of certain symptoms—arrests for drunken driving are obviously rare in cultures where the standard conveyance is a bicycle. Such variability clearly does not invalidate the diagnosis of alcoholism.

Conversely, schizophrenia appears to be an organic, probably largely genetic illness whose occurrence and symptomatic expression would seem to be far less subject to social context. However, even here cultural variation would be expected in the content of delusions, for example, or in the necessity of delimiting pathological hallucinations from culturally consonant ones such as those that might occur in the context of religious ceremony. There is also some evidence that schizophrenia may have a better prognosis in developing than in developed countries.

However, apart from these caveats, consistency of the clinical picture across cultural groups is of no less relevance to validity than is clinical consistency within the same culture, a previously cited validity indicator (3). If we have identified by its clinical manifestations a distinct psychiatric entity, the manifestations should be relatively consistent wherever that entity occurs. Since we recognize that the occurrence of an illness and certainly some symptoms may be influenced by social context, intercultural and even intracultural inconsistencies do not necessarily invalidate the construct, but at least we would hope to be able to explain why differences occur. In fact such explanations could offer important clues to the etiology of the illness.

Unfortunately, as desirable as it is to compare illness expression cross-culturally, there is considerable practical difficulty in doing so. Most such attempts have been based on a comparison of independent studies, each done within a single cultural context. It is well known that even subtle differences in any one of a number of areas including illness definition, sample selection, symptom ascertainment, or data analysis can produce important differences in results. Typically investigators trying to compare results between countries have to account for major differences in all four of the above areas. It becomes virtually impossible to separate true differences in rates or symptoms from those due to design artifact.

In order to use cross-national data to assess the consistency of clinical manifestations of psychiatric disorders, we need to go beyond the stage of comparing prevalence rates of disorders across national boundaries and examine, as the International Pilot Study of Schizophrenia (IPSS) (4) and the US/UK study (5) have attempted to do, the symptomatic expression of disorder. But this is an enterprise that is fraught with much difficulty because with national or cultural boundaries come differences in language and possibly of illness concepts. Kleinman, for example, has claimed that a diagnostic nomenclature, like DSM-III, that has been developed in one country or region of the world may not be applicable in other countries or regions (6). In the study of illness etiology, differences in prevalence between cultural groups and the examination of risk factors or social variables that may relate to these differences are certainly relevant. But before intercultural variation can be used for this purpose, we need some assurance that we are in fact using the same diagnostic language, or that the same language is even applicable. If it is true that a taxonomy developed in the West seems to Far Eastern colleagues to be inappropriate or inapplicable, the discovery of differential prevalence of an illness between East and West may simply be irrelevant.

The development and widespread usage of DSM-III provides an opportunity to test cross-national relevance of illness definitions. Since the definitions in DSM-III are relatively specific, use of this taxonomy connotes more than simple acceptance of its diagnostic labels and general illness concepts, as might be the case with a less specific taxonomy such as DSM-II or ICD-9.

CROSS-NATIONAL ACCEPTANCE OF DSM-III

There has been some systematic exploration of the cross-national acceptability and utility of DSM-III. Spitzer et al. reported commentary and some data on DSM-III usage from investigators and clinicians in 18 countries in a volume published 3 years after DSM-III (7). Contributors' comments at that point were mostly general, but largely favorable. Especially interesting was the survey of more than 50 senior psychiatrists throughout the People's Republic of China reported by Kuo-Tai and Shan-Ming. Even at this early date, they found that most respondents had studied DSM-III, were favorable toward it, and had applied it in clinical and research work. All of the respondents felt it had already had a marked influence on psychiatric diagnosis in China (8).

In 1985, Mezzich et al. reported the results of a survey sponsored by the World Psychiatric Association of 175 "expert diagnosticians" in 52 countries spanning all continents (9). Nearly as many of the respondents used DSM-III as used ICD-9, and 46% rated DSM-III high on "usefulness" whereas only 29% so rated the ICD-9. This preference was found in every region of the world except Africa, and even there only 14% rated DSM-III as of low usefulness, compared to 27% for the ICD-9.

The question we seek to address, however, is not the overall usefulness of the DSM-III or general favorable feelings toward it, but rather the cultural appropriateness of its specific illness definitions. By now, clinicians outside the United States have had some 8 years to become familiar with DSM-III in various clinical contexts and to draw conclusions about the appropriateness of its definitions in their particular environment. We therefore decided to survey opinion on this specific issue and to sample the thoughts of general psychiatric clinicians rather than designated experts.

In order to do this we sent a questionnaire to psychiatric colleagues in 27 countries. As in the previous international surveys on DSM-III, the sampling design was one of convenience. We sent five copies of the questionnaire to each correspondent and asked him to distribute them to practitioners known to be at least acquainted with DSM-III. A self-addressed envelope was attached to each questionnaire so the completed form could be returned directly to us, although the original recipients were invited to copy and distribute more of the forms if they wished. So far as we could tell, our colleague in Taiwan was the only to do so. He was especially generous, and we received 52 returns for the five that we sent him. We received no response from colleagues in Lebanon, East Germany, and Colombia and do not know whether these requests were ever received. Setting aside the three countries from which we had no response and counting the generous response from Taiwan separately, we received 88 questionnaires from the 23 remaining countries (a response rate of 77%). Including the Taiwan data, the tables and figures described below are based on 140 responses from 24 countries. (The Taiwan data were analyzed separately, but since rates differed little from overall rates, they were merged.)

It is sure to please its publisher to know that 93% of the respondents owned their own copy of DSM-III (Table 1). Although most were required to use ICD to code their clinical diagnoses, the DSM-III was preferred either as the exclusive nomenclature, or in concert with other diagnostic systems.

We next asked the respondents to state their preferred diagnostic system in three contexts: clinical work, teaching, and research (Fig. 1). Thirty-seven percent indicated an exclusive preference for the DSM-III definitions for clinical work, and an additional 60% preferred the DSM for some disorders, leaving only 3% who preferred some other system for all diagnoses. Exclusive preference for DSM-III rises to 56% for teaching and to 69% for research work. Exclusive preference for some other taxonomy is 5% or less in all three types of usage. Eighty-two percent of the respondents said they "often" refer to the DSM-III definitions.

PERCEIVED APPROPRIATENESS OF DSM-III ILLNESS DEFINITIONS

The possible responses regarding the appropriateness of specific DSM-III definitions included two indicating the definition is appropriate in the respondent's

TABLE 1. *Ownership and use of DSM-III(R) cross-nationally*

Question	Positive (%)
Do you own a copy of DSM-III?	93
Do you have access to a copy?	100
Are you required to code diagnoses using a particular nomenclature?	84
Which one?	
ICD	68
DSM-III	32
Other	0
Which is your preferred nomenclature?	
ICD	18
DSM-III	50
Mixture of DSM-III and others	32

N = 140 responses from 24 countries.
Of those required to use ICD exclusively, 65% said they preferred DSM-III for their own clinical work.

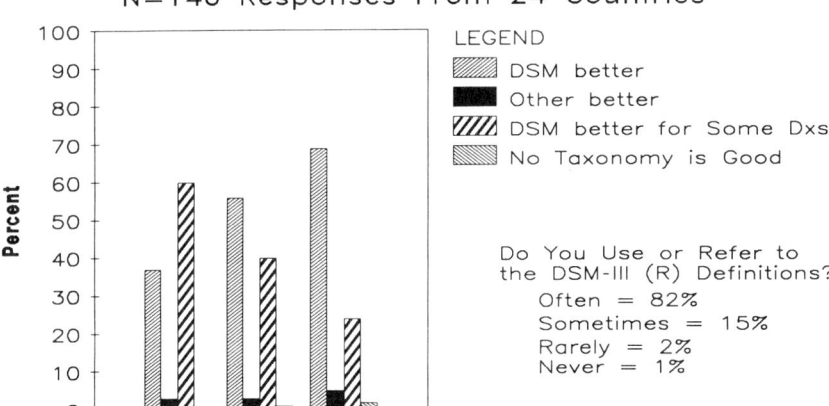

FIG. 1. Comparison of DSM-III (R) and other taxonomies for clinical work, teaching, and research.

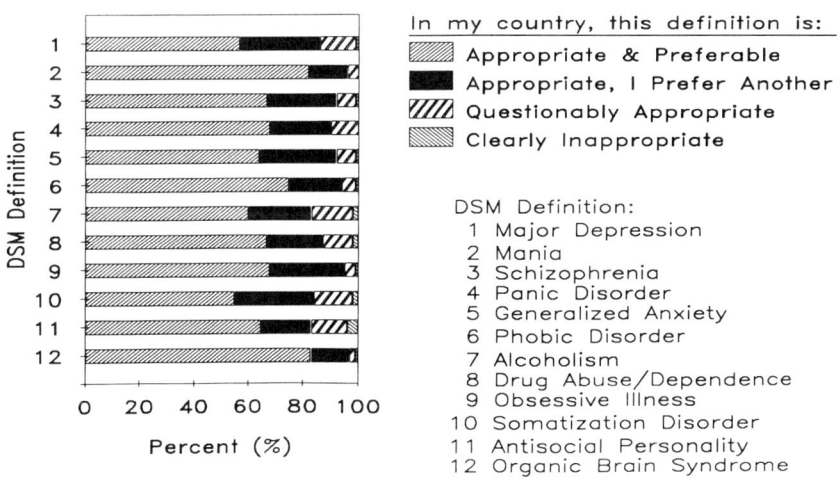

FIG. 2. Appropriateness of DSM-III (R) diagnostic definitions.

cultural context, and two indicating questionable or outright inappropriateness (Fig. 2). It is clear that most respondents consider the DSM-III definitions to be appropriate in their country, whether or not they personally prefer a different definition. The sum of these two "appropriate" categories is 90% or above for a majority of the diagnoses and 80% or higher for all of them. The "clearly inappropriate" category was less than 1% for eight diagnoses, and less than 5% for all. The four with the lowest appropriateness ratings were alcohol, drug, antisocial personality, and somatization disorders. For the first three, socially disapproved behaviors play a major role in diagnosis, and it is not surprising that social disapproval varies by culture. The fourth diagnosis, somatization disorder, was found inappropriate primarily in Germany, Sweden, and Puerto Rico. It was found acceptable in Asia and other Latin American countries.

DIAGNOSTIC PREVALENCE RATES

We would certainly anticipate that the prevalence of some diagnoses would be influenced by social context and perhaps those most likely to be so are the substance use disorders. The importance of social context for substance use criteria is suggested by the results noted in Fig. 2, and in a separate study indicating major cross-national differences in the lifetime prevalence of alcoholism (10). But societal mores might also have considerable influence on other disorders. Recent studies in psychiatric epidemiology using consistent definitions in several different countries enable us to explore this.

The Epidemiologic Catchment Area (ECA) survey (11) conducted in the United States in the early 1980s captured widespread attention outside of this country, and there have now been several population surveys similar to the ECA, i.e., large samples of respondents drawn from the general population and personally interviewed with the Diagnostic Interview Schedule (DIS) (12). Since, with few exceptions, the same diagnoses were ascertained and the diagnostic scoring program was that developed for DSM-III in St. Louis, it is possible to use these data to see what the relative prevalence of various diagnoses is. We have summarized these findings by ranking diagnoses according to lifetime prevalence rates within each country and examining the rank order correlation between countries. The diagnoses included are all of those shown in Fig. 2 plus anorexia nervosa (which had not been included on our above noted questionnaire). The cultural regions or groups are non-Hispanics in the United States (represented by the combined five-site ECA data); ECA data on Hispanics in Los Angeles (labelled MexAm on graphs); population surveys done in Edmonton, Canada (Edm) (10), Puerto Rico (PR) (10), Munich, Germany (Mun) (13), Christchurch, New Zealand (CCh) (14), Seoul, Korea (10), Shanghai, China (15); and three surveys done in Taiwan (10): metropolitan Taipei, nonmetropolitan townships, and rural villages.

The full correlation matrix for the rank ordering by prevalence of these 13 diagnoses in the 10 cultural regions is overwhelming, but Table 2 summarizes the re-

TABLE 2. *Rank order correlations (SPEARMAN) for lifetime prevalence of DIS/DSM-III diagnoses; data from 11 cultural regions*

	Correlations	
Range of Values		
Lowest	.65	(New Zealand and rural Taiwan)
Highest	.98	(New Zealand and Edmonton, Canada)
Mean correlation across all regions	.82	
Mean for U.S. vs. all other regions	.80	
Asia		
Mean for all Asian regions	.86	
Mean for U.S. vs. all Asian regions	.73	
Mean for Puerto Rico vs. Asian regions	.92	
Hispanic		
Two Hispanic regions	.95	
North America		
U.S. and Edmonton, Canada	.91	
Christchurch, New Zealand		
Mean for Christchurch, New Zealand vs. all other regions	.78	

sults. The lowest cross-site correlation is between Christchurch, New Zealand, and the rural Taiwan sample at .65. Correlations with New Zealand were not uniformly low; in fact, the highest correlation (.98) is between Christchurch and Edmonton, Canada. The mean correlation between the Asian regions is .86, but further evidence that a taxonomy developed in the West seems to transfer well to non-Western countries is the fact that the mean correlation between the U.S. and the six Asian regions is .73. The mean correlation between Puerto Rico and the Asian sites (.92) is even higher than the inter-Asian one. In other words, correlations within cultural groupings are high, but those between cultural groups are either just as high or do not fall greatly.

SYMPTOMATIC EXPRESSION OF PSYCHIATRIC DISORDER

Perhaps the question of greatest interest in a discussion of cross-national evidence for validity is whether or not there is similarity of symptomatic expression of the major disorders across cultural groups. Again it is difficult to equate va-

TABLE 3. *Rank order correlations of DSM-III alcohol symptoms between cultural regions*

Region	Correlation with St. Louis (ECA Data)
All other ECA sites (Mean)	.95
Mexican Americans in Los Angeles	.97
Edmonton, Canada	.94
Puerto Rico	.94
Christchurch, New Zealand	.94
Taipei, Taiwan	.79
Seoul, Korea	.69
American Indians (22)	.59
Shanghai	.56
Mean correlation	.80

lidity with consistency, but if there is a good deal of similarity in the relative prevalence of individual symptoms among those given a particular diagnosis, this suggests that the diagnostic category may reflect a natural grouping of psychopathology.

We have previously examined cross-national symptom data for alcoholism and found much similarity in relative symptom rates among diagnosed alcoholics despite considerable differences in the diagnostic prevalence rates (10). Table 3 supplements these findings for alcoholism with recently obtained data from additional sites. Again we have used rank order correlations to examine the relative prevalence of symptoms used in the DSM-III definition as ascertained by the DIS interview. The comparison here is between St. Louis, where the criteria and the interview were developed, and other cultural regions for which we have data, with the other ECA sites shown for comparison.

Recently, we have also acquired data for the symptoms of major depression from some of these same sites (16). This is fortunate for an enquiry about validity, since the appropriateness of a Western definition of depression, a psychiatric disorder of perennial interest, has been questioned for non-Western cultures (6). The five regions for which we report data are the five ECA sites in the United States; Edmonton, Canada; Puerto Rico; Munich, Germany; and Taipei, Taiwan. (Findings from the other two sites in Taiwan are similar to those from Taipei.)

First we see that there is similarity across these five regions regarding the number of DSM-III depressive systems by diagnostic category (Figure 3). In the Munich sample, those with no affective disorder had a higher symptom count, but the mean counts were correspondingly higher in the two illness categories as well. Thus, the DSM-III definition provides as good a discrimination between categories in Munich as it does elsewhere.

We are also able to calculate between-site rank order prevalence correlations for individual depressive symptoms. In the matrix shown in Table 4, correlations are

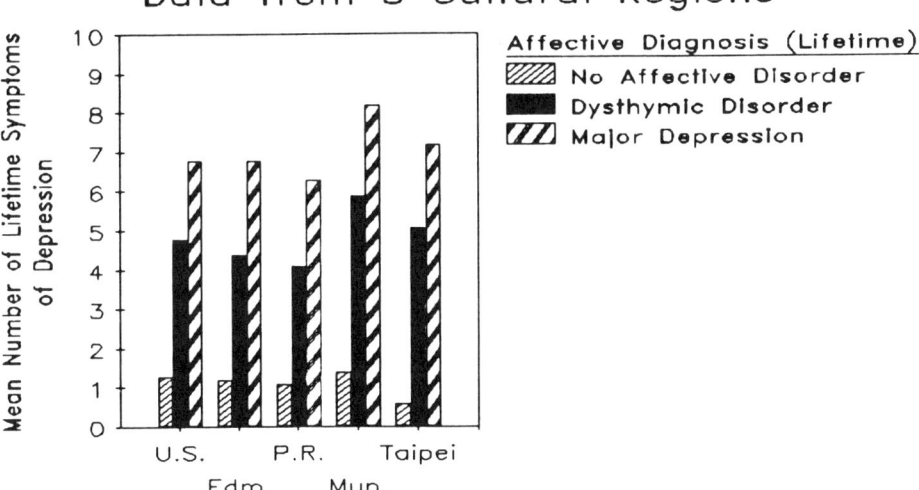

FIG. 3. Mean number of lifetime major depressive symptoms by affective diagnosis.

seen to range from .69 to .92. However, cross-national correlations are lower for men than for women as reflected in the means also shown in Table 4. This sex differential pertains for major depression and dysthymia, although the correlations among those with no depression do not differ by sex.

RISK FACTORS FOR PSYCHIATRIC DISORDER

Lastly, we have had some opportunity to examine risk factors for one diagnosis, alcoholism. In a separate paper (10), we showed an association between anti-

TABLE 4. *Rank order frequency correlations (SPEARMAN) for depressive symptoms in women with DSM-III major depression*

	Puerto Rico	Munich, West Germany	Edmonton, Canada	Taipei, Taiwan
United States (ECA 5-site data)	.86	.92	.88	.81
Puerto Rico	—	.82	.77	.69
Munich, West Germany	—	—	.88	.85
Edmonton, Canada	—	—	—	.87

Mean Correlation for Women = .84
Mean Correlation for Men = .57

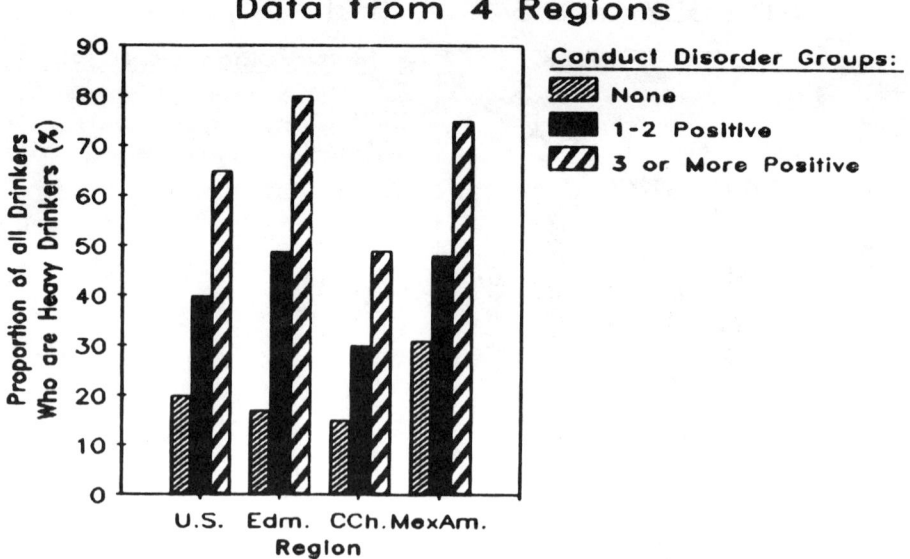

FIG. 4. Association of childhood conduct disorder and heavy drinking.

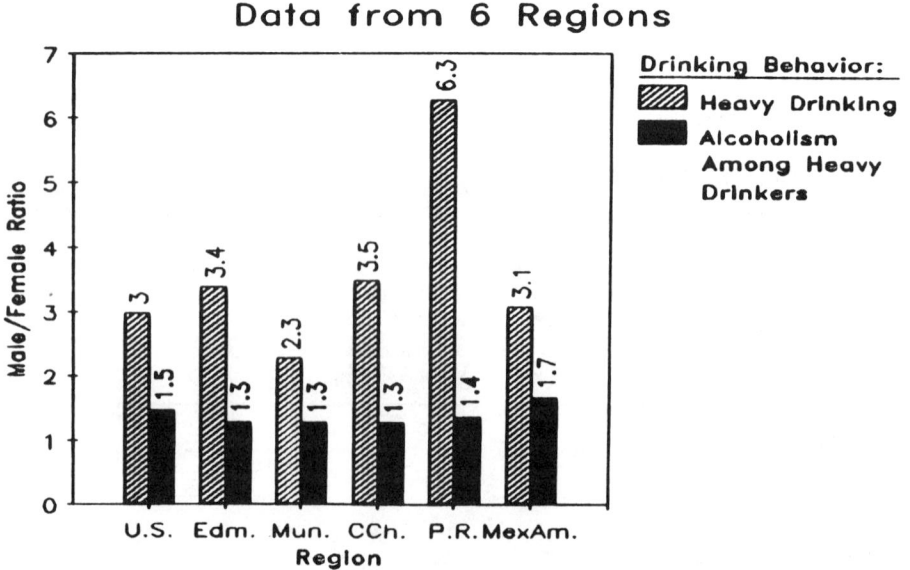

FIG. 5. Sex ratios for heavy drinking and alcoholism among heavy drinkers.

social personality disorder (ASP) and alcoholism that is consistent across cultures. We also noted that the lower the population prevalence of alcoholism, the stronger its relationship with ASP. However, it may be questionable to consider antisocial personality as a risk factor for alcoholism since they are both adult disorders; it is just as likely that drinking is a risk factor for antisocial behavior as vice versa.

We now have data for childhood conduct problems for several countries and can examine the consistency of the relationship between this antecedent and heavy drinking as an adult. This relationship is highly consistent across the four regions for which we have data (Fig. 4).

Being male is a known risk factor for alcoholism. The sex differential could occur because of a lower tolerance for alcohol among women, a greater social stigma attached to their drinking, or both. In Figure 5 we have disaggregated sex as a risk factor for heavy drinking and for alcoholism among heavy drinkers in order to examine this. Consistent with a social stigma hypothesis, there is considerable variation in the male/female ratio for heavy drinking ranging from a low of 2.3 in Munich to 6.3 in Puerto Rico. In contrast, the sex ratio for alcoholism after controlling for heavy drinking is considerably lower and highly consistent between sites.

DISCUSSION OF RESULTS

The results of this and previous surveys suggest that far from being inapplicable in countries or regions of the world other than that in which it was developed, the DSM-III definitions not only have widespread utility but are actually preferred by a majority of clinicians, even those in non-Western countries. The book by Spitzer et al. (7) suggested widespread acceptance of the American classification, but at that early date endorsements might have applied more to the concept of highly specific ("operational") definitions per se rather than concurrence with the particular definitions proposed. Similarly, the survey by Mezzich et al. (9) did not ask respondents to comment specifically on the appropriateness of the DSM-III definitions, but it did attest to the feeling in virtually every corner of the world that the taxonomy is useful. The sampling of the present survey is more limited in scope than Mezzich's, but the results, specifically focused on the issue of appropriateness of the criteria, are just as positive.

The findings here suggest much consistency of psychiatric diagnostic variables across widely divergent cultural groups. This is not prima facie evidence of validity of diagnostic constructs. But the fact that the consistency has been tested in population rather than in clinical samples and is seen in many spheres including perceived utility and appropriateness of DSM-III, relative prevalence of diagnoses, ranking of symptom prevalence within diagnostic groups, correlates of illness, and risk factors suggests that these findings are not just an artifact resulting from the fact that the symptom and diagnostic data were all from the same interview and scoring program (i.e., the DIS in translation). In fact, these findings support the validity of both the DIS and DSM-III in population samples, since consistent results were obtained in very different cultures.

It has been suggested that the widespread diffusion of the DSM-III could be considered an example of psychiatric imperialism and that it is inappropriate to apply a set of criteria developed in a highly industrialized nation, with stresses and disorders characteristic of modern society, to vastly different cultures. However, it seems to us difficult to support a charge of imperialism. It is likely that DSM-III has been imported by willing users rather than exported by its developers. The fact that even a majority of those *required* to use another diagnostic system own a personal copy of DSM-III and prefer its definitions for their own clinical work supports this view.

On the other hand, it is not our intention to imply that the DSM-III definitions per se are superior to other specific definitions that have been or might be developed. We suspect that the wide endorsement of DSM-III is not necessarily for its definitions per se, but is because its definitions are more specific than its predecessors' have been. The point of this article is to examine the cross-national clinical consistency of psychiatric syndromes, not to hold a popularity contest for a particular set of definitions.

A certain degree of similarity between countries is perhaps guaranteed by comparing data from the DIS since the same set of symptoms is used at each site. Therefore, we have not argued that the same universe of symptoms characterizes specific disorders across sites. What we have done here is to show that within the universe of items ascertained by the DIS, there is a striking cross-site agreement about their relative frequency. If the list of symptoms covered by DSM-III approximates the universe of symptoms of these disorders in all cultures, this finding argues that the symptom structure of the disorders studied may be universal.

There are a number of shortcomings in the present study. For example, the DSM-III survey of psychiatrists we report is hardly comprehensive. We sent only five questionnaires to each correspondent, and there is no guarantee that their subsequent distribution was to an unbiased sample of clinicians familiar with DSM-III. Also, the breadth of our diagnostic comparison is limited. For example, it would be of great interest to be able to examine the perceived appropriateness of alternative sets of highly specific criteria cross-nationally. With the present data set we can compare the Feighner criteria (17) and the RDC (18) as well as DSM-III, but for many diagnoses there are few differences between these three sets of definitions. It would be of greater interest to compare results for ICD-10 (19) criteria with those of the DSM, since they differ more. We will not be able to examine the question further until new population studies using ICD-10 criteria become available.

There are some other shortcomings we will be able to correct. First, the analyses presented are based on those data we now have available. In the future we will be able to study other diagnoses and add samples from other countries where surveys are now being carried out. Second, the analyses we have performed here are not very sophisticated. It would be of interest to supplement the correlational symptom data with multivariate techniques. For example, Kendell, in his classic volume on diagnosis, reviews studies of the cross-national replication of cluster and factor analyses of symptoms in clinical populations (20). More recently, Rubio-Stipec has applied this technique using DIS data from population samples in Puerto Rico and Los Angeles (21). Lastly, it would be of great interest to assess other diagnoses and go beyond single disorders to examine comorbidities and diagnostic interactions such as those suggested to occur between depression and somatization.

Our present method, completing a set of analyses on our data and asking collaborators to replicate them in their data, is probably inadequate to these more sophisticated types of analyses for a number of reasons. However, we have recently received funding to undertake a pilot project in which data from the three Taiwan sites (total N, about 11,000) will be merged with the ECA data from the United States (total N, about 20,000) to form a common data bank. In the future we plan to expand the data bank to include many of the other DIS-based population surveys mentioned here. Such a data library will provide a unique opportunity for cross-cultural collaboration and will permit collaborators to compare cross-national findings regarding illness prevalence, illness expression, correlates, and risk factors in ways never before possible.

ACKNOWLEDGMENTS

This research was supported by United States Public Health Service grants MH 31302, DA 04001, Research Scientist Development Award MH 00617 (Dr. Helzer), MH 36230, and the MacArthur Foundation Risk Factor Network.

The authors wish to thank Drs. Lee N. Robins (St. Louis), Hans-Ulrich Wittchen (Munich), and Norman Sartorius (Geneva), who gave helpful comments on this paper. We would also like to thank Drs. Eng-Kung Yeh (Taipei), Roger C. Bland (Edmonton), Hans-Ulrich Wittchen (Munich), Elisabeth Wells (Christchurch), C.R. Lee (Seoul), William T. Liu (Chicago/Shanghai), and Spero M. Manson (data on American Indians) for sharing survey data with us, and colleagues from many other countries who participated in the distribution and completion of questionnaires.

REFERENCES

1. Kraepelin, E. (1904): Vergleichende Psychiatrie. *Zentralbl Nervenheilk Psychiatr*, 27:433–437.
2. Kraepelin, E. (1906): *Psychiatrie: Ein Lehrbuch fur Studierende und Arzte*. Barth, Leipzig.
3. Robins, E. and Guze, S. B. (1970): Establishment of diagnostic validity in psychiatric illness: Its application to schizophrenia. *Am J Psychiatry*, 126:983–987.
4. World Health Organization. (1973): *The International Pilot Study of Schizophrenia*. World Health Organization, Geneva.
5. Cooper, J. E., Kendell, R. E., Gurland, B. J., Sharpe, L., Copeland, J. R. M., and Simon, R. (1972): *Psychiatric Diagnosis in New York and London*. Oxford University Press, New York.

6. Kleinman, A., and Good, B. (1985): *Culture and Depression: Studies in the Anthropology and Cross-Cultural Psychiatry of Affect and Disorder.* University of California Press, Berkeley.
7. Spitzer, R. L., Williams, J. B. W., and Skodol, A. E. (eds.). (1983): *International Perspectives on DSM-III.* American Psychiatric Press, Washington, D.C.
8. Kuo-Tai, T., Shan-Ming, Y. (1983): The impact of DSM-III on Chinese psychiatry. In *International Perspectives on DSM-III,* edited by R. L. Spitzer, J. B. W. Williams, and A. E. Skodol. American Psychiatric Press, Washington, D.C.
9. Mezzich, J. E., Fabrega, H., Mezzich, A. C., and Coffman, G. A. (1985): International experience with DSM-III. *J Nerv Ment Dis,* 173:738–741.
10. Helzer, J. E., Canino, G. J., Yeh, E.-K., Bland, R. C., Lee C. K., Hwu, H. G., and Newman, S. Alcoholism—North America and Asia: A comparison of population surveys with the DIS. (Submitted for publication.)
11. Regier, D. A., Myers, J. K., Kramer, M., Robins, L. N., Blazer, D. G., Hough, R. L., Eaton, W. W., and Locke, B. Z. (1984): The NIMH Epidemiologic Catchment Area Program: Historical context, major objectives, and study population characteristics. *Arch Gen Psychiatry,* 41:934–941.
12. Robins, L. N., Helzer, J. E., Croughan, J., and Ratcliff, K. S. (1981): National Institute of Mental Health Diagnostic Interview Schedule: Its history, characteristics, and validity. *Arch Gen Psychiatry,* 38:381–389.
13. Wittchen, H.-U., and Bronisch, T. (1988): Use, abuse and dependence on alcohol in West Germany—Lifetime and six-month prevalence in the Munich follow-up study. In: *The Prevalence and Symptoms of Alcoholism: A Coordinated Analysis of Population Data from Ten Countries,* edited by J. E. Helzer and G. J. Canino. Oxford University Press *(in press).*
14. Wells, J. E., Bushnell, J. A., Joyce, P. R., Hornblow, A. R., and Oakley-Browne, M. A. (1988): Alcohol abuse and dependence in New Zealand: Data from Christchurch. In: *The Prevalence and Symptoms of Alcoholism: A Coordinated Analysis of Population Data from Ten Countries,* edited by J. E. Helzer and G. J. Canino. *(Submitted for publication.)*
15. Wang, C. H., Liu, W. T., Zhang, M. Y., Yu, E. S. H., Xia, Z. Y., Fernandez, M., Lung, C. T., Xu, C. L., and Qu, G. Y. Alcohol use, abuse and dependency in Shanghai. In: *The Prevalence and Symptoms of Alcoholism: A Coordinated Analysis of Population Data from Ten Countries. (Submitted for publication.)*
16. Helzer, J. E. (1988): The symptoms of depression. Presented at the annual meeting of the American Psychiatric Association, Montreal, Canada.
17. Feighner, J. P., Robins, E., Guze, S. B., Woodruff, R. A., Winokur, G., and Munoz, R. (1972): Diagnostic criteria for use in psychiatric research. *Arch Gen Psychiatry,* 26:57–63.
18. Spitzer, R. L., Endicott, J., and Robins, E. (1978): Research diagnostic criteria: Rationale and reliability. *Arch Gen Psychiatry,* 35:773–782.
19. World Health Organization. *Tenth Revision of the International Classification of Diseases (ICD-10).* World Health Organization, Geneva *(in preparation).*
20. Kendell, R. E. (1975): *The Role of Diagnosis in Psychiatry.* Blackwell Scientific Publications, London.
21. Rubio-Stipec, M., Shrout, P., Bird, H., Canino, G., and Bravo, M. Empirically defined scales of the Diagnostic Interview Schedule. *(Submitted for publication.)*
22. Manson, S., Shore, J. H., Baron, A. E., Ackerson, L., and Neligh, G. (1988): Alcohol abuse and dependence among American Indians. In: *The Prevalence and Symptoms of Alcoholism: A Coordinated Analysis of Population Data from Ten Countries,* edited by J. E. Helzer and G. J. Canino. *(Submitted for publication.)*

DISCUSSION

Dr. Lebensohn: Your paper confirms what Joe Zubin said, that there are political factors involved in making a diagnostic scheme for any given country. This was shown clearly by the fact that the People's Republic of China was very enthusiastic about accepting DSM-III. Can you tell us anything at all about what happened in the Soviet Union in this regard?

Dr. Helzer: I don't think the Soviet Union contributed to the book about international perspectives on DSM-III.

Dr. Spitzer: I don't recall a single letter from the Soviet Union. We had a lot of interest from Hungary, Czechozlovakia, and Poland. There is a Hungarian translation.

Dr. Lebensohn: Do we know anything about the Soviet Union's current diagnostic scheme?

Dr. Spitzer: I have read bits and pieces about it, but they don't really enable me to put any coherent picture together. I am afraid I can't make any intelligent comment about the scheme there.

Dr. Klein: In the countries you studied, was there a wide range of prevalence rates?

Dr. Helzer: For alcoholism there certainly was. I don't have prevalence data yet for depression. We organized the APA symposium by having each of us do analyses of interest to us on our own data, and then distributing those analyses to the other participants and asking them to replicate them. My specific interest was in the symptoms, and those results I showed you here today. Someone else will be presenting prevalence data.

Dr. Zubin: You have shown the similarities in symptoms across cultures. Could Bob Kendell comment about differences between the United Kingdom and the United States?

Prof. Kendell: There appear to be remarkably few, apart from the substance use disorders. David Goldberg has administered his General Health Questionnaire to population samples all over the world, and it is remarkable how stable the factor structure of these sets of ratings is, suggesting that the patterning of neurotic or minor psychiatric symptoms is very similar worldwide, not at all what most of us would have expected. Certainly, I would have started off assuming that, although major disorders like schizophrenia might be very similar, the patterning of minor symptoms would differ a great deal cross-culturally. But it doesn't appear to, which is fascinating, as well as being rather good news.

Dr. Spitzer: We had a very interesting experience in revising the DSM-III casebook. We made a concerted effort to get cases from non-U.S. countries, and we particularly asked for cases which would be difficult to classify in DSM-III and DSM-III-R. We found that in the Western countries, the cases we received were, by and large, of similar difficulty to cases in this country. The exceptions were in the non-Western countries, such as Africa and the Far East, particularly those cases involving dissociative disorders and psychoses where the issues of culturally sanctioned religious experiences become involved. There it was very difficult to fit the cases into any DSM-III or DSM-III-R categories.

Dr. Paula Clayton: In an earlier presentation of your alcohol data you showed an association between other diseases and alcoholism. Mania was one of them; was that finding replicated across cultures?

Dr. Helzer: Yes it was. The earlier data did show comorbidities across several countries, and we saw similar patterns of comorbidity between countries. Mania showed a stronger comorbidity than did depression; that was a consistent finding.

The Validity of Psychiatric Diagnosis, edited by
Lee N. Robins and James E. Barrett.
Raven Press, Ltd., New York © 1989.

Diagnostic Grammar and Assessment: Translating Criteria into Questions

Lee N. Robins

Department of Psychiatry, Washington University School of Medicine, St. Louis, MO 63110

Over the last 10 years, a number of efforts have been made by our group to turn the formal diagnostic criteria of various psychiatric diagnostic systems, including the Feighner criteria, the RDC, DSM-III and DSM-III-R, ICD-9, and ICD-10, into interview questions that when asked by lay interviewers or clinicians produce answers which can be combined by computer to make diagnoses consistent with those criteria. The goal was to construct standardized interviews appropriate for use in the general population that would function more like a psychiatrist does during a clinical assessment than had previous interviews designed for this use. That is, they would be tightly tied to official diagnostic criteria; they would endeavor to distinguish clinically significant symptoms from the trials and tribulations of everyday life; and they would attempt to exclude symptoms entirely explained by physical illness or conditions or by the ingestion of alcohol or other drugs. The goal was not to write an interview equivalent to the behavior of particular psychiatrists; instead the aim was to come as close as possible to what the ideal psychiatrist would do if he properly interpreted and rigorously followed the criteria in the diagnostic systems being assessed.

Our group has produced a series of interviews, the best known of which is the Diagnostic Interview Schedule (DIS), which has appeared in four versions, and is about to appear in a fifth. Our newest enterprise is an interview named the Composite International Diagnostic Interview (CIDI) (1), written for the WHO/ADAMHA Task Force on Diagnostic Assessment, which combines the DIS with PSE items. This interview is currently undergoing field tests in 19 sites around the world.

Deciding whether these interviews actually do what they are supposed to do—i.e., accurately make specific diagnoses according to the existing nomenclatures for both treated and untreated persons—has been a challenging task. There have now been a variety of validity studies of the DIS, most of which were reviewed by Burke (1a). The studies covered by his review were in every case test-retest comparisons between results obtained when lay interviewers administered the interview and when clinicians either repeated the DIS, used other assessment methods, or combined the two. Yet we knew from the beginning that judging the DIS's validity on the basis of its agreement with a clinician's judgment was questionable, because the original purpose of structured interviews was to overcome the well-known unreliability of clinical judgment. Since none of these studies presented evidence that the clinician's assessment was itself valid, discrepancies may or may not have indicated invalidity. The most we can conclude may be that when clinicians and lay interviewers choose the same diagnosis from among the large number available to both, assessments are likely to be valid, because agreement by chance alone in that situation is so unlikely. By this unsatisfactory criterion, as Burke's review shows, there is considerable support for the validity of the DIS in the hands of a lay interviewer, but there are also sufficient discrepancies to support those who doubt its validity. Since Burke's review, several other clinician-lay interviewer test-retest studies have been published (2-10) These studies, like earlier ones, show considerable but not perfect agreement of the lay interviewers' results with the clinicians'.

Unfortunately, as Kendell (11) has pointed out, there are no easy and widely accepted alternatives to clinicians' assessments for evaluating the validity of diagnostic instruments. Although many would agree that prediction of future events is a better validity criterion than physicians' concurrent assessment, prediction has two important drawbacks: first, it does not provide the rapid answer that reinterview by a psychiatrist does, and second, it is not possible to say how good prediction has to be to demonstrate perfect validity. While agreement with an expert has as its goal identical results, i. e., concordance of 100%, future behaviors are only probabilistically related to current diagnosis. For example, those with a particular diagnosis at initial assessment should be more likely to show its symptoms in the future than those without that diagnosis. However, we know that disorders may remit, and so some correctly diagnosed positive cases will have none of these symptoms in the follow-up period. We also know that new cases can arise, and persons with subclinical symptomatology can continue to show an occasional symptom, so that some of those correctly identified as unaffected initially should display symptoms of the disorder in the follow-up period. Knowing the proportion of correctly diagnosed positives and negatives who will show symptoms in the interval between assessments requires knowing expected rates of remission, incidence, and progression, data not now available for any disorder. Other outcomes, such as future treatment for the disorder or proportion of family members who will have the disorder, are equally probabilistic and the probabilities equally unknown.

While prediction has these serious drawbacks as a measure of validity, it can help to evaluate whether or not the clinician's assessment is a satisfactory yardstick against which to assess a lay interviewer's assessment. If the clinician interview was more often correct than the lay interview, it should better discriminate between the futures of positive and negative cases. One predictive study (12) found that persons identified as having depressions through the DIS administered by a lay interviewer were more likely to be depressed 6 months later than persons initially depression-free, whereas those few depressions recognized by their primary care physician were not more likely to be depressed 6 months later than those not recognized. Psychiatrists' assessments should be expected to be better predictors of future course, however, than those of primary care physicians. A year after the St. Louis Physician Reexamination was used to assess validity of the lay interviewers' DIS for respondents in the Epidemiologic Catchment Area (ECA) study, a second interview was carried out by lay interviewers in which the DIS was repeated and information asked about treatment experience in the interval. Helzer et al. (13) used responses to this follow-up interview to compare the predictive power of the lay interviewer's diagnosis and the psychiatrist's diagnosis in the St. Louis Physician's Reassessment Study. They found that there was little to choose between the clinician and lay interviewer in their ability to predict future responses, suggesting that the clinician's reinterview might be no more valid than the lay interviewer's. We have done some further analyses of these follow-up data, with some small changes in method. First, we have combined depressive episode and dysthymia, since most of the differences in the St. Louis Physician Reexamination between lay and psychiatrist's depressive diagnoses were accounted for by the disagreement between depression and dysthymia, diagnoses which share most symptoms. Dysthymia is a diagnosis that has been little used by Washington University psychiatrists. We have also limited the symptom responses to be predicted to symptoms occurring *between* interviews, to eliminate any possible effects of rehearsal of past symptoms during the earlier interviews. We present results for alcohol abuse/dependence and depression/ dysthymia, the two most common disorders.

First we report on the initial concordance of the DIS with the physicians' reassessment. For both diagnoses, specificity was higher than sensitivity, and negative predictive value higher than positive, as is generally true in studies of normal populations, where levels of disorder are low (Table 1). By all four measures, alcohol disorders were more validly reported than depressive disorders, but both were de-

TABLE 1. *Validity of lay interviews (N = 333; positive cases oversampled)*

	Alcohol/ Abuse/ Dependence	Depressive Episode/ Dysthymia
Sensitivity[a]	71%	70%
Specificity[b]	95	88
Pos. Predictive Value[c]	76	63
Neg. Predictive Value[d]	93	91

[a] % positive by lay DIS, given positive by clinician
[b] % negative by lay DIS, given negative by clinician
[c] % positive by clinician, given positive by lay DIS
[d] % negative by clinician, given negative by lay DIS

tected reasonably accurately, using the psychiatrist's independent interview as the yardstick.

We next compare lay interview diagnoses that are "valid" (because they are confirmed by the psychiatrist's diagnosis) with "invalid" lay interview diagnoses (those not confirmed by the psychiatrist) in their ability to predict responses at reinterview a year later (Table 2). This comparison is somewhat hampered by the small number of invalid alcohol disorders. Relative risks show how much persons with a positive diagnosis at the time of the initial interview exceed persons without one in meeting five criteria that should be met by more persons with than without the diagnosis. The five outcome criteria are: a history of the same disorder in members of the immediate family (parents, siblings, and offspring over 15), experiencing a critical symptom within the interval year (heavy drinking for alcoholics, suicidal thoughts or attempts for depressives), experiencing any other symptom of the particular disorder within the interval year, having sufficient symptoms of the disorder within the interval year to meet full diagnostic criteria, and having discussed symptoms of that particular disorder with a doctor during the interval year. The final relative risk is obtained by dividing the mean number of these five predictive criteria met by positive cases by the mean number met by those without a positive diagnosis. We find that the validated diagnoses are better than those not validated in predicting that these criteria will be met. But the striking finding is that even diagnoses judged invalid because not confirmed by a psychiatrist predicted more positive responses than did negative diagnoses. To the extent that prediction of the future validates the diagnosis, this suggests that the "invalid" lay-interviewer interviews may not all have been incorrect, although an alternative tenable interpretation is that the respondents *were* misdiagnosed, but a higher proportion of these invalid positives than negatives developed the disorder or showed subclinical symptoms of it in the following year.

When we compare the predictive power of clinicians' and lay interviewers' di-

TABLE 2. *Predictive power of valid and invalid lay interviewer diagnoses (wave 2 responses)*

	Relative Risks*			
	Alcohol		Depression	
	"Valid" (45)	"Invalid" (14)	"Valid" (52)	"Invalid" (31)
Positive family history	2.5	1.1	2.5	3.5
Interval history				
Heavy drink or suicidal thoughts	8.0	7.2	3.0	2.1
Any other symptom	8.4	4.2	2.5	2.0
Met full criteria	14.5	0.0	5.5	2.9
Told doctor	1.8	0.0	4.3	1.0
Positive responses (Mean)	5.3	2.5	3.1	2.4

*Compared with negatives.

TABLE 3. *Comparing psychiatrists' and lay interviewers' diagnoses as predictors of mean number of future positive responses*

		Relative risks (Positive/negative diagnosis)	
	Total	"Valid" or confirmed	"Invalid" or not confirmed
Alcohol			
Lay	4.6	5.3	2.5
Psychiatrist	5.2	5.8	3.7
Depression/dysthymia			
Lay	2.8	3.1	2.4
Psychiatrist	3.0	3.1	2.8

agnoses directly (Table 3), we find that overall the clinicians have a bit of an edge over the lay interviewers, supporting the choice of clinicians as the standard against which to judge lay interviewers. However, when psychiatrists' diagnoses were confirmed by lay interviewers' diagnoses, they predicted the future better than when they were not confirmed, suggesting that psychiatrists, like lay interviewers, may be imperfect diagnosticians. Indeed, the chief message of these results appears to be that two heads are better than one, since both lay interviewers' results and psychiatrists' results are better when confirmed by the other. They also suggest that a diagnosis based on a standardized interview has considerable predictive power even when it is not confirmed by a clinician.

Other kinds of results have become available that appear to have a bearing on the validity of a standardized interview in lay interviewers' hands. These include a remarkable consistency across studies in different sites and cultures in the prevalence rates of specific diagnoses (13-16); the fact that the demographic risk factors for specific diagnoses that were initially identified in clinical studies regularly appear (e.g., the excess of women among depressives (15a), of men among those with alcohol disorders (14), of very young adults among drug abusers (17)); and the fact that rank orders of the prevalence of individual symptoms of specific disorders correlate highly across sites and cultures (18, 19).

While this amassing evidence is viewed as encouraging by some, others stress the fact that the agreements between clinicians and lay interviewers administering the DIS separately are far from perfect. But perhaps one should not expect agreements between psychiatric assessments to surpass those for other assessments in medicine. When levels of agreement between lay interviewers' diagnoses using standardized psychiatric interviews and clinician assessments are compared with agreements between various methods of suspecting breast cancer and biopsy results (20), or between readings of radiographic results by experts (21, 22), standardized psychiatric interviews are found to achieve validity levels well within the range for diagnostic techniques that have been widely accepted as useful to medical practice. While there is less than perfect validity for each of these measures, no one would suggest dispensing with x-rays or the palpation of lumps before something better—and affordable—becomes available. Our standardized psychiatric interviews do much better than chance. Because they improve our state of knowledge, we need to continue using them while we try to improve or replace them with something better. At present, we have no better method for assessing psychiatric illness than the standardized interview. It may well be most accurate in the hands of a clinician, but it is not economically feasible to have all epidemiological studies carried out by psychiatrists, so long as lay interviewers do reasonably well.

More interesting than deciding whether standardized interviews are "valid" or "invalid" in some global sense is trying to understand how the grammar of current diagnostic systems influences the agreement we can expect between clinicians and lay interviewers. I use the term "grammar" because diagnosis is much like a language. The criteria include elements that have special relations to each other like parts of speech—symptoms (nouns?); severity (adjectives?); clustering (verbs?); age of onset, frequency, and duration (adverbs?). The computer algorithms for combining these criteria can be parsed like sentences. That the grammar of diagnosis plays an important role in validity is suggested by the observation that some diagnoses are regularly found to be more valid than others no matter what setting the study was carried out in or how validity was assessed. Since the same general methods have been followed for each diagnosis in deciding how questions are to be written to match the criteria and how responses to those questions are to be combined by computer to make diagnoses, finding a regular difference between disorders in measured validity suggests that the source of these differences may lie not in the interview so much as in the way the Diagnostic Manual it follows describes and combines the criteria.

In every validity study of the DIS and CIDI, substance abuse disorders (abuse and dependence taken together) have been found to be exceptionally valid. Depressive disorders have a middle rank. Results have been variable for schizophrenia and panic disorder; in some studies they have been found quite invalid, in others about as valid as depression, but never as valid as substance abuse. Because most of the studies available have compared diagnoses made according to DSM-III criteria, and most have data on both alcohol abuse or dependence and major depressive episode, we will pay particular attention to differences in the grammars of these two diagnoses in DSM-III. But we will also note difficulties that other diagnoses present, difficulties that we have become particularly aware of as we update the DIS and CIDI so that they can be used to make DSM-III-R diagnoses.

In trying to understand this variation in validity, we will look both at the content of symptoms and at how symptoms and other criteria are combined to reach diagnostic decisions.

CONTENT

We begin with symptom content. The purpose of writing a highly structured interview is to relieve the interviewer of the need for making judgments in so far as possible. This is achieved by specifying question wording exactly, even including the phrases to be used in following up on positive responses, and phrasing questions so that only a very limited range of responses is possible (yes-no, a number, or selection from among a few alternatives that can be read to the respondent). This limited range of responses makes it possible to enter responses directly into the computer without the interviewer's needing to exercise judgment as to which category best includes the answer. But a highly structured interview does not necessarily relieve *the respondent* of the need for judgment. He or she must listen to the question and decide into which of the fixed categories his own history best fits.

Studies of the reliability of opinion surveys have shown that opinions on topics of great interest to the respondent that he had had many previous occasions to express were reported reliably, although opinions on topics that were not salient to him, or worse where his opinion had to be formed on the spot during the interview, were both highly unstable and much influenced by the respondent's surmises as to the interviewer's attitudes on the subject (23).

The situation is probably much the same for questions about one's psychiatric history. When the question asks about something the respondent has often thought about before in the very language in which the question is phrased, reliability and validity are high. But when the question asks the respondent to summarize his experiences in a new way, a way that has not already been laid down in memory, the answer will be unreliable, probably susceptible to surmises about what the interviewer wants or expects to hear, and almost certainly dependent on the respondent's motivation to cooperate and his current mood.

Responses to substance abuse questions may be reliable because respondents have thought of themselves as using or not using certain drugs; arrest for drunkenness or possession of illicit drugs is a salient event, the memory of which may be reinforced by a subsequent trial and confinement; family members' complaints about substance abuse are usually persistent and clear; and it is conventional in our society to count one's drinks, if only because we pay by the drink. In contrast, questions about depressive symptoms are not so easy to answer. Take retardation as an example. It is not common to have thought about whether one has moved or talked more slowly than normal for a period of 2 weeks or more. To answer that question, one has to decide within the very brief interval that social convention allows between question and response what is normal for oneself, whether there was ever a period different from that normal pattern, and how long that different period lasted. It is easy to imagine that on having to make those calculations a second time during the validation assessment, one might come up with a different answer. For years, surveyors of mental health in the community argued that they could not ask about substance abuse because the questions were so "sensitive" that they would not be answered honestly. It seems to be the case that the degree of instant judgment required is a much more important determinant of accuracy than is the social acceptability of the symptom asked about.

The proposition that it is the availability of the item in memory rather than its sensitivity that affects reliability and presumably validity is consistent with the results found for the reliability of individual depressive symptoms in the ECA sample as measured by the frequency with which they are reported again a year later (in Wave 2) after having been reported in a first interview (in Wave 1) (Table 4). (Data from four of the five ECA sites are included here—all but New Haven, where in Wave 2 the questions about occurrence at any time in the past were replaced with questions about occurrence since the last interview.) Relative risks of affirming the initial report are calculated by dividing rates of reporting ever having had the symptom in Wave 2 for persons who reported it in Wave 1—and so definitely should also have had it by Wave 2 a year later—by rates of reporting by persons who had not yet had it by Wave 1, and so should be positive in Wave 2 only if the symptom occurred for the first time in the intervening year. Results are presented separately for those with many or few symptoms in Wave 1 because those with many symptoms are both more likely to repeat any particular Wave 1 symptom in Wave 2 and to report for the first time at Wave 2 symptoms that were not reported in Wave 1. Since some depressive symptoms are rarely reported unless many other symptoms are reported, our assessment of the relative reliability of particular symptoms would be confounded by the reliability attributable to severity if we had failed to control on initial number of symptoms.

TABLE 4. *Report of depressive symptoms after one year*

Among 18 symptoms	Relative risk* of reporting when many or few Wave 1 symptoms	
	Few (1–4)	Many (5+)
1. Trouble concentrating	2.6	1.9
2. Dysphoria for 2 weeks	2.7	1.6
3. Death thoughts	2.5	2.5
5. Insomnia	3.1	2.3
5. Fatigue	2.4	2.5
5. Slowed thinking	2.7	2.4
6. Retardation	3.7	2.4
7. Weight gain	3.5	3.1
8. Weight loss	3.7	2.9
9. Feeling worthless	5.3	2.5
10. Loss of libido	3.3	4.4
11. Agitation	4.3	3.7
12. Wanted to die	6.6	3.3
13. Appetite loss	5.5	3.5
14. Hypersomnia	4.6	4.5
15. Dysphoria for 2 years	9.8	3.5
17. Thoughts of suicide	16.7	7.5
18. Attempted suicide	54.6	17.7

*Percent reporting the symptom in Wave 2 among those who reported it in Wave 1 divided by percent reporting the symptom in Wave 2 among those who did not report it in Wave 1.

By far the most reliably reported depressive symptom is the suicide attempt, even though it is probably also the most "sensitive." It is reported 15 times as reliably as retardation (54.6/3.7) by those with few symptoms, and 7 times as reliably as retardation by those with many symptoms. (Relative risks are higher for those mildly than severely symptomatic at Wave 1 because a higher proportion of the severely affected with no prior attempt had one in the intervening year.) Unlike retardation, suicide attempts are memorable events with no required duration, and since they are clearly not part of one's usual behavior, no judgment is needed as to whether there has been a change from the normal state. Further, they are recorded in the memory in just the words used in the question—"attempted suicide." Since we have no outside verification, we don't know how valid these reports of suicide attempts are, but they certainly are the most reliable depressive symptom by a very large factor. It is notable that suicidal *acts* are much more reliable than suicidal *thoughts,* presumably because acts are more definite and more memorable.

Another difference between alcohol and depressive diagnoses is that DSM-III specifies the etiological role of alcohol in symptoms of alcohol abuse, but does not specify the role of depression in its symptoms. The B criterion for Alcohol Abuse, for example, is "Impairment in social or occupational function due to alcohol use." Consequently, one of the DIS questions asks "Have you ever had job troubles because of drinking?" Criterion B for a Major Depressive Episode says only "At least four of the following symptoms have each been present nearly every day for a period of at least two weeks." So the DIS asks "Has there ever been a period of two weeks or longer when you lost your appetite?", not "Were you ever so depressed that you lost your appetite for two weeks or longer?" Since in following DSM-III we do not link appetite loss to depression in the main question, we have to do complex probing to rule out physical explanations for the appetite loss. No such probing is required for the question about job troubles due to alcohol.

PARSING THE DIAGNOSTIC STRUCTURE

Alcohol diagnoses are like simple compound sentences; they only require the occurrence of symptoms from at least two categories. The diagnosis of a depressive episode, in contrast, is a sentence full of subordinate clauses and other grammatical intricacies. While alcohol diagnoses have no exclusion criteria, a depressive episode is ruled out if (Criterion C) there has ever been preoccupation with a mood-incongruent delusion or hallucination or bizarre behavior in the absence of an affective syndrome (i.e., at a time other than during a depressive episode), or (Criterion D) the episode was superimposed on schizophrenia, schizophreniform disorder, or paranoid disorder, or (Criterion E) it is due to an organic mental disorder or uncomplicated bereavement. Hallucinations and delusions are defined in the section on schizophrenia, but bizarre behavior is undefined. Not knowing precisely what should be included as bizarre behavior, we put no question into the DIS to ask about its presence, providing an opportunity for disagreement between the DIS and a clinician if the clinician judges it to be present. The DIS makes the diagnoses of schizophrenia and schizophreniform disorder, but not paranoid disorder, providing another opportunity for disagreement if the clinician should make that diagnosis. The DIS assesses organic mental disorders by giving the Folstein-McHugh Mini-Mental State Exam. That exam detects *current* cognitive impairment, but does not really assess current organic mental disorder (since it gets false positives associated with poor education, for example). Further, because the DIS gets no historical information about the onset of the cognitive impairment, it cannot determine whether a past depressive episode was or was not explained by organic disorder. Our compromise was to score depressive episodes both with and without exclusions for the current diagnosis of cognitive impairment and the diagnosis ever in one's lifetime of schizophrenia and schizophreniform disorder. Clearly these DIS rules do not perfectly match the DSM-III exclusion criteria. But even had we been able to get precise measures of the excluding diagnoses, we could expect more invalidity for depression than for alcohol disorders because when a disorder can be excluded by the presence of any of a number of other diagnoses, a diagnostic error in one diagnosis will have a ripple effect, causing errors in other diagnoses. In the grammar of diagnosis, such exclusion rules are restrictive clauses, which cannot be removed without changing the meaning of the sentence/diagnosis. DSM-III-R has reduced the number of excluding diagnoses, but they are by no means all gone. Criteria C, D, and E from DSM-III are still there for a depressive episode, and so it will continue to be more difficult to be correct about depressive disorders than alcohol disorders.

Alcohol disorders not only have no exclusion criteria, they do not require clustering. There is nothing in DSM-III that says that alcohol symptoms must appear in the same time span, while a depressive episode requires that there be dysphoric mood "associated with" (which we interpreted to mean temporally associated with) other symptoms of the depressive syndrome. While the associated symptoms have a clear duration requirement—2 weeks each, there is no clear duration requirement for dysphoria. We made the arbitrary decision that dysphoria had to be present for 2 weeks as well. DSM-III-R has changed the definition of clusters. It says that five symptoms, one of which must be dysphoric mood or loss of interest, must have been present during the same 2-week period; it no longer specifies a duration requirement for any single depressive symptom, including dysphoria. So clustering remains, but the duration specified has been shifted from symptoms to the cluster. We have called clustering a diagnostic "verb." The grammars of all diagnoses have verbs, but some are simple intransitive verbs like "to be." Clustering is very like "get" in the sense of "get together"—an originally transitive verb that now also serves as an intransitive one, but still communicates a sense of acting on others. In alcohol, the symptoms just have to exist; for a depressive episode they have to get together. But it is not entirely clear how much togetherness is required. The fact that DSM-III and DSM-III-R do not specify the number of symptoms that need to co-occur on a particular day or the number of days they need to overlap can lead to disagreements.

Affective (mood) disorders are even more complex than we have shown so far. Indeed, they are more like paragraphs than sentences. They depend on linking the two affective episodes, manic and depressive, and their "near misses," hypomania and dysthymia, into more complex hierarchical patterns. Bipolar disorders, both mixed and depressive, for example, require both a manic and depressive episode, but the mixed type requires that they alternate. Major depression requires both the presence of a depressive episode and the lifelong absence of a manic episode; cyclothymic disorder requires symptoms of both depression and mania but never meeting criteria for either; dysthymia requires either never meeting criteria for a depressive episode or at least having 2 years of depressive symptoms before meeting the criteria; and atypical bipolar and atypical depression require an absence not only of depressive and manic episodes but of cyclothymia and dysthymia. An error in diagnosing a depressive episode or a manic episode will affect each of these diagnoses, because for each they serve either as a positive or exclusion criterion.

The comparative simplicity of the structure of the alcohol diagnoses may explain their relative validity when compared with depression, but even alcohol disorders are not perfectly valid when measured by agreement between lay interviewer and clinician. One reason may be that the DSM-III diagnostic criteria do not always match the clinician's views. When the Manual prescribes a diagnosis the clinician does not feel is present, he may simply not follow the rules. It is formally possible for a person to meet DSM-III criteria for alcohol dependence with only two symptoms, one indicating tolerance, another indicating social problems. Any one who drinks heavily and regularly will probably develop tolerance, and if he or she has a relative or friend who regularly tells him that they do not like his drinking so much, he can qualify as alcohol dependent, because criticism from family members over a 1-month period plus tolerance equals dependence. If there are no other symptoms and no more serious impairment than family complaints, many clinicians would be reluctant to make a diagnosis of alcohol dependence. (DSM-III-R has made the criteria somewhat stricter; it will be interesting to see how much difference this makes practically.)

DSM-III encourages multiple diagnoses, and computer programs written for the DIS relentlessly identify every diagnosis a respondent meets. Because clinicians, in contrast, are highly motivated to explain the current symptom presentation, their interest in secondary diagnoses may be limited to diagnoses which help to account for the current clinical picture. It is probably the combination of the "softness" of DSM-III's alcohol criteria and the frequent irrelevance of early substance abuse to the onset of other disorders much later in life that explains why validation studies that compare DIS diagnoses with clinical records find the most common discrepancy between the two to be the absence of an alcohol diagnosis in the clinical record. Where these discrepancies occur, it is likely that the DIS fits the formal statements in DSM-III better than the clinical record does, but it does not match clinical practice.

In addition to disagreements about the minimum number of symptoms required to define a diagnosis and the appropriateness of noting secondary diagnoses, the very specific criteria of DSM-III may sometimes account both for clinicians' straying from the written word and for unreliability in respondents' reporting. According to DSM-III, a diagnosis of panic disorder requires three attacks within a 3-week period. Respondents do not count attacks like drinks, and they may be particularly inaccurate about relating number of attacks to time intervals. Panic disorder has had uniquely low rates of agreement between lay interviewers and clinical assessment, but failure of agreement rests on this criterion of three attacks in 3 weeks. There is generally good agreement on which symptoms were present during the worst panic attack. Because clinicians are aware that the three-attacks-in-3-weeks criterion asks for a precision that respondents often cannot provide, they may use their own best guess rather than taking a response to this question literally. The computer cannot respond so flexibly.

DSM-III-R has replaced some of the numeric criteria for DSM-III diagnoses with terms like "often," "frequent," and "persistent" (terms which we shall see later have their own problems), but a number of arbitrary cut points remain that are likely to cause diagnostic disagreements because they will be answered unreliably and because they limit clinicians' options. Attention deficit disorder, for example, must have its onset before age 7, and the tic disorders must have theirs before age 21. What will a clinician do if a patient gives a history of attention problems beginning at age 8 or tics beginning at age 22? Probably he will ignore the rule, while a computer will go its relentless way in disqualifying all cases above the specified cut point. Clinicians also believe some symptoms are more pathognomonic than others, even when the Manual treats them all equally. A clinician with a patient who has only four of the five symptoms required for a depressive episode in DSM-III-R may be tempted to make the diagnosis if one of the symptoms present is suicidal ideation. Such minor clinical rebellions make for apparent "invalidity" when a highly structured interview is compared with a clinician's evaluation, because the computer follows the rules that call for counting symptoms when that is what the Manual says to do. The clinician may be right in some deeper sense, while the DIS may adhere more closely to the literal statement in the Manual.

Another threat to diagnostic validity lies in bad diagnostic grammar—by which I mean illogical statements in DSM-III or DSM-III-R. One of the chief motivations for revising DSM-III was to remove these, and the effort has been largely successful, but a few have still slipped through in III-R. Take the criteria for a panic attack, for example. The D criterion requires that four symptoms more than once developed and increased in severity within 10 minutes of the first symptom. By my calculation, that means there have to be five symptoms altogether (one plus four more within 10 minutes) in at least two attacks ("more than once"). However, the C criterion clearly states that a minimum of four symptoms in one attack is sufficient.

"Bad grammar" also occurs when "obsolete or archaic" terms are introduced that harken back to DSM-II, when each person was to be given only a single diagnosis. As an example, consider the term "disturbance" in the DSM-III-R criteria for a manic episode. Criterion D says, "At no time during the disturbance have there been delusions or hallucinations for as long as two weeks in the absence of prominent mood symptoms." But if there were no mood symptoms, the manic episode was not in progress. The word "disturbance" seems to imply that what happened before or after the manic episode and the episode itself were all part of a single disorder, although DSM-III-R's grammar allows for the possibility that there were two discrete disorders. Because the Manual mentions no requirement for temporal continuity between the manic episode and the period of the "disturbance" when the manic episode was not active, close observance of the stated rules would require that someone who develops a delusional (paranoid) disorder at 60 after having had a manic episode at 30, must now be defined as never having had the manic episode. Yet clinicians who "speak" Modern Diagnosis (DSM-III-R) rather than Middle Diagnosis (DSM-II) or Old Diagnosis (DSM-I) would be unlikely to follow that rule.

ELLIPTICAL GRAMMAR

The statements in the Diagnostic Manual sometimes require interpretation on the part of the person writing questions to match them because they are incomplete and nonspecific. They are like elliptical sentences. As an example, the question "May I talk to you for a minute?" can be answered "Not now." "Not now" has neither a subject nor a predicate, but it can be expanded from the context to the form "Unfortunately, I am busy at the moment, but I will be available later." But other possible expansions are also possible with quite a different sense, for instance, "Can't you see that I am busy; leave me alone." The difficulty with ellipsis is being sure exactly what was omitted when we have to rely on context to fill in the missing parts of speech.

As the author of questions to be used in the general population by people who lack the context supplied by clinical training, I have to fill in the parts that are omitted for them. Unfortunately, I can't be sure that I do it correctly. Indeed, sometimes I am too unsure of what has been omitted to try to replace it at all. Replacement is particularly problematic when criteria taken literally seem to omit distinctions between normal and pathological behavior, and when criteria are vague with respect to frequency or severity. Examples of criteria that appear to include normal behavior are the childhood criteria for antisocial personality in DSM-III-R. If one followed their language literally and asked "Have you been physically cruel to animals?" and "Have you deliberately set fires?", responses might include "I stepped on a roach in my house," "I went hunting," and "I'm a Boy Scout and had to pass my fire-starting test." To avoid such answers, I wrote questions adding in restrictions that I thought the criteria implied. For example, our question about fire-setting asks whether the respondent ever started a fire in a situation where someone else's property was likely to be damaged. The problem with this solution is that my judgment as to what a criterion "really" means may not match a clinician's interpretation of the same item. It is easy to imagine that not everyone would agree that our questions have "face validity."

We also have to impose our own definitions when criteria include words like often or frequently, because if we ask respondents whether they have had a symptom frequently, they reply, "It's happened five times; I don't know whether you'd call that frequent." We have arbitrarily decided that a plural means at least twice, while "often" or "frequently" means at least three times. We can be certain that these definitions will not be applied by all clinicians; as a result some degree of "invalidity" becomes inevitable.

The Diagnostic Manual gives many examples that help us to write questions, but these examples are almost always preceded by the phrase "such as" and they end with "etc." These words clearly imply that other unlisted behaviors or feelings would also meet this criterion, but here context gives us inadequate clues as to what they might be. Our solution is to cover only examples specifically listed, recognizing that our coverage will be incomplete—and that a clinician may accept other evidence for the presence of the symptom being assessed. Our solution becomes even more problematic when examples appear in the text but not in the boxed criteria. Our general rule is to write questions to match the boxed criteria, not the text, but sometimes we have to violate that rule. In DSM-III-R, for example, there are no examples of simple phobias in the boxed criteria section. Clearly, it would be disastrous to use the phrase in the boxed criteria in a standardized interview: "Have you ever had such an unreasonable fear of a circumscribed stimulus that you tried to avoid it?" We have instead resorted to the examples in the text.

CONCLUSION

The recent developments in psychiatric nosology represented by the Feighner criteria, RDC criteria, DSM-III, DSM-III-R, and now ICD-10, which is still in preliminary form, represent a marked improvement in clarity and detail of criteria over their predecessors. It is just this clarity and detail that encouraged the production of standardized interviews to cover specific diagnoses. However, attempts to transform those criteria into simple questions to be asked of members of the general population reveal that the ultimate in clarity of criteria and logic of the grammar of diagnosis has not yet been achieved. The elliptical constructions, the complex diagnostic structures, the imprecise statement of criteria, all consign any standardized interview derived from them to showing up as less than perfectly valid when its validity is measured against clinicians' diagnostic assessments, even when both attempt to make diagnoses as they believe the Manual intended them to. Recognition of these problems may appear to be pointing the finger at others, but it is not. In this chapter, I have stressed the problems I faced as the author of a standardized interview, but I participated in writing many of the very criteria in DSM-III and III-R that later gave me trouble.

The development of diagnostic systems and the development of assessment tools are symbiotic. Comparisons between the manual and standardized interviews reveal errors in the interview; honest attempts to translate the criteria as stated in the Manual into interview questions reveal grammatical difficulties in the criteria. As both profit from the interactions between them, we can expect improvements in our diagnostic nosology and in our assessment tools for use in clinical and community settings. Meanwhile, we would be better off working toward such improvements of both manual and interview than in bewailing our failure to achieve near-perfect agreement between any standardized diagnostic instrument and the yardstick of clinical judgment. We have not yet reached the state of perfection in either diagnosis or interview construction that justifies discarding standardized interviews because lay interviewers and clinicians do not always come to identical results. Lack of perfect agreement will certainly be with us until the diagnostic systems are exquisitely precise, logical, and complete and the diagnostic interviews interpret them absolutely correctly. And even then, we will be plagued by the fact that respondents, for no good reason that we know, sometimes change their stories between interviews. If we continue the symbiosis between diagnostic nosology and its standardized assessment, we can look forward to a long future of improvement in both. Let us welcome the future diagnostic systems, DSM-IV and ICD-10, and the future diagnostic instruments that will attempt to assess them, PSE-10, DIS-IV, SCID-II, and CIDI-II

ACKNOWLEDGMENTS

This work was supported in part by grants MH 17104, MH 00 334, MH 33883, MH 31302, DA-04001, and the MacArthur Foundation Network in Health and Protective Factors.

This was delivered as the Presidential Address to the The American Psychopathological Association's 78th Annual Meeting, March 5, 1988.

REFERENCES

1. Robins, L. N., Wing, J., Wittchen, H.-U., Helzer, J. E., Babor, T. F., Burke, J. D., Farmer, A., Jablenski, A., Pickens, R., Regier, D. A., Sartorius, N., Towle, L. H. The Composite International Diagnostic Interview (CIDI): An epidemiologic instrument suitable for use in conjunction with different diagnostic systems and in different cultures. *Arch Gen Psychiatry* 1988;45:1069–1077.
1a. Burke, J. D., Jr. Diagnostic categorization by the Diagnostic Interview Schedule (DIS): A comparison with other methods of assessment. In Rose, R. M., Barrett, J. E. (eds.) *Mental Disorders in the Community*. New York: Guilford Press, 1986; pp. 255–285.
2. Breslau, N., Davis, G. C. Post-traumatic Stress Disorder: The etiologic specificity of wartime stressors. *Am J Psychiat*, 1987;144:578–583.
3. Canino, G. J., Bird, H. R., Shrout, P. E., Rubio-Stipec, M., Bravo, M., Martinez, R., Sesman,

M., Guzman, A., Guevara, L. M., and Costas, H. The Spanish Diagnostic Interview Schedule:Reliability and concordance with clinical diagnoses in Puerto Rico. *Arch Gen Psychiatry,* 1987;44:720–726.
4. Erdman, H. P., Klein, M. H., Greist, J. H., Bass, S. M., Bires, J. K., and Machtinger, P. E. A comparison of the Diagnostic Interview Schedule and clinical diagnosis. *Am J Psychiatry,* 1987; 144:1477–1480.
5. Hwu, H. G., Yeh, E. K., Chang, L. Y., Chinese Diagnostic Interview Schedule. I. Agreement with psychiatrist's diagnosis. *Acta Psychiatr Scand.* 1986;73:225–233.
6. Laessle, R., Pfister, H., Wittchen, H. U. Risk of rehospitalization of psychotic patients. *Psychopathology* 1987;20:48–60.
7. Schulberg, H. C., Saul, M., McClelland, M., Ganguli, M., Christy, W., Frank, R. Assessing depression in primary medical and psychiatric practices. *Arch Gen Psychiatry* 1985;42:1164–1170.
8. Spengler, P. A., Wittchen, H. U. Procedural validity of the standardized symptom questions for the assessment of psychotic symptoms: A comparison of the DIS with two clinical methods. *Comprehensive Psychiatry* 1988;29:309–322.
9. Teplin, L. A. The criminality of the mentally ill: A dangerous misconception. *Am J Psychiatry* 1985;142:593–599.
10. von Korff, M., Sharpiro, S., Burke, J. D., Teitlebaum, M., Skinner, E. A., German, P., Turner, R. W., Klein, L., Burns, B. Anxiety and depression in a primary care clinic: Comparison of Diagnostic Interview Schedule, General Health Questionnaire and practitioner assessments. *Arch Gen Psychiatry* 1987;44:152–156.
11. Kendell, R. Clinical validity. In Robins, L. N., Barrett, J. E. (eds), *The Validity of Psychiatric Diagnosis,* New York: Raven Press, 1989;305–324.
12. Schulberg, H. C., McClelland, M., Gooding, W., Frank, R. Six-month outcome for medical patients with major depressive disorders. *J. Gen Int Med,* 1987;2:312–317.
13. Helzer, J. E., Spitznagel, E. L., McEvoy, L. The predictive validity of lay Diagnostic Interview Schedule diagnoses in the general population. *Arch Gen Psychiatry* 1987;44:1069–1077.
14. Helzer, J. E., Canino, G. J., Hwu, H. G., Bland, R. C., Newman, S., and Yeh, E. K. Alcoholism: A cross-national comparison of population surveys with the Diagnostic Interview Schedule. In Rose, R. M., Barrett, J. E. (eds.), *Alcoholism: Origins and Outcome,* New York: Raven Press, 1988.
15. Regier, D. A., Boyd, J. H., Rae, D. S., Burke, J. D., Locke, B. Z., Myers, J. K., Kramer, M., Robins, L. N., George, L. K., Karno, M. One month prevalence of psychiatric disorders in five epidemiologic catchment area sites. *Arch Gen Psychiatry,* 1988;45:977–986.
15a. Weissman, M. M., Leaf, P. J., Holzer, C. E. III, Myers, J. K., Tischler, G. L. The epidemiology of depression: An update on sex differences in rates. *J Affective Disorders* 1984;7:179–188.
16. Surtees, P. G., Sashidharen, S. P. Psychiatric morbidity in two matched community samples: A comparison of rates and risks in Edinburgh and St. Louis. *J Affective Disorders* 1986;10:101–113.
17. Robins, L. N., Helzer, J. E., Przybeck, T. Substance abuse in the general population. In Barrett, J. (ed.), *Mental Disorders in the Community: Findings from Psychiatric Epidemiology,* Chapter 2. New York: Guilford Press, 1987.
18. Anthony, J. C., Ritter, C. J., von Korff, M. R., Chee, E. M., and Kramer, M. (1986): Descriptive epidemiology of cocaine use in four U.S. communities. *Nat'l Inst Drug Abuse Res Monogr Ser,* 67:283–289.
19. Helzer, J. E., and Canino, G. The implications of cross-national research for diagnostic validity. Presented at the American Psychopathological Association Annual Meeting, March 3-5, 1988. In: L. N. Robins and Barret, J. E. (eds.) *The Validity of Psychiatric Diagnosis,* New York: Raven Press, 1989;247–262.
20. Gohagen, J. K., Rodes, N. D., Blackwell, C. W., Darby, W. P., Farrell, C., Herder, T., Pearson, D. K., Spitznagel, E. L., and Wallace, M. D. (1980): Individual and combined effectiveness of palpation, thermography, and mammography in breast cancer screening. *Preventive Med,* 9: 713–721.
21. Felson, B., Morgan, W. K. C., Bristol, L. J. et al. (1973): Observations on the results of multiple readings of chest films in coal miner's pneumoconiosis. *Radiology,* 109:19–23.
22. Norden, C., Philipps, E., Levy, P. et al. Variation in interpretation of intravenous pyelograms. *Am J Epidemiol* 1970;91:155–160.
23. Sudman, S., Bradburn, N. M. *Response Effects in Surveys.* Chicago: Aldine, 1974. Ch. 4.

The Validity of Psychiatric Diagnosis, edited by
Lee N. Robins and James E. Barrett.
Raven Press, Ltd., New York © 1989.

Reliability Considerations in Planning Diagnostic Validity Studies

Joseph L. Fleiss* and Patrick E. Shrout*,**

*Division of Biostatistics, Columbia University School of Public Health, New York, New York 10032; and **New York State Psychiatric Institute, New York, New York 10032*

INTRODUCTION

When examining the validity of a given diagnostic system, one should be sure that classifications made according to that system are as reliable as possible. Random misclassification error attenuates the validity of a categorical scale just as random measurement error attenuates the validity of a numerical scale (1). Increasing the sample size will overcome the diminished power of a test to find statistically significant correlations between the diagnostic system and external validity criteria, but will not overcome the bias in estimating such measures of validity as odds ratios, relative risks, phi coefficients, or point biserial correlation coefficients.

Reliability might be improved by making revisions in the system, but then it would be the validity of the new system that would be under examination, not the validity of the original one. Further, as Carey and Gottesman (2) showed, validity might actually worsen as reliability improves. One might, for example, make the criteria for a given diagnostic category so limited but so precise that interexaminer agreement on presence versus absence is excellent but the patients one ends up with as cases of that disorder are atypical of the population of cases.

In the context of diagnostic systems that are associated with structured interview schedules, rating scales, and checklists, reliability will be improved without changing the system by more careful phrasing of the questions to be asked, the items to be rated, and the decision rules to be employed. Careful training of the diagnosticians will also improve reliability. An appreciable degree of unreliability may remain, though. This chapter studies replication as the method for overcoming the unreliability that remains in a diagnostic system—without changing the system—in order that the validity studies to be undertaken are as valid as possible.

The chapter will focus on the practical problem of determining whether one or two independent diagnosticians are required for obtaining a reliable diagnosis on a patient. Before this problem is addressed there will be a review of the classical linear model for the reliability of a numerical variable, followed by a derivation of the kappa coefficient that is different from the way Cohen originally derived it (3) but that will be useful in the sequel.

The kind of validity study being considered here is one in which psychiatric patients who are diagnosed as having a certain disorder according to a given system—for example, schizoaffective disorder according to the Research Diagnostic Criteria (4)—will serve as the cases in a case-control study or as the probands in a family study. The controls are to come from an entirely different source population, such as the community or a facility for treating physically ill patients. This kind of study was the one considered first by Carey and Gottesman (2) in their seminal article.

A LINEAR MODEL FOR A NUMERICAL VARIABLE

The classical linear model for a numerical variable (e.g., a patient's total score on the Hamilton Depression Rating Scale [5]) is

$$X = T + E, \tag{A}$$

where X denotes the observed score, T represents the underlying steady-state value or so-called true score, and E represents the random measurement error made in obtaining the observed score (6). The two unobservable quantities T and E are assumed to be uncorrelated and to have variances σ_T^2 and σ_E^2. The variance of X is therefore equal to $\sigma_T^2 + \sigma_E^2$, and the correlation between a pair of replicate measurements on a subject,

$$X_1 = T + E_1$$

and

$$X_2 = T + E_2,$$

is equal to

$$R = \frac{\sigma_T^2}{\sigma_T^2 + \sigma_E^2} \tag{B}$$

R is known as the intraclass correlation coefficient of reliability, and is seen to be interpretable as the proportion of the variance of observed scores due to patient-to-patient variability in true scores. Most of the untoward effects of unreliability, including biased estimates of correlation and regression coefficients, false positives and false negatives on screening tests, and larger sample sizes than otherwise necessary, are expressible mathematically as functions of R (7,8).

A reliability study in which each subject is measured independently two or more times produces the requisite quantities for estimating the reliability coefficient, using the methods of analysis of variance (9, 10). One of the most important uses of the estimated reliability coefficient is in determining the number of replicate measurements to be made on each subject in the substantive study that will follow the reliability study, with the mean of those measurements serving as the datum for a subject. If R is the reliability coefficient from equation B, and if each subject is measured m times and the m measurements are averaged, the Spearman-Brown formula (6) gives

$$R_m = \frac{mR}{1 + (m - 1)R} \quad \text{(C)}$$

as the reliability coefficient for the mean.

If the investigators demand a reliability of, say, R* for the observations to be obtained in the substantive study, the Spearman-Brown formula yields

$$m = \frac{R^*(1 - R)}{R(1 - R^*)} \quad \text{(D)}$$

as the number of replicate measurements to be obtained and averaged on each subject. (Equation D follows from C by replacing R_m by R* and solving for m.) For example, if R = 0.67 but the investigators require a reliability coefficient of R* = 0.8, they should plan to have each subject measured

$$m = \frac{0.8(1 - 0.67)}{0.67(1 - 0.8)} = 2$$

independent times on the variable under consideration.

A feature of the model represented by equation A that must be born in mind is that the "true score" T does not represent a subject's score on some fundamental underlying ideal variable. Rather, T should be understood to represent the mean score for a subject across many hypothetical replicate measurements. T is therefore a subject's underlying value on whatever construct it is that the variable is actually measuring, not necessarily the value on the underlying construct one hopes the variable is measuring.

A RELIABILITY MODEL FOR DIAGNOSIS

In turning our attention to the reliability of diagnoses instead of quantitative measures, we make use of kappa, the most common reliability measure for categorical ratings. We summarize the derivation of a version of kappa that is appropriate for reliability studies involving a large pool of diagnosticians (11, 12). We use Greek letters or capital Latin letters to denote population parameters. Their sample estimators are denoted by a caret placed over the Greek letter or the Latin letter set in lower case.

Consider a simple reliability study in which each of a sample of n subjects is examined twice, with each examination resulting in a binary categorization: the patient is judged to satisfy or not to satisfy the criteria for the diagnosis under investigation. The two examinations, by two different examiners, are assumed to be independent but are not assumed to be necessarily by the same two examiners for all patients. The pair of examiners responsible for examining and diagnosing one patient may be different from the pair responsible for examining and diagnosing another.

The results of such a reliability study may be summarized by three quantities, the numbers n_0, n_1, and n_2 of patients for whom none, one, or both of a pair of examiners made a classification into the category of interest. (For convenience, such classifications will be referred to as "positive".) Let the corresponding proportions be denoted by $p_i = n_i/n$ for $i = 0, 1, 2$. The observed proportion of agreement is then

$$p_{obs} = p_0 + p_2 \qquad (E)$$

The chance-expected proportion of agreement may be developed as follows. Of the $2n$ categorizations that were made in all, a total of $2n_2 + n_1$ were positive and $2n_0 + n_1$ were negative. The corresponding proportions of positive and negative ratings are, say,

$$p = \frac{2n_2 + n_1}{2n} = p_2 + p_1/2 \qquad (F)$$

and $q = 1 - p = p_0 + p_1/2$. The proportion of agreement expected if the examiners were merely making classifications at random with the relative frequencies p and q is then

$$p_{exp} = p^2 + q^2, \qquad (G)$$

and

$$\hat{\kappa} = \frac{p_{obs} - p_{exp}}{1 - p_{exp}} = \frac{p_2 - p^2}{pq} \qquad (H)$$

Generalizations of this version of kappa have been published (13–15).

The version of kappa just derived is related to measures commonly used to quantify the chances of correct diagnostic classification, sensitivity and specificity. These measures are defined with reference to a patient's "true diagnostic status," to the classification of a patient as positive or negative according to the criteria of the given system, not to the classification according to the criteria of some underlying ideal system (see Kaye [16] and Kraemer [17] for a debate concerning this model).

The following model is a variation of one initially proposed by Kraemer (1). Let

$$\pi = \text{"true" prevalence,}$$

the proportion of patients in the population whose true status is positive, let

θ = sensitivity,

the chances that a truly positive patient will be correctly classified as positive by a typical examiner, and let

$$\phi = \text{specificity},$$

the chances that a truly negative patient will be correctly classified as negative by a typical examiner. Then P, the prevalence based on single diagnoses on each patient, is equal to

$$P = \theta\pi + (1 - \phi)(1 - \pi), \tag{I}$$

and p_2, the proportion of patients in the reliability study both of whose diagnoses were positive, estimates

$$P_2 = \theta^2\pi + (1-\phi)^2(1-\pi). \tag{J}$$

The parameter that $\hat{\kappa}$ estimates is easily shown to be

$$\kappa = \frac{\pi(1-\pi)}{PQ}(\theta + \phi - 1)^2, \tag{K}$$

where $Q = 1 - P$. This identity, first derived by Kraemer (1), has been analyzed by several investigators (18–20).

As Carey and Gottesman (2) pointed out, the kappa coefficient is particularly relevant to those validity studies in which patients diagnosed as positive will be compared to those diagnosed as negative. Here, however, only those identified as positive will be enrolled in the validity study. The parameter that is informative about the trustworthiness of a single diagnosis of positive is the positive predictive value, the probability, denoted by V, that a patient who is diagnosed once, and receives a diagnosis of positive, is truly positive:

$$V = \frac{\theta\pi}{\theta\pi + (1-\phi)(1-\pi)} \tag{L}$$

The calculation of V requires knowledge of the three parameters θ, ϕ, and π. If the value of the true prevalence π could be specified, and if $\hat{\kappa}$ and p are available from a reliability study conducted on a sample from the population of interest, then sensitivity and specificity could be estimated by means of the equations

$$\hat{\theta} = p\left(1 \pm \sqrt{\hat{\kappa}\frac{q(1-\pi)}{p\pi}}\right) \tag{M}$$

and

$$\hat{\phi} = q\left(1 \pm \sqrt{\hat{\kappa}\frac{p\pi}{q(1-\pi)}}\right) \tag{N}$$

Within these equations, either both signs are to be taken as positive or both as negative. If π is close to p, one sign will generally produce an estimate outside of the interval from 0 to 1; the other sign will then be the correct one. Assume for simplicity that for the data one has at hand, the correct sign happens to be positive. The estimate of positive predictive value is then, say,

$$v = \pi \left(1 + \sqrt{\hat{\kappa}\,\frac{q(1-\pi)}{p\pi}} \right) \tag{O}$$

For fixed values of π, p and q ($=1-p$), v increases as $\hat{\kappa}$ increases.

In practice, one would postulate a range of reasonable values for the true prevalence π (this range should include the estimated prevalence, p), and examine the values of v over this range. If the values are deemed to be high throughout the range, the validity study could safely rely on single diagnoses to identify the positives. If not, judgments made by two or more diagnosticians would have to be obtained and combined in order to identify putative positives with confidence. In specifying what constitutes a "high" positive predictive value, one would likely require that half or more of one's putative positives should be true positives. Thus v should, at the very least, exceed 0.5 throughout the range of plausible π's.

EXAMPLE

Suppose that the results of a reliability study of n=50 patients each diagnosed twice are as in Table 1. The obtained value of $\hat{\kappa}=0.52$ would ordinarily suggest only modest reliability, but that value is not useful by itself when only the purported positives are of interest. For true prevalences varying between 0.20 and 0.40, positive predictive value varies from a low of 0.64 to a high of 0.94 (see Table 2). The value of 0.64, occurring at $\pi=0.2$, means that slightly more than one out of every three putative positives will actually be a true negative. Some investigators will be willing to tolerate an error rate of this magnitude; they would then proceed to identify the patients eligible for the validity study on the basis of just a single diagnosis. Investigators who feel that an error rate of one-third is too great will have to rely on at least two diagnoses per patient.

TABLE 1. *Results of a hypothetical reliability study*

Pattern of duplicate diagnoses	Proportion of patients
Both positive	$0.20 = p_2$
One positive	$0.20 = p_1$
Neither positive	$0.60 = p_0$

p = observed prevalence = 0.3

$$\hat{\kappa} = \frac{0.20 - (0.30)^2}{0.30 \times 0.70} = 0.5238$$

TABLE 2. Characteristics of the rule that identifies positives on the basis of one diagnosis (for the study in Table 1)

Prevalence (π)	Sensitivity ($\hat{\theta}$)	Specificity ($\hat{\phi}$)	Positive Predictive Value (v)
0.20	0.9633	0.8658	0.642
0.25	0.8745	0.8915	0.729
0.30	0.8066	0.9171	0.807
0.35	0.7520	0.9434	0.877
0.40	0.7062	0.9708	0.942

THE "TWO-OUT-OF-TWO" RULE

A sensible rule for identifying cases with the disorder under study when patients are examined twice is to have a patient classified as positive only if both diagnosticians agree that the disorder is present. Patients with one-out-of-two or zero-out-of-two diagnoses of that disorder are classified as negative. A patient whose first diagnosis was of some other disorder would not have to be diagnosed again, because such a patient could not possibly end up classified as positive.

The Spearman-Brown formula does not predict the reliability of the two-out-of-two rule. To assess its reliability, one has to analyze the rule probabilistically in terms of the parameters π, θ and ϕ, and determine what the resulting positive predictive values are. As an example of the mathematical analysis, consider the determination of the sensitivity and specificity of the new rule. Sensitivity is now the probability that a true positive will be called positive by the two-out-of-two rule. It is equal to, say,

$$\theta_2 = \theta^2$$

Specificity is now the probability that a true negative will be called negative by the new rule. It is equal to, say,

$$\phi_2 = \phi + (1 - \phi)\phi = \phi(2 - \phi).$$

The proportion of putative positives in the population based on the two-out-of-two rule, P_2, simplifies to the expression in equation J.

The calculation of kappa requires determining the probability, say P_{++}, that a patient would be classified as a positive both times if the two-out-of-two rule could be applied twice. If we assume, as we did earlier, that a large pool of diagnosticians are available, and that they are all characterized by the same sensitivity and specificity, then P_{++}, the probability that two examiners say that the condition is present and that another two examiners also say that the condition is present, is identical to the probability that four examiners all say that the condition is present,

$$P_{++} = \theta^4\pi + (1-\phi)^4(1-\pi).$$

The population value of kappa for the new rule is then equal to

$$\kappa_2 = \frac{P_{++} - P_2^2}{P_2(1-P_2)} = \frac{\pi(1-\pi)(\theta^2 - (1-\phi)^2)^2}{(\theta^2\pi + (1-\phi)^2(1-\pi))(1-\theta^2\pi - (1-\phi)^2(1-\pi))}. \quad (P)$$

Using the estimators of θ and ϕ given in equations M and N, one may estimate κ_2 as

$$\hat{\kappa}_2 = \frac{p\left(\hat{\kappa}q(1-2\pi) + 2\sqrt{\hat{\kappa}pq\pi(1-\pi)}\right)^2}{\pi(1-\pi)(p+\hat{\kappa}q)(1-p(p+\hat{\kappa}q))} \quad (Q)$$

The positive predictive value for the two-out-of-two rule, finally, is,

$$v_2 = \frac{\theta_2\pi}{\theta_2\pi + (1-\phi_2)(1-\pi)} = \frac{\theta^2\pi}{\theta^2\pi + (1-\phi)^2(1-\pi)}, \quad (R)$$

which may be estimated as

$$v_2 = \frac{p\pi + \hat{\kappa}q(1-\pi) + 2\sqrt{\hat{\kappa}pq\pi(1-\pi)}}{p + \hat{\kappa}q} \quad (S)$$

Estimates of these parameters for the illustrative data set appear in Table 3. Throughout the entire range of reasonable values for the underlying prevalence, positive predictive value exceeds 92.5%; at the upper end of the range, positive predictive value is nearly perfect. Curiously, the value of kappa declines over the interval even as positive predictive value increases. In fact, $\hat{\kappa}_2$ is less than $\hat{\kappa}$ over most of the upper half of the interval. The sharply declining values of $\hat{\kappa}_2$ reflect the sharply declining sensitivity values for the two-out-of-two rule: because the specificity values for this rule are all nearly equal to unity,

$$\hat{\kappa}_2 \approx \frac{\pi(1-\pi)}{p_2(1-p_2)}\hat{\theta}^4 = \frac{\pi(1-\pi)}{0.2 \times 0.8}\hat{\theta}^4 \quad (T)$$

TABLE 3. *Characteristics of the rule that identifies positives on the basis of two diagnoses (for the study in Table 1)*

Prevalence (π)	Sensitivity ($\hat{\theta}_2$)	Specificity ($\hat{\phi}_2$)	Kappa ($\hat{\kappa}_2$)	Positive Predictive Value (v_2)
0.20	0.9280	0.9820	0.8281	0.928
0.25	0.7647	0.9882	0.6643	0.956
0.30	0.6506	0.9931	0.5440	0.976
0.35	0.5655	0.9968	0.4495	0.990
0.40	0.4987	0.9992	0.3718	0.997

(Recall that p_2 is the observed proportion of patients called positive by two examiners.) In contrast, it is the exceptionally high values for specificity that produce such excellent positive predictive values. Because $\hat{\phi}$ is nearly equal to 1.0, it is extremely unlikely that a patient who is negative will, according to the two-out-of-two rule, be incorrectly identified as positive. As a result,

$$v_2 = \frac{\hat{\theta}^2 \pi}{\hat{\theta}^2 \pi + (1 - \hat{\phi})^2(1 - \pi)} = \frac{\hat{\theta}^2 \pi}{\hat{\theta}^2 \pi} = 1.$$

A price must be paid for the excellent positive predictive value that the two-out-of-two rule achieves. Suppose that the substantive study is to involve a sample of 100 putative positives. With the rule that calls for a single diagnosis on each patient, a total of $N_1 = 100/p = 100/0.3 = 333$ patients will have to be evaluated in order that one may expect to end up with 100 presumed positives. The expected number of evaluations, say E_1, is also equal to 333.

With the two-out-of-two rule, a total of $N_2 = 100/p_2 = 100/0.2 = 500$ patients will have to be evaluated, 50% more than N_1. If patients are evaluated at a uniform rate over time, it will take, on the average, 50% longer for 100 presumed positives to be identified with the two-out-of-two rule than with the rule of relying on a single diagnosis. The expected number of evaluations, E_2, is nearly twice E_1. Thirty percent of the 500 patients, those whose first diagnosis is positive, will be evaluated a second time; the remaining 70% will not require a second evaluation. Thus,

$$E_2 = (0.3 \times 500) \times 2 + (0.7 \times 500) \times 1 = 650.$$

DISCUSSION

The selection of patients with a given disorder for a prospective or a case-control validity study has been used as an example of a situation in which reliability analyses may be misleading with respect to diagnostic validity (2). We analyzed this diagnostic problem using a simple probability model and found that positive predictive value, the proportion of purported cases who actually have the disorder according to the criteria of the diagnostic system under analysis, increases with kappa, the measure of diagnostic reliability. Under this same model, we showed that positive predictive value can be improved, for fixed levels of reliability, by following a two-out-of-two rule for patient selection: two independent diagnosticians have to agree that a patient is a case in order for the patient to be eligible for the validity study. We derived an estimate of the reliability of this rule, and found that in some cases the reliability of the diagnosis based on two assessments actually was less than the reliability of an individual assessment. This finding is different from the usual result, based on the Spearman-Brown formula, that reliability increases as information from several assessments is pooled. The classical result applies to averages of ratings, which are continuous rather than categorical. Because the selection problem requires a composite binary classification, the Spearman-Brown result does not hold.

Our results and selection rules would be different if the diagnostic problem were to identify both cases and noncases from a single population. In that instance both the positive predictive value and the negative predictive value will have to be large. The kind of selection rule that would be analyzed calls for taking as positive those patients so diagnosed by two independent assessments, and taking as negative those patients so diagnosed also by two independent assessments. Patients for whom the assessments lead to different results would either be dropped from further consideration or, if resources existed, would be assessed a third time and classified according to the majority of the three. Such rules have been proposed (21), but they have been rarely implemented because of the cost of triple assessments.

The statistical model we used in our analyses was the simplest possible. We assumed that all patients who were truly positive were characterized by a single sensitivity value, and that all who were truly negative were characterized by a single specificity. Alternative models have been proposed in which patients differ in the degree to which they fit a set of diagnostic criteria. Under such models it is hypothesized that there exist prototypical cases who have a higher probability of being correctly diagnosed than other cases (22). One may, in fact, postulate that sensitivity and specificity vary continuously in a population of patients. While such models have received some attention (1, 23), work is needed to determine the generalizability of results obtained with simple models such as the one we employed.

It is clear that if patients do vary in the probability of being correctly diagnosed, then the two-out-of-two rule that we studied may lead to biased samples of cases. For example, if high levels of some types of social functioning make certain patients difficult to diagnose correctly then such patients will tend to be underrepresented in case groups constructed using the two-out-of-two rule. While this bias may not be important in a randomized pharmacologic study, it would be very serious in risk factor research.

In practice the elimination of such bias is difficult, not because of the mathematics involved in characterizing the heterogeneity among cases, but because of the cost of the repeated assessments needed to identify the elusive cases. For example, potential bias could be reduced (but not eliminated) by modifying the rule we studied to be a two-out-of-three rule. This modification would call for double assessments of all patients in the initial pool, and a third "tie-breaker" assessment of all patients for whom there was initial diagnostic disagreement. The value of such extra cost and effort will only become apparent when data are collected that are informative about how heterogeneous patients are.

Throughout our discussion we have assumed that a reliability study would be conducted prior to selection of patients, regardless of the selection rule employed. Without estimates of kappa and of the proportions diagnosed as cases by one and by pairs of raters, it would be difficult to plan the selection rule for the validity study. It should be noted that such estimates cannot be transported easily between studies of different populations. It is risky to rely on estimates from the literature unless the previous studies focused on similar populations with similar diagnostic criteria. Thus, whenever new clinical populations or new diagnostic criteria are studied, it is desirable to conduct a new preliminary reliability study. While such efforts add to the cost of the entire research endeavor, the added expense is well worth it.

ACKNOWLEDGMENTS

This research was supported in part by grant MH30906 from the National Institute of Mental Health. Professor Helena Chmura Kraemer of Stanford University reviewed an earlier version of this chapter; we are grateful for her critique.

REFERENCES

1. Kraemer, H. C. (1979): Ramifications of a population model for κ as a coefficient of reliability. *Psychometrika*, 44:461–72.
2. Carey, G., Gottesman, I. I. (1978): Reliability and validity in binary ratings. *Arch Gen Psychiat*, 35:1454–9.
3. Cohen, J. (1960): A coefficient of agreement for nominal scales. *Educ Psychol Meas*, 20:37–46.
4. Spitzer, R. L., Endicott, J., and Robins, E. (1978): Research Diagnostic Criteria (RDC): Rationale and reliability. *Arch Gen Psychiat*, 35:773–82.
5. Hamilton, M. (1960): A rating scale for depression. *J Neurol Neurosurg Psychiat*, 23:56–62.
6. Lord, F. M., and Novick, M. R. (1968): *Statistical Theories of Mental Test Scores*. Addison-Wesley, Reading, Massachusetts.
7. Shrout, P. E., and Fleiss, J. L. (1981): Reliability and case detection. In: *What Is a Case?* edited by J. Wing, P. Bebbington, and L. N. Robins. pp. 117–128: Grant McIntyre, London.
8. Fleiss, J. L. (1986): *The Design and Analysis of Clinical Experiments*. Wiley, New York.
9. Bartko, J. J. (1966): The intraclass correlation coefficient as a measure of reliability. *Psychol Rep*, 19:3–11.
10. Shrout, P. E., and Fleiss, J. L. (1979): Intraclass correlations: Uses in assessing rater reliability. *Psychol Bull*, 86:420–8.
11. Fleiss, J. L. (1975): Measuring agreement between two judges on the presence or absence of a trait. *Biometrics*, 31:651–9.
12. Landis, J. R., and Koch, G. G. (1977): The measurement of observer agreement for categorical data. *Biometrics*, 33:159–74.
13. Fleiss, J. L., Nee, J. C. M., and Landis, J. R. (1979): The large sample variance of kappa in the case of different sets of raters. *Psychol Bull*, 86:974–7.
14. Fleiss, J. L., and Cuzick, J. (1979): The reliability of dichotomous judgments: Unequal numbers of judges per subject. *Appl Psychol Meas*, 3:537–42.
15. Kraemer, H. C. (1980): Extension of the kappa coefficient. *Biometrics*, 36:207–16.
16. Kaye, K. (1980): Estimating false alarms and missed events from inter-observer agreement: A rationale. *Psychol Bull*, 88:458–68.
17. Kraemer, H. C. (1982): Estimating false alarms and missed events from inter-observer agreement: Comment on Kaye. *Psychol Bull*, 92:749–54.
18. Grove, W. M., Andreasen, N. C., McDonald-Scott, P., Keller, M. B., and Shapiro, R. W., (1981) Reliability studies of psychiatric diagnosis: Theory and practice. *Arch Gen Psychiat*, 38:408–13.
19. Spitznagel, E. L., and Helzer, J. E. (1985): A proposed solution to the base rate problem in the kappa statistic. *Arch Gen Psychiat*, 42:725–8.

20. Shrout, P. E., Spitzer, R. L., and Fleiss, J. L. (1987): Quantification of agreement in psychiatric diagnosis revisited. *Arch Gen Psychiat,* 44:172–7.
21. Dohrenwend, B. P., Shrout, P. E. (1981): Toward the development of a two-stage procedure for case identification and classification in psychiatric epidemiology. In: *Research in Community and Mental Health,* volume 2, edited by R. G. Simmons, pp. 295–323: JAI Press, Greenwich, Connecticut.
22. Maxwell, A. E. (1977): Coefficients of agreement between observers and their interpretation. *Brit J Psychiat,* 130:79–83.
23. Sandifer, M. G., Fleiss, J. L., and Green, L. M., (1968): Sample selection by diagnosis in clinical drug evaluations. *Psychopharm,* (Berl) 13:118–28.

DISCUSSION

Dr. Donald Klein: We have been working on reliability of diagnosis problems for quite a while. We had two independent raters rate 104 anxiety patients. The kappa's that we obtained for most diagnoses were really quite nice, .8 to .9. The literature says that above .8 is good, .5 is getting weak, and less than .5 is unacceptable. For obsessive-compulsive disorder, we got kappas of .3. The question is, what do we do about it? Do we train our raters better? Do we change our system of listing the questions? What are we doing wrong?

Obsessive-compulsives were about 5% of the patient group that we worked with. Under the exact model, Kraemer's model, you take the sample kappa, plug in estimates of base rate, and you can derive estimates of sensitivity and specificity. As the estimate of base rate I took when both raters agreed the disorder was present. By this procedure the sensitivity and specificity were both around .9. The positive predictive value was lousy because of the many false positives, but, although we were stuck with a low base rate, it was reassuring to have the sensitivity and specificity above .9. I did not have to go back and revise the diagnostic plan, or do any more training.

Dr. Fleiss: But don't forget that the positive predictive value was poor. If one of the purposes of the classification is to rule out obsessive-compulsive disorder, you can trust a negative classification, but for other purposes, like trusting classification based on a single judgment, the system isn't good enough, even though sensitivity and specificity are high.

Dr. Klein: The question is, what needs fixing? If you don't recognize that the sensitivity and specificity are actually high, you will go back and start redoing your interview, or your training. If you know sensitivity and specificity are high but there is a low positive predictive value, then you should do something like multiple iterative ratings to decide who does or does not have the disorder. Saying "the kappa is too low" gives the message, "improve your methods." I don't think that is the right message. First you should estimate sensitivity and specificity. If high, you need multiple reexaminations.

Dr. Fleiss: I would agree. You cannot go by the value of kappa alone.

Dr. Grove: Would you comment on the implications of shifting from a one-out-of-one inclusion rule to a two-out-of-two inclusion rule from the standpoint of who gets sampled? When sensitivity and specificity vary along a continuum, as you shift from one-out-of-one to two-out-of-two inclusion rules, you are selecting farther up the continuum to which the sensitivity and specificity are related, perhaps a severity continuum. You are selecting differently, which might affect findings in a validity study.

Dr. Fleiss: You are absolutely right. If the true model is something other than the model that we assumed in order to get some results, we will be selecting atypical cases. With the two-out-of-two rule, we will select those who are the more severe, the more obvious, the more classic, and we will likely be missing less typical but still true cases.

But I want to learn how robust these rules are. They have going for them that they are simple to evaluate, which should not be denigrated. Nevertheless, we must ask how robust are the rules and properties derived from the simple model; how do they hold up when a more realistic model is applied? We have to evaluate this.

Dr. Grove: Even with a one-out-of-one selection rule, you are selecting atypical cases. But you are probably selecting more atypical ones when you go to a two-out-of-two rule.

Dr. Zubin: As a former statistician who has fallen behind the times, I have a question for the statisticians who are present. There are a variety of ways that the fourfold table is being dealt with. On the one hand, you have specificity and sensitivity, and you have positive and negative predictive value. From signal detection theory, you also have the "criterion" and the "sensitivity." Can somebody pull together these various aspects of the same fourfold table, and tell us the relation between these different indices?

Dr. Fleiss: I am afraid it is a lost cause. There is a correlation of 1.0 between the number of new journals and the number of new measures for the fourfold table in any given year. It is hopeless.

Dr. Shrout: In our work, one result was that *under certain circumstances,* reliability does not relate to validity in the way we would normally assume. This result relates to Dr. Klein's point that a reliability or .30 might be good enough if you are interested only in negative predictive value of specificity, but are not interested in positive predictive value or sensitivity. Statements have been made during this meeting that reliability is not needed for validity. Such summary statements can be misleading in their generality. Dr. Klein's comments, and our results about obtaining a good validity coefficient with a poor kappa, arise from the specific context where only one of two validity criteria is considered—the other is ignored. In other words, if sensitivity is considered, specificity is ignored; if positive predictive value is considered, negative predictive value is ignored. In these situations, one can obtain the results that we have reported, but from them it would be a mistake to conclude generally that one need not worry about reliability.

In its formal definition, reliability is said to be the absence of random error. Intuitively we know that if we throw error into a diagnostic system, it is likely to cause trouble. It is only when we carefully analyze the fourfold table, with all its complexity, that we can determine whether or not the error has done damage to the distinction that is most of interest.

Dr. Fleiss: I am in complete agreement.

The Validity of Psychiatric Diagnosis, edited by
Lee N. Robins and James E. Barrett.
Raven Press, Ltd., New York © 1989.

Having a Dream:
A Research Strategy for DSM-IV

Robert L. Spitzer and Janet B.W. Williams

*Department of Psychiatry, Columbia University,
New York State Psychiatric Institute,
New York, New York, 10032*

One evening, after we put our two young sons, Noah (1) and Ezra, to bed, we decided it was now time to start working on the paper that Dr. Robins had asked us to present at the 78th Annual Meeting of The American Psychopathological Association on the kind of psychiatric research that we thought is needed for the development of DSM-IV. We reviewed the program for this meeting and noted the roster of distinguished speakers who would review the advances that have been made in establishing the validity of psychiatric diagnoses and appropriate research strategies for the future. Having been asked by the Program Committee to present our views of what kind of research is needed for DSM-IV as the last talk of the meeting, we wondered what we could say that would add to what would already have been presented.

We went to bed troubled, not knowing how to approach the paper. At about 3 a.m. the phone rang. The senior author answered it and was startled to hear the friendly voice of the Director of the Division of Clinical Research of the NIMH. He apologized for the hour of his call and asked that we both get on the phone. He then explained that he had just come from an emergency meeting with the new Director of NIMH. A somewhat awkward situation had developed. Due to an accounting error, an enormous amount of federal funds was available and had to be committed within the next few weeks. Any delay would undoubtedly result in the loss of these funds. A hastily assembled study group had concluded that the funds would best be allocated to research focused on providing an empirical base for the development of DSM-IV.

Because of our past association with DSM-III and DSM-III-R, we had been chosen to write the Request for Proposals (RFP) that would specify the research to be done. We were not to be concerned with funding limitations.

The following is the RFP.

RFP FOR RESEARCH FOCUSED ON DEVELOPING DSM-IV

Beginning in 1980, DSM-III, and more recently its revision (DSM-III-R), has provided researchers with a common language with which to study mental disorders. This RFP is to solicit proposals from investigators interested in contributing to the further development of psychiatric nosology, as embodied in the next revision, DSM-IV, expected to go into effect in 1993. Because of the need to have results in early 1992, proposals will be quickly reviewed with an accelerated start date to allow for 6 months of intake, 2 years of follow-up, and 6 months of data analysis and preparation of final recommendations.

BACKGROUND

The Impact of Research on DSM-III and DSM-III-R

The major innovations and conceptual changes in DSM-III were based on nosologic research of the two preceding decades. The development of specified diagnostic criteria for virtually all of the specific diagnoses of DSM-III was based on the experience of researchers with the Feighner Criteria (2) and the Research Diagnostic Criteria (3). The DSM-III multiaxial system was a derivative of earlier, largely European, research on multiaxial systems (4). The U.S./U.K. Study indicated the overly broad definition of Schizophrenia that was used in this country in the 1960s, and together with the results of many family and follow-up studies of psychoses (5,6), led to the more restricted DSM-III definition of Schizophrenia. Epidemiologic studies of depression resulted in the elimination of the DSM-II diagnosis of Involutional Melancholia (7). Research into the treatment of phobias and other anxiety disorders, both in this country (8) and in England (9), led to the identification of specific anxiety disorders such as Panic Disorder, Generalized Anxiety Disorder, and the differentiation of Social Phobia, Simple Phobia, and Agoraphobia.

Research findings also played an important role in many of the changes embodied in DSM-III-R. Recent family and follow-up studies of psychoses (10) called into question the validity of the DSM-III requirement that Schizophrenia have an onset prior to age 45, resulting in the elimination of this criterion in DSM-III-R. Descriptive and treatment studies of "Seasonal Affective Disorder" (11,12) led to the inclusion in DSM-III-R of a specification for "seasonal pattern" of several Mood Disorders. The numerous studies of the clinical characteristics of "PMS" led to the inclusion in DSM-III-R, albeit in an appendix, of Late Luteal Phase Dysphoric Disorder (13,14).

DSM-III-R DIAGNOSTIC CRITERIA FIELD TRIALS

During the process of revising DSM-III, it became clear that for several diagnoses for which there was considerable controversy as to how to define the disorder, it would be valuable to conduct field trials that examined proposed diagnostic criteria. The purpose of these field trials was to examine the feasibility of proposed criteria for the disorders, and to determine the optimal number of items to require for maximizing sensitivity and specificity, using the clinicians' diagnoses as the criterion. Three field trials were conducted: the first focused on Autistic Disorder, the second on the Disruptive Behavior Disorders (Attention-deficit Hyperactivity Disorder, Oppositional Defiant Disorder, Conduct Disorder), and the third on Self-defeating Personality Disorder.

In all three field trials, advisory committee members were able to reach a consensus on the set of items comprising the diagnostic criteria though at times with great difficulty. The focus of the research, then, was to determine the precise algorithm that would be applied to the item to make the diagnosis. The two field trials for the childhood disorders were collaborative efforts conducted in clinical services that specialized in the diagnoses being studied. The participating clinicians were experts in the area of interest, and many were also members of the respective DSM-III-R advisory committees. The inclusion criteria for the study insured that there were an adequate number of appropriate control cases for the diagnoses being studied. For example, in the study of Autistic Disorder, control subjects included children with the clinical diagnosis of Pervasive Developmental Disorder Not Otherwise Specified (PDDNOS), as well as children with serious chronic behavioral difficulties, but not within the spectrum of Pervasive Developmental Disorders.

As noted above, the criterion diagnoses were made by expert clinicians who had available to them, in addition to their own interviews, chart material, and in many cases, information from informants. Thus, this validity criterion conforms to the concept of the LEAD standard (15), which refers to a clinical validity criterion that includes Longitudinal observations made by Expert clinicians utilizing all data available, including referral notes and family informants. However, in this study the LEAD standard was without the "L" since there was no provision for longitudinal follow-up. To illustrate the usefulness of a collaborative effort for providing an empirical base for decisions about a particular set of diagnostic criteria, the method and results of the Autistic Disorder Field Trial are described.

The Advisory Committee on Pervasive Developmental Disorders (PDD) agreed on a list of 16 items to be included in the diagnostic criteria for Autistic Disorder, the only specific category within the class of PDD. These items were conceptually grouped into three areas: A: impaired reciprocal social interaction (five items), B: impaired verbal and nonverbal communication (six items), and C: restricted repertoire of activities (5 items). Members of the advisory committee differed in the importance that they attached to these three areas and disagreed as to whether certain key items in each group should be required for the diagnosis.

Fifteen centers participated in evaluating 223 children given a clinical diagnosis of Autistic Disorder, 109 with PDDNOS, and 174 with other severe chronic behavioral disturbances ("Other"). To analyze the data, eight algorithms summarizing the information contained in the 18 items were compared in terms of sensitivity (proportion of cases diagnosed clinically as Autistic Disorder that were diagnosed with the algorithm as Autistic Disorder), specificity (proportion of cases diagnosed clinically as PDDNOS or Other that were not diagnosed with the algorithm as Autistic Disorder). In addition, the total predictive value (TPV), i.e., the proportion of all cases diagnosed correctly as either Autistic Disorder or not Autistic Disorder, was calculated. Table 1 presents the results for the three algorithms that achieved high total predictive values and were the final contenders for the recommended algorithm.

The first algorithm used a "polythetic" model, in which the 16 items were treated equally regardless of their *a priori* grouping, and the total number of items that were present determined the diagnosis. Using this model, a cut-off of at least 8 of the 16 items maximized the total predictive value (.85) and resulted in nearly equally high sensitivity (.86) and specificity (.84). Some members of the advisory committee objected to this algorithm on the grounds that it allowed the diagnosis to be given to children who did not have any of the core disturbances, such as the first items from groups A and B. They proposed the second algorithm, employing a mainly "monothetic" model, in which certain core features were required to make the diagnosis. Although conceptually attractive, as can be seen from Table 1, this algorithm markedly sacrificed sensitivity for a slight increase in specificity, and yielded a total predictive value that was not as high as the first algorithm. The third algorithm used a mixed model that combined the requirements of the first algorithm (any 8 of the 16 items) with a requirement that some features be present from each of the three groups of symptoms. This algorithm was finally selected since its total predictive value was as high as the first algorithm and, with the availability of PDDNOS as a diagnosis, there appeared to be some advantage in having specificity slightly higher than sensitivity. That is, it was felt to be less objectionable for DSM-III-R to make a diagnosis of PDDNOS when a clinician would diagnose Autistic Disorder, than to have the diagnostic criteria require that a child be diagnosed as having Autistic Disorder when a clinician would not give that diagnosis.

TABLE 1. *Autistic disorder field trial results*

Algorithm	Sens	Spec	TPV
I. Purely polythetic: Any 8 of the 16	.86	.84	.85
II. Mainly monothetic: A1 or 3 from A and B1 or 3 from B	.72	.87	.81
III. Mixed model: Algorithm I and 2 from A, 1 from B, and 1 from C	.80	.89	.85

Although the DSM-III-R Diagnostic Criteria Field Trials were extremely useful in revising the criteria, the method used had serious limitations. First of all, it was limited to the study of algorithms (ways of combining criteria) and did not evaluate alternative sets of criteria. The only criterion items studied were those on which the advisory committees had achieved consensus; no items about which there was a marked disagreement within the committees were studied. The field trial of Autistic Disorder criteria would have benefited from including two variables about which the committee was divided: the age at onset (included in the DSM-III criteria for Infantile Autism) and the presence or absence of a physical disorder that could account for the syndrome. The other serious limitation of the method was that the validity criterion was limited to descriptive validity using expert diagnosis as the criterion (referred to at this meeting as "delimitation from other disorders"). Other validity criteria for diagnosis, such as stability over time, familial aggregation, and differential response to therapy, were not used.

PRIORITIES FOR RFP FOR FOCUSED DIAGNOSTIC RESEARCH

This RFP is designed to support focused research that will provide an empirical base to the developers of DSM-IV. The research must be directed toward addressing at least one of the following questions.

(a) For established diagnoses (categories whose basic validity is not in question): among alternative criteria sets, which criteria set has the most validity? Table 2 presents established diagnoses in DSM-III-R about which there have been some disagreement as to how they should optimally be defined.

TABLE 2. *Established diagnoses needing further study*

Autistic Disorder
Disruptive Behavior Disorders
    Attention-deficit Hyperactivity Disorder
    Conduct Disorder
    Oppositional Defiant Disorder
Schizophrenia
Schizophreniform Disorder
Schizoaffective Disorder
Brief Reactive Psychosis
Major Depression
Seasonal Pattern of Mood Disorders
Dsythymia
Cyclothymia
Generalized Anxiety Disorder
Social Phobia
Somatization Disorder
Somatoform Pain Disorder
Narcissistic, Histrionic, Borderline
    Personality Disorders

TABLE 3. *Diagnoses of Questionable Validity*

Identity Disorder
Multi-infarct Dementia
Undifferentiated Attention-deficit
   Disorder
Melancholia subtype
Intermittent Explosive Disorder
Dependent and Passive Aggressive
   Personality Disorders

(b) For diagnoses of questionable validity: should the category be retained in the DSM-IV classification? Table 3 lists DSM-III-R diagnoses whose basic validity has been seriously questioned.

(c) For nonofficial diagnoses: should the category be added to the DSM-IV classification? Categories to be considered include the three categories that are included in Appendix A of DSM-III-R: Late Luteal Phase Dysphoric Disorder, and Self-defeating and Sadistic Personality Disorders. Other categories to be considered are Paraphilic Coercive Disorder (16,17), which was initially proposed for inclusion in DSM-III-R, the concept of "Atypical Depression" (18), and a category that might be called Victimization Disorder, for individuals who experience maladaptive changes in self-esteem and judgment as a result of having been physically or psychologically mistreated (19).

Although the primary focus of the research will address at least one of these three questions, ancillary benefits from the research are anticipated. For example, the research may provide data that will be useful in modifying the text of DSM-IV, e.g., the description of associated features, prevalence, sex ratio, and familial pattern. In addition, the data may be useful in determining how categories are classified, e.g., if Schizoaffective Disorder is best grouped with Schizophrenia and whether Dysthymia should be classified as a Personality Disorder or as a Mood Disorder.

STUDY DESIGN

The study should have a "multiplex design," which has the following elements:

(a) Multiple centers. This should be a collaborative effort involving several centers that differ in theoretical perspective with regard to such issues as definition, treatment, and etiology of the disorders. This will ensure generalizability and acceptability of the findings and study recommendations.

(b) Multiple experts at each site. At least two clinicians at each study site should have extensive clinical experience with the diagnoses being studied.

(c) Multiple diagnostic criteria sets. Special attention should be given to developing appropriate diagnostic criteria sets so that alternative conceptions of the diagnoses can be compared. The first step in doing this is to identify the issues that need to be considered in developing the multiple diagnostic criteria sets.

Investigators who have critiqued the DSM-III and DSM-III-R definitions of Dysthymia (20,21), for example, have suggested changes that address the following issues: the content of the symptom list (e.g., somatic, cognitive, and functional impairment items), the diagnostic threshold (how many symptoms should be required?), age at onset (should it begin before adulthood?), mode of onset (should insidious onset be required?), and finally, primary versus secondary (should cases that develop secondary to another disorder be included?). Investigators who have critiqued the DSM-III and DSM-III-R definitions of Major Depression have sugested changes that address many of the same issues. For example, Akiskal has suggested that the symptom list for Major Depression give greater prominence to evidence of psychomotor disturbance (22). Gershon has suggested that the validity of Major Depression would be greatly increased by requiring marked functional impairment (23).

(d) Multiple external validators. The proposed research should make use of a variety of external validators. The expert clinician's diagnosis at intake should make use of all available data, such as chart material and informants. This diagnosis should be reassessed at the 2-year follow-up with the advantage of longitudinal information. The investigator should address the issue of possible confounding of this LEAD standard with information about the other external validators. Other external validators that should be considered for inclusion in the study are response to somatic therapies, familial aggregation, stability over time, and laboratory tests of biological variables. It is recognized that it may not be possible for all collaborating centers to collect data using the same validators. For example, some centers may not be able to include specialized laboratory data or a double-blind, random, placebo-control drug study.

TRANSLATING THE RESULTS INTO RECOMMENDATIONS FOR DSM-IV

As Kendler et al. (10) have noted in a discussion of the changes in the psychotic disorders section of DSM-III-R, the use of familial aggregation as a validator may yield results that are inconsistent with results from the use of stability over time as a validator. Therefore, the investigator should address the integration of discordant external validity results into a final recommendation for DSM-IV.

MUST IT BE ONLY A DREAM?

Dear Reader: You knew from the start that it was only in our dreams that we were asked to prepare an RFP focused on research toward the development of DSM-IV. Our choice of this fanciful literary device to get your attention should not preclude your consideration of this research strategy as a serious and not entirely unrealistic goal. Although in our dream we were told not to worry about fiscal constraints, we recognize that such constraints are a reality. However, the multiplex research strategy that we have proposed need not be prohibitively expensive if it can fit into ongoing clinical and research work. The DSM-III-R Diagnostic Criteria Field Trials were modest in scope compared to what we are proposing, in that they did not include a comparison of multiple criteria sets and multiple external validators. However, multiple clinicians in multiple centers were involved and, because the work largely fit into ongoing clinical and research activities, the costs of the projects were minimal.

CONCLUSION

Research had a major impact on both DSM-III and DSM-III-R. We have proposed a multiplex research strategy for collecting data that is an elaboration of a strategy that was particularly helpful in developing criteria for several of the diagnostic categories of DSM-III-R. We believe that this research strategy is an unusually efficient method for providing an empirical base for further revisions in our official classification of mental disorders.

REFERENCES

1. Spitzer, R. L., and Williams, J. B. W. (1984): Research couple finds novel use for *Archives*. *Archives of General Psychiatry*, 41:632.
2. Feighner, J. P., Robins, E., Guze, S. B., Woodruff, R. A., Winokur, G., and Munoz, R. (1972): Diagnostic criteria for use in psychiatric research. *Arch Gen Psychiatry*, 26:57–63.
3. Spitzer, R. L., Endicott, J., and Robins, E. 1978): Research diagnostic criteria: Rationale and reliability. *Arch Gen Psychiatry*, 35:773–789.
4. Williams, J. B. W. (1985): The multiaxial system of DSM-III: Where did it come from and where should it go? I. Its origins and critiques. *Arch Gen Psychiatry*, 42:175–180.
5. Cooper, J. E., Kendell, R. E., Gurland, B. J., Sharpe, L., Copeland, J. R. M., and Simon, R. (1972): *Psychiatric Diagnosis in New York and London: A Comparative Study of Mental Hospital Admissions*. Oxford University Press, London.
6. Spitzer, R. L., Andreasen, N. C., and Endicott, J. (1978): Schizophrenia and other psychotic disorders in DSM-III. *Schizophr Bull*, 4:489–511.
7. Weissman, M. M. (1979): The myth of involutional melancholia. *JAMA*, 242:742–744.
8. Klein, D. F., Zitrin, C. M., and Woerner, M. (1978): Antidepressants, anxiety, panic and phobia. In *Psychopharmacology: A Generation of Progress* edited by M. A. Lipton, A. DiMascio, and K. Killamn, pp. 1401–1410. Raven Press, New York.
9. Marks, I. (1969): *Fears and Phobias*. Academic Press, New York.
10. Kendler, K. S., Spitzer, R. L., and Williams, J. B. W. Psychotic disorders in DSM-III-R. *(Submitted for publication.)*
11. Rosenthal, N. E., Sack, D. A., Gillin, J. C., Lewy, A. J., Goodwin, F. K., Davenport, Y., Mueller, P. S., Newsome, D. A., and Wehr, T. A. (1984): Seasonal affective disorder: A description of the syndrome and preliminary findings with light therapy. *Arch Gen Psychiatry*, 41:72–80.
12. Terman, M. On the question of a mechanism in the phototherapy for seasonal affective disorder: Considerations of clinical efficacy and epidemiology. *J Biological Rhythms*, (in press).
13. Halbreich, U., Endicott, J., and Nee, J. (1982): The diversity of premenstrual changes as reflected in the premenstrual evaluation form. *Acta Psychiatr Scand*, 65:46–65.
14. Rubinow, D. R., Roy-Byrne, P., and Hoban, M. C. (1984): Prospective assessment of menstrually related mood disorders. *Am J Psychiatry*, 141:684–686.
15. Spitzer, R. L. (1983): Psychiatric diagnosis: Are clinicians still necessary? *Compr Psychiatry*, 24:399–411.
16. Berlin, F. S. (1986): Interviews with five rapists. *Am J Forensic Psychiatry*, 7:11–41.

17. American Psychiatric Association. (1985): *Draft: DSM-III-R In Development—10/5/85*. American Psychiatric Association, Washington D. C.
18. Liebowitz, M. R., Quitkin, F. M., Stewart, J. W., McGrath, P. J., Harrison, W. M., Markowitz, J. S., Rabkin, J. G., Tricamo, E., Goetz, D. M., and Klein, D. F. (1988): Antidepressant specificity in atypical depression. *Arch Gen Psychiatry*, 45:129–137.
19. Ochberg, F. (ed.) (1988): *Post-traumatic Therapy and Victims of Violence*. Brunner-Mazel, New York.
20. Kocsis, J. H., and Frances, A. J. (1987): A critical discussion of DSM-III dysthymic disorder. *Am J Psychiatry*, 144:1534–1542.
21. Akiskal, H. S. (1983): Dysthymic disorder: Psychopathology of proposed chronic depressive subtypes. *Am J Psychiatry*, 140:11–20.
22. Akiskal, H. S. (1987): Personal communication.
23. Gershon, E. S., Weissman, M. M., Guroff, J. J., Prusoff, B. A., and Leckman, J. F. (1986): Validation of criteria for major depression through controlled family study. *J Affective Disorders*, 11:125–131.

DISCUSSION

Dr. Alan Frances: I was asked to comment on the process of revising DSM-III-R criteria for DSM-IV. This conference could not have been timed better in preparation for our work. We are planning to have a methodological workshop soon to deal with practical issues, and this conference has helped to frame some of the more general problems in a way that we would never have been able to do otherwise. The conference began with a focus on the 1970 Robins and Guze paper on validation of psychiatric diagnosis. In that paper the initial statement of clear validation principles and the initial provision of clear diagnostic criteria was a kind of paradigm shift in psychiatry. Its impact was responsible for really changing our field, not just diagnostically, but in general.

However, as the results came in, one finding was that the categories weren't as clear, except under very special circumstances, as we might have liked. They were certainly not clear in research settings and in community settings. What do you do next? You could shift paradigms yet again, from a classical categorical paradigm in which disorders are regarded as diseases, to a prototypal paradigm which is more probabilistic and in which disorders are regarded as interesting syndromes that need to be understood. However, in doing this, as Sam Guze pointed out, we mustn't lose the medical model. There could not be a worse time to abandon the medical model than at present, when we are finding such wonderful ways of applying molecular biology and the neurosciences to understanding psychiatric disorders. As we get prototypal and even, in some cases, dimensional, it doesn't mean giving up the medical model. We have to accommodate the medical model. I don't think that will be hard to do, but it has to be thought out.

What does this mean in practice? Maybe not a lot. In terms of criteria development, I think of the prototypal model as being probabilistic, with the expectation that there will be heterogeneity within categories and fuzzy data sets between categories. When you begin to think more of polythetic than monothetic criteria sets, it is not an enormous change, but perhaps involves the same items organized in various ways.

Another issue is how to regard comorbidity. For some people it has been upsetting that in many studies patients will meet criteria for three, four, or five different diagnoses. Within a simple medical model, where these diagnoses are seen as diseases, that is a terrible problem. Within the prototypal model, there is less concern about differential diagnosis and more concern about how well a patient approximates the prototype. Within this model it is fine to have multiple diagnoses, as long as epistemologically we realize that we are just gaining information. We are not necessarily saying that the patient has four diseases. We have to rethink what comorbidity means. We have been using it in a different way than it is used in general medicine. Comorbidity at the descriptive level is not the same as having two separate diseases; it is rather adding information. Don Klein has used the term "syndromal complexity" for this, but there are other ways of looking at it.

What this means in practical terms is that "diseases" are going to come out of work that someone else will be doing, or such is my guess. The diseases will come out of work in neuroscience, in molecular biology, and with other validators. Clinicians from Kraepelin through DSM-III committee members have tended to categorize in various ways, but without information from other disciplines, it is unlikely that we are going to make progress in understanding the underlying important etiologies and pathogenesis. Our job is to provide the basis for the studies being done as well as they can be, so that a Barney Carroll can be satisfied that confusing findings are not all due to a diagnostic problem, but may also be due to a test problem.

Another issue is how do we review the literature? We have lots of data that have been reported, but how do we aggregate those data? We would like to convene a methods conference soon to discuss when and where meta-analytic techniques may be useful in this regard, and how to put together what is known. We hope to have literature reviews in each of the diagnostic areas. We may be overly ambitious, but when the DSM-IV document finally appears we hope to provide a companion volume that will say how we got there—what the literature shows in each diagnostic area; what it doesn't show; and what needs to be done next. Here a particularly difficult question was raised by Bruce Dohrenwend: how do we reconcile differences which appear between studies using patients from clinical settings and studies using high-risk populations or community populations? This is a very tough problem, and there is not an easy answer for it. Related to this problem is the question of the purpose of DSM-IV. Some years ago, following a special issue of *Schizophrenia Bulletin* on classification, several authors pointed out that the DSM-III definition of schizotypal personality was not a good definition for family members of schizophrenics. They tended to be less odd, more flat, more schizoid, less schizotypal, and to have more negative symptoms and fewer positive symptoms. But these family member schizoid types don't come for treatment, which raises the question: should DSM-IV criteria be geared to the best validated group, the family members of schizophrenics, or should it be geared more to those patients who actually appear in clinical settings? How do you balance the various needs for the classification, since you do not want to meet the needs of just one constituency? The patients who appear in primary care settings who receive diagnoses may look different than the patients who appear in the university clinics where most of the treatment studies are done. Should we be accounting for mixed, milder symptom pictures within the diagnostic system? Again, a question without an answer, but an important question.

Diagnostic validators present another issue. When to include a validator within the diagnostic criteria is one of the underlying questions of this conference. If you have a sore throat, you are not satisfied with a diagnosis of "sore throat"; you would like to know whether there is a strep infection, and so the laboratory test result becomes the diagnosis. Hopefully in psychiatry, as time goes on, we will have convincing tests that provide etiologic and pathogenic information. A question with the tests we have now is: are they really validating the diagnostic construct, or are they diagnostic tests? The answer is easy for some tests. The literature on CAT scans in schizophrenia indicates CAT results validate the concept of poor prognosis schizophrenia, because in that group there are abnormalities, but an individual CAT scan doesn't really categorize a patient. Clearly this is a case of a validator that is useful for construct validity, useful for saying something about the diagnosis, but useless as a diagnostic test. But what about tests that are close to being useful, such as DST and REM latency in depression? Here we have to review the literature; at the present time I am not prepared to make a statement. I would want to see the data, but we have to recognize that a test almost always works best at its introduction because at that time the diagnostic comparison groups are more sharply drawn. As we start testing patient groups that are at the boundaries of the diagnosis, and these patients are common, the tests tend to have more difficulties. For the official nomenclature we have to decide how well a test has to perform in mixed populations before we include it as an actual part of the diagnostic criteria versus seeing it as a validator for the diagnosis.

Finally, everyone is asking me how much are you going to change DSM-III, and how are you going to change it. I am hopeful that we will have at least 500 people actively involved in this process. Lots of people are going to be making lots of decisions, and the result shouldn't be any one person's product. My own bias is to be conservative about the text, and especially about the criteria, at this point. If there is a tie score, or lots of contention, my own bias is that the winner should be the incumbent. We should not change criteria unless there is a clear reason that people can agree on. We have to develop creative ways for researchers to use the document which do not involve changing the criteria. For instance, we might have an Appendix of criteria that almost made it, so that people who are developing research instruments for assessment will not be limited to only official DSM-III criteria in their studies. It is a terrible problem. DSM-III criteria have rather restricted people's attention too much; other criteria that were seriously considered need to be studied. I think an Appendix can be a very useful middle zone between changing the system and at the same time giving people a shot at the future.

Dr. William Coryell: A point needs to be made about the rate of revision of existing criteria. I participated to a limited extent in the DSM-III-R proceedings and deliberations. I talked to many other people who participated more, and I have concluded that the only sure thing when one of these committees meets is that there will be revisions. If there is data to bear on revisions, they will influence committee members. If there is no data, revisions will take place anyway, but they will be determined by other things, namely the actual membership of the committee and the person who is running the committee.

Out in the field there is a touchingly naive assumption that revisions represent progress, and so I have a proposal to speed up the rate of progress: convene more committees for a shorter period of time, and just vary the membership a little bit each time. We will have a lot more revisions, and we can move the field along much faster. Perhaps this would not really be progress, but then maybe it would, and why not try?

However, I think there are some real drawbacks when these revisions are made official. One is the resulting confusion in teaching residents. It is confusing to try to remember the various changes, and it is upsetting to patients to get rediagnosed every 5 years. I thus applaud the conservative approach to revision that Alan Frances proposed.

Dr. Grove: In comparing DSM-III-R to DSM-III, I noticed that a number of categories are defined more polythetically. You did this for the autistic criteria. When you went from version one to version three, the specificity went up a little and the sensitivity went down a little. Could the same result have been accomplished by shifting the cut point from eight to nine?

Dr. Spitzer: Possibly, but I don't know what the effect would have been on the total predictive value. I suspect it would have dropped.

Dr. Grove: Not necessarily.

Dr. Spitzer: It might have stayed the same. What that exercise showed is that it is not always clear what you should do when you have alternative criteria sets. The reason we moved away from a strictly polythetic approach was the clinical argument that important conceptual clarification would be lost by adopting a purely polythetic model. The reason for change wasn't just to raise the specificity, but for teaching purposes, to emphasize the importance of looking at the three components before making a diagnosis.

Dr. Carroll: I liked Allen Frances' outline of the process of revision to develop DSM-IV. Concerning the laboratory test area, I want to remind people that no external validator can do better than the diagnostic system against which it is being compared. Consider the area of boundary conditions around major depression, and the uses of REM latency or DST. That is the very area in which the iterative process is an appropriate strategy. But as long as the validation is limited to a comparison of external laboratory measures against clinical features, it is impossible to make any progress, and it is very likely that type 2 errors can be introduced. We need some way to resolve this issue. My recommendation is to bring in additional external validators so that the initial two under comparison can be sorted out a little better.

Dr. Jack Barchas: Bob Spitzer's approach to DSM-IV is right on target. It is exactly the way it ought to be done, and it fits very well with what Allen Francis proposed.

Dr. Cloninger: DSM-III and DSM-III-R were a necessary and invaluable phase of getting national, and to some extent international, consensus on the way to define diagnoses. We are now moving into a phase where we will be emphasizing actual empirical validation. That is what this conference has been about. I am excited to see that we can move beyond the phase of committee judgments to a phase of empirical validation of diagnostic categories, as was embodied in the Robins and Guze 1970 paper.

The Validity of Psychiatric Diagnosis, edited by
Lee N. Robins and James E. Barrett.
Raven Press, Ltd., New York © 1989.

Clinical Validity

R. E. Kendell

*Department of Psychiatry, University of Edinburgh,
Royal Edinburgh Hospital, Edinburgh, EH10 5HF, Scotland*

Few psychiatric disorders have yet been adequately validated and it is still an open issue whether there are genuine boundaries between the clinical syndromes and normality. In the long run validation depends on the elucidation of etiological processes. There are, however, a number of strategies which clinicians could use, but at present rarely do, in order to improve and validate existing classifications. Most of these involve studying populations which have been deliberately chosen to represent a broader grouping than a single diagnostic category, or even a group of related categories.

INTRODUCTION

Until about 20 years ago, psychiatric research was gravely handicapped by the low reliability of our diagnoses. It was commonplace for different psychiatrists to attribute different diagnoses to the same patients, particularly if they themselves had been trained in different centers. This was so for a variety of reasons. In the first place, they elicited different phenomena, partly because their interviewing styles were different and also inconsistent, and partly because they were attributing different meanings to a wide range of technical terms like thought disorder and passivity experience. Their usually unstated assumptions about which clinical phenomena were needed to establish particular diagnoses were also different. So too were the assumptions they made about the etiology of the disorders they so confidently diagnosed. During the last two decades these problems have largely been solved by a series of methodological advances. Structured interviews have reduced variation in interviewing styles to manageable proportions, and the widespread adoption of semantic or operational definitions both for individual clinical phenomena like confusion and for syndromes like schizophrenia has greatly improved the reliability of both.

Unfortunately, although we have learned how to make reliable diagnoses we still have no adequate criterion of their validity, and the achievement focuses attention on the failure. Reliability is concerned with the defining characteristics of a class, and the criteria which must be met in order to establish class membership. Validity is concerned with the correlates of class membership. Reliability is easily measured. Validity is more nebulous, though the more important correlates a class has, over and above its defining characteristics, the less likely is its validity to be questioned. Psychologists are accustomed to distinguishing several different kinds of validity—construct, concurrent, content, predictive, and so on—and although these are useful distinctions in some contexts, it is important not to allow them to obscure the fact that in the context of clinical psychiatry, statements about diagnostic validity are essentially statements about predictive power, and hence about practical utility. Among other things, this implies that the validity of a diagnostic concept, or of a diagnostic distinction, is not an absolute quality of that diagnosis or that distinction, but may vary with the context to some extent. Most of us do not regard insanity as a valid concept because we do not find it useful in contemporary clinical practice, but that does not necessarily mean that it was not a valid concept in a 19th century law court.

ETIOLOGY AND VALIDITY

There is a longstanding and now deeply rooted assumption in medicine that the most valid diagnoses are those whose etiology is known; a corollary is that the most effective way of establishing the validity of a clinical syndrome is to elucidate its etiology. Both these assumptions are usually justified, but again the reasons are largely practical. There is nothing inherently preeminent about etiology. It is simply an empirical finding that most etiologically based classifications are more useful—because they embody a wider range of implications—than purely clinical classifications. A classification of fevers based on the identity of the infective organism is more useful, for example, than one based on the characteristics of the pyrexia and the accompanying exanthem, and a classification of tumors based on histology is more useful than one based simply on the patient's symptoms and physical signs. This is the basis of our preoccupation with etiology. Modern clinical science is largely focused on the elucidation of underlying mechanisms because experience has taught us that this is almost always the most effective way of predicting outcome, of acquiring new and more effective therapies, and—most important of all—of preventing disorders developing in the first place. Although some individual clinical scientists may insist that they are motivated by an interest in knowledge for its own sake, which is why they devote their time to, for example, trying to elucidate the etiology of Alzheimer's disease, clinical science itself is explicitly an applied science and its preoccupation with underlying mechanisms is a quest not for knowledge itself but for power—the power to predict outcome and the power to prevent or to diminish suffering and disability.

Whether or not these utilitarian arguments are accepted, it can be assumed that the validity of the clinical syndromes currently recognized will eventually be established, or undermined, by etiological discoveries. Many will probably also assume that the majority of these discoveries are unlikely to be made by clinicians, either psychiatrists or clinical psychologists. They will be made by neuropharmacologists, neuropathologists, experimental psychologists, molecular biologists, or geneticists.

In this chapter, there will be discussed what clinicians themselves can do by the exercise of their own clinical skills to improve the validity of psychiatric classifications. It can, of course, be argued that we have already done all we can. We have identified at least the major syndromes, we have provided relatively unambiguous operational definitions, and now, so the argument goes, it is up to others to elucidate the etiology. Indeed, it could be argued that from now on the research time of most clinicians would be better spent in other ways: on therapeutic trials perhaps, or on comparisons of the cost effectiveness of different methods of health care delivery. Although this is not an unreasonable argument, this author believes it to be ill-advised for the following reasons.

CLINICAL SYNDROMES

Irrespective of whether it is a clinician or a scientist who eventually unlocks the secrets of schizophrenia and bipolar disorder, success is much more likely if the syndromes in question have been accurately identified to begin with. Noguchi was able to demonstrate that general paralysis was due to syphilitic infection of the brain only because the alienists of the 19th century had been able to discriminate fairly accurately between general paralysis and other forms of insanity. And Goldberger was able to demonstrate that pellagra was due to a dietary deficiency only because his predecessors had been able to distinguish pellagra from other psychoses.

Of course, delineation of a clinical syndrome does not always precede etiological discovery. Fölling identified phenylpyruvic acid in the urine of mental defectives before anyone had described the fair hair and other clinical characteristics associated with phenylketonuria. Indeed, the clinical syndrome was only recognized after the metabolic abnormality had been clarified, and the same was true of most other aminoacidurias. But although accurate identification of the clinical syndrome is not a necessary preliminary, it undoubtedly increases the likelihood that attempts to elucidate etiology will be successful. Geneticists exploring the etiology of schizophrenia and bipolar disorder currently have high hopes that studies of the DNA of large pedigrees with several members all manifesting the same syndrome will make it possible to identify the genes transmitting these disorders, but one "false positive" may invalidate the whole elaborate chain of inference on which identification of the locus of the putative gene depends.

There are other reasons why it is important to distinguish between one syndrome and another as accurately as possible. It was only after Sydenham had demonstrated that "the pox" was actually two distinct syndromes, chicken pox and small pox, that it was possible to predict with any accuracy who would almost certainly recover and who would remain scarred for life and was in danger of dying. And only after physicians had learned to distinguish between the renal and the cardiac forms of dropsy was it possible to predict which patients were likely to benefit from digitalis.

A clinical syndrome consists of a cluster of related symptoms with a characteristic time course, and in a psychiatric context these symptoms may be either abnormal behaviors or abnormal or distressing subjective experiences, or a mixture of the two. There are, therefore, two elements to the concept: a group of correlated symptoms and a more or less distinctive temporal evolution. For most of medical history, syndromes have been identified intuitively by gifted physicians on the basis of their personal clinical experiences. They saw a pattern where others saw only confusion, or they saw a different pattern than had their predecessors. Sometimes they were simply more astute observers than other physicians. Sometimes, like Kraepelin, they also kept better clinical records over longer periods of time. Either way, the identification of the new syndrome was essentially an imaginative insight which could not be reduced to any formal rules of procedure. In the last two generations we have developed a variety of techniques for replacing or at least facilitating this intuitive process—rating scales, structured interviews, formal follow-up and family studies, and elaborate forms of multivariate analysis for developing or testing new classifications. It has to be admitted, however, that the fruits of these technological innovations have so far been rather meager. Classifications of mental disorders have become much more complex but this is mainly because we have enlarged our sphere of interest to encompass the disorders of childhood and old age, and many comparatively minor disorders our predecessors rarely encountered. Our classification of the so-called functional psychoses is still basically Kraepelin's classification and the few fundamental changes that have been made, like the distinction between unipolar and bipolar affective disorders, we owe to Leonhard's imaginative insight, not to our new technologies.

VALIDATION STRATEGIES

1. Syndrome Identification

Several fairly distinct strategies are available for establishing the validity of a clinical syndrome (see Table 1). The first of these is the first of Robins' and Guze's "five phases," the initial description of the syndrome.(1) In the past this was wholly dependent on the "imaginative insight" of the clinician and this is probably still an indispensable starting point. In theory the multivariate procedures known generically as cluster analysis are capable of recognizing syndromes, or at least recognizing clusters of correlated symptoms, without any prior identification by a clinician, and various forms of cluster analysis were enthusiastically adopted for that purpose in the 1970s.(2) Such enterprises were not very successful, however, for a variety of reasons. The number of variables used in the analysis has to be substantially less than the number of patients, and as the number of variables on which a patient, or indeed any human being, can be rated is almost limitless, the initial choice of variables is crucial. This means that the clinician has to start with a shrewd idea of which symptoms or other characteristics are likely to be the best discriminators. Validating the clusters generated by clustering programs is an-

TABLE 1. *Validators of clinical syndromes*

1. Identification and description of the syndrome, either by "clinical intuition" or by cluster analysis.
2. Demonstration of boundaries or "points of rarity" between related syndromes by discriminant function analysis, latent class analysis, etc.
3. Follow-up studies establishing a distinctive course or outcome.
4. Therapeutic trials establishing a distinctive treatment response.
5. Family studies establishing that the syndrome "breeds true."
6. Association with some more fundamental abnormality—histological, psychological, biochemical, or molecular.

other problem. There are innumerable forms of cluster analysis based on different mathematical definitions of similarity; some are synthetic, others analytic, and many will generate clusters even from artificial data sets known to have a single multivariate normal distribution. Confidence in the validity of mathematically generated clusters of this kind can be bolstered by demonstrating that the same groupings are produced by different clustering procedures, or that the same syndromes are identified from different data sets. But the fundamental problem of validation still remains, and it has to be admitted that none of the 200 or so psychiatric syndromes we currently recognize was originally identified by cluster analysis. Indeed, cluster analysis has proved to be more useful as a means of validating traditional clinical syndromes than of generating new ones. Everitt and his colleagues were able to demonstrate, for example, that clusters representing the syndromes of mania, melancholia, and schizophrenia were generated by two quite different clustering procedures from two different data sets, one American and the other English (3).

2. Identification of Boundaries

Discriminant function analysis has been more widely used as a validating procedure. If there is a genuine boundary or "point of rarity" between two related syndromes—between melancholia and other depressions, for example, or between schizophrenic and affective psychoses—patients with mixed symptomatology should be less common than typical members of the two syndromes; the "grays," in other words, should be outnumbered by the blacks and the whites (Fig. 1). Discriminant function analysis is a means of testing whether or not this is so. It cannot generate new groupings and, as with clustering procedures, the clinician has to decide which of innumerable possible items or ratings to employ as potential discriminators. But if a bimodal distribution of scores can be demonstrated on the discriminant function, and this bimodal distribution is replicated in additional sets of data, the validity of the distinction is powerfully supported. The distinction in question may either be between two related syndromes, or between one syndrome and all other mental disorders, or between a syndrome and normality, depending

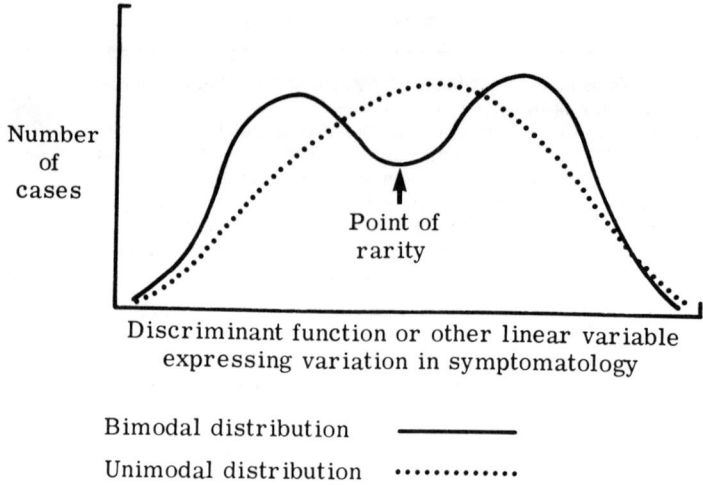

FIG. 1. Variation in symptomatology expressed by a linear variable.

on the focus of interest. Although it may under some circumstances be possible to generate a bimodal distribution of scores on a discriminant function even when there is no "point of rarity" in nature (4,5), this is not a fatal objection to the use of discriminant functions, because in practice it has proved remarkably difficult to produce a bimodal distribution of scores from psychiatric data except in the patient population used to generate the function in the first place. Cloninger and his colleagues in St. Louis succeeded in demonstrating a boundary between schizophrenia and other forms of mental disorder (6), but so far most attempts to demonstrate natural boundaries between different depressive syndromes, or between schizophrenic and affective psychoses, have been unsuccessful.

3. Outcome Studies

Outcome provides the most important and the most widely applicable criterion of validity available to the clinician. This is because the ability to predict the future course of events, and to alter this if need be, have always been the primary functions of medicine; and this in turn is why follow-up studies play so prominent a part in clinical research. Indeed, a more or less distinctive course has always been inherent in the concept of a syndrome. There are, of course, many aspects to outcome. Two syndromes may be distinguished by a difference in outcome over the course of a few days, or over 20 years. They may differ in the speed or completeness of recovery, in their tendency to relapse, in the stability of their phenomenology, in their mortality, or in their liability to lead to particular end states such as suicide or a "defect state." It is not enough, however, to demonstrate that two syndromes characteristically have a different outcome. It has to be demonstrated that this difference in outcome is attributable to the diagnostic difference and not to some other difference associated with this, such as age or age of onset, or social class, sex ratio, or physique. Even if this is done, though in practice it rarely is, the fact that there is a statistically significant difference between the mean outcome scores of members of two diagnostic groupings does not prove that the distinction between the two syndromes is valid, any more than the demonstration that there was a statistically significant difference in mortality between fat men and thin men would prove that there was some fundamental difference between the asthenic and the obese. In order to prove that a difference in outcome is due to a qualitative rather than a purely quantitative difference between two diagnostic groupings, it has to be demonstrated that the relationship between outcome and symptomatology is nonlinear (Fig. 2). To pursue the analogy with the mortality of fat men and thin men, it would have to be demonstrated that mortality increased suddenly beyond a particular weight or weight/height ratio rather than increasing slowly and steadily with increasing weight.

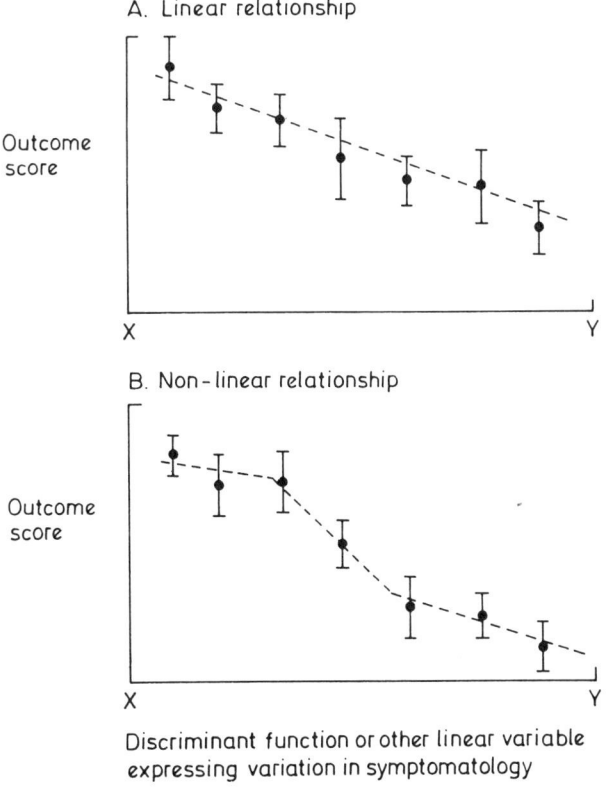

FIG. 2. Relationship between symptomatology and outcome when symptomatology is converted to a linear variable.

4. Therapeutic Trials

Response to treatment is another important criterion of validity. It is important to appreciate, though, that treatment response is simply one aspect of outcome, and that in a therapeutic trial one is simply studying outcome under conditions designed to isolate the effects on outcome of the therapeutic agent in question and to minimize, or control for, the effects of other influences. In some branches of medicine treatment response has made an important contribution to the validation of clinical concepts. The validity of the distinction between hypochromic and pernicious anemia, for example, was strongly reinforced by the demonstration that pernicious anemia responded only to vitamin B_{12}, while the more common hypochromic anemias responded to oral iron. The validity of the distinction between pulmonary sarcoidosis and pulmonary tuberculosis was likewise powerfully reinforced by the demonstration that sarcoidosis responded to steroids but not to antituberculous agents.

In psychiatry, although Klein has used his technique of "pharmacological dissection" with some success to develop new classifications of anxiety disorders (7), treatment response has contributed little so far to the validation of psychiatric syndromes. This is because most of our effective therapies—psychological treatments like cognitive therapy and response prevention as well as physical treatments like neuroleptics, antidepressants, and ECT—are not syndrome specific; they are partially effective across a range of related syndromes. Moreover, none of them is invariably effective in the treatment of any syndrome no matter how narrowly that syndrome is defined. This is rather dispiriting, but it is important to recognize that treatments which are specific to a single disorder are uncommon in any branch of medicine. Antibiotics, steroids, beta blockers, and calcium antagonists all possess valuable therapeutic properties across a range of unrelated disorders; and as Max Hamilton once observed, the fact that bruises, dysmenorrhea, rheumatic fever, and rheumatoid arthritis all respond to aspirin does not entitle us to assume that they share a common etiology.

5. Family Studies

The fifth criterion of validity available to the clinician is evidence that a syndrome "breeds true," i.e., that first degree relatives have a raised lifetime risk for that syndrome, and that syndrome alone. This is evidence of validity despite the fact that breeding true may sometimes be the product of cultural rather than genetic transmission (mediated, for example, by dietary customs or behaviors predisposing to particular infections). For even if genetic factors are not responsible, a syndrome will only breed true if it is fairly stable and well delineated. In fact there is evidence from family, twin, and adoption studies that there is an important genetic component to the etiology of many psychiatric syndromes, including schizophrenic and affective disorders, Alzheimer's disease, alcoholism, and obsessional disorders.

Until quite recently it was not established that any psychiatric syndromes bred true. It had, of course, been claimed several times that there was a raised incidence of schizophrenia but not of affective illness in the relatives of schizophrenics, and a raised incidence of affective illness but not of schizophrenia in the relatives of manic depressives. But the relatives had not been assessed blindly; they were known to be the relatives of schizophrenics (or manic depressives) by whoever assessed them and for that reason the claim was suspect. Only since Tsuang (8) and others (9-11) have carried out family studies in which the relatives were examined and diagnoses assigned to them in ignorance of the probands' diagnoses have we really possessed evidence that schizophrenia and some forms of affective disorder do indeed "breed true."

6. Biological Correlates

The sixth and last criterion of validity is evidence that the syndrome is habitually associated with some more fundamental abnormality—histological, biochemical, physiological, psychological, or molecular. The discovery of relationships of this kind is commonly the vital clue leading to understanding etiology. But they are explicitly outside the bounds of this chapter largely because they have eluded us for so long that we would be wise to assume that they are comparatively unlikely to be discovered by clinicians.

* * * *

Ninety years have now elapsed since Kraepelin first provided the framework of a plausible classification of mental disorders. Why then, with so many potential validators available, have we made so little progress since that time?

CONTINUITY OR DISCONTINUITY

One important possibility is that the discrete clusters of psychiatric symptoms we are trying to delineate do not actually exist but are as much a mirage as discrete personality types. We are very reluctant to take this possibility seriously, partly because the whole weight of medical history is against it. Even so, we ignore the possibility at our peril. It would certainly explain why we are having such difficulty agreeing where to draw the boundaries between one syndrome and another; why we are so frequently driven to employing terms like anxiety depression, schizoaffective disorder, and borderline state; and why none of our therapies is specific to a single disorder.

The most effective way of finding out whether or not we are dealing with continuous variation, approximating to a multivariate normal distribution of symptom scores, is by discriminant function analysis or conceptually similar techniques like latent class analysis. Many attempts have been made to demonstrate a bimodal distribution of scores on a discriminant function in order to demonstrate the existence of discrete types of depressive illness, or the existence of a "point of rarity" between depression and anxiety states, or between schizophrenia and other disorders. Unfortunately, most of them have been unsuccessful. Either no bimodal distribution of scores could be obtained even in the data set used to generate the discriminant function (12), or bimodality failed to survive cross-validation on a second data set (13), or the claims of the original investigators could not be confirmed by others (14). Only Cloninger's demonstration of a point of rarity between schizophrenia and other mental disorders has survived cross-validation (6), and even this has yet to be confirmed by other investigators.

Recent attempts to demonstrate the existence of discrete types of depressive disorder by latent class analysis of the SADS ratings generated by the Collaborative Study on the Psychobiology of Depression have been no more successful than earlier English studies (15). It seems, therefore, that discrete psychiatric syndromes are either rare and elusive, or simply nonexistent. Of course, this may simply be because our techniques for demonstrating bimodality and nonlinearity are too weak, and require larger numbers and more reliable ratings than we can produce. And even if discrete syndromes are indeed nonexistent, this does not mean that there may not be important discontinuities at some more fundamental level.

There is no reason why a qualitative neurophysiological abnormality should necessarily be associated with a unique symptom complex. We know that carriers of the Huntington gene may present with a wide variety of psychiatric syndromes, including dysthymic, major depressive, schizophrenic, and anxiety disorders (16). There is also evidence to suggest that the gene responsible for Tourette's syndrome may manifest itself as obsessive-compulsive disorder as well as, or even instead of, Tourette's syndrome itself or other motor tics (17). Indeed, individuals who are genetically identical may develop psychiatric disorders which are strikingly and consistently different (18). But the lack, or at least the rarity, of identifiable discontinuities in symptomatology does make it difficult for us to be confident that we are identifying and describing valid categories. The old aphorism that classification is "the art of carving nature at the joints" loses its force if nature has no joints.

THE HIERARCHY OF SYMPTOMS

Multivariate techniques like discriminant function analysis and latent trait analysis are essentially cross-sectional; they examine relationships between the symptoms elicited on a single occasion. There is no reason in principle why variables of other kinds should not be included in the analysis. At times items such as personality ratings and the outcome, or response to treatment, of previous episodes of illness are included, but the main focus of interest is usually on current symptomatology. Perhaps this is where we are going wrong; perhaps we would be more successful if we paid more attention to the sequence in which symptoms appear and disappear.

It is well established that psychiatric symptoms tend to be arranged in a loose hierarchy (19). The most common and often the first to develop are disturbances of mood, like anxiety and depression. Next come a variety of symptoms such as phobic anxiety, obsessional rituals, agitation, severe insomnia, apathy, anhedonia, retardation, and impairment of concentration, which are less common than mood disturbances and rarely encountered in their absence. Finally come psychotic symptoms— hallucinations, delusions, and incoherent speech—which are relatively uncommon and usually the last symptoms to develop and the first to remit.

It is still uncertain to what extent this hierarchy is simply an artifact, a device to enable psychiatrists to make a single diagnosis in each patient, and to what extent it is an important and neglected natural phenomenon. Part of the reason for the uncertainty is that our habits of thought are so strongly based on hierarchical assumptions that we are often unaware of the full range of our patients' symptoms. If a patient describes alien thoughts intruding into his consciousness, or hearing several voices discussing him among themselves, we immediately focus our attention on these phenomena because they establish the diagnosis. We may not bother to enquire whether he is also experiencing panic attacks, or has checking rituals, or feels miserable, because these have no bearing on diagnosis, and even if we are aware of the presence of these other symptoms we pay little attention to them because they are "less serious" and do not determine treatment.

Our hierarchical assumptions also have important implications for psychiatric epidemiology. Most psychiatrists regard it as well established that depressive disorders are more common than anxiety disorders. This is not, however, because depression is more common than anxiety. It is largely a consequence of the fact that, at least until DSM-IIIR was published last year (20), depression came higher up our hierarchy than anxiety, so that a patient who had symptoms of both anxiety and depression was regarded as having a depressive disorder, rather than an anxiety disorder, or both disorders simultaneously.

FOUR RESEARCH STRATEGIES

What kinds of clinical research are most likely to clarify the unresolved issues just described, and so enable the generation of better and more useful classifications in the future? Singled out are four kinds of study that have rarely been carried out in the past.

A. Prospective Follow-Up Studies Based on Serial Interviews

Until quite recently, most follow-up studies have been based on assessment on two occasions, first during an index episode of illness, and then once more months or years later. The focus of interest has usually been on the overall course of the illness or on which features of the index episode best predicted some aspect of outcome. Only rarely has a single cohort of patients been interviewed repeatedly using a structured interview in order to establish the detailed patterning of symptomatology on more than one occasion. It is very striking, for example, that throughout the long dispute about the classification of depressions, which has now rumbled on for two generations, no one has ever followed a substantial series of patients through a series of successive episodes in order to find out how often the symptomatology, and hence the type of depression, changes from one episode to the next, or whether there are systematic changes in symptomatology with increasing age or chronicity.

Although they are expensive and difficult to organize, repeated interviews at intervals of days or weeks are the only reliable way of determining the sequence in which individual symptoms develop and remit, and serial interviews at intervals of months or years—either at regular intervals or at the time of each successive relapse—are the most effective way of assessing syndrome stability. Studies of both kinds are now starting to appear in the literature. Indeed, Kovacs (21) and Beiser (22) both described studies of the latter kind during this conference. A recent study at the Maudsley Hospital of 70 patients recovering from depressive illnesses was based on ratings of mood every 48 hours and of bodily symptoms and psychomotor and cognitive performance every 7 days for a period of 6 weeks (23). Last year Tyrer and his colleagues in Nottingham described a prospective study in which 78 patients with depressive, anxiety, and phobic neuroses were given a Present State Examination on four occasions over 2 years (24), and Biehl in Mannheim has reported a similar study in which 70 first onset schizophrenics were all reassessed with structured interviews 2, 3, and 5 years after their initial assessment (25). The Nottingham study is particularly interesting because the investigators deliberately started with a cohort consisting of a spectrum of neurotic syndromes rather than a single diagnostic category, and so were able to assess the frequency of transitions between depressive disorders and anxiety disorders in both directions. Their findings, incidentally, do not suggest that there is any fundamental difference between the two.

B. Therapeutic Trials Involving a Broad Spectrum of Diagnostic Categories

The majority of clinical trials are based on patients attributed to a single diagnostic category because the question at issue is whether treatment A is more or less effective than treatment B, or more effective than placebo, in the treatment of disorder X. This was not always so, however. In the early 1960s clinical trials were mounted to compare the efficacy of phenothiazines and tricyclics in mixed populations of schizophrenics and depressives (26) or even in unselected mental hospital admissions (27), and as Overall and his colleagues observed, the results "did not confirm the specificity of action ordinarily attributed to antipsychotic and antidepressant drugs" (26). Despite such warnings, or perhaps because of them, few trials since that time have been designed to find out where the therapeutic range of treatment A begins and ends, though such information might well help us to decide where to draw the boundaries between one syndrome and another as well as how to interpret that treatment's mode of action.

However, a number of drug trials have been carried out in which two different antidepressants, or an antidepressant and an anxiolytic, have been compared across a broad range of depressions, or a mixture of depressions and anxiety states, and the differential response of various diagnostic subgroups to the two drugs have then been compared. In this way we have learned, for example, that tricyclic antidepressants are equally effective in so called "neurotic" and "endogenous" depressions (28), and that tricyclic antidepressants are more effective than anxiolytics in anxiety states as well as depressions (29,30). Such information has obvious relevance to the validity of the distinctions between endogenous and neurotic depressions, or between depressions and anxiety states. It is rare, though, for contemporary therapeutic trials to transgress major diagnostic boundaries. The potential of such studies is well illustrated by a trial recently carried out by Johnstone and her colleagues at Northwick Park (31).

In this trial, 120 newly admitted psychotic patients were randomly allocated to receive either pimozide, lithium, or both, or neither for 4 weeks, regardless of whether their symptoms were schizophrenic, affective, or a mixture of the two. The study was conducted double-blind and its results were very interesting. Pimozide, a selective antagonist of D_2 dopamine receptors, was highly effective in relieving hallucinations, delusions, incoherence of speech, and incongruity of affect, whether or not these symptoms were associated with a mood disturbance and whether or not the patient met either DSM-III or CATEGO criteria for either a schizophrenic or an affective psychosis. Lithium, on the other hand, was effective in combatting elevation of mood whatever the setting but was without effect on hallucinations and delusions. As there was no apparent relationship between drug response and diagnostic category, the validity of the distinction between schizophrenic and affective psychoses was not supported. Indeed, in Johnstone's words, "the model of psychotic illness which would best fit these results would be dimensional rather than categorical." Despite their potential, however, it must be recognized that trials of this kind raise important ethical issues, for they involve treating some patients with a drug or other therapy which conventional psychiatric opinion would regard as inappropriate, and simultaneously withholding, at least temporarily, an effective therapy.

C. Family Studies Involving a Broad Spectrum of Diagnostic Categories

In 1980 Tsuang and his colleagues in Iowa set new standards for the design and execution of family studies in psychiatry. They interviewed over 1,500 first degree relatives of proband groups who had been diagnosed using operational criteria. They succeeded in interviewing a high proportion of all living relatives, they used structured interviews and, most important of all, the relatives were interviewed blind to proband diagnosis (8). Others have used the same basic methodology subsequently (9–11). In every case, however, the study was based on a group of probands attributed either to a single diagnostic category, or to two or three related diagnostic categories using a single set of operational criteria. The results of such studies provide accurate estimates of the morbid risk for a variety of different disorders in the first degree relatives of the restricted proband group or groups as defined, but that is all.

What we need are similar large-scale family studies in which the proband group is more comprehensive, like the psychotic patients on whom Johnstone's drug trial was based (31), and that include, for example, the inconvenient patients with "schizoaffective" symptomatology as well as those meeting strict operational criteria for schizophrenic and/or affective disorders. A data base of this kind would make it possible to examine the consequences of drawing the boundaries between syndromes in different places (in relatives as well as in probands). In that way, we could learn with some precision which syndromes coaggregate, and how broadly it is possible to define individual categories like schizophrenia and bipolar disorder without their propensity to breed true breaking down. Tsuang's family study demonstrated that Feighner schizophrenia and Feighner affective disorders both "bred true" (32). This is obviously important, but it does not tell us whether this would have occurred if broader criteria had been used, and it tells us nothing about the status of the many patients who were excluded because they exhibited combinations of symptoms which did not meet Feighner criteria for either syndrome.

D. Twin Studies Involving Alternative Definitions of Syndromes

There is a substantial genetic contribution to the etiology of many psychiatric syndromes. This genetic component is strongest and best documented for bipolar disorder and schizophrenia, but it is significant in many others, including unipolar depressive disorders, obsessional disorders, and alcohol dependence. Heritability can be calculated from concordance rates in monozygous and dizygous twins. In principle, therefore, the heritabilities associated with a variety of alternative operational definitions of a single syndrome can be compared to identify the precise constellation of clinical characteristics most closely associated with hereditary transmission. However, this requires data from a large and well documented population of twins, in which one or both has the syndrome in question.

Although few suitable data sets exist, McGuffin and his colleagues at the Institute of Psychiatry in London have at least been able to illustrate the potential power of this method (33). Using data from the Maudsley Twin Register accumulated by Slater and Shields, they applied six alternative operational definitions of schizophrenia to 22 MZ and 33 DZ twin pairs and calculated the heritabilities associated with each. They found major differences. Spitzer and Endicott's RDC definition and the Feighner definition were both associated with a heritability of about 0.8, whereas Schneider's first rank symptoms appeared to have a heritability of zero. These should be regarded as preliminary findings, partly because the number of twin pairs was not large and more particularly because the diagnostic allocations were based on case summaries which did not always include all the necessary information, but they do serve to illustrate the potential of the method.

CONCLUSION

Clearly none of the four types of clinical research advocated here is easy or straightforward. Prospective follow-up studies with frequent serial interviews and large-scale family studies are both expensive and difficult to organize. The former may also take a decade or more to establish long-term outcome and syndrome stability. Therapeutic trials based on a broad spectrum of diagnostic categories may raise serious ethical problems. The kind of twin study I am advocating requires comprehensive and carefully standardized information about large numbers of psychiatrically ill twins. Nonetheless, this author is convinced that we will learn little that is new and important about the validity of our clinical syndromes unless we adopt such approaches. Their most important element is a willingness to investigate—either by prospective follow-up, therapeutic trial, or family study—a cohort of subjects who have been deliberately picked to represent a population which is more comprehensive than any single diagnostic category.

In the past we have almost invariably based our research on populations which we believed to be diagnostically homogeneous. Our starting point was a population of schizophrenics, appropriately defined, or a population of depressives. We have often had control groups, of course, either psychiatrically healthy people or members of a different diagnostic category, but comparisons of this kind are of little value in determining where the boundaries between one syndrome and another should be drawn, or for deciding whether there *are* any valid boundaries to be found. Studying populations of schizophrenics or phobics implicitly assumes that schizophrenia and phobic disorder are valid diagnostic categories, and some believe that we do not yet have the evidence to justify such assumptions.

It may be, of course, that the validity of our clinical syndromes can only ultimately be established, or tested, by laboratory scientists, or at least by clinicians using the methods of laboratory science. In the long run that is certainly so. At the present time, however, it is striking how many of the physiological, pharmacological, neuropathological and endocrine abnormalities first identified in members of one diagnostic category, like schizophrenia or "endogenous" depression, are subsequently found in other diagnostic categories also. It does not seem, therefore, that our syndromes are yet sufficiently well delineated and validated to be handed over to others for further investigation. We must go on trying to improve our classifications by the further development and application of our own clinical and epidemiological skills. But if we do carry out the kinds of studies described here, the results may not be comforting.

ACKNOWLEDGMENTS

This chapter was presented as the Paul Hoch Award Lecture at the annual meeting of the American Psychopathological Association in New York, New York on March 4, 1988.

REFERENCES

1. Robins, E., and Guze, S. B. (1970): Establishment of diagnostic validity in psychiatric illness: Its application to schizophrenia. *Am J Psychiatry*, 126:983–987.
2. Everitt, B. S. (1974): *Cluster Analysis*. Heinemann, London.
3. Everitt, B. S., Gourlay, A. J., and Kendell, R. E. C. (1971): An attempt at validation of traditional psychiatric syndromes by cluster analysis. *Br J Psychiatry*, 119:399–412.
4. Grayson, D. A. (1987): Can categorical and dimensional views of psychiatric illness be distinguished? *Br J Psychiatry*, 151:355–361.
5. Grove, W. M., and Andreasen N. C. (1989): Quantitative and qualitative distinctions between psychiatric disorders. In: *The Validity of Psychiatric Diagnosis*, edited by Lee N. Robins and James E. Barrett. Raven Press, New York.
6. Cloninger, C. R., Martin, R. L., and Guze, S. B., et al. (1985): Diagnosis and prognosis in schizophrenia. *Arch Gen Psychiatry*, 42:15–25.
7. Klein, D. F. (1989): The pharmacological validation of psychiatric diagnosis. In: *The Validity of Psychiatric Diagnosis*, edited by Lee N. Robins and James E. Barrett. Raven Press, New York.
8. Tsuang, M. T., Winokur, G., and Crowe, R. R. (1980): Morbidity risks of schizophrenia and affective disorders among first degree relatives of patients with schizophrenia, mania, depression and surgical conditions. *Br J Psychiatry*, 137:497–504.
9. Weissman, M. M., Gershon, E. S., Kidd, K. K., et al. (1984): Psychiatric disorders in the relatives of probands with affective disorders. *Arch Gen Psychiatry*, 41:13–21.
10. Baron, M., Gruen, R., Rainer, J. D., et al. (1985): A family study of schizophrenic and normal control probands: Implications for the spectrum concept of schizophrenia. *Am J Psychiatry*, 142:447–455, 1985.
11. Kendler, K. S., Gruenberg, A. M., and Tsuang, M. T. (1985): Psychiatric illness in first-degree relatives of schizophrenic and surgical control patients. *Arch Gen Psychiatry*, 42:770–779.
12. Kendell, R. E., and Gourlay, A. J. (1970): The clinical distinction between psychotic and neurotic depression. *Br J Psychiatry*, 117:257–260.
13. Brockington, I. F., Kendell, R. E., Wainwright, S., et al. (1979): The distinction between the affective psychoses and schizophrenia. *Br J Psychiatry*, 135:243–248.
14. Abou-Saleh, M. T., and Coppen, A. (1984): Classification of depressive illnesses: Clinico-psychological correlates. *J Affective Disord*, 6:53–66.
15. Young, M. A., Scheftner, W. A., Klerman, G. L., et al. (1986): The endogenous sub-type of depression: A study of its internal construct validity. *Br J Psychiatry*, 148:257–267.
16. Caine, E. D., and Shoulson, I. (1983): Psychiatric syndromes in Huntington's disease. *Am J Psychiatry*, 140:728–733.
17. Pauls, D. L., Towbin, K. E., Leckman, J. F., et al. (1986): Gilles de la Tourette's syndrome and obsessive compulsive disorder. *Arch Gen Psychiatry*, 43:1180–1182.
18. McGuffin, P., Reveley, A., and Holland, A. (1982): Identical triplets: Non-identical psychosis? *Br J Psychiatry*, 140:1–6.
19. Sturt, E. (1981): Hierarchical patterns in the distribution of psychiatric symptoms. *Psychol Med*, 11:783–794.
20. American Psychiatric Association. (1987): *Diagnostic and Statistical Manual of Mental Disorders (3rd Edition, revised)* [DSM-III-R]. American Psychiatric Association, Washington, D.C.
21. Kovacs, M., and Gatsonis, C. (1989): Stability and change in childhood-onset depressive disorders: Longitudinal course as a diagnostic validator. In: *The Validity of Psychiatric Diagnosis*, edited by Lee N. Robins and James E. Barrett. Raven Press, New York.
22. Beiser, M., (1989): Temporal stability in the major mental disorders. In: *The Validity of Psychiatric Diagnosis*, edited by Lee N. Robins and James E. Barrett. Raven Press, New York.
23. Lader, M., Lang, R. A., and Wilson, G. D. (1987): *Patterns of Improvement in Depressed In-Patients*. Maudsley Monograph No. 30. Oxford University Press, Oxford.
24. Tyrer, P., Alexander, J., Remington, M., et al. (1987): Relationship between neurotic symptoms and neurotic diagnosis: A longitudinal study. *J Affective Disord*, 13:13–21.
25. Biehl, H., Maurer, K., Schubart, C., et al. (1986): Prediction of outcome and utilization of medical services in a prospective study of first onset schizophrenics. *Eur Arch Psychiatr Neurol Sci*, 236:139–147.
26. Overall, J. E., Hollister, L. E., Meyer, F., et al. (1964): Imipramine and thioridazine in depressed and schizophrenic patients. *J Am Med Association*, 189:605–608.

27. Klein, D. F., and Fink, M. (1963): Multiple item factors as change measures in psychopharmacology. *Psychopharmacologia*, 4:43–52.
28. Ball, J. R. B., and Kiloh, L. G. (1959): A controlled trial of imipramine in treatment of depressive states. *Br Med J*, 2:1052–1055.
29. Johnstone, E. C., Owens, D. G. C., Frith, C. D., et al. (1980): Neurotic illness and its response to anxiolytic and antidepressant treatment. *Psychol Med*, 10:321–328.
30. Lipman, R. S., Covi, L., Rickels, K., et al. (1986): Imipramine and chlordiazepoxide in depressive and anxiety disorders. *Arch Gen Psychiatry*, 43:68–77, 79–85.
31. Johnstone, E. C. Personal communication, 1987.
32. Feighner, J. P., Robins, E., Guze, S. B., et al. (1972): Diagnostic criteria for use in psychiatric research. *Arch Gen Psychiatry*, 26:57–63.
33. McGuffin, P., Farmer, A. E., Gottesman, I. I., et al. (1984): Twin concordance for operationally defined schizophrenia: Confirmation of familiality and heritability. *Arch Gen Psychiatry*, 41:541–545.

DISCUSSION

Dr. William Coryell: We have recently completed a study such as you described. It was a blind family study of psychotics, and we made it a point to include the troublesome patients. We thus included a consecutive series of nonmanic psychotics, and our largest group was RDC schizoaffective. We found that schizoaffectives had an intermediate morbid risk for affective disorder among relatives. When we subdivided schizoaffectives according to the RDC criteria, however, they fell very nicely into mainly schizophrenic and mainly affective groups. The mainly affectives were indistinguishable from the psychotic major depressives in terms of morbid risk for affective disorder; the mainly schizophrenics, the schizophrenics, and the controls were similar in terms of morbid risk for affective disorder. It was very noncontinuous with a nice, clean dividing point. The follow-up data showed the same thing.

A general point: in your presentation you frequently made analogies with medical history. I have a hard time imagining why the realm of psychiatric illness might turn out to be dimensional without any precedent in medicine for this. I can imagine some illnesses turning out to be dimensional, but to have all psychiatric disorders turn out to be dimensional would be incredible. It is more parsimonious to conclude that so far our methods are inadequate than to conclude that all disorders will turn out to be dimensional.

Dr. Kendell: I am delighted to hear what you found in your family study, and I look forward to seeing it published. With respect to your general points about the nature of mental disorders, yes, it would be surprising if they were quite different from medical disorders, and I share your view that we probably ought to assume that they are fundamentally rather similar. But, of course, we always assume that the future is going to be like the past, and we are always being proved wrong. The trick is to know when the future is going to be different. It is important not to lose sight of the fact that a brain is a more complex mechanism by several orders of magnitude than a heart or a kidney. It would be surprising, therefore, if its disorders did not turn out to have some unexpected and unique features.

Dr. Zubin: After Bob's wonderful synthesis of the approaches to bring some order out of the chaos that we are suffering in the realm of diagnosis, let me comment about the recent renewed interest in diagnosis. After World War II, there was an attempt at doing away with diagnosis completely. Someone, whose name I no longer recall, said, "Let us call the people who respond to insulin 'dysglycolic' as their diagnosis, the people who respond to ECT 'dysoxic,' and the people who respond to psychosurgery as 'dysenzymatic.' Let us do away with standard diagnosis, and only consider response to treatment and outcome." There was, of course, a danger in this procedure because these treatments have since disappeared. Applying the notion of outcome to treatment as a basis for diagnostic categories may be a snare and a delusion because we know full well that both outcome and evaluation of treatment are surrounded by so many uncontrollable variables. The social network determines whether a patient is going to get better or not in many instances, despite diagnosis or anything else. Premorbid personality may determine outcome, as well as the effect of treatment, and the ecological niche the patient occupies may be a determinant. In our search for validation criteria, outcome of illness or outcome of treatment are not solid approaches.

Incidentally, in your list of fundamental abnormalities, you spoke of the histological, the psychological, the biochemical, and the molecular. For some reason you left out the psychophysiological, but you did mention it later.

As to the matter of the distinction between the dimensional and the typological approaches, there is something fundamentally different between these approaches. Most people who apply the dimensional approach use factor analysis. Most people who apply the typological approach utilize clustering techniques. The clusterers have one flaw. Because there are so many items, they tend first to do a factor analysis in order to reduce the number of items before they cluster. Therein lies the danger, because by doing a factor analysis on these items, they may be destroying the very essence of what clustering tends to be. This may produce linearity where none exists. It may produce continuity where none exists, because to do a factor analysis you must have continuity, linearity, and so on. One of the reasons why the typological or categorical approach has not succeeded may be that we have failed to take into consideration this flaw.

Dr. Cloninger: In our attempts to demonstrate discreteness in psychiatric disorders, Dr. Guze and I have been successful whereas earlier attempts often were not. One reason may be that we used large sample sizes in both the criterion and the replication samples. Another may be that we have always used large general samples that have had an unrestricted range of clinical variation. Would you comment on the extent to which some of the earlier failures to demonstrate points of rarity could be limited by the restricted range and sample size of the populations?

Dr. Kendell: Your work was superior in many respects. You had large samples, and you had a better understanding of some of the mathematical limitations of the techniques. Of course, it is very important to recognize that failure to demonstrate bimodality never proves anything, because it is always possible that with a different selection of items, you would get it. I would still like to see other people repeat your findings before I am 100% convinced.

Dr. Cloninger: Have you attempted to replicate the discriminate function that was derived in your original samples? In those samples it appeared to me that your first four or five items were remarkably similar to ours, and yet you included a large number of items that were individually nonsignificant which could have added noise to your results. Would it be possible for you to attempt to replicate our criteria?

Dr. Kendell: I certainly haven't done it yet, and it may not be possible. The computer we used went to the graveyard long ago, and I rather doubt whether Ian Brockington or I have a usable data set any longer, but it might be possible.

Dr. Lebensohn: Thirty-one years ago, at the 1957 meeting of the American Psychiatric Association, I had the pleasure of arranging what was then called a "Theoretical Symposium" on psychiatric nosology. At that symposium we had four panelists: One was a historian, Ilza Veith. The second was a philosopher, Dr. Reid of the University of Maryland. The third was a clinical psychiatrist, Thomas Szasz. The fourth was a biologist, Garrett Hardin, with an interest in comparative linguistics. I invited him because he had written an extraordinary paper about the meaninglessness of the term protoplasm, pointing out that protoplasm had something like 17 different definitions. He also pointed out that in the course of the history of any science, calling something by a name often confuses rather than clarifies. Dr. Hardin originally called his paper on psychiatric nosology "Name Calling, or the Threat of Clarity.*"

---

*Hardin, G. (1957): The threat of clarity, *Amer. J. Psychiat.*, 114(5):392.

He also pointed out that the word "ether," which was once used to describe what we now call "space," actually impeded the course of science. As far as psychiatric terminology is concerned, why indulge in name calling? If the name means nothing, why use it? I raise this not only for the historical significance but also for the philosophical implications.

Dr. Kendell: As Karl Popper emphasized, it is important that all definitions be read from right to left, not from left to right. We are just using words like schizophrenia as a convenient shorthand for what would otherwise be a statement running to two paragraphs about combinations of symptoms. There is no such thing as schizophrenia. It is just a shorthand symbol. But Hardin was right. We keep confusing the issue by allowing our symbols to "reify."

Dr. Kramer: I enjoyed your outline of steps to be taken to assure better classification. You stimulated me to think about issues that need further discussion, particularly those related to follow-up. It seemed to me that in your discussion of follow-up you presented an idealized situation in which the subjects were never permitted to experience additional treatments once an initial treatment plan was formulated and implemented. Furthermore, you did not specify how long the subjects were to be followed in order to determine outcome: 1 year, 2 years, or throughout his or her lifetime. Another factor is that over a period of time patients may change living arrangements, marital status, occupation, and so on. Patients may also develop intercurrent infections and diseases, additional events which may in some way change the course of the initial illness. Consider the less developed areas of the world where, for example, 60% of a population may survive to the age of 25, and the survivors to that age will experience very high mortality rates during their subsequent lifetimes. You would then have the mortality of the study subjects to take into account in a follow-up study.

I think it is essential that some specification be made of the duration of follow-up. If you have to wait 25 years, for example, to obtain the information needed to make a diagnosis, you will never obtain data needed to answer questions that are very relevant to understanding the course and outcome of a specific type of mental disorder.

Dr. Kendell: You are absolutely right. In any long-term follow-up study, you have no control over the treatments people receive. You have no control over life events either, and you are implicitly assuming that they either have relatively little effect on course or that they are randomly distributed between the different groups, and both those assumptions may be wrong. That is a very important limitation of all long-term follow-up studies. Nonetheless, I think most of us are convinced that there are important things to be learned from long-term follow-up. For example, I think we have all learned important things about schizophrenia from the three big continental European studies that have been published in the last 10 years, all of them extending over 20 years or more. We would never have learned these things without somebody anticipating the need for such studies 25 or 30 years ago. But I quite agree about the limitations.

Dr. Kramer: Don't misunderstand me. I was not saying that follow-up studies are not important, but that, for developing operational criteria for arriving at a diagnosis, there needs to be a cutoff point.

Dr. Kendell: I wasn't suggesting that you should delay making a diagnosis until the follow-up is completed. But I was saying that from studies of this kind there are important things to be learned which are relevant to our classification.

Subject Index

Subject Index

A

Acting out symptoms
 DSM-III analysis, 118–120
 GOM analysis of, 118–120
Adjustment, disorder with depressed mood (ADDM)
 in children, 63,65–66,71
 prognosis in, 65–66
Affective disorders
 alcoholism and, 254–257
 classification of, 224–225
 cultural influences in, 254–255
 cyclothymic temperament and, 218–219
 depressive temperament as, 222, 226
 diagnostic validity of, 225–226, 273
 DSM-III classification, 26–27,105, 217
 hyperthymic temperament and, 219–221
 irritable temperament as, 224–225
 mood disorders and, 217
 schizophrenia and, 5,7
 sleep in, 226
Age
 in childhood depression, 58,61–62, 67–68
 hypersomnia and, 61–62
 symptom change and, 61–62
Alcoholism
 ASP disorders and, 255–257
 cultural factors and, 254–257,261
 dependence and, 273
 depression and, 271
 diagnostic interview in, 266–267
 diagnostic validity of, 272,273
Alzheimer's disease
 EEG in, 193

 linkage studies in, 166,194
 neurochemical studies of, 194
Antisocial personality disorder (ASP)
 alcoholism and, 255–257
 criminality and, 153
 criteria for, 18
 cytogenic markers for, 153–154
 DSM-III diagnosis, 18
 DSM-III-R and, 275
 GOM analysis, 118–119
 validation of, 33
Anxiety disorders
 bimodality and, 131–133
 depression and, 106,117–118
 DSM-III diagnosis, 107,117–118
 GAD and, 107,146–147
 genetics of, 146–147
 GOM analysis, 117–118
 imipramine and, 208–210
 PD as, 146–147
 pharmacological validation, 208–210
Attention deficit disorder (ADD), TS and, 145
Autistic disorder diagnosis
 criteria for, 296–297
 in DSM-III-R, 295–297
 field results in, 296–297
 program for, 295–296
Autopsy results
 diagnostic validity and, 185
 in MDD, 183–185
 in PDD, 192–193

B

Bimodality
 anxiety and, 131–133
 diagnosis and, 131–133
 psychiatric disorders and, 129–133

327

328   SUBJECT INDEX

Biological classification, diagnostic validity of, 19–21
Bipolar affective disorder
  genetic studies of, 147–148
  unipolar disease and, 147–148
Bipolar disorders
  childhood depression and, 64,65,74
  in children, 97–98
  definition of, 74
  genetic linkage in, 143–144,166, 168–171
  hyperthymic personality and, 220–221
  risk of, 64

C

Childhood-onset depression
  ADDM in, 63,65–66,71
  age and, 58,59,61–62,67–68
  bipolar disorders and, 64,65,74
  changes in, 57–58,60,61–62,67–68
  DD in, 60,63,64–65,70–71
  diagnostic validity, 60,62–66
  diagnostic verification, 60–61,75
  DSM-III and, 59,68,69
  follow-up in, 60
  homogeneity of, 70
  hypersomnia and, 61–62
  ISC use in, 59
  MDD in, 60,61–62,63–64,70–71
  MDD/DD in, 60
  prognosis in, 58–59,62–66,67–68, 69–71
  recovery in, 62–63
  stability in, 57–58,62–66,67–68
  study methods, 59–61
Children
  adjustment disorders in, 74–75
  conduct disorders in, 74
  depressive disorders in, 57–75
  dysthymia in, 98
  eating disorders in, 73–74
Classification, see Psychiatric nosology

Classification models
  anthropology and, 21–22
  atheoretical, 29–30,32
  biological, 19–21
  diagnostic validity and, 19,21,24,33
  DIS as, 42–43
  DSM-III as, 26–27,29,104–105
  folk, 21–23
  prototype, 23–24
  psychological testing as, 24–26
  reliability and, 24–26,28–29
  significance of, 26–31
  validity and, 28,33–34
Clinical examinations, semistructured
  computer use in, 40–41
  DIS in, 42–46
  interview in, 39,40–42
  multimethod approach in, 46–50
  PSE and, 39
  PSS in, 39–40
  validity of, 39
Clinical syndromes
  boundary identification in, 309–310, 313–314
  clinical validity of, 307–308
  clustering and, 309
  etiology and, 307
  family studies in, 312–313,318,319, 321
  identification of, 308–309
  outcome and, 310–311
  pharmacology and, 207–208,312
  twin studies in, 318
  validity of, 308–309,319
Composite international diagnostic interview (CIDI), nature of, 263
Compulsive disorders
  diagnosis of, 109
  internal consistency analysis, 109
Computed tomography (CT)
  in MDD, 185
  in PDD, 193
Criminality, genetic markers for, 153
Cross-national research

cultural factors and, 247–248,249,
253–257
diagnostic prevalence rates and,
252–253
diagnostic validity and, 247–259
DSM-III acceptance and, 249–252
DSM-III definitions and, 249–251
DSM-III diagnosis and, 247,249–
252,257–258
ECA data and, 259
risk-factors and, 255–257
symptomatic expression of disorders
and, 253–255
Cultural factors
affective disorders and, 254–255
alcoholism and, 254–257
diagnostic validity and, 247–248,
249,257–258,260
in symptom expression, 253–255
Cyclothymic temperament
affective episodes in, 223–224
bipolar nature of, 218–219
depressive personality and, 223–224
diagnosis of, 218–219
manic episodes in, 223

D

Depressive disorders
in adults, 58
alcoholism and, 271
anxiety and, 107
in children, 57–75
clinical features in, 236–238
consistency of analysis in, 105–107
diagnosis of, 127–128,229,236–
238,241–242,264–266
drug-free interval in, 244
DSM-III diagnosis of, 105–107,
117–118,229
DST diagnosis of, 229,232–234,
236,240
exclusion criteria in, 271–272
GOM analysis of, 117–118
IDD and, 106–107

melancholia and, 106
pharmacological validation, 211
psychosocial aspects of, 244
psychotic features of, 106
relapse in, 58
sleep disturbances in, 236
subtypes of, 137,314
symptoms of, 117–118,270–272
Depressive temperament
affective episodes in,223–224,226
criteria for, 221–224
cyclothymic temperament and,
223–224
sleep in, 222
Dexamethasone suppression test
(DST)
clinical features and, 237–238
in depression, 229,232–234,236–
238,240
laboratory validity of, 232–234,
236–238,240
melancholia and, 233–234
placebo response and, 240
sensitivity of, 235,237
sleep EEG and, 236
specificity of, 235,237
Diagnosis
analytical methods in, 133–138,
139–141
association markers in, 152–153
bimodality and, 129–133
bitangentiality criterion in, 133–136
of childhood depression, 60,62–66
classification of, 1,19–26,323
cluster analysis of, 134–135
cytogenic markers in, 153–154
etiology and, 128,129–130,163–
173
familial aggregation and, 144–145
family studies and, 3,5–6,137–138,
312–313,317–318
follow-up in, 2,3–5
genetics and, 137–138,143–155
impairment ratings and, 37

Diagnosis (*contd.*)
  interviews in, 36,263–268
  LCA analysis of, 136
  linkage markers in, 149–154,164–173
  mode of onset and, 81
  multiple, 273
  multivariate analysis of, 135–136
  objective measures in, 36–38
  overlap in, 127–128
  pharmacological, 203–213,312, 316–317,321–322
  prevalence rates and, 252–253,261
  probability of, 238–240
  psychological tests in, 2,24–26
  reliability of, 25–26,230–237,279–289
  of schizophrenia, 3–7
  stability of, 57,77–78
  symptoms and, 268–275,314–315, 316
  syndromes and, 128–129
  twin studies and, 318
  validity of, 35–38,77,241–242,319
Diagnostic interview
  in alcohol disorders, 266–267
  by clinician, 264–267
  content of, 268–271
  in depressive disorders, 264–266, 270–271
  in DIS, 263–268
  by lay person, 264–267
  predictive value of, 264–265
  symptom content and, 268–271
  validity of, 265–268,269
  wording of, 269,274–276,277
Diagnostic interview schedule (DIS)
  in depression, 264–265,271
  development of, 42
  DSM-III and, 43–44,258
  follow-up in, 43
  GOM and, 115,116,117
  interviewer and, 263–265
  schizophrenia and, 272
  validity of, 38,42–46,263–264,268

Diagnostic validity
  age and, 67–68
  assessing, 16–18,19,127–128,177–178,247
  biological correlates and, 313
  bitangentiality criterion and, 133–136
  in childhood depression, 60,62–66
  classification and, 19–26,29,279, 323
  of clinical syndromes, 306
  criteria for, 2,7,17–18,29–31,32, 36–38,97,239–242,263,264, 295,305,310–313
  cross-national research and, 247–259
  cultural factors in, 247–248,249, 257–258,260
  diagnostic grammar and, 274–275
  of DIS, 38,42–46,263–264
  of DST, 229,232–234
  epidemiology and, 35
  etiology and, 306–307
  exclusion criteria for, 2
  family studies in, 5–6,11,13–15, 17,79,312–313,317–318
  five phases for, 1–3,13–15
  follow-up studies and, 2,3–5,11, 315–316,319,323
  interview and, 36,263–268
  laboratory testing and, 177–195, 229–242
  multimethod approach to, 46–50,54
  by outcome, 310–311
  of PERI, 38
  pharmacological evidence and, 203–213,312
  phases of, 1–3,11,13–15
  prediction and, 264
  prognosis and, 3,4,5,57
  of PSE, 38
  psychological tests and, 2,24–26
  reliability and, 24–25,28–29,178, 233,279–289
  in Robins-Guze method, 11,32

of SADS, 38
in schizoaffective disorders, 85–88
of schizophrenia, 1–7,54–55,108–109,319
screening scales and, 36,37–38,41–42,53
sensitivity of, 233–234,239,295
social factors and, 247–248
specificity and, 233–234,239,295
temporal stability and, 57,77,85–90
undiagnosed cases and, 2,5,14,16
DNA probes
in linkage studies, 165,171–173
of psychiatric disorders, 171–172,173
DSM-III diagnosis
acceptance of, 250–252
alcoholism and, 254,271,272,273
of antisocial personality, 18,33,118
anxiety disorders and, 107,117–118
atypical cases and, 14,17,105
in childhood depression, 59,68,69
cross-national findings and, 247,249–252,257–259
cultural factors and, 248,254–255,257–258
definitions in, 250–252
of depressive disorders, 105–107,117–118,255,271
design of, 9,26–27,104–105
DIS and, 43–44,258
epidemiology and, 35,38
exclusion criteria in, 272
GOM analysis and, 114–121
ICD-9 and, 249,258
internal consistency of, 99,104–105
MDD and, 254–255
multiple diagnosis and, 273
of organic brain syndromes, 111
of personality disorders, 109–111,217
prevalence rates of, 252–253
psychiatric classification and, 26–27,29
question wording and, 274–276

in schizoaffective disorders, 85–88
in schizophrenia, 91,93,95,108–109
in schizophreniform disorders, 89
in schizotypical disorders, 110
in stability studies, 79,80,89
in substance abuse, 109
usefulness rating of, 249–252
validity of, 43–44,217,247
world-wide use of, 250–252,260–261
DSM-IV diagnosis
depressive types in, 224–225
DSM-III and, 294
hyperthymic temperament in, 224–225
nosology in, 294
research required for, 297–298
study design, 298–299
DSM-III-R diagnosis
antisocial criteria in, 275
autistic disorder field trial, 295–297
comorbidity and, 301–302
criterion for, 274,295
diagnosis requiring study and, 297–298
diagnostic validators for, 302–303
DSM-III and, 274
field trials of, 294–297
grammar in, 274–275
literature review for, 302
revision of, 301–303
Dysthmic disorder (DD)
bipolar disorders and, 64–65
in children, 60,63,64–65,70–71
risk estimates, 64–65

E

Eating disorders, in children, 73–74
Electroencephalograms (EEG)
in epilepsy diagnosis, 238–239
in MDD, 184,185–187,189
in mood disorders, 191
in PDD, 193–194,195

Electroencephalograms (*contd.*)
  probability of diagnosis and, 238–239
  in REM sleep, 186–187,189,201
  in sleep, 185–187
Epidemiologic catchment area (ECA) program
  cross-national findings and, 259
  depressive symptoms and, 117–118
  diagnostic prevalence and, 252–253
  DIS and, 252
  GOM and, 114–118
  purpose of, 114–115
Epidemiology
  diagnostic methods and, 35
  DIS in, 42–46
  of first generation studies, 35–36
  in Israel, 47–49
  of psychological disorders, 35–50
  screening scales and, 36,37–38
  of second generation studies, 36–37
  third generation studies, 38
  validity of, 35,42–46
Etiology
  bimodality and, 131
  clinical syndromes and, 307
  psychiatric disorders and, 128,129–131
  validity and, 306–307

F

Family studies, *see also* genetic studies
  in diagnosis, 3,5–7,137–138
  diagnostic stability and, 79
  in diagnostic validation, 11,13–15, 17,79,312–313,317–318,321
  linkage markers and, 168
  psychopathology and, 97
  in Robins-Guze method, 11
  of schizophrenia, 3,5–7
  in syndrome identification, 312–313
Folk classification
  anthropology and, 21–23
  in diagnosis, 21–23

Follow-up studies
  in childhood depression, 60,62–66, 67–68
  in diagnostic validation, 11,315–316
  in DIS, 43,45
  duration of, 4
  family in, 5–6
  in Robins-Guze method, 11
  of schizophrenia, 3–6
  serial interviews in, 315–316

G

Generalized anxiety disorders (GAD)
  DSM-III diagnosis of, 107
  genetics of, 146–147
Genetics
  of ADD, 145–146
  of anxiety disorders, 146–147
  applications of, 155
  association markers and, 152–153
  of bipolar disorders, 143–144,147–148
  of criminality, 153
  diagnosis and, 143–155
  DNA probes and, 165,171–172, 173
  familial coaggregation and, 144–145
  linkage and, 138,143,155,161,163–173
  linkage markers and, 149–154
  of manic-depression, 143
  of OCD disorders, 145–146,160
  in psychiatric nosology, 163–173
  of schizophrenia, 148–149
  in syndrome distinctions, 137–138
  of TS, 145–146,160
  in twin studies, 318
Grade of membership (GOM) analysis
  "acting out" symptoms and, 118–120
  antisocial behavior and, 118–119
  applications, 114–120,125
  consistency of analysis and, 113–118

of depressive symptoms, 117–118
DIS and, 115,116,117
DSM-III diagnosis and, 114–117
ECA program and, 114–118
procedure, 113–114
somatization disorders and, 115–117

H

Hyperthymic temperament
bipolar personality of, 220–221
depressive temperament and, 220, 221
diagnosis of, 219–221
personality profile of, 219
REM sleep in, 220
Hypomanic, *see* hyperthymic
Hypothalamic-pituitary-adrenal cortex (HPA) axis
in MDD, 188–189,235
validity of, 235

I

ICD-9 diagnostic criteria
acceptance of, 250
in major mental disorders, 80,82–85
RDC comparison, 90–92
in schizoaffective disorders, 85–86
in schizophrenia, 82–85,90–91,93
usefulness of, 249
Imipramine
in anxiety disorders, 208–210
in depression, 211
pharmacological validation and, 208–210,211
Impairment ratings, validity of diagnosis and, 37
Internal consistency analysis
of anxiety disorders, 107
assessment of, 112–113,123
coefficient alpha and, 101
demographic factors in, 124
of depressive disorders, 105–107
of DSM-III diagnosis, 99,104–112

factor analysis and, 101–102
GOM and, 113–120,125
of organic brain syndrome, 111
of personality disorders, 109–111, 118–120
principles of, 99–104,120–121
problems of, 102–103
psychometrics and, 99–101
of schizophrenia, 108–109,111
substance abuse and, 109
Interviews
ISC in, 59
in Israel, 47–48
in PSE, 39
in PSS, 39–40
psychiatric disorder incidence and, 36–37
in semistructured clinical examinations, 39
serial, 315–316
symptom development and, 316
Interview schedule for children (ISC), childhood depression and, 59
Inventory to diagnose depression (IDD)
depression diagnosis and, 106–107
DSM-III and, 106–107
Irritable temperament
hyperactivity in, 224
operational definition of, 224–225

K

Kappa coefficient
depression and, 23
diagnostic concordance and, 230–231
diagnostic validity and, 281–282, 284,285,288,290
as laboratory measure, 230–231

L

Laboratory studies
autopsy as, 183–185,192–193

Laboratory studies (*contd.*)
  baseline for, 235–236
  clinical features and, 236–238
  combinations of, 236
  diagnostic validity and, 229–242
  of DST, 229,232–234,235,236, 237–238,240
  EEG as, 184,185–187,189,191, 193–194,195,235–236
  functional measures and, 235–236
  HPA as, 188–189,235
  Kappa coefficient and, 230–231
  listing of, 184
  of MDD, 183–192
  in mood disorders, 191
  motor activity measurements in, 187–188
  neurochemical, 190–191,194–195
  neuroendocrines as, 188–190
  in PDD, 192–195
  probability of diagnosis and, 238–240
  in psychiatric diagnosis, 177–179, 181
  purpose of, 179–180
  radiographic methods in, 184,185, 193
  relevance of, 239–240
  reliability of, 230–232
  rules for, 230–240
  sensitivity of, 233–234,239
  specificity of, 233–234,239
  statistical concerns in, 182
  treatment response and, 240
  value of, 195,200,244–245
Latent class analysis (LCA), in diagnostic distinctions, 136
Linkage markers
  in Alzheimer's disease, 166,194
  in bipolar disease, 166,168–170
  clinical value of, 151
  in diagnosis, 149–150,151
  disease mutation and, 151–152
  disequilibrium and, 151–152
  DNA probes and, 165
  etiology based, 164
  gene identification and, 166–167
  limitations of, 171–173
  nature of, 164–165,167
  penetrance and, 168,169,171
  phenotype definition in, 172,173, 175
  in psychiatric nosology, 165–173
  risk identification and, 168–171
  study methods in, 165

M

Manic-depressive illness, genetic diagnosis, 143
Major depressive disorder (MDD)
  autopsy results in, 183–185
  bipolar disorders and, 64
  in children, 60,61–62,63–64,70–71
  clinical diagnosis of, 183,191
  CT scan in, 185
  EEG studies in, 185–187
  HPA in, 188
  laboratory studies of, 183–192
  motor activity measurements in, 187–188
  neurochemical studies of, 190–191
  neuroendocrine studies of, 188–190
  PET scan in, 185
  prevalence correlations in, 254–255
  radiographic findings in, 184,185
  risk estimates for, 63–64
  in women, 254–255
Major mental disorders
  DSM-III use in, 79,80,82–83
  ICD-9 measure of, 80,82–84
  RDC use in, 79,80,83–84
  study methods, 77–82
  temporal stability of, 77–95
  walking wounded in, 82
  working wounded in, 82
Melancholia
  DST diagnosis, 233–234

depression and, 106
DSM-III diagnosis, 106
Mood disorders
  cyclothymic temperament and, 218–219
  laboratory studies of, 191,192
  pharmacological validation of, 211
Motor activity
  in MDD, 187–188
  in schizophrenia, 187,188
Multimethod screening, diagnostic validity of, 46–50,54

N

Neurochemical studies
  of Alzheimer's disease, 194
  catecholamines in, 190
  of MDD, 190–191
  of PDD, 194
Neuroendocrine studies
  HPA in, 188–189
  in MDD, 188–190
  thyroid function and, 189

O

Obsessive-compulsive disorders (OCD)
  as genetic disease, 145–146,160
  pharmacological validation of, 215
  TS and, 145–146,160
Organic brain syndromes
  DSM-III diagnosis, 111
  internal consistency analysis of, 111

P

Panic disorder
  agoraphobia and, 146
  genetics of, 146–147
Paranoid disorders, internal consistency analysis of, 109,110
Pathogenesis, of psychiatric disorders, 177–178,180,203

Personality disorders
  cyclothymic temperament and, 218–219
  DSM-III diagnosis, 109–111,217
  GOM analysis of, 118–119
  hyperthymic temperament and, 219–221
  internal consistency analysis of, 109–111
  pharmacological validation of, 211
  in Robins-Guze diagnosis, 217
  validation of, 217
Pharmacological diagnosis
  in anxiety disorders, 208–210
  behavioral similarities of drugs in, 205–206
  chlorpromazine in, 204–205
  clinical toxicity and, 204
  comorbidity and, 206–207
  in depression, 211,212,216
  drug response and, 206–208
  effects of treatment and, 204
  imipramine and, 208–210
  in OCD, 215
  pathophysiology and, 203–204, 216
  of personality disorders, 212
  of pseudoneurotic schizophrenia, 204–205,215
  of schizophrenia, 204–205,215
  of subgroups, 204–205
  symptoms and, 207–208
  syndromes and, 207–208
  value of, 212–213,215–216
Placebo response
  diagnostic validity and, 240
  DST and, 240
Positron emission tomography (PET)
  in MDD, 185
  in PDD, 193
Present state examination (PSE)
  diagnostic validity of, 38
  rating procedure in, 39
  in stability estimates, 79,80

Primary degenerative dementia (PDD)
  autopsy results in, 192–193
  CT scan in, 193,195
  EEG in, 193–194,195
  laboratory diagnosis of, 192–195
  neurochemical studies of, 194
  PET scan in, 193
Probability
  EEG studies and, 238–239
  laboratory diagnosis and, 238–240
Prognosis
  age and, 61–62,67–68
  in childhood depression, 58–59,62–66,67–68,69–71
  family studies and, 5–6
  prediction of, 4–5,57
  in schizophrenia, 3–5,7,90
  in schizophreniform behavior, 90
Prototype classification, in diagnosis, 23–24,32–33
Psychiatric disorders
  categorization of, 68–69
  childhood-onset depression as, 57–71
  diagnosis of, 68–69
  epidemiology of, 35–37
  etiology of, 128,129–130
  evolution of, 94–95
  genetics of, 143–155
  incidence of, 36
  laboratory studies of, 182,183
  major mental, 77–95
  nosology of, 163–173
  objective measures of, 36–37
  pathogenesis of, 177–178,180
  prevalence of, 35
  prognosis in, 4–5,57
  prototypical class of, 68–69
  screening scales in, 36,37–38
  stability of, 57,77–95
  statistical concerns in, 182
  temporal stability of, 77–95
  untreated cases and, 36
Psychiatric epidemiology research interview (PERI)
  interview in, 46
  in Israel, 47–48
  in multimethod diagnosis, 46,47–48
  validity of, 38,40
Psychiatric nosology
  clinical validity and, 305,308
  development of, 294,322–323
  DSM-III and, 294
  DSM-IV and, 294
  etiological basis of, 163,173,308
  goal of, 163,173
  linkage markers in, 164–173
  reliability of, 279
Psychiatric status schedule (PSS)
  interviews in, 39–40
  validity of, 39–41
Psychological tests
  as classification model, 24–26
  in diagnosis, 2
  reliability and, 24–26
Psychometrics
  indicators and, 100
  internal consistency and, 99–101

R
RDC
  DSM-III comparison, 90–91
  ICD-9 comparison, 90–92
  in schizoaffective disorders, 85–88, 90–91
  schizophrenia and, 83–84,90–91
  stability determinations and, 79,80, 83–84
Reliability of diagnosis
  assessing, 25–26
  classification and, 279
  clinical validity and, 305
  criterion for, 305
  diagnostic validity and, 24–25,28–29,178,233,279–289
  improvement of, 279
  Kappa coefficient and, 230–231, 281–282,284,285,288,290
  in laboratory studies, 230–232

linear model for, 280–281
a model of, 281–285,290
patient selection and, 287,288
probability and, 238–240
of psychological testing, 24–25
tests of, 24–25
two examiners or one, 279–280, 282,285
"two-out-of-two" rule in, 285–287, 288,290
validity and, 28–29,291,305–306
REM sleep
depression and, 220
EEG in, 186–187,189,201,235
DST and, 236
hyperthymic temperament and, 220
in MDD, 235–236
specificity of, 235–236
Robins-Guze method
in affective disorders, 217
clinical syndromes and, 308–309
concepts in, 9–11
five-phase approach of, 13–15
impact of, 11–13
implications of, 16
internal consistency of, 99
limitations of, 13–14
literature citations of, 11–13
personality disorders in, 217
validation phases of, 11,13–15,32, 127,308–309

S

Schedule for affective disorders and schizophrenia (SADS)
diagnostic validity of, 38,47–49
Israeli use of, 47–49
Schizoaffective disorder
diagnostic validity of, 85–88
DSM-III in, 85
genetics of, 148–149
RDC in, 85–88
stability of, 85–88
Schizophrenia

affective disorders and, 5,7
clinical description, 4–5
diagnosis, 3–7,54–55,90,108–109, 319
in DIS, 272
DSM-III and, 26–27,82–85,90–91, 93,108–109
evolution of, 94–95
family studies of, 3,5–6,148
follow-up studies of, 3–6
genetics of, 148–149
heterogeneity of, 204–205
ICD-9 diagnosis, 82–83,90–91,93
internal consistency analysis of, 108–109
nomenclature in, 3
pharmacological validation, 204– 205,208
prognosis in, 3–5,7,90
pseudoneurotic, 208
RDC diagnosis, 83–85,90–93
relapsing, 94
stability of, 83–85,88–89,91–95
subgroups in, 94–95,108–109, 204–205
Schizophreniform disorder
diagnostic validity of, 88–90,108
in DSM-III-R, 89
prognosis in, 90
schizophrenia and, 89
stability of, 88–90
Schizotypical disorder
diagnosis of, 109,110
genetics of, 148–149
Screening scales
as identifiers, 53
validity of, 36,37–38,41–42,53
Sleep, *see also* REM sleep
DST and, 236
in depressive personality, 222,223, 226,236
in hyperthymic temperament, 220, 221
in MDD, 185–187
in mood disorders, 191

Somatization disorders
  DIS diagnosis, 116
  DSM-III diagnosis, 116–117
  GOM analysis, 115–117
Stability
  in childhood depression, 57–58,62–66,67–68
  of diagnosis, 57,78,92,98
  DSM-III use and, 79,80,82–83
  estimation of, 77–82
  ICD-9 measure of, 80,83–95
  in major mental disorders, 77–95
  mode of onset and, 81
  PSE use in, 79,80
  RDC estimation of, 79,80,83
  scales for, 81–82
  of schizoaffective disorders, 85–88
  of schizophrenia, 82–85,92
  of schizophreniform disorder, 88–90,92
  temporal, 77–95
  validity and, 85–90,95,98
Substance abuse, DSM-III diagnosis, 109

T

Therapeutic trials
  of antidepressants, 317
  diagnosis by, 312,321–322
  diagnostic validity and, 316–317
Tourette's syndrome, (TS)
  as genetic disease, 145–146,160
  OCD and, 145–146,160
"Two-out-of-two" rule
  application of, 285–287
  diagnostic reliability and, 285–287,288,290

U

Undiagnosed cases
  in DSM-III, 17
  Feighner criteria and, 17
  in Robins-Guze method, 14,16
  validation of, 2,5,14,16,17

V

Validity, *see also* diagnostic validity
  biological correlates, 313
  etiology and, 306–307
  in laboratory studies, 234–235
  measures of, 234–235,319
  predictive, 234–235
  therapeutic trials and, 312,316–317